This book by Robert Walters apprehends the coming storm in the financial world of the digital finance economy. We are almost into it, and should blockchain technology and cryptocurrency become a universal currency of world trade, disputes in that area are bound to arise. Arbitration and mediation seem to be on the forefront to solve these issues, and an in-depth understanding of the subject will give lawyers a competitive edge. Professor Robert Walters is a great researcher in this field and his constant academic pursuits in the form of his second book is indeed a must read for those who need to understand the various facets. I strongly recommend this to all students, bar and bench, professors and businessmen alike.

Justice Vineet Kothari, *Former Acting Chief Justice, Gujarat and Madras High Courts, Former Judge, Rajasthan & Karnataka High Courts, Senior Advocate, Supreme Court of India, India*

I have worked with Dr Walters in India. We have advised both the Indian and Australian Governments as part of a grant on the governance of data, cybersecurity, artificial intelligence, critical and quantum technologies and the law. This book is at the cutting edge of the new digital finance economy. The transformation that tokens will bring to the world economy will be significant. The technology of blockchain is at the forefront of this new economic activity, and this book highlights the gaps in the current day legal frameworks. The book offers a way forward and allows technologist, regulators, and the finance sector to better understand the commercial legal dilemmas related to licensing, tax, insurance, intellectual property and transnational arbitration law. I recommend this book to whoever is interested in the token and blockchain economy.

Deepak Sharma, *Arna Capital, United States*

The financial world is undergoing rapid transformation. While digital finance and tokens are not new concepts, their integration with blockchain, digital wallets, and stable coins is reshaping the global financial landscape. This book is highly recommended, and having worked with the author, Dr. Walters, for over two decades, I can attest to his deep expertise in navigating complex cross-border transnational law.

Dr. Walters has an exceptional ability to translate his practical experience as a solicitor and international arbitrator into a forward-looking legal framework. His deep understanding of digital wallets and stable coins as tools for seamless cross-border payments, combined with his insights into how banks are adopting advanced workflows, positions him as a leader in this field. His work lays the foundation for new opportunities in the digital economy, enabling it to thrive and drive further innovation.

Andrew Paynter, *Chief Executive Officer and Founder, BAWN Consulting Group, Australia*

The author Dr Walters expertly navigates the fast-evolving landscape of fintech, digitisation and tokenisation. The book combines clear explanations with real-world case studies, making complex concepts accessible to both novices and experts. The comparative narrative of the various laws of numerous countries (including the EU) is an excellent overview for people needing to have that birds eye view and deeper understanding of the legal challenges that lie ahead.

Readers will appreciate the insightful analysis on issues including taxation, IP and insurance issues. Long story short – the writing is concise yet rich and full with information/analysis and references to laws and authorities, which makes this a very useful book in a transformative sector. It is a must-read for anyone looking to grasp the future of finance. Highly recommended for those wanting to know more!

Lawrence Tan, *Founding Partner, Elden Law, Singapore*

Digital Finance Law

This book assesses the rapidly changing landscape of digital finance regulation. Focusing on the laws of banking-finance, tax, insurance, intellectual property (patents and copyright) and international commercial arbitration, it also delves into the regulation of tokens and the laws pertaining to its development, use, and transaction.

The book undertakes a comparative study of civil and common law jurisdictions such as Australia, India, Japan, Singapore, United Kingdom, European Union, and the United States. It explores how each jurisdiction is at various stages of developing its digital economy and providing banking and financial regulations for crypto-digital assets such as tokens. It also highlights the potential for global regulatory change and collaboration, such that there is a robust, efficient, and harmonised framework of standards, codes and law. The book asserts that blockchain technology will be a disruptive force to commercial law and will be important to taxation and insurance laws (smart contracts), as well as the technology that supports them. Due to the rapid transformation in regulatory landscape, the laws compared were as at November 2024. Since then there have been changes. It also expands on how international arbitration agreements will require more extensive knowledge on data and cybersecurity due to the use of expert evidence that involves blockchain, code, and cybersecurity, amongst other technological elements that facilitate smart contracts and token transactions.

A book of keen interest to scholars of finance law, digital finance, and comparative law, as well as legal practitioners.

Robert Walters is an Associate Professor Law and Director Technology Law and Legal Research, Victoria University-Australia, Adjunct Professor European Faculty of Law, Advisor Corporate Insolvency Centre Gujarat National Law University, India, Honorary Lecturer Liverpool Law School, United Kingdom, Adjunct Research Fellow University Western Australia. Dr Walters is a practicing Solicitor and International Arbitrator, holding an LLB (Victoria), MPPM (Monash), PhD Law (Victoria), and been engaged by national governments to address commercial and private law matters across the digital economy.

Routledge Research in International Commercial Law

Available titles in this series include:

International Commercial and Marine Arbitration
Georgios l. Zekos

International Commercial Arbitration and the Arbitrator's Contract
Emilia Onyema

Jurisdiction and Arbitration Agreements in International Commercial Law
Zheng Sophia Tang

Progressive Commercialization of Airline Governance Culture
Jan Walulik

Economic and Environmental Regulation of International Aviation
From Inter-National to Global Governance
Steven Truxal

Combining Mediation and Arbitration in International Commercial Dispute Resolution
Dilyara Nigmatullina

Non-State Rules in International Commercial Law
Contracts, Legal Authority and Application
Johanna Hoekstra

Commercial Law in the South Pacific
Mohammed L Ahmadu and Bridget Fa'amatuainu

Digital Finance Law
Common and Civil Law
Robert Walters

Digital Finance Law

Common and Civil Law

Robert Walters

Routledge
Taylor & Francis Group
LONDON AND NEW YORK

First published 2025
by Routledge
4 Park Square, Milton Park, Abingdon, Oxon, OX14 4RN

and by Routledge
605 Third Avenue, New York, NY 10158

Routledge is an imprint of the Taylor & Francis Group, an informa business

British Library Cataloguing-in-Publication Data
A catalogue record for this book is available from the British Library

Library of Congress Cataloging-in-Publication Data
Names: Walters, Robert (Barrister at law), author.
Title: Digital finance law: common and civil law/Robert Walters.
Description: Abingdon, Oxon [UK]; New York, NY: Routledge, 2025. | Series: Routledge research in international commercial law | Includes bibliographical references and index. | Contents: Finance and banking – Taxation – Insurance – Intellectual property law [patents copyright] – International arbitration.
Identifiers: LCCN 2024048863 (print) | LCCN 2024048864 (ebook) | ISBN 9781032842042 (hardback) | ISBN 9781032842059 (paperback) | ISBN 9781003511687 (ebook)
Subjects: LCSH: Internet banking–Law and legislation. | Finance–Law and legislation. | Financial services industry–Law and legislation. | Capital market–Law and legislation
Classification: LCC K1066 .W357 2025 (print) | LCC K1066 (ebook) | DDC 346/.08–dc23/eng/20241017
LC record available at https://lccn.loc.gov/2024048863
LC ebook record available at https://lccn.loc.gov/2024048864

ISBN: 9781032842042 (hbk)
ISBN: 9781032842059 (pbk)
ISBN: 9781003511687 (ebk)

DOI: 10.4324/9781003511687

Typeset in Galliard
by Deanta Global Publishing Services, Chennai, India

Contents

Foreword

This book authored by my close friend and mentee Associate Professor and Legal Practitioner Dr. Robert Walters addresses the salient issue of tokenisation in digital financing, both globally and in key domestic jurisdictions. It highlights the importance of tokens in blockchain technologies, encompassing codes, algorithms, and related instruments of machine learning. The significant benefit of the book is in outlining the fluidity of developments in blockchain technology and the pervasive importance of tokens in cross-border digital financing.

The target audience consists of key figures struggling to address complexities in digital financing. That audience includes industry personnel engaged in financing digital products, legal practitioners advising on the use of such products, and academics studying digital financing, blockchain technology, and the use of tokens.

The book is appropriate and comprehensive in its examination of diffuse domestic laws governing intellectual property, notably in relation to patents and copyright, international commercial arbitration, insurance law, taxation, and the regulation of digital technology. Importantly, the book focuses on the expanding but inconsistent use of digital tokens in blockchain and smart computing in an era of digital innovation, undermined by errors in digital design and confusion in the application of that design.

A primary challenge addressed by the author in the book is the divergence in national and international laws that regulate digital technology and financing. It explores that divergence comprehensively, focusing on the digitalisation of finance in major trading nations. It also recognises limitations in accessing up-to-date information, such as those stemming from fluid developments in digitalisation and its regulation in some countries.

In responding to these challenges, the author stresses the urgent need to resolve differences in national and international regulatory regimes. The essential purpose is to achieve greater consistency in the regulation of digital financing chains. The related challenge is to explore methods used to regularise the adoption and implementation of tokens in digital financing.

The book's fundamental value lies in identifying the pitfalls in divergent regulatory reform measures adopted by national legislatures and courts.

Its functional focus is to highlight disparities between local, regional, or international codes and conventions adopting digitalisation in finance inconsistently, if at all. Its strategic value is to highlight the problematic divide between domestic, regional, and global institutions that fail to govern tokenism in digital finance, those that do so limitedly, and those that do so extensively but often inconsistently. The book's essential innovative contribution is to provide readers with valuable insight into identifying legal inconsistencies and methods of redressing them in commercial practice and in the application of law to that practice.

At the same time, the book avoids dictating peremptory measures by which state and international regulators should seek to coalesce inconsistent laws governing digitalisation and tokenisation. Those are decisions for regulators themselves to make. However, the book provides a valuable tool by which to enable them to do so.

This work is highly recommended because of its expansive coverage of a critical area of finance law that has received wholly inadequate attention to date. Its parameters extend from the regulation of digital finance to the impact of digital technologies on intellectual property and taxation. It extends further to the salient adaptation of dispute resolution measures to accommodate these innovations, such as through international commercial arbitration.

Finally, the book stresses the urgent demand in finance markets to address these issues, not only timely but also comprehensively. The risk of the global disruption of finance and ancillary commercial markets being perpetuated through regulatory inertia and confusion is too great to bear. This book concentrates on limiting that risk by preparing commercial practitioners, lawyers, and academics to address gaps in digital finance regulation that are urgently required at this critical juncture. It is in this critical respect that the book is valuable reading to those engaged in this fluid and dynamic field of law.

Emeritus Professor, Dr Leon Trakman
International, Arbitrator – Barrister
University of New South Wales – Australia

Problem Definition

This book expands on the previous book titled *Robert Walters Commercial & Arbitration Law of the Digital Economy: A Comparison of Asian, European and North American Jurisdictions*, Routledge, 2024.

The tokenisation of the digital and financial economy will bring about profound changes worldwide if fully realised. It will create as many challenges as it will benefits in the short to medium term. A central theme of this book is tokens that are applied, governed, and used over blockchain technology and smart contracts. This book highlights the complex technology arrangements, specifically blockchain, that can be used to govern and facilitate token transactions, including code, machine learning, and algorithms. It will address the laws of intellectual property (patents and copyright), international commercial arbitration, insurance (contracts), and tax, as they pertain to tokens in the current period. To be clear, the book is not making the case for regulation and placing restrictions on blockchain. Rather, it addresses the relevant laws that will be important for the use of tokens in and across international borders.

Pertinent too, the book further highlights how smart contracts and token agreements developed on a blockchain can be used for the commercial governance of tokens. In relation to intellectual property, tokens have emerged as providing two components such as an IP right, and the laws regulating these rights (patents and copyright, such as the authentication process). The national laws are far from settled to provide certainty in investment and trade in these new products. There is no international agreement on what the legal landscape should look like.

The book places a special emphasis on discussing blockchain evidence used in arbitration and the rules of evidence pertaining to arbitration. This will challenge the current-day arbitration laws and rules. The book does not address the confidentiality of the person or parties over blockchain. This is an area of further research and can, in part, be addressed through confidentiality\non-disclosure agreements like any other industry, such as defence that allows for government intervention when required.

Centrally, the challenges posed by the possible tokenisation of the economy are yet to be fully realised. Nation-states and jurisdictions are all at different stages of developing their respective legal frameworks for tokens. There are many unanswered questions. This book addresses some of those complex questions related to tax, insurance, and intellectual property.

Notwithstanding the above, this timely and important book compares the commercial laws of Australia, India, Indonesia, Japan, Liechtenstein, Singapore, the United Kingdom (UK), Switzerland, the European Union (EU), and the United States (US). At various stages throughout the book, it will also compare the laws of China. This is because Liechtenstein and Switzerland have been early developers of the law for tokens. Most noteworthy is that the book does not comment on what China should do to reform its laws or their policy approach. The discussion regarding China is limited to patent and copyright law. The book aims to highlight areas that may be beneficial for all economies to collaborate and build a coherent and consistent framework.

By examining these jurisdictions comparatively, it provides an in-depth understanding of the gaps in the respective national laws, in order to better manage future economic and geopolitical shocks.

The most pressing challenge that needs to be addressed is the overall lack of international agreement and developing law for tokens. There is an urgent need to reconcile the current non-alignment among economies. The failure to develop agreed international law and standards will result in another area of commercial law being highly fragmented. This, in and of itself, will only complicate international digital finance and the evolving token economy once fully commercialised. It will be complex for practitioners of digital finance products, and those who need to resolve commercial disputes.

1 Introduction

1.1 Digital Finance and FinTech

One of the most pressing challenges facing the commercial world is the evolution of digital finance, the benefits and challenges of which are far from being fully understood. At the time of writing, governments, regulators, and policymakers around the world were grappling with ways to keep pace with the transformation of technology that provides a pathway to digital finance products and services. A central position taken throughout this book is that tokens and the tokenisation of the economy are inextricably linked to smart contracts and, in turn, to blockchain technology.

Digital finance, which is used for commercial transactions today, has been developing in different forms for a number of decades. For more than a century, different types of digital finance have been developed and applied to transactions and to investment products. Finance and the money derived from these products has been, and continues to be one of the 'fundamental inventions that support human societies, from the first forms of account-based money and commodity money, through the development of fiat money and on to new digital forms of money'.[1] Interestingly, the history of money comprises four historical and current-day periods: i) 3000 BCE–1300; ii) the modern era; iii) 1300–1950; and the digital era; iv) 1950–present). Digital finance has been described as 'financial services that are provided for over the internet through digital devices and platforms'.[2] Digital finance is also referred to as FinTech[3] or decentralised finance.[4] According to Douglas Arner, Janos Barberis, and Ross Buckley, '"Financial technology" or "FinTech" refers to

1 Shreepad Shukla, *Historical Context and Key Features of Digital Money Tokens*, Barclays (2020), p. 2.

2 P Ozili, Impact of Digital Finance on Financial Inclusion and Stability, *Borsa Istanbul Review*, *18* (4) (2018), 329–340. https://doi.org/10.1016/j.bir.2017.12.003

3 Douglas Arner, Janos Barberis, Ross Buckley, The Evolution of FinTech: A New Post-Crisis Paradigm, *University of Hong Kong Faculty of Law Research Paper, 2015*/047 (2015).

4 P Ozili, Decentralised Finance Research and Developments Around the World. *Journal Bank, Finance Technology*, *6* (2) (2022), 117. https://doi.org/10.1007/s42786-022-00044-x

DOI: 10.4324/9781003511687-1

the use of technology to deliver financial solutions. The term's origin can be traced to the early 1990s and referred to the "Financial Services Technology Consortium"'.[5] Thus, the emergence of FinTech is relatively recent.

FinTech has generally relied on the support of technology for its growth and development over the past three decades. Arner, Barberis, and Buckley reaffirm this point, stating that FinTech today is a marriage of 'financial services and information technology. However, the interlinkage of finance and technology has a long history. In fact, technological developments have long been intertwined and mutually reinforcing'.[6] Noteworthy too, when tracing the development of FinTech, the authors expand on the periods above, stating that in 1838 the telegraph began to be used commercially. Nearly 30 years later, the laying of the first successful Transatlantic cable in 1866 provided the 'fundamental infrastructure for the first major period of financial globalisation in the late 19th century'.[7] Two decades after World War II, came 'the introduction of the Automatic Teller Machine (ATM) in 1967 by Barclays Bank that marked the codmmencement of the modern evolution of today's FinTech. The impact of the ATM led Paul Volcker, former chairman of the US Federal Reserve (1979–1987), to famously state in 2009, while commenting on the role of financial innovation in the GFC [Global Financial Crisis] of 2008 'the most important financial innovation that I have seen in the past 20 years is the automatic teller machine, that really helps people and prevents visits to the bank and it is a real convenience'.[8] Moreover, other national and international events have also shaped and influenced the evolution of the financial system. For instance, the Asian Banking Crisis of 1997[9] had a significant impact on economies, which resulted in law reform to ensure that states' economies would be in a better position to manage risk. Also, the terrorist[10] attacks on New York in 2001 and the ensuing response from governments around the world had significant impacts on financial markets. More recently, from 2022 to 2024, the world has experienced a heightened level of transnational conflict and geopolitical tension. This includes, but is not limited to, the

5 Douglas Arner, Janos Barberis, Ross Buckley, The Evolution of FinTech: A New Post-Crisis Paradigm [2015], *University of Hong Kong Faculty of Law Research Paper, 2015/047*, 2–3.

6 Ibid., p. 3.

7 Ibid.

8 Ibid., p. 5. The authors refer to Paul Volcker, The Only Thing Useful Banks Have Invented in 20 Years Is the ATM, *New York Post* (2009). http://nypost.com/2009/12/13/the-only-thing-useful-banks-have-invented-in-20-years-is-the-atm/

9 Frederic S Mishkin, Lessons from the Asian Crisis, *Journal of International Money and Finance, 18* (4) (1999), 709. https://doi.org/10.1016/S0261-5606(99)00020-0 See also, Salim Rashid, The Asian Financial Crisis. In *Economic Policy for Growth,* Springer (2000). https://doi.org/10.1007/978-1-4615-4537-8_9

10 Vincent Richman, Michael Santos, John Barkoulas, Short- and Long-Term Effects of the 9/11 Event: The International Evidence, *International Journal of Theoretical and Applied Finance, 8* (7), p. 947. https://doi.org/10.1142/S021902490500327X

war in Ukraine, the conflict in the Middle East, and the tensions in the Indo Pacific Region.

These conflicts have arisen along with further developments in and by regional blocs and intergovernmental organisations, such as the BRICs [Brazil, Russia, India, China, South Africa, Iran, Egypt, Ethiopia, and the United Arab Emirates].[11] The BRICs announced in early 2024 that the group of member countries is developing a 'blockchain-based payment system that will be used called BRICS Pay'.[12] The European Union has had a single currency for more than two decades,[13] with implementation in 1999, and are grappling with what the token economy will look like.

Against the backdrop of the above, Anjan Thakor,[14] notes that 'FinTech is part of the process of evolving financial innovation. In reference to the Financial Stability Board (FSB), Thakor notes that the FSB defines FinTech as 'technologically enabled financial innovation that could result in new business models, applications, processes, or products with an associated material effect on financial markets and institutions, and the provision of financial services'.[15] Importantly, the FSB noted that it was premature to specifically or narrowly define FinTech in 2017; arguably, this is still the case today, seven years later. This is because the regulatory framework and law are far from being formally established and agreed upon by most nation-states. The FSB highlights how various definitions of FinTech have emerged, and 'innovation or similar terms that were identified is that they designate an innovative service, business model (which can be provided by an incumbent bank or a non-financial company) or a new-technology start-up in the financial industry'.[16] Notably, the FSB's definition of FinTech has been adopted by the Basel Committee on Banking Supervision.[17] Doing so, at what I call the intermediate stages of FinTech development because society is past the early stage, requiring a high level of discretion. This is because the current status of FinTech, digital finance, and tokens is very fluid, and in some cases unpredictable. Nevertheless, a formal definition evolving as a collective or singular noun for each of these terms will be predicated on the judiciary, governments, regulators, industry, and

11 BRICs, International Bar Association. https://www.ibanet.org/Expanding-BRICS-bloc-challenge-international-order

12 INTELLNEWS, *BRICS Announce a Blockchain-Based Payment System to Create A Common Currency* https://www.intellinews.com/brics-announce-a-blockchain-based-payment-system-to-create-a-common-currency-318710/

13 Maastricht Treaty 1992, *Official Journal of the European Union, C 191*: Creating the Economic and Monetary Union.

14 Anjan V. Thakor, Fintech and Banking: What Do We Know? *Journal of Financial Intermediation* (2019), 2.

15 Ibid., See also Bank for International Settlements, *Sound Practices: Implications of Fintech Developments for Banks and Bank Supervisors. Basel Committee on Banking Supervision* (February 2018). https://www.bis.org/bcbs/publ/d431.pdf

16 Ibid.

17 Ibid.

the market. Nonetheless, and more specifically, between '1866 to 1967, the financial services industry, while heavily interlinked with technology, has generally remained an analogue industry, which Arner and Barberis have named 'FinTech 1.0'.[18] On the other hand, tokens can be traced back over a number of centuries. During the 20th century, there were studies undertaken with animals whereby tokens were used for exchanges/transactions.[19] Similar to FinTech, tokens have developed an economy of their own that is interlinked with other digital financial sectors and products. Arguably, these developments have led to the growth of the token economy, which began to take hold in the 1980s.[20] The token economy has much to offer the world, although it comes with its own challenges. First, today's regulatory landscape is far from settled. This book will discuss and compare some of the evolving regulatory challenges to be addressed. Second, the compliance issues related to money laundering and fraud are yet to be fully understood. This begs the question: will tokens be an enabler of criminal activity such as cybercrime and money laundering? A third pertinent question arises: is society ready for a token economy? Fourth, what is the reach of a token economy? This book will draw upon the work largely undertaken by Douglas Arner, Janos Barberis, and Ross Buckley, who have been instrumental in shaping and influencing the developing legal framework for FinTech.

Essentially, FinTech is comprised of: i) credit, deposits, and capital-raising services; ii) payments, clearing and settlement services, including digital currencies; iii) investment management services; and iv) insurance.[21] In reaffirming the timeframe above of the development of the financial sector more broadly, FinTech, digital finance, and tokens, collectively, fall within the following timeframes over the past century.

While digital finance or tokens are not present in the diagram above, arguably these two concepts[22] fall under the FinTech umbrella and, more broadly, that of the digital finance[23] or digital money[24] economies. Nevertheless, they

18 Maastricht Treaty 1992, *Official Journal of the European Union C 191*: Creating the Economic and Monetary Union.

19 S Ferreri, Token Economy. In FR Volkmar, (eds) ,*Encyclopaedia of Autism Spectrum Disorders* Springer (2013). https://doi.org/10.1007/978-1-4419-1698-3_198 Referring to, John Wolfe, Effectiveness of Token Rewards for Chimpanzees. *Comparative Psychology Monograph, 11* (5, Series No. 60) (1936).

20 AE Kazdin, The Token Economy: A Decade Later, *Journal of Applied Behaviour Analysis, 15* (1982), 431–445.

21 Ibid.

22 Matteo Foglia, Giampiero Maci, Vincenzo Pacelli, FinTech and Fan Tokens: Understanding the Risks Spillover of Digital Asset Investment, *Research in International Business and Finance, 68* (2024). https://doi.org/10.1016/j.ribaf.2023.102190

23 Baxter Hines, *Digital Finance: Security Tokens and Unlocking the Real Potential of Blockchain*, Wiley (2021), p. 94.

24 Jayanth Rama Varma, Blockchain in Finance, *Vikalpa, 44* (1) (2019), 1–11. https://doi.org/10.1177/0256090919839897

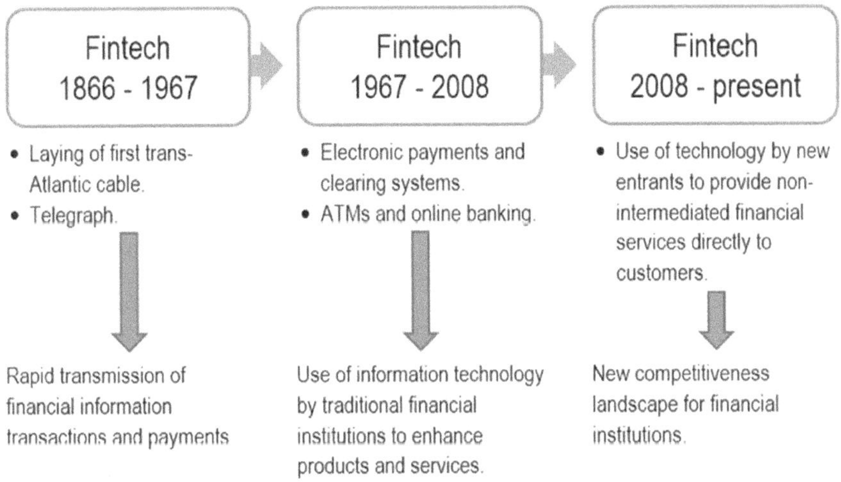

Figure 1.1 The Evolution of FinTech

Source: Anjan V. Thakor Anjan V Thakor, Fintech and Banking: What Do We Know? *Journal of Financial Intermediation* (2019), 2.

are all implementing blockchain technology. These sectors have been evolving gradually over a long period of time. For decades, financial data and information have been transmitted internationally, and this is now a fundamental feature of the modern-day economy.

1.1.1 Defining Digital Finance, FinTech, Tokens

Notwithstanding the above, the World Bank has defined the terms separately:

> Digital financial services are financial services which rely on digital technologies for their delivery and use by consumers.
>
> FinTech is digital technologies that have the potential to transform the provision of financial services. Spurring the development of new, or, modify existing business model, applications, processes and products.[25]

The above definitions were established in 2020, and digital finance has been extended to include services. That is, the World Bank has extended the definition to include services within digital finance, which is the way that these concepts are discussed in this book. Importantly, the above definition relies on a

25 Ceyla Pazarbasioglu, Alfonso Garcia Mora, Mahesh Uttamchandani, Harish Natarajan, Erik Feyen, Mathew Saal, *Digital Financial Services*, World Bank (2020). https://pubdocs.worldbank.org/en/230281588169110691/Digital-Financial-Services.pdf

level of technology to facilitate the operation and application of digital finance and FinTech. Both concepts have brought a level of economic efficiency to the financial sector by making payments simpler, more efficient, and cheaper. This is because people do not have to travel to make a payment; they can simply make payments from their home or office. On the other hand, there is no single definition of tokens. The most recent definition of tokens was offered by Jose Gorrido[26] who notes that there is no settled definition, but describes a token as:

> a unit of value that an organisation creates to self-govern its business model, and empower its users to interact with its products, while facilitating the distribution and sharing of rewards and benefits to all of its stakeholders.[27]

This is a broad definition that allows tokens to apply to anything and possibly everything. In a further development, UNIDROIT (International Institute for the Unification of Private Law)[28] states that a token constitutes a digital asset, which has been established according to Principle 6, which states that a person has 'control' of a digital asset if:

(a) subject to paragraphs (2) and (3), the digital asset, or the relevant protocol or system, confers on that person:
(b) (i) the exclusive ability to prevent others from obtaining substantially all of the benefit from the digital asset;
  (ii) the ability to obtain substantially all of the benefit from the digital asset; and
  (iii) the exclusive ability to transfer the abilities in sub-paragraphs (a)(i), (a)(ii) and (a)(iii) to another person; and

the digital asset, or the relevant protocols or system, allows that person to identify itself as having the abilities set out in paragraph (a). A 'change of control' means a transfer of the abilities in sub (2) paragraph (1)(a) to another person, and includes the replacement, modification, destruction, cancellation, or elimination of a digital asset, and the resulting and corresponding derivative creation of a new digital asset (a 'resulting digital asset') which is subject to the control of another person. (3) An ability for the purposes of sub-paragraph (1)(a) need not be exclusive if and to the extent that: (a) the digital asset, or the relevant protocol or system, limits the use of, or is programmed to make

26 Jose Garrido, *Digital Tokens: A Legal Perspective*, IMF (2023), WP/23/151.
27 Ibid., p. 7.
28 UNIDROIT, *Item No. 4 on the Agenda: Adoption of Draft UNIDROIT Instruments (c) Principles on Digital Assets and Private Law*, 2023. https://www.unidroit.org/wp-content/uploads/2023/04/C.D.-102-6-Principles-on-Digital-Assets-and-Private-Law.pdf

changes to, the digital asset, including change or loss of control of the digital asset; or (b) the person in control has agreed, consented to, or acquiesced in sharing that ability with one or more other persons.[29]

The emphasis placed on the word 'control' is highly significant because it assumes a level of possession. However, possession in this context is not the same as possession as normally understood and applied in criminal law.[30] Rather, UNIDROIT applies the concept of custody according to Principle 10.[31] It remains to be seen whether countries will adopt this approach. Importantly, international organisations such as UNIDROIT view tokens as a form of digital asset, which is often referred to as a 'digital token'.

Notwithstanding the above, the developments and innovations in technology and the implementation of blockchain continue to expand and are a key component of the developing token economy. Tokens, as a singular economic activity, are in the early stages of establishing a market that is represented by digital tokens.[32] The token economy is creating a framework whereby 'asset ownership is recorded on a distributed electronic ledger, and value exchange is peer-to-peer and automated with decentralised computer programmes called "smart contracts"'.[33] To delineate and analyse the various elements of the token economy, the use of smart contracts will also be discussed later in this book as they relate to arbitration. Arbitration is a legal mechanism that allows parties to resolve legal disputes outside of the traditional court process. Post World War II, there has been a steady transformation of technology, leading

29 Ibid., Principle 6.

30 Ibid., p. 39.

31 Ibid., Principle 10, *Custody* (a) 'custodian' means a person who provides services to a client pursuant to a custody agreement as defined in paragraphs (3) and (4), and is acting in that capacity; (b) 'sub-custodian' means a custodian who provides services to another custodian pursuant to a custody agreement as defined in paragraphs (3) and (4), and is acting in that capacity; (c) 'client' means a person to whom a custodian provides services pursuant to a custody agreement as defined in paragraphs (3) and (4). (2) A custodian 'maintains' a digital asset for a client if: (a) that custodian has control of the digital asset; or (b) that custodian enters into a custody agreement, as defined in paragraph (3), with a sub-custodian with respect to the digital asset in the circumstances set out in paragraph (4). (3) Subject to paragraph (4), an agreement for services to a client in relation to a digital asset is a 'custody agreement' if: (a) the service is provided in the ordinary course of the service provider's business; (b) the service provider is obliged to obtain (if this is not yet the case) and to maintain the digital asset for the client; and (c) the client does not have the exclusive ability to change the control of the digital asset within the meaning of Principle 6(2). (4) An agreement to which paragraph (3) applies is not a custody agreement if it is clear from the agreement that, if the service provider enters into an insolvency-related proceeding, the digital asset would be part of the service provider's assets available for distribution to its creditors. (5) The relationship between the custodian and the client may exist notwithstanding that the client may be acting in any capacity on behalf of a third party in relation to the digital asset.

32 Mary Lacity, Horst Treiblmaier, *Blockchains and the Token Economy: Theory and Practice*, Palgrave MacMillan (2022), p. 3.

33 Ibid., p. xxxi.

to its increasing use by the financial sector, particularly in cross-border transnational transactions. As a result there are complex commercial disputes that arise and arbitration is viewed as a mechanism to resolve legal conflicts.

Digital finance has various descriptions depending on the technology used. For instance, 'decentralised finance is financial services offered on a public blockchain over the internet'.[34] Most noteworthy is that decentralised finance is on a public, not a private, blockchain. According to Ozili Peterson, this form of finance goes 'a step further by offering digital financial services on a public database known as blockchain over the internet'.[35] That further step has been achieved through blockchain technology that:

> records information that cannot be changed once recorded. It is often described as a digital ledger of duplicate transactions that are spread across many computer networks. Decentralised finance operates on blockchain technology, and the advantages of blockchain technology to users is that it eliminates delays and failure of intermediaries, it reduces the cost of transactions, and reduces credit risk when used in lending. An example of products formed out of blockchain technology include Bitcoin, Ethereum, Litecoin, Cardano, Polkadot, Bitcoin Cash, Stellar and Chainlink.[36]

Digital transactions and digital investment products are two different things. Apart from transactions and investments, digital finance also involves money, financing, payments, insurance, and advice. Just as important is the technology that supports these financial activities, such as blockchain, distributed ledger technology (DLT), social networks, person-to-person (P2P), big data analytics, and other enablers.[37] However, this does not fully account for the technology that underpins blockchain. For instance, blockchain is supported by advanced technology comprising algorithms. On the other hand, the technologies used by consumers across the digital financial landscape have been defined as agents.[38] It is these agents that are the technology enablers of the new and exciting transformation of digital financial products. It is this technology that is capturing, storing, aggregating, and using knowledge that has been generated over the blockchain.

With the financial sector's transition to digital enablers and agents, the regulation of this developing sector continues to be, one of the most pressing

34 P. Ozili, Decentralized Finance Research and Developments Around the World, *Journal of Bank, Finance Technology*, 6 (2) (2022), 117. https://doi.org/10.1007/s42786-022-00044-x

35 Ibid., p. 117.

36 Ibid.

37 A Pal S Gopi KM Lee, FinTech Agents: Technologies and Theories, *Electronics*, 12 (15) (2023), 3301 https://doi.org/10.3390/electronics12153301

38 Ibid., pp. 1–2.

challenges.[39] For some time, the regulatory approach to digital finance has been highly fragmented. Most compelling is the lack of a uniform, and agreed international approach. This, however, is to be expected. Nation-states will be reviewing the economic and social implications of new technologies for their local economies. Inevitably, there is a level of international competition, requiring nation-states to view the regulatory landscape from their local perspective. One of the most significant challenges for regulators has been the capture and use of data by the sector.[40] Arguably, data is the lifeblood of the financial sector. Without personal and commercial data, transactions and the use of both current and historical financial products would not exist. To illustrate this point, take a person born in 1950. That person has seen the transition of financial products from the humble cheque, which, it could be argued, is a type of token, to the ATM that provides access to cash 24 hours a day. Then the credit or debit card emerged, enabling a person to engage in transactions without having to carry or use cash. While not often discussed, these cards could be seen as a form of token, even though they are never physically exchanged between individuals. The next step in the development of the digital and token economy was the introduction of online banking, enabling the client or customer to make payments or transfer money from home, obviating the need to physically go to a bank or other financial institution to accomplish the transaction. Around the same period, the smartphone was developed. Its applications (apps) could link the user to the Internet, enabling payments to be made in-store and in real time. It has facilitated online banking and transactions, gradually doing away with the credit card. More recently, the use of facial recognition[41] and finger print technology is either being trialled or used to allow people to make payments. Over time, there has been a gradual departure from the use of cash or 'physical money'.

Today, digital finance technology has accelerated, enabling individuals and entities who have an internet connection to access various forms of financial products online.

Gomber et al. introduced the three-dimensional digital finance cube (depicted above). These dimensions are: i) Digital Finance Business Functions, ii) relevant Technologies and Technological Concepts, and iii) Institutions providing digital finance solutions.[42] The formal and functional arrangements of technology that underscore digital finance in the modern period

39 I Kapsis, Artificial Intelligence in Financial Services: Systemic Implications and Regulatory Responses, *Banking and Financial Services Policy Rep.*, *39* (2020), 1–21.

40 Raghuram Rajan, Luigi Zingales, Financial Dependence and Growth, *The American Economic Review*, *88* (3), (1998), 559–586. https://www.nber.org/system/files/working_papers/w5758/w5758.pdf

41 Emi Moriuchi, An Empirical Study of Consumers' Intention to Use Biometric Facial Recognition as a Payment Method, *Psychology & Marketing*, *38* (2021), 1741–1765. https://doi.org/10.1002/mar.21495

42 Ibid.

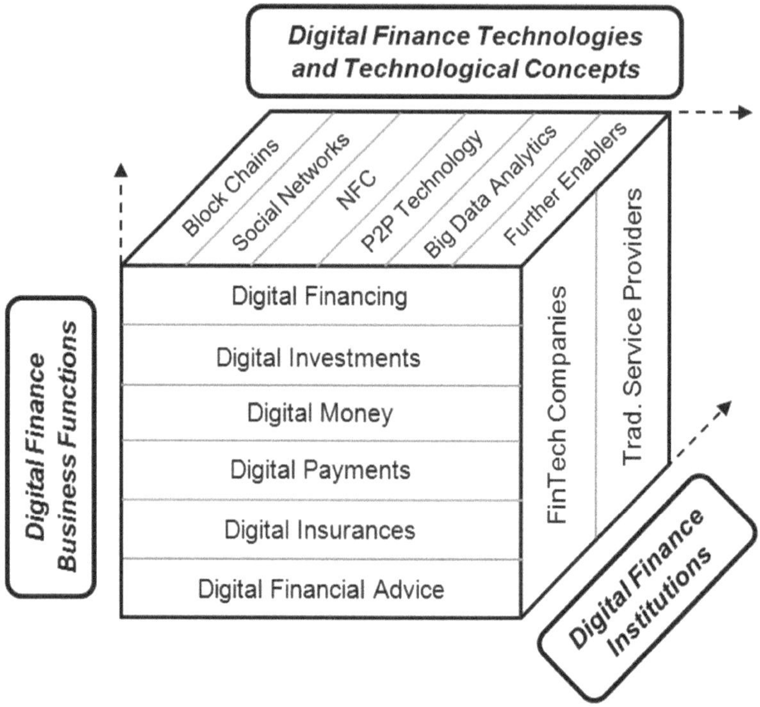

Figure 1.2 The Developing Digital Economy

Source: Gomber et al. Peter Gomber, Jascha-Alexander Koch, Michael Siering, Digital Finance and FinTech: Current Research and Future Research Directions, Working Paper *Journal of Business Economics* (2017), 537–580.

are complex. Not only are there more sophisticated products on the market; these are available to more consumers across the world, provided that they are connected to the Internet. The ensuing question is: what does this mean for society? Another pertinent question is: how has the theory of society generally responded to the evolution of finance and digital finance?

Up to this point in the book, the focus has been on the formal and functional aspects of digital finance and tokens, not on banks. Undoubtedly, the banking system has also been implementing increasingly sophisticated technology, increasing the efficiency of its systems. Arguably, this has allowed banks to broaden their customer base by offering different products. For developing economies, digital finance 'raises the question of whether or not it can be a solution for achieving banking stability in light of both the positive and/or negative effects of financial inclusion on financial stability'.[43] This

43 Frank Antwi, Yusheng Kong, Investigating the Impacts of Digital Finance Technology on Financial Stability of the Banking Sector: New Insights from Developing Market Economies,

is understandable, as developing economies might not have well-structured, formulated, or mature banking or financial regimes, or a legal framework to support the sector. Antwi and Kong, referring to an earlier study by Belinda Del Gaudioet et al.,[44] make the point that even though 'technological changes are commonly perceived to be associated with the growth of an economy as a whole, the beneficial effect and the relative importance of IT, especially in the banking industry, are still under debate'.[45] Therefore, this is an area requiring vigilance and further research.

Just as important as the above is that both the banking and financial sectors play a vital role in ensuring the stability of society. While their primary goal is to return a profit to shareholders, they also have a role to play in terms of public interest: to ensure that there is a level of financial stability for all of society (see theory). Furthermore, the public interest in regard to digital finance has involved the expansion of microfinance entities and products. Another perspective on digital financial inclusion is to see it as providing 'low-cost digital access to financial services, with a particular emphasis on economically underserved demographics,[46] and has assisted in alleviating poverty.[47] The core principles that have emerged from digital finance inclusion are:

- equal access of citizens to financial services provided via digital technologies;
- consistent contractual relations between digital financial service providers and clients;
- available infrastructure for digital provision of financial services;
- adjusted activities of financial institutions and their agents, the protection of consumer rights in digital financial services; and
- increased control over the additional risks (or relocating existing ones) arising in the financial services process using digital technologies.[48]

This level of equality that has found its way into the sector offers new forms of contractual arrangements for digital finance products. They have become a lot

Cogent Business & Management, 10 (3) (2023). https://doi.org/10.1080/23311975.2023.2284738

44 Ibid., referring to Belinda L. Del Gaudio, Claudio Porzio, Gabriele Sampagnaro, Vincenzo Verdoliva, How Do Mobile, Internet and ICT Diffusion Affect the Banking Industry? An Empirical Analysis, *European Management Journal, 39* (2) (2021), 327–332. https://doi.org/10.1016/j.emj.2020.07.003

45 Ibid.

46 Svitlana Naumenkova, Svitlana Mishchenko, Dmytro Dorofeiev, Digital Financial Inclusion: Evidence from Ukraine, *Investment Management and Financial Innovations, 16*(3) (2019), p. 194.

47 Ceyla Pazarbasioglu, Alfonso Garcia Mora, Mahesh Uttamchandani, Harish Natarajan, Erik Feyen, Mathew Saal, *Digital Financial Services*, World Bank (2020). https://pubdocs.worldbank.org/en/230281588169110691/Digital-Financial-Services.pdf

48 Svitlana Naumenkova, Svitlana Mishchenko, Dmytro Dorofeiev, Digital financial inclusion: Evidence from Ukraine*Investment Management and Financial Innovations, 16* (3) (2019), 197.

more accessible than they have been at any other time in history. While banks are heavily regulated across the world, there are still shortcomings in terms of their governance. This has been well documented over decades that have seen substantial economic shocks, resulting in extensive law reform. What is evident is that banks are now being forced to expand their products and services through online banking and the use of tokens[49] such as a stablecoin.

1.1.2 Developments in Tokenomics

Given these developments, it is not surprising that other scholars have proposed other theories to explain this transition throughout the financial sector. Pierluigi Freni, Enrico Ferro, and Roberto Moncada posit that the theory of tokenomics is a new development. They assert that 'in tokenomics, innovation is put forward by designing the rules governing the playground in a way that the stakeholders' behaviour aligns with the goal pursued'.[50] This has required a shift from the passive observation of the ecosystem's reaction to a change to the active design of the ecosystem's constituent laws, aimed at reaching the desired outcome. The tokenisation process, as well as the shift to tokenomics, revolves around the token.[51] Arguably, it is a form of decentralised finance within the broader area of digital finance.

Importantly, the term 'tokenomics' can be used to describe different aspects of a blockchain project such as: 1) the number of tokens issued and the way they are issued (vesting schedule, airdrops, etc.); 2) the economics of a consensus algorithm, largely referred to as crypto-economics; and 3) the general structure of the system, including game-theoretic and economic incentives.[52] Stylianos Kampakis argues that there is a place for auditing the process and application of tokenomics and offers the following explanation: 'the goal of a tokenomics audit is to convince an informed but sceptical reader that the properties and claims of a project are true, given the current and foreseeable conditions in the world'.[53]

Viewed this way, Kampakis' statement is project-based rather than theory-based. This is because it emphasises 'price stability (for stablecoins) or appreciation; creating a store of wealth against inflation; and ensuring real-world utility

49 James Eyers. ANZ the First Bank to Mint an Australian Dollar Stablecoin, *The A$DC, Financial Review* (2022), https://www.afr.com/companies/financial-services/anz-the-first-bank-to-mint-an-australian-dollar-stablecoin-the-a-dc-20220323-p5a743

50 Svitlana Naumenkova, Svitlana Mishchenko, Dmytro Dorofeiev, Digital Financial Inclusion: Evidence from Ukraine. *Investment Management and Financial Innovations, 16* (3) (2019), 197.

51 Ibid.

52 Stylianos Kampakis, *Auditing Tokenomics: A Case Study and Lessons from Auditing a Stablecoin Project*, Centre for Blockchain Technologies, University College London, UK (2022). https://doi.org/10.31585/jbba-5-2-(1)2022

53 Ibid., p. 25.

of the token'. On the other hand, Alfonso Carvalho compares tokens and their financial capacity and capability with that of the traditional financial sector. In drawing these comparisons, he focuses on the values of the related token to a particular good or service.[54] Problematic though is that the current regulatory and economic framework for tokens requires further research. Carvalho is right to take this early view because there is a need to understand the interrelationship between the traditional economy and the new economic trend.

Sadykhov, Goodell, and others reaffirm the views of the aforementioned scholars, referring to this transition as the decentralised token economy or tokenomics,[55] more specifically in relation to tokens themselves. According to Sadykhov and Goodell, this theory relates to the exchange of tokenised goods and services between economic participants. This theory facilitates the analysis of existing policy-setting mechanisms for pricing and risk management to ensure financial stability. Even though the authors do not define a token, they explain that it is a 'process of issuing tokens that represent a digital asset, where the rules and behaviours governing the asset are controlled by smart contracts with the outcomes stored on a blockchain'.[56] Further, Sadykhov and Goodell state that tokenomics is a distinct theory developed to accommodate an economic system that is set apart from other economic systems and includes, but is not limited to, blockchain protocol and smart contract provisions that allocate specific resources such as coins and tokens.[57] This economic system interacts with the broader economic system through a level of market capitalisation involving tokens, and the technology supporting the efficiency of the process. They also argue that this theory is needed to 'achieve controlled and regulated distribution of tokens'.[58] Thus, the authors align tokenomics with the technology itself whereby programs and applications are run in Web 3.0.[59] Tokenomics involves decentralised applications,[60] decentralised autonomous organisation,[61] decentralised finance, [62] and game finance.[63] Moreover, toke-

54 Alfonso Carvalho, *Tokenomics Design and their Parallels in Traditional Finance*, Working Paper (2022).

55 R Sadykhov G Goodell D De Montigny M Schoernig P Treleaven, Decentralized Token Economy Theory (DeTEcT): Token Pricing, Stability and Governance for Token Economies *Front. Blockchain* 6 (1298330) (2023). https://doi.org/10.3389/fbloc.2023.1298330

56 Ibid., p. 1.

57 Ibid., p. 2.

58 Ibid., p. 2.

59 Ibid., in referring to P Treleaven, A Greenwood, H Pithadia, J and Xu, *Web3.0 Tokenization and Decentralized Finance* (2022). https://papers.ssrn.com/sol3/papers.cfm?abstract_id=4037471

60 Ibid., in referring to *Blockchain Distributed Ledger Technologies – Vocabulary* (2023). https://www.iso.org/obp/ui/#iso:std:iso:22739:dis:ed-2:v1:en

61 Ibid., in referring to N. Reiff, *Decentralized Autonomous Organization* (2018). https://www.investopedia.com/tech/what-dao

62 Ibid., referring to R. Sharma, *Decentralized Finance* (2022) https://www.investopedia.com/decentralized-finance-defi-5113835

63 Ibid., referring to E Glover, *Inside GameFi: What It Is, How It Works, Why It's Popular* (2022). https://builtin.com/blockchain/gamefi

nomics[64] has also been applied to include elements of game theory,[65] where it can be applied to predict possible responses from market participants.[66] These concepts have one common denominator: they all apply and use blockchain technology or smart contracts over a distributed ledger. Tokenomics has been designed to establish a new 'framework that models token economies, performs pricing and introduces regulatory control mechanism'.[67] Although the current regulatory framework is in the early stages of development, and it is far from being agreed upon at a nation-state, supranational or international level.

According to the emerging scholarly work in this area, tokenomics is seen as a form of tokenisation.[68] Arguably, the term 'tokenisation' applies to sectors of the economy that have been tokenised. Today, tokens are being used across the economy at a functional level and in different forms. On the other hand, the tokenisation of all areas of the trading and investment economy is far from being fully realised. Nevertheless, tokenomics considers blockchain tokens as a tool facilitating the exchange of value within the blockchain, while the process of tokenisation involves digital or real-world assets that are assigned a digital representation (token) that can be traded on the blockchain.[69] More specifically, this process allows any kind of value to be managed and exchanged as a digital asset, indicating the ability to shift from economics to tokenomics, with stakeholders reacting to changes, that is, to token economics, requiring them to adjust to the tokens.[70] Marin et al. refer to tokenomics as the process of transforming value into tradeable tokens or coins, creating a self-governed economic system with rules set by token designers.[71] The authors take the view that one of the major benefits of this new economic theory is that the tokens themselves will provide 'improvements in asset liquidity through expanded investor pools, transaction efficiency, and transparency, obliging to the anti-laundry money laws in financing the infrastructure'.[72] Should this be fully real-

64 Pierluigi Freni, Enrico Ferro, Roberto Moncada, Tokenomics and Blockchain Tokens: A Design-Oriented Morphological Framework, *Blockchain: Research and Applications*, 3 (1) (2022).

https://doi.org/10.1016/j.bcra.2022.100069 A consistent theme applied by this theory is the use of blockchain technology.

65 Von Neumann and O. Morgenstern, *Theory of Games and Economic Behavior*, Princeton University Press (1944) examines the behaviour based on games and strategies.

66 Domas Golysenko, *Game Theory in Tokenomics* (2024). https://blacktokenomics.com/game-theory-in-tokenomics-design/ To apply game theory in this situation, is to utilise a mathematical study of strategic interactions where the outcome of an individual's decision depends on the choices of others.

67 Ibid., p. 16.

68 O Marin, T Cioara, L Toderean, D Mitrea, I Anghel, Review of Blockchain Tokens Creation and Valuation, *Future Internet* (2023), p. 7. https://doi.org/10.3390/fi15120382

69 Ibid.

70 Ibid.

71 Ibid.

72 Ibid.

ised, the world may experience a reduction in economic shocks. However, the jury is still out in relation to this proposition. It has not yet been fully understood what, if any, geopolitical influences or criminal activity can result from the use of tokens and threaten to subvert the current economic regime. While tokenomics as a new theory of economics is shaping the way policymakers and regulators will approach the governance of this activity more broadly, it will become an important feature of society in general. This is evident when one considers the theory of society in the context of the financial sector's development for more than a century. The next section will briefly draw upon the theory of society proposed by key philosophers such as John Rawls, Max Weber, and John Rawls, amongst others.

1.1.3 Theory of Society and Tokenomics

Society cannot function without a clear and certain framework or regime that provides a high level of governance in all sectors, including finance. Importantly, and particularly in this era of rapid technological developments, the law has to provide and continue to provide a high level of certainty that has been enjoyed worldwide for centuries. In 1651, Thomas Hobbes argued that the 'essential role of the law is to provide a system that allows the parties to have trust in receiving their performance under a binding agreement'.[73] Hobbes' stance is still highly relevant today, especially in terms of commercial activities that are now being conducted via the Internet. The use and application of tokens based on blockchain technology and the application of smart contracts are a form of binding agreement established online. As such, the binding agreement inherent in a smart contract is established by a system that provides a high level of trust between the relevant parties.

More than a century later, Georg Wilhelm Friedrich Hegel (1770–1831) became notable for his social philosophy explained in his book, *Science of Logic*. Arguably, this can be interlinked with the broader theory of society and transcends 'subject-matters of human reflection, such as metaphysics, epistemology, law, ethics, politics, theology, arts, and history'.[74] Society requires these subject matters in order to function. Hegel applied concepts such as law and technology to the science of logic through the 'universal representation but a systematic semantical structure that includes sides or moments and inner semantical references to other concepts'.[75] According to Hegel, each

73 Thomas Hobbes, *Leviathan* (first published 1651, Penguin 1985) passim. In Maren K. Woebbeking, The Impact of Smart Contracts on Traditional Concepts of Contract Law, *JIPITEC*, 10 (2019), 113.

74 Gianfrancesco Zanetti, Mortimer Sellers, Stephan Kirste, *Handbook of the History of the Philosophy of Law and Social Philosophy Volume 2: From Kant to Nietzsche*, Springer Nature (2023), p. 129.

75 Ibid., p. 130.

concept, taken by itself and isolated from others, leads to a contradiction.[76] For instance, the law is a completely separate concept and is used to govern society, and therefore, it is a societal function that is only beginning to be fully realised by modern-day technology. Likewise, the concept of technology is different from that of the law. Generally, it is well understood that any technological innovation will come well before any law has been developed by the government to regulate its use. It is only when society demands that a level of regulation and law be developed to minimise any adverse economic, social, environmental, or national security threats, that regulation will be established. There is no better example than social media today, which has governments around the world continuing to respond to societal demands to strengthen the regulation of access, use, and transmission of personal data. Hence, and in alignment with Hegel's philosophy, I agree that for a proper, functioning token economy, there is a need to integrate regulation/law and technology. Put another way, this philosophy can be applied to data protection/data flow laws and cybersecurity laws in general, yet there is currently a significant gap because tokens and much of the digital finance landscape remain unregulated.

In turn, one of the most highly-regarded English legal theorists is John Austin, who proposed the top-down theoritecal approach where rules are imposed on society by certain authorised entities.[77] Across the digital financial sector, this has been far from the case. It could be argued that to date, and in many respects, what prevails in this sector is analogous to the Wild West. Austin posits that laws are commands of a sovereign. The sovereign is the nation-state. This is certainly evident in recent times, with nation states developing data and cybersecurity laws. Over the past century, nation-states have been refining the law of finance, which has culminated in the gradual development of laws pertaining to digital finance and tokens. Austin refers to these as positive laws, which establish recommendations requiring certain things to be done in a certain way. There is no better example in finance law today than the requirement that an entity must have a licence to conduct and provide financial and banking services and products. A licence issued under a legal regime by the nation-state allows for an entity to provide financial and banking services. For tokens, a similar requirement is beginning to emerge in some countries such as the United States and Singapore.

In addition to the aforesaid philosophers, it is also worth mentioning the renowned British philosopher, Jeremy Bentham, who called for the 'rationalisation of the laws according to the principle of utility and their systematic codification'.[78] He applied the concept of utility to his work and defined law as

76 Ibid.
77 Ibid., p. 3.
78 Ibid., p. 12.

> an assemblage of signs declarative of a volition conceived or adopted by the sovereign in a state, concerning the conduct to be observed in a certain case by a certain person or class of persons, who in the case in question are or are supposed to be subject to his power: such volition trusting for its accomplishment to the expectation of certain events which it is intended such declaration should upon occasion be a means of bringing to pass, and the prospect of which it is intended should act as a motive upon those whose conduct is in question.[79]

Arguably, there is some similarity between Bentham's philosophy and Austin's position: that the law is adopted by the sovereign and observed by certain persons, ostensibly including all of society. Therefore, as laws develop for tokens and digital finance, they will apply to all of society within the borders of the sovereign state.

Another leading British legal theorist was Albert Venn Dicey, who advocated for and argued that 'parliamentary sovereignty and the rule of law are complementary. Parliament's sovereignty is only expressed through the Acts of Parliament'.[80] Most noteworthy is how Dicey applied the theory of the rule of law by 're-proposes the principles, values, and standards of the common law, identifying them with those of liberal philosophy'.[81] Even though Dicey was applying the theory of the rule of law and constitutionalism to a level of judicial power, the rights of the people were central to these theories. In terms of the modern period of technology and the law, people's rights are increasingly at the forefront of issues considered by policymakers and regulators, particularly in relation to electronic data. Data is the backbone of digital finance and will be for the token economy. Likewise, as I have stated, cybersecurity will be just as important. These are important to the theory of society because they ensure that certain societal norms are established for all, and not just a few.

Bentham and Dicey were the predecessors of Immanuel Kant, whose studies in the fields of 'philosophy, physics, and mathematics'[82] were significant and influential. This is an important point because modern-day technology, specifically quantum technology, is largely based on physics and mathematics. Mathematics underpins the technology of blockchain and, in turn, tokens and other areas of the digital finance economy. Kant believed that the doctrine of right was at the forefront of the development of the law, and that private right requires public right, which is enjoyed only within a legal state.[83]

79 Ibid., p. 14.
80 Ibid., p. 79.
81 Ibid., p. 82.
82 Ibid., p. 193.
83 Ibid., p. 203.

American political philosopher John Rawls, affirmed that a 'good society is the greatest achievement of individual interests for the greatest number of citizens, and the role of the political realm is to protect individuals by leaving them unhindered in pursuit of their interests'.[84] This position taken by Rawls can be directly related to today's financial sector. Arguably, while the financial system has a high level of control over the population, no matter where one resides, indirectly, its function allows individuals to pursue their own interests. For Rawls, the process of active participation extends across the public sphere.[85]

Although Rawls was discussing individual interests in the context of citizenship, a relationship can be drawn between the citizen and the token economy. They are mutually exclusive, yet they co-exist because, without humans (citizens of a state), the development of the technology that supports the token economy would not exist.

On the other hand, Max Weber succinctly states: 'man sought to acquire, by his own hands, the work of nature that he needed for his nourishment, clothing, and protection against the cold and the weather'.[86] Weber went on to say that in order to maintain his or her existence, the individual was already – and always would be – dependent upon social relationships with others. Taking a broader economic perspective, Weber wrote that:

> the economy of the household included brothers, cousins, sisters-in-law to the furthest degree, and unfree household servants; they were all subjected to a military-like power; or else, those whom cold and the death of livestock robbed of their possessions wished to live by [even] the oldest of all legal principles, namely having to become the slaves of the physically triumphant and of the owners of property. The family of this sort is the oldest economic community. They produced goods through common work and consumed them in common.[87]

Here, Weber's description of the household economy suggests that the exchange of products is a form of tokenised economy, albeit local at that time. For instance, the token was a product, such as an animal, that was exchanged for grains. Weber goes on to explain the extent to which this historical practice was embedded in the economy, calling it a 'community of exchange that encompasses within it an increasing number of other economic actors and activities'.[88] In other words, the evolution of token exchanges began in a very small way to become, as society has grown and become more sophisticated,

84 John Rawls, *A Theory of Justice*, Belknap Press (1971), p. 227.
85 Ibid.
86 Max Weber, Stock and Commodity Exchanges [Die Börse (1894)]. *Theory and Society*, *29* (3) (2000), p. 306. https://www.jstor.org/stable/3108485
87 Ibid., p. 306.
88 Ibid., p. 307.

a community of exchange that now relies increasingly on technology that facilitates transactions between individuals and entities.

More specifically, John Locke explained his political philosophy in his work, *Two Treatises of Government*, published anonymously in 1689.[89] As highlighted by Lee Ward, Locke's philosophy focused on five specific areas: 1) a state of nature, 2) individual natural rights, 3) a right of revolution, 4) rejection of republican ideas of civic virtue, and 5) endorsement of the traditional English constitutional separation of powers. Locke's position on separation of powers is well entrenched in many jurisdictions, within and by the law, although often blurred politically. Locke's philosophy can easily be applied to the modern token economy. In fact, the jurisdictions compared in this book all subscribe, in part, to elements of Locke's view of society. The exception is the European Union, as it is not constitutionalised. To explain: in 2004, the European Council approved the *Constitutional Treaty*,[90] however, this would fail, and the *Lisbon Treaty*[91] was established to replace it because the Irish people opposed the constitution. Despite this constitutional hurdle for the European Union, the EU continues to use a single currency and has embraced the notion of individual natural rights. It is these natural rights that are embedded in democratic jurisdictions that give individuals the freedom to develop and innovate across economic sectors. Without natural rights, technological advancements would be significantly constrained until governments became fully aware of the potential negative impacts they may have on society in general.

Also significant is how, the past two decades in particular have seen the increasing adoption of technology. It could be argued that while capitalism has enabled and facilitated these innovations, a type of socialism has emerged beyond what the general population would understand. Robert van der Veen and Philippe van Parijs, drawing on Karl Marx's earlier works and his 1859 *Critique of the Political Economy*, argue that the

> development of the productive forces is fettered under advanced capitalism: the productivity of labour grows at a rate that is lower than it would be if relations of production were if socialism were substituted for capitalism. This is because profit maximization, which competition forces capitalists to seek, does not necessarily coincide with the maximization of labour productivity or – what comes down to the same thing – with the minimization of the amount of labour that is required directly (as living labour) or indirectly (as means of production) to produce one unit of output.[92]

89 John Locke, Lee Ward, *Two Treatises of Government*. Focus, 9th Edition (2016), p. xii.
90 Treaty Establishing the Constitution for Europe, *Official Journal of the European Union*, *C 310*.
91 Treaty of Lisbon, *Official Journal of the European Union, C 83/171* (2010).
92 Robert van der Veen, Philippe van Parijs, A Capitalist Road to Communism. *Theory and Society*, *15* (5) (1986), 635–639. http://www.jstor.org/stable/657301

Put another way, capitalism is a transient form of production[93] that has shaped the way technology has developed. It has shaped the financial sector for more than a century. However, in industry parlance today, does the technology invariably create a greater level of socialism?

In regard to society, the stark reality is that it is influenced and shaped by a number of factors such as democracy, socialism, economics, the state of nature, the social contract, and, today, the Internet of Things (IoT). Some scholars have argued that capitalism is being transformed as a consequence of the development and expansion of IoT. This transformation has been defined by Shoshana Zuboff as a form of surveillance capitalism, which is a new economic order that claims human experience is a free raw material used for hidden commercial practices of extraction, prediction and sale.[94] Zuboff posits that the level of access that technology has to individuals allows these entities to obtain a 'dominance over a data society, challenging democracy itself'.[95] If this is true, and I have no reason to argue otherwise, when applying Zuboff's position to the theory of society and to blockchain technology, it can be argued that the surveillance of tokens can be undertaken more easily because a wallet address is automatically published on the blockchain. Yet, this is likely to be different when the wallet is on a public, private, or consortium blockchain. This is because, as their titles suggest, a public blockchain is open for all to see. On the other hand, a private blockchain is limited to the parties, and thus, there is a level of restricted access and traceability. A consortium blockchain allows for a group of entities to enter and use the blockchain, with restrictions to those that are not part of the consortium. However, the issue of transparency or surveillance has to be weighed against the benefits that this technology provides by enabling multiple transactions of a single token to be tracked and traced. The very notion that society is changing as a result of digital transformation has been viewed by scholars as being of benefit to the 'sovereign state, as it limits the number of entities the state is obliged to collaborate with for the purpose of various forms of supervision over end users of the digital market'[96] including digital finance. The result of this transformation is that private entities are now able to undertake activities once thought of as being the responsibility of the sovereign only. Put another way, private entities that have access to and control of the Internet platforms that individuals use can easily be monitored. Despite some disadvantages, the technology has improved system efficiency, making financial transactions simpler and easier. Also, in many countries worldwide, the technology allows and encourages citizens to interact with the government.

93 Ibid., p. 640.

94 Shoshana Zuboff, *The Age of Surveillance Capitalism. The Fight for a Human Future at the New Frontier of Power* (2019), p. 8.

95 Ibid., p. 1.

96 Marek Ratajczak, *Digital Finance and the Future of the Global Financial System*, Routledge, 1st ed. (2022), p. 100.

On the other hand, Peter Berger and Thomas Luckmann make the point that the transformation of a social world is generally based on historical events. As mentioned earlier in this book, historical events from around the world, whether economic, social, geopolitical, or conflict-related, have all shaped the economy, particularly the finance sector. Berger and Luckmann also point out that

> historically the creators of the first social world, say A and B, 'can always reconstruct the circumstances under which their world and any part of it was established … and their recollection explains how their world and any part of it was established'.[97]

The authors go on to state:

> ideology is taken on by a group because of specific theoretical elements that are conducive to its interests. For example, when an impoverished peasant group struggles against an urban merchant group that has financially enslaved it, it may rally around a religious doctrine that upholds the virtues of agrarian life, condemns the money economy and its credit system as immoral, and generally decries the luxuries of urban living.[98]

In applying this theory or notion to the modern period of technology, is society in general already enslaved? Also pertinent to this question or observation is the fact that with the concentration of technology that facilitates digital finance for a few across the world, which has resulted in a level of monopolisation. That said, it is argued that this is inevitable with any new innovation. Go back more than 100 years to when the first motor vehicle was manufactured: the company that developed this technology monopolised the automotive industry for some time. Thus, if the enslavement analogy is applied to the token economy, government and regulators will need to strike a balance between providing a pathway to innovation and encouraging competition across the sector, in order to ensure that no single entity holds all the rights.

The various theories related to society and the law, discussed briefly above, indicate that society will undergo a significant transformation as a result of changes in the financial sector, particularly with regard to tokens and the digital finance economy. The transformation of society has been remarkable when we consider that over the centuries, people have used a range of tokens to conduct transactions, moving from clay, paper, and metal tokens (amongst many others) to the modern-day token introduced by technology. The major difference is that the earlier tokens were tangible: physically held, used, and

97 Peter Berger, Thomas Luckman, *The Social Construction of Reality*, Penguin Books (1967), p. 79.

98 Ibid., p. 141.

transacted between individuals and entities. Today, the modern token is not as tangible because it is developed by technology and requires a technological device (e.g. a smartphone, which is the tangible item). A person does not physically hold the modern-day token. That said, the nation-state and supranational polity of the EU need to establish laws to regulate the safe exchange of such tokens. The laws can be informed by the above and other well-established philosophers. Most importantly, any rules that are established must ensure that the rule of law is retained, based on a set of principles and values pertaining to each of the sovereigns. This will ensure that the legal framework will be coherent, and not a highly fragmented regime. For financial stability and certainty, legal convergence is essential in this new area of the economy.

1.2 Technology – Digital Finance and Tokens

The technology that is supporting the development of an increasing number of digital financial products is difficult for laypersons to understand, particularly those who do not have a technology background. This section briefly discusses the development of artificial intelligence (AI) technology that is used by digital finance platforms to facilitate transactions. It traces some of the theories that have emerged to support the development of AI. Blockchain, which is underpinned by AI technology,[99] is having a significant impact on the digital finance landscape. While most commentators and scholars discuss this technology in the context of the modern period, computers and AI have been researched and discussed by scholars for more than five decades.

In 1947, Alan Turing,[100] regarded as the 'father of artificial intelligence', stated that 'computing machines all have a central mechanism or control and some very extensive form of memory'.[101] It is this reference to memory that has developed artificial intelligence. Over time, as computers became more sophisticated and the number of data entries increased at an unprecedented rate, the memory has expanded. These early steps eventually led to the development of AI as we know it today.

Importantly, Turing notes that the humble book, which can be viewed by the human eye, is a form of memory captured in written script for other humans to read. Moreover, at the time of writing, in order for a digital computer to exercise a level of 'intelligence', much larger capacities than are yet available must be provided.[102] The digital computer was developed as

99 John McCarthy. *First Order Theories of Individual Concepts and Propositions*, Stanford University (2000), pp. 21–23, http://jmc.stanford.edu/articles/concepts/concepts.pdf

100 Alan Turing, *Lecture to the London Mathematical Society* (20 February 1947). https://www.vordenker.de/downloads/turing-vorlesung.pdf

101 Ibid., p. 2.

102 Ibid., p. 5.

a machine 'intended to carry out any operations which could be done by a human computer'.[103]

Most noteworthy, Turing stated that the 'digital computer is an old one, whereby, Charles Babbage, Lucasian Professor of Mathematics at Cambridge from 1828 to 1839, planned such a machine, called the Analytical Engine, but it was never completed'.[104] The development of AI began to take off between 1957 and 1974 when computers could store more information and became faster, cheaper, and more accessible. Machine-learning algorithms also improved, and people got better at knowing which algorithm to apply to their problem.[105]

On the other hand, John McCarthy and Patrick Hayes, when writing about this topic in 1969, made the point that:

> A computer program capable of acting intelligently in the world must have a general representation of the world in terms of which its inputs are interpreted. Designing such a program requires commitments about what knowledge is and how it is obtained. Thus, some of the major traditional problems of philosophy arise in artificial intelligence.[106]

Viewed this way, what can emerge from AI is a computer program that can perform certain functions. During the earlier period, the development of AI was largely based on 'mathematical theorems, transforming one symbolic expression into another by given rules, integrating expressions composed of elementary functions, determining chemical compounds consistent with mass-spectrographic and other data'.[107] The application of a philosophy of intelligence to the theory of computer development has resulted in significant transformations across society. In defining this philosophy, in 1969, McCarthy and Hayes expressed the view that 'a machine is intelligent if it solves certain classes of problems requiring intelligence in humans, or survives in an intellectually demanding environment'.[108] In the early stages of computer development, the intelligence that a computer has depends on what is input by humans. Put another way, a human has traditionally had to input data, which translates to a level of intelligence. However, the above definition originally was based on two elements: 'the epistemological and the heuristic'.[109] First, the

103 Alan Turing, Computing Machinery and Intelligence, *Mind, 49* (1950), 433–460. https://redirect.cs.umbc.edu/courses/471/papers/turing.pdf

104 Ibid., p. 438.

105 Rockwell Anyoha. *The History of Artificial Intelligence*, 2017. https://sitn.hms.harvard.edu/flash/2017/history-artificial-intelligence/

106 John McCarthy, Patrick Hayes, Some Philosophical Problems from the Standpoint of Artificial Intelligence. *Machine Intelligence* (1969), 1. http://www.inf.ufsc.br/~mauro.roisenberg/ine6102/leituras/mcchay69.pdf

107 Ibid., p. 2.

108 Ibid., p. 3.

109 Ibid., p. 5.

> epistemological part is the representation of the world in such a form that the solution of problems follows from the facts expressed in the representation. Second, the heuristic part is the mechanism that on the basis of the information solves the problem and decides what to do.[110]

In reference to the 1950s to 1960s, 'artificial intelligence so far can be regarded as devoted to the heuristic part of the problem'.[111] The subsequent development of computer systems and AI has resulted in the collection, storage, and use of knowledge. It is the knowledge that comes from the data, which is aggregated by human input, that provides a level of computer intelligence.

In 1977, a study undertaken by Ira Goldstein and Seymour Papert noted that AI represented a new style of thinking about cognition that 'is having an important impact on the study of language'.[112] The authors expand on language, stating that

> 'frame theory' is an AI approach to representing knowledge that generalises the linguistic notion of case grammars in a manner that allows the representation not only of syntactic knowledge, but also procedural knowledge for how to construct a parse as well as related semantic, contextual, and thematic facts.[113]

Further, they argue that the fame itself is a system or systems 'developed in equal measure from problems arising-from the construction of adequate theories for vision, for memory, for logical reasoning, and for the comprehension of language'.[114] The frame theory leads to the logical conclusion that knowledge and information are framed within a computer AI system in order to solve problems.

In the late 1970s, the theory of knowledge pertaining to AI was represented in three forms: knowledge representation, knowledge utilisation and knowledge acquisition.[115] One of the most complex questions arising in the early 1980s was: how is it possible to acquire knowledge important for problem solving in such a way that a computer facilitates the transfer of expertise from humans to symbolic data structures that constitute the representation of knowledge by the machine?[116] This was viewed as one of the most complex hurdles to overcome, since the data collected and input into an AI system must be able to solve problems encountered by humans. Generally, these

110 Ibid.
111 Ibid.
112 Ira Goldstein, Seymour Papert. *Artificial Intelligence, Language, and the Study of Knowledge*, Massachusetts Institute of Technology (1977), p. 84.
113 Ibid., p. 89.
114 Ibid.
115 Edward Feigenbaum, *Knowledge Engineering: The Applied Side of Artificial Intelligence*, Stanford University (1980), p. 2. https://apps.dtic.mil/sti/tr/pdf/ADA092574.pdf
116 Ibid.

data structures have all but been fully addressed today. The early beginnings of AI development revealed the complexities that scientists and developers wanted to address so that AI could be used to solve human-related problems for humans. Today, society is experiencing the way data has been aggregated into large quantities of knowledge to resolve health, environmental, and social problems for the human population. In the same year, decision theory was formulated,[117] highlighting the early concerns regarding the application of algorithms. Algorithms are an essential component of AI, involving machine learning from the captured data and, in turn, making predictions.

Allen Newell[118] describes knowledge as a 'physical structure that can fill the functional role, and is never filled directly'.[119] Indeed knowledge is not 'necessarily seen and is the result of interpretive processes operating on symbolic expressions, and it requires both processes and data structures'.[120] However, it must be said that Newell was defining knowledge in the context of technology and the computer. Therefore, in practice, the theory of knowledge is an approximation that Newell refers to as the symbol level. In turn, the symbol level describes how

> information-processing agents arrive at actions by means of search for problem spaces, and search of global data bases that map structures which are representations of given knowledge to structures. These are then representations of task-state knowledge that create representations of solutions.[121]

Newell concludes that:

> approximation is such that the representation at the symbol level can be seen as knowledge plus the access structure to that knowledge. At the computer systems level it features 1) a complete absence of structure, as characterized at the configuration level; 2) no specification of processing mechanisms, only a global principle to be satisfied by the system behaviour; 3) a radical degree of approximation that does not guarantee a deterministic machine; and 4) a medium that is not realised in physical space in a passive way, but only in an active process of selection.[122]

117 Jerome Feldman, Decision Theory and Artificial Intelligence II: The Hungry Monkey, *Cognitive Science 1* (1977), 158–192. Decision theory helps a symbolic problem-solver search for the best plan that achieves a given goal. It is the technology as a whole that today is able to solve complex problems.

118 Allen Newell, The Knowledge Level, *AI Magazine*, *2* (2) (1981), 1–20. Originally delivered as the Presidential Address, American Association for Artificial Intelligence, AAAI80, Stanford, CA, August 1980.

119 Ibid., p. 11.

120 Ibid.

121 Ibid., p. 12.

122 Ibid., p. 19.

By 1989, Newell went a step further and extended the theory of knowledge to the theory of psychology [123] and cognition.[124] Despite Newell's shift in perspective, it can be argued that knowledge and psychology are closely intertwined. This is because psychology is a form of knowledge that is informed by the capture of information. Put another way, Ira Goldstein, in his Seymour Paper, put forward the theory of intelligence.[125] One could be excused for assuming that the authors were theorising intelligence in terms of artificial intelligence. On the other hand, in fact, understanding intelligence is not the 'identification of a few powerful techniques, but rather the question of how to represent large amounts of knowledge in a fashion that permits their effective use and interaction'.[126]

Even more compelling, more than 40 years after Newell formulated his theory, it can be argued that there is a clear pathway forward although there is a lack of agreed global principles that govern AI. Thus, for Newell, the theory of knowledge and representation corresponds to how AI uses terms in (evolving) everyday scientific practice. It is a refinement of several fundamental features of adaptive systems that have been well articulated, and it has nothing that is incompatible with foundational work in logic.[127] Fast forward to 2024, and this theory of knowledge has not changed all that much. What has changed is the quantity and quality of data that is now available through computers and AI systems that now learn from the knowledge with which they have been supplied (machine learning). Nikolos Gurney and David Pynadat[128] recently put forward the theory of the mind in AI, which underpins much of human social cognition.[129] Gurney and Pynadat draw upon the above theories of language, cognition, and psychology that contribute to large language models that now make up AI, particularly machine learning.

1.2.1 Machine Learning [ML]

In addition to the previous section, one could also be forgiven for assuming that ML is also a recent phenomenon in the same way as digital finance and

123 Allen Newell, Artificial Intelligence and the Concept of Mind (1973). In Ira Goldstein, Seymour Papert, *Artificial Intelligence, Language, and the Study of Knowledge*, Massachusetts Institute of Technology (1977).

124 Allen Newell, *The 1987 William James Lectures United Theories of Cognition*, Carnegie-Mellon University. http://iiif.library.cmu.edu/file/Newell_box00022_fld01506_doc0001/Newell_box00022_fld01506_doc0001.pdf

125 Ira Goldstein, Seymour Papert, *Artificial Intelligence, Language, and the Study of Knowledge*, Massachusetts Institute of Technology (1977), p. 85.

126 Ibid.

127 Allen Newell, The Knowledge Level, *AI Magazine*, *2* (2) (1981), 1–20. Originally delivered as the Presidential Address, American Association for Artificial Intelligence, AAAI80, Stanford, CA, August 1980.

128 Nikolos Gurney, David Pynadat, *Spontaneous Theory of Mind for Artificial Intelligence* (2024). https://arxiv.org/pdf/2402.13272v1

129 Ibid., p. 1.

the technology that supports it. In fact, in 1959, after conducting a series of experiments, AL Samuel wrote that computer games contained some level of AI or ML.[130] Samuel noted how the experiments were able to demonstrate that a 'device contained a level of learning schemes which outperform an average person and that such learning schemes may eventually be economically feasible as applied to real-life problems'.[131] More than six decades later, this level of ML has not only been extensively modified and updated; today, it is performing at a level close to human learning. It is important to note that this book is not discussing the in-depth level of ML technology and comparing it with the scientific learning levels of humans. This section is providing an overview of ML and how it is used in the technology that supports digital finance and tokens. Put another way, in 1949 and a decade before Samuel, McCulloch made the observation that in order to 'compute as we do, a machine must have some kind of memory. A level of memory was applied to the humble clock/punch-card used to record an employee's start and conclusion of the work day'. That is, the punch/clock card was a very simple small computer that had to record and memorise a time, in order to mark the card with a time or symbol at the start or conclusion of the working day.[132]

In 2024, ML combined with other technology, such as AI and quantum computing, is beginning to substantially change the technological landscape of digital finance and tokens. The most substantial change is the quantity and quality of data that is captured by applications and the services derived from that data. The profound changes and challenges are only beginning to be fully realised. Scholars and practitioners have been researching and developing practical solutions in this area, not only by advancing the technology itself but also, informing governments and regulators of the need for a level of regulation. For instance, blockchain technology has been a significant disruptor of the FinTech sector that enables functional improvements and innovations in existing business models, or even disruption through the creation of new business models and innovative products and services (disruptive, enhancing user experience).[133] Blockchain technology relies on algorithms and ML[134] to improve its operation and application to digital financial products.

130 AL Samuel, Some Studies in Machine Learning Using the Game of Checkers *IBM J. Res. Dev., 3* (1959), 210–229.

131 Ibid.

132 S Warren, C McCulloch. The Brain as a Computing Machine, *Electrical Engineering, 69* (1949), 492. https://journal.emergentpublications.com/Article/6ab86c78-c4e7-43a8-aeeb-ffb95fd0eb7c/academic

133 P Gomber, RJ Kauffman, C Parker, BW Weber, On the Fintech Revolution: Interpreting the Forces of Innovation, Disruption, and Transformation in Financial Services, *Journal of Management Information Systems, 35* (1) (2018), 220–265. https://doi.org/10.1080/07421222.2018.1440766

134 Coinbase. https://www.coinbase.com/en-au/blog/blockchain-for-ai See also IMI Blockchain, *Blockchain. & Machine Learning Use Cases & Key Benefits in Major Industries* https://imiblockchain.com/blockchain-machine-learning/

Another way to view ML is as a subgroup of AI.[135] Sarah Chojecki and Sophie Nappert, in referring to Jay D. Aronson, Gregory Scopino, and Maxi Scherer, state that ML is:

> the science of creating computing systems that are programmed to arrive at logical conclusions about the world through exposure to, and processing of, data. While machine learning concepts have existed since the early stages of AI, its prominence grew with the advent of big data. Unlike expert systems that rely on pre-determined norms encoded in a program, machine learning programs leverage extensive sample data to extract relevant algorithms. Learning algorithms … make other algorithms, enabling computers to self-generate programs. This process is achieved by identifying repeat patterns in the data. Employing statistical and probabilistic methods, machine learning algorithms calculate the probability of specific outcomes based on the extracted algorithms.[136]

The interaction of all the parts of the scientific process that makes up ML is complex and difficult to understand but can be simply reduced to a function. The technology functions by combining the various components of the system to produce an outcome. This is analogous to the functioning of a motor vehicle: all of the components of an engine perform separate but important functions that allow the engine, as a whole, to operate. AI and ML have functional attributes very similar to those of a motor engine. It is the next phase of this function that is even more important to the learning process. In other words, as the authors note, 'by continually analysing data over time, machine-learning algorithms can refine their models to produce increasingly accurate results'.[137]

Based on the above, it is argued that over time, as the ML is afforded more data, it will become more proficient at resolving problems. This is no different from the way the human brain operates: as the human ages and transitions from child to adult, the brain learns from the input of data, instructions, and undertaking physical functions. Over time, the human reaches a level of proficiency enabling him/her to perform certain tasks.

135 Sarah Elisabeth Chojecki, Sophie Nappert, Evidence in International Arbitration through the Looking-Glass of the Digital Economy. In Nassib G Ziadé (ed), *BCDR International Arbitration Review* (© Kluwer Law International; Kluwer Law International, 2021, 8 (1)) pp. 121–122. See also, Jay D Aronson, Computer Vision and Machine Learning for Human Rights Video Analysis: Case Studies, Possibilities, Concerns, and Limitations, *Law & Social Inquiry*, *43* (4) (2018), 1188 at 1193. Gregory Scopino, op. cit., fn 17, p. 26 (quoting Pedro Domingos, *The Master Algorithms: How the Quest for the Ultimate Learning Machine Will Remake Our World*, Basic Books, 2015, p. 6. Maxi Scherer, Artificial Intelligence and Legal Decision-Making: The Wide Open? Study on the Example of International Arbitration, *Queen Mary School of Law Legal Studies Research Papers*, *318* (23 May 2019). https://ssrn.com/abstract=3392669

136 Ibid.

137 Ibid.

However, ML has several problematic elements such as the potential for bias and the infringement of rights, segregating certain ethnic and religious groups in society. This is an area requiring further research and is outside the scope of this book. Chojecki and Nappert also highlight how deep learning is another category of ML that has significantly advanced technological capabilities that accelerate the collection, analysis, and interpretation of vast amounts of data (big data) and facilitated the extraction of complex patterns and features that were previously challenging to uncover.[138] Moreover, deep learning has played a pivotal role in advancing the highly discussed field of generative AI by providing the necessary methodologies and algorithms to train models capable of generating new content, encompassing images, music, and text, along with Large Language Model-based systems (LLMS).[139] Today, society is experiencing profound changes due to technology that is able to learn from itself and the functions it performs.

The technological innovations described above have led to the development of blockchain – a technology that has become central to digital finance and tokens. The three types of blockchain are described below, classified according to their degree of decentralisation:

- *Public blockchains*: A blockchain that anyone in the world can read, anyone in the world can send transactions to and expect to see them included if they are valid, and anyone in the world can participate in the *consensus process* – the process for determining what blocks get added to the chain and what the current state is. These blockchains are generally considered to be fully decentralised.
- *Consortium blockchains*: A blockchain where the consensus process is controlled by a pre-selected set of nodes; for example, one might imagine a consortium of 15 financial institutions, each of which operates a node and of which ten must sign every block in order for the block to be valid. The right to read the blockchain may be public or restricted to the participants. These blockchains may be considered partially decentralised.
- *Fully private blockchains*: A blockchain where write permissions are kept centralised to one organisation. Read permissions may be public or restricted to an arbitrary extent. Likely applications include database management, auditing, etc., internal to a single company, and so public readability may not be necessary in many cases at all, though in other cases public auditability is desired.[140]

138 Ibid., p. 129.
139 Ibid.
140 Vitalik Buterin, *On Public and Private Blockchains* (2015). https://blog.ethereum.org/2015/08/07/on-public-and-private-blockchains/

The three blockchain types are distinguished by their level of decentralisation or centralisation. The public and private aspects of blockchain have different levels of security. That is, fully private blockchains require 'cryptographic authentication',[141] providing a high level of security. Another advantage is that under the consortium model, the 'rules can be changed',[142] further enabling another layer of security. Private blockchains are 'cheaper, the nodes have a higher level of trust and connectivity, and faults can be quickly addressed, translating into better privacy protection'.[143] On the other hand, a public blockchain provides a level of 'freedom, neutrality and openness, while protecting against coercion'.[144] These security mechanisms provide a higher level of cybersecurity, although there still remains a level of vulnerability. Hence, despite the sophistication of blockchain technology, cybersecurity remains a concern for digital finance and tokens. The next section briefly discusses cybersecurity threats.

1.2.2 Cybersecurity

Cybersecurity has emerged as a potential threat to blockchain technology and the digital finance sector. While an in-depth exploration of these issues is outside the scope of this book, a significant amount of scholarly and governmental research is emerging, highlighting the vulnerabilities of personal and financial data captured by blockchain technology. This poses significant challenges for governments and regulators.

Jayanth Varma highlights some of the challenges that have emerged from the application of blockchain. Varma notes that blockchain has a 'Byzantine fault tolerance that deals with nodes that malfunction and function maliciously'.[145] Varma explains that this has come to

> prominence with the rise of hacking and cyber-attacks. Criminal gangs might be content to steal money, terrorist group and nation state adversaries seek to inflict catastrophic damage by corrupting or destroying data. The blockchain provides strong defence against this attack because of (a) replication of the data across large number of nodes running on completely different computer networks and (b) cryptographic integrity checks.[146]

Vinden Wylde and others found that the vulnerabilities are not limited or restricted to a single sector. The vulnerabilities of data, privacy, and financial/commercial information are a concern for all 'companies, organisations,

141 Ibid.
142 Ibid.
143 Ibid.
144 Ibid.
145 Jayanth Rama Varma, Blockchain in Finance, *Vikalpa*, *44*(1) (2019), 1–11. https://doi.org/10.1177/0256090919839897
146 Ibid.

businesses, government institutions and the general public in adopting, promoting and utilising blockchain technology'.[147] They note that other challenges have also emerged because data security management systems and legal frameworks, such as ISO 27001 and the *European Union General Data Protection Regulations*,[148] may not be able to address the shortcomings of blockchain security measures.

More specifically, globally, ethical and legal challenges significantly differ. This is because consent and trust in the public and private sectors regarding the deployment of the required management strategies to protect data are directly related to the accountability and transparency systems in place to deliver certainty and justice.[149] This will become evident throughout this book, which demonstrates that there is no agreed international approach, and nation-states are developing their own legal and policy frameworks. That said, some nation-states are waiting for others to take the lead and will then follow suit by developing a framework that considers and compares other frameworks before developing their own. Arguably, this is a common practice around the world.

However, without more research and information, the full extent of cybersecurity-related issues is not fully understood. Further, it is not fully understood whether current-day cybersecurity laws will address the vulnerabilities posed by blockchain technology. That being the case, research has demonstrated that 'financial cybercrime is positively correlated with immutability, smart contract, distributed ledger technology and consensus algorithms'.[150] The importance of this issue and its potential impact on the broader economy was highlighted in 2018 by the World Economic Forum, where it was stated that 'cybercrime and frauds are part of a trillion-dollar industry as financial industries are spending more than $8.2 billion on these crimes'.[151] These types of crimes are expected to increase over the coming decade as state and non-state actors find sophisticated ways of gaining access to technology systems and infrastructure. The following chart, which pertains to the United States, highlights the problem and the extent of the vulnerability of data up to and including 2021.[152]

147 Vinden Wylde, Nisha Rawindaran, John Lawrence, Rushil Balasubramanian, Edmond Prakash, Ambikesh Jayal, Imtiaz Khan, Chaminda Hewage, Jon Platts, Cybersecurity, Data Privacy and Blockchain: A Review *SN Computer Science*, *3* (2), 127. https://doi.org/10.1007/s42979-022-01020-4

148 Ibid.

149 Ibid.

150 Pvheanushaa Patmanathan, Kavitha Arunasalam, Kahyahthri Suppiah, Dhamayanthi Arumugam, The Effectiveness of Blockchain Technology in Preventing Financial Cybercrime, *E3S Web of Conferences, 389* (07022) (2023). https://doi.org/10.1051/e3sconf/202338907022

151 Ibid., p. 2.

152 Ibid., referring to Identity Theft Resource Centre (2021). Retrieved from Insurance Theft Resource Centre. https://www.idtheftcenter.org/post/identity-theft-resource-center-2021-annual-data-breach-report-sets-new-record-for-number-of-compromises/

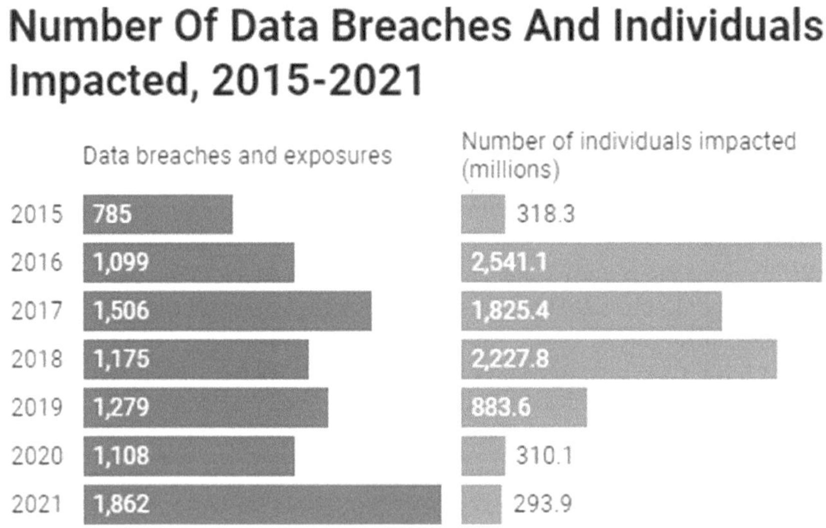

Figure 1.3 Data Breaches 2015–2021

In taking a broader view that includes intellectual property and other commercial activities, for the period between 2002 and 2003, it was reported that:

> Cybercrime can take many forms – identity fraud, data theft, ransomware attacks, copyright infringement, and phishing campaigns are just some examples. Organisations consider the loss of personally identifiable information of customers or employees as one of the most dangerous outcomes of cyberattacks. The loss of sensitive information can have serious repercussions for companies, such as damaged reputation and loss in revenue.[153]

This statement outlines the functional operation of cybercrime activity, which many criminal laws around the world are attempting to deal with. It is outside the scope of this book to compare the criminal laws pertaining to these offences. This is evident in the criminal activity and loss of crypto (token) currency that was estimated to be USD $610 million between 2021 and 2022.[154] This highlights the vulnerability of tokens to financial loss, as well as the privacy infringements and identity theft.

153 Statista, *Cybercrime and Security*. https://www.statista.com/markets/424/topic/1065/cyber-crime-security/#statistic1

154 Ibid., total value of cryptocurrency lost to and recovered from theft and other attacks between March 2020 and February 2022. https://www.statista.com/statistics/1285057/crypto-theft-size/

Importantly, cybercrime within the financial sector, including digital finance, is generally recognised as falling within criminal law. The developing and ensuing challenges for governments and regulators are highly problematic since the extent of the identified criminal activities includes, but are not limited to:

- *Exchange scams* involve cybercriminals opening a fraudulent cryptocurrency exchange service, enticing victims to purchase cryptocurrency through the exchange, and then closing the exchange and absconding with the victims' money;
- *Scam wallets* are fraudulent cryptocurrency wallets used by cyber criminals to illicitly draw away some or all of the cryptocurrency transferred to them by victims;
- *Mining scams* involve promises of high returns to lure victims to invest in cryptocurrency mining operations, but victims rarely receive a payout from their investments;
- *Fraudulent cryptocurrency investment apps and websites* are created by cyber criminals using the names and/or logos of legitimate companies to attract investors under the pretense of providing authentic cryptocurrency investment services; and
- *Pump-and-dump schemes* involving cryptocurrencies are becoming widespread.[155]

These cybersecurity breaches and criminal activities that are occurring despite the sophistication of blockchain technology have the potential, it can be argued, to be a major disruptor of the finance sector. There is no international legal framework that can guide nation-states to address these issues and to ensure a coordinated approach. More needs to be undertaken to address the aforementioned issues at the international level. One way to achieve this is to further expand existing and developing trade agreements and model laws, among others. This begs the question: is it time for the world community to develop an international treaty or convention to address the gaps transnationally? A failure to do so would only embolden those individuals and entities involved in money laundering, fraud, and the loss of identity and commercial-financial data. For these reasons, more needs to be done at national, bilateral, multilateral, and international levels.

Although there are international conventions that address money laundering,[156] and as nation-states continue to grapple with how to regulate

155 David S Kerr, Karen A Loveland, Katherine Taken Smith, Lawrence Murphy Smith, Cryptocurrency Risks, Fraud Cases, and Financial Performance, *Risks, 11* (3) (2023), 51. https://doi.org/10.3390/risks11030005

156 *United Nations Convention against Transnational Organized Crime* (Palermo, Italy, in December 2000). https://www.unodc.org/documents/treaties/UNTOC/Publications/

these new activities, it is arguable that the current international framework needs to be expanded. I argue that, to a large extent, the current international conventions generally deal with money laundering as it pertains to the existing banking and financial sector and the various regulatory regimes. Therefore, it could be argued that unless digital finance and tokens are regulated in the same way, they could fall outside of the current international framework. Having stated that, as long as this activity is viewed as a form of money, prima facie, Article 14 of the United Nations Convention against Corruption, 2003, clearly states measures to prevent money laundering and requires each party to institute a regulatory regime for 'banks and non-bank financial institutions, including natural or legal persons that provide formal or informal services for the transmission of money or value'.[157] The issue related to the concerns expressed in this book is that Article 14 might not apply at this point in time because jurisdictions have not established a regulatory regime specifically for digital currency and tokens.

Of note is the UN Vienna 1988 Convention Article 3.1, which defines money laundering as:

> the conversion or transfer of property, knowing that such property is derived from any offense(s), for the purpose of concealing or disguising the illicit origin of the property or of assisting any person who is involved in such offense(s) to evade the legal consequences of his actions.[158]

Centrally, this broad definition is likely to include tokens and other forms of digital finance pertaining to property. It could also encompass the use of the technology to facilitate the transfer of such property. More recently in 2022, scholars in Australia undertook a review of court decisions involving cryptocurrency (a form of tokenisation) and 'found that matters involving cryptocurrency have appeared in administrative tribunals, trial courts and appellate courts throughout all Australian jurisdictions'.[159] The study also found that cryptocurrency has 'been used by offenders in the commission of criminal offences, notwithstanding the underlying technology such as blockchain to facilitate the activity'.[160] This continues to be an area requiring much-needed research.

TOC%20Convention/TOCebook-e.pdf and *The United Nations Convention against Corruption* (2003). https://www.unodc.org/documents/treaties/UNCAC/Publications/Convention/08-50026_E.pdf

157 Ibid., Article 14.

158 *United Nations Convention against Illicit Traffic in Narcotic Drugs and Psychotropic Substances* (Vienna, 20 December 1988).
https://treaties.un.org/doc/Treaties/1990/11/19901111%2008-29%20AM/Ch_VI_19p.pdf Ratification by National States List. https://treaties.un.org/pages/ViewDetails.aspx?src=TREATY&mtdsg_no=VI-19&chapter=6&clang=_en

159 Arron Lane, Lisanne Adam, Crime and Cryptocurrency in Australian Courts, *Monash University Law Review*, *48* (3) (2022), 182.

160 Ibid., p. 186.

In regard to the aforementioned criminal use of technology and tokens in particular, blockchain technology in its current state of development does not offer a solution to governments and regulators. As explained by Jonno Newman, Global Investigator at TRM Labs and former cybercrime training supervisor with the South Australia police:

> Cryptocurrency [token] investigations were previously seen as a niche and specialized field. However, time has shown that crypto is not exclusive to cybercrime, and that more traditional offending can also have a crypto nexus. The good news is that the transparent and often traceable nature of the blockchain means the use of cryptocurrencies can provide law enforcement with additional avenues of investigation. With increased investments into foundational training and blockchain intelligence tools, the capabilities of law enforcement agencies around Australia have increased exponentially. Current capabilities are vastly different to 2020, and we are reaping the dividends in the form of real-world results.[161]

It is this new frontier of using and applying technology to investigate criminal activities that will be beneficial to governments and law enforcement around the world. Blockchain technology is by no means the silver bullet; however, it does provide greater transparency and traceability of activity and the ability to identify wallets. However, these wallets do attract[162] criminal activity. The next section identifies and discusses the types of tokens that are currently in use, and their categorisation.

1.3 Categories of Tokens

As explained in the previous section, the tokenisation of assets and the economy will require sophisticated technology such as blockchain. Most noteworthy is that tokens will be able to be used to tokenise assets. In other words, it will require assets of any kind to be digitally represented on a distributed ledger; hence, those assets are represented in token form. With blockchain technology, an asset such as real estate is converted into a token that is assigned a value. This real estate then becomes tokenised and can be used within the

161 TRM, *Crypto-related Crime in Australia: What Court Records Tell Us, and What Lies Ahead* (2023). https://www.trmlabs.com/post/crypto-related-crime-in-australia-what-court-records-tell-us-and-what-lies-ahead Note, also there are crypto wallets that are custodial wallets, web wallets, mobile wallets, desktop wallets, hardware wallets, metal wallets, and paper wallets. A wallet is really a user interface that allows you to query your cryptocurrency's underlying blockchain for information, receive funds from other users, and send funds to others by writing transactions to the blockchain. KRIPTOMAT, What is a blockchain wallet? https://kriptomat.io/blockchain/what-is-a-blockchain-wallet/

162 Sabine Houy, Phillip Schmid, Alexandre Bartel, Security Aspects of Cryptocurrency Wallets – A Systematic Literature Review, *ACM Computing Surveys*, *561* (2023). https://doi.org/10.1145/3596906

blockchain. It can also be used in smart contracts that also rely on blockchain. The emerging tokenisation of the economy can apply to both tangible and non-tangible assets. This includes the use of stablecoins.

To date, tokens have been grouped under four categories:

- Fungible Token (FT) – a token that is capable of mutual substitution among individual units
- Non-Fungible Token (NFT) – a token that is not capable of mutual substitution among individual units;
- Security Token – a token with specific characteristics that meets the definition of financial instrument or other investment instrument under applicable legislation in the relevant jurisdiction; and
- Utility Token – a token that can be used by its owner to access goods or services.[163]

The above categories of token can fall into either the NFT or FT category. These categories represent the many emerging sectorial tokens that have emerged or are being developed. Commercially, they can be used for both goods and services, performing a functional transaction, and having a certain value. Jose Garrido argues that tokens:

> coexist with existing commercial instruments, but remarkably, can perform additional functions that are out of reach for commercial instruments. The connection with smart contracts means that tokens can have *any* content, and therefore are not subject to the constraints of a limited number of instruments as it is the case in commercial law. Tokens do not experience the typical limits of the literality principle, either. Through smart contracts, it is possible to include the complex suite of rights that a shareholder has, for instance.[164]

By specifically addressing the governance of tokens via smart contracts, commercially, these contracts are becoming increasingly popular and are being used in many areas of the legal profession. Smart contracts are digital agreements that use blockchain technology to manage property transactions, data, and other digital tasks. The benefit of using smart contracts is that they are tamper-proof.

163 R Sadykhov, G Goodell, D De Montigny, M Schoernig, P Treleaven, Decentralised Token Economy Theory (DeTEcT): Token Pricing, Stability and Governance for Token Economies, *Front. Blockchain*, *6* (1298330) (2023). https://doi.org/10.3389/fbloc.2023.1298330

164 Ibid., p. 20.

In addition to the above, there are sub-categories of tokens. For instance, security tokens,[165] infrastructure tokens, and energy tokens,[166] real estate tokens,[167] agriculture tokens,[168] fan tokens,[169] amongst others. Of note is that the securities tokens have emerged as specific to the current financial market of securities. The development of sectorial tokens is important to note because the above sectors are all regulated differently. A significant question is: will specific sector-based regulation impede or complicate the use of tokens? As this area of the economy develops, more tokens will be made available across more sectors.

Against the backdrop of the above, in the future, tokens will provide the EU's 'financial sector between EUR 27 to 55 billion annually, and is an opportunity for freed financial resources well beyond USD $100 billion that could be redeployed to generate incremental returns'.[170] One way that tokens benefit the economy is by allowing assets, including illiquid assets, to be accessed by more investors and to be traded. They enable fractionalisation whereby investors can purchase fractions of an asset; hence, their usefulness as a risk management tool.[171] Conversely, they pose a risk to potential increase 'financial stability'.[172] It is by minimising any risks to financial stability that the economy can ensure consumers retain a high level of trust and confidence. Arguably, the full risks associated with the tokenisation of the economy are far from being understood. There needs to be sectorial research as well as broader national-economic research in order to develop frameworks that can minimise any adverse impact on nation states. Because the level of property rights assigned to tokens is not fully understood, the next section briefly examines recent developments in this area.

165 LCX, *Security Tokens.* https://www.lcx.com/introduction-to-security-tokens/

166 Cointree, *Three Crypto Infrastructure Projects Building the Next Generation of the Internet* https://www.cointree.com/learn/crypto-internet-infrastructure-projects/

167 Chainlink, *What Is Tokenised Real Estate?* https://chain.link/education-hub/tokenized-real-estate

168 Agrotoken. https://www.agrotoken.com/en/home

169 Matteo Foglia, Giampiero Maci, Vincenzo Pacelli, FinTech and Fan Tokens: Understanding the Risks Spillover of Digital Asset Investment, *Research in International Business and Finance, 68* (2024). https://doi.org/10.1016/j.ribaf.2023.102190

170 *UK Finance: Unlocking the Power of Securities Tokenisation* (2023), p. 10. https://www.ukfinance.org.uk/system/files/2023-07/Unlocking%20the%20power%20of%20securities%20tokenisation.pdf

171 Ibid. See also Asia Securities Industry and Financial Markets Association (ASIFMA) (2021). https://www.asifma.org/wp-content/uploads/2021/06/tokenised-securities-in-apac-a-state-of-play-june-2021-final-1.pdf

172 Carapella, Francesca, Grace Chuan, Jacob Gerszten, Chelsea Hunter, Nathan Swem, *Tokenization: Overview and Financial Stability Implications, Finance and Economics Discussion Series 2023-060.* Washington: Board of Governors of the Federal Reserve System (2023). https://doi.org/10.17016/FEDS.2023.060

1.3.1 Intellectual Property (IP) Rights

The reach of digital finance and tokens extends to blockchain, which is creating another layer of property rights. The technology 'allows virtual disintermediation and automatisation of property transactions, which might help to design future platforms, intended to facilitate cross-border transactions within the EU and worldwide'.[173] Moreover,

> users of these blockchain-based platforms may create the so-called 'digital tokens' or 'coloured coins' that aim to represent rights over different types of 'real world' assets. By transferring a digital token, the parties aim to transfer the ownership or other property rights over the asset represented by the token without the intervention of traditional intermediaries.[174]

Furthermore, because smart contracts operate on blockchain, they are, in turn, sequenced by 'computer codes that automatically execute pre-established instructions thanks to the use of functions (executable code)'.[175] Specifically, 'smart contracts allow for a particular cryptocurrency or asset to be transferred almost immediately between two virtual wallets. In order to do so, parties create the so-called "tokens" or "coloured coins", a digital asset intended to represent a right'.[176] This brief section does not include the IP application processes of the jurisdictions being compared. Neither does it compare court decisions on the eligibility of IP rights afforded to tokens.

Despite the above, there are a number of areas of IP rights (discussed later in this book) that pertain to digital finance and tokens. These include copyright, trademarks, and patents. This section will deal only with patents. The application of a patent framework to the area of NFTs is still undergoing development. Joshua Fairfield has taken the position that:

> NFTs contain a component, the token itself, that is conceptually distinct from the abstract intellectual property rights. The token demands legal characterisation, and the obvious legal characterization is personal property. NFTs stand as a new and powerful grounding example of digital personal property, one that is capable of resisting the dominant online narrative whereby assets that are supposedly 'sold' to consumers are in fact merely licensed.[177]

173 Rosa M Garcia-Teruel, Héctor Simón-Moreno. The Digital Tokenization of Property Rights. A Comparative Perspective *Computer Law & Security Review*, *41* (2021), 1. https://doi.org/10.1016/j.clsr.2021.105543

174 Ibid.

175 Ibid., p. 3.

176 Ibid.

177 Joshua Fairfield, Tokenized: The Law of Non-Fungible Tokens and Unique Digital Property, *Indiana Law Journal*, *97* (4), Article 4 (2022). https://www.repository.law.indiana.edu/ilj/vol97/iss4/4

While this section does not address the specific requirements of patent applications using NFTs, the law is being applied to artwork that has been generated by artificial intelligence and is therefore not eligible for a patent. In 2022, Godfrey Benjamin informed the community through Blockchain News that

> Artsy Monke collection was generated using text descriptions instead of reference images, pushing a new frontier previously uncommon in AI-generated artworks. We were able to take all ten thousand Bored Ape NFT images, and feed those into the machine as a loose canvas to frame the generative art.[178]

In a recent United States case of *Thaler v Vidal*[179] the court explained how such patent or copyright protection would not be applicable. This is arguably another new area of law that is far from being developed. I believe that it will not so much require patent law to be amended, as rely on courts to decide if or when general IP law will apply to NFTs. Even though there is considerable research required over the coming years to confirm patent eligibility for NFTs, some scholars have begun to highlight the benefit of offering general IP rights to NFTs. Eli Kraizberg asserts that 'NFTs are claimed to securitize "ownership rights short of use", and as such they may potentially serve as a substitute for the need to replace the reliance on the legal protection provided by intellectual property rights'.[180] Tokens and the ensuing challenges faced by IP rights have a long way to go before becoming a mature area of law. It is argued, however, that as certain rights begin to be established as norms for blockchain technology, the legal landscape could be transformed. It remains to be seen whether any IP rights applicable to NFTs will automatically align with today's legal framework. In my view, should IP rights be lost or diluted by blockchain technology, there could be disastrous impacts on trade and investment. The current status of IP rights related to tokens, particularly NFTs, is not settled and regulators around the world need to address this issue as a matter of urgency. Generally, it is arguable that the current legal framework for IP will apply to digital finance products in most circumstances. Moreover, NFTs come under copyright and trademark law. However, for tokens, more work is needed in regard to IP.

178 Godfrey Benjamin, Cloned Bored Ape NFT Emerges through Google AI Technology, *Blockchain News* (2022). https://blockchain.news/news/cloned-bored-ape-nft-emerges-through-google-ai-technology Referred to in Runhua Wang, Jyh-An Lee, Jingwen, Unwinding NFTs in the Shadow of IP Law, *American Business Law Review* (2024), 33–40.

179 *Thaler v Vidal*, No. 21-2347 (Fed. Cir., Aug. 5, 2022), in Runhua Wang, Jyh-An Lee, Jingwen, Unwinding NFTs in the Shadow of IP Law. *American Business Law Review* (2024), 33–40.

180 Eli Kraizberg, Non-Fungible Tokens: A Bubble or the End of an Era of Intellectual Property Rights, *Financial Innovation*, *9* (32) (2023). https://doi.org/10.1186/s40854-022-00428-4

1.3.2 International Law

The United Nations Commission on International Trade Law (UNCITRAL) adopted the Model Law on Electronic Transferable Records (MLETR) in 2017.[181] This section discusses the MLETR, otherwise known as the Model Law, and its relevance to international arbitration. The Model Law is specific to the transferability of electronic records and defines an 'electronic record' as 'information generated, communicated, received or stored by electronic means'.[182] Professor Henry Gabriel described the MLETR as a

> legal framework to validate electronic transferable records. The Model Law does not provide technological guidance on how this is to be achieved, nor does it provide guidance on how the underlying substantive law of paper instruments and documents can be adjusted to conform to their electronic equivalents.[183]

Hence, the Model Law provides generic rules that can be applied to various types of electronic transferable records, enabling the use of various models whether based on registry, token, distributed ledger, or other technology.[184] More specifically, Article 7 in relation to the legal recognition of an electronic transferable record, requires a level of consent:

> to the use of an electronic transferable record is a general one and applies to all instances where an electronic transferable record is used under the Model Law and to all parties involved in the life cycle of the electronic transferable record.[185]

The ensuing question is how could or would consent apply to tokens on blockchain (distributed ledger)? Accordingly, the Model Law has addressed this issue by directing that:

> consent to the use of an electronic transferable record in systems that lack a centralized operator, such as some token-based and distributed ledger-based systems, may be implicit and inferred by circumstances such as exercise of control of the record or performance of the obligation contained in the record.[186]

181 The United Nations Commission on International Trade Law (UNCITRAL) adopted the Model Law on Electronic Transferable Records (MLETR) in 2017. https://uncitral.un.org/en/texts/ecommerce/modellaw/electronic_transferable_records
182 Ibid., Article 2.
183 Henry Gabriel, The UNCITRAL Model Law on Electronic Transferable Records, *Uniform Law Review*, 24 (2019), 261.
184 Ibid., p. 23. https://uncitral.un.org/sites/uncitral.un.org/files/media-documents/uncitral/en/mletr_ebook_e.pdf
185 Ibid., p. 33.
186 Ibid.

Moreover, Article 13 governs the time and place of electronic transferable records, which is based on a technology-neutral approach compatible with systems based on registry, token, distributed ledger, or other technology.[187] The above directs this issue back to the application of the Model Law, whereby, according to Article 1, it applies the 'principle of technological neutrality entails adopting a system-neutral approach, enabling the use of various models whether based on registry, token, distributed ledger or other technology'.[188] The MLETER is relevant to digital finance and tokens because they are used in transferable transactions and know no national borders. A record is generated from the data input, which is then afforded a token that is transferable and is a fundamental feature of this economic activity.

1.3.3 *Transnational Arbitration*

It has been well documented that international arbitration provides a suitable and effective means of resolving complex transnational commercial and investor-state disputes. Chapter 6 discusses international arbitration in more detail, together with the increasing use of blockchain within arbitration. It is well understood that arbitration can be used to resolve token[189] disputes, such as those that have been assigned to a contract or a smart contract established on blockchain. The 2023 UK *Dispute Resolution Rule* states that 'a digital asset includes a crypto asset, digital token, smart contract or other digital or coded representation of an asset or transaction; and a digital asset system means the digital environment or platform in which a digital asset exists'.[190] On the other hand, there is no clear definition of a token. With the current regulatory frameworks being unclear and uncertain, over the coming years, there are likely to be investor-state arbitration disputes that arise from the use of tokens.

1.4 Structure and Methodology

This book provides a comparative study of the laws that will support the development and use of tokens, smart contracts, and digital finance products over a blockchain and to a lesser extent other distributed ledgers. Max Rheinstein's[191] comparative legal research approach is adopted for the study of laws, legislative texts, and judicial decisions from various countries. The second phase of

187 Ibid., p. 50.
188 Ibid., p. 23.
189 Sir Geoffrey Vos, Francis Bautista. *ADR in the Blockchain Ecosystem: A Primer* (2023). https://arbitrationblog.kluwerarbitration.com/2023/12/14/adr-in-the-blockchain-ecosystem-a-primer/ See
190 *Digital Dispute Resolution Rules.* https://27221500.fs1.hubspotusercontent-eu1.net/hubfs/27221500/UKJT%20work/Digital%20Dispute%20resolution%20rules.pdf
191 Max Rheinstein. Comparative Law – Its Functions, Methods and Usages, *Arkansas Law Review, 415* (1968), 416.

this approach involves the study of foreign law and the legal systems (including legislation and case law) which are currently in force. This approach is different from that of the comparative approach taken by Peter de Cruz, who considers the linguistic and terminological problems and the cultural differences between legal systems,[192] amongst others.

On the other hand, Clive Schmittoff asserts that the function of comparative law is to find a system of legal abstractions based on the results of factual comparison or as a special branch of the science of law. This is because it would be too difficult and impractical to discuss the historical beginnings, cultural, religious, and other influences that have shaped the current-day legal frameworks of the respective states. Edward Eberle, on the one hand, is of the view that when applied to law, comparisons can provide insights into another law, our law and, just as importantly, our own perceptions and intuitions – a self-reflection that can often yield insights into our view of the law.[193] On the other hand, Eberle raises the following questions:

- Do we see law as only rules – commands that channel us along prescribed paths?
- Do we see law as filtered through the lens of our own law and native predispositions associated with our home territory?
- Is this a form of cognitive lock-in which colours or even blinds us?
- Or do we see law as only illusion?
- Do we sense a disjunction between law as written versus law as applied or as practiced within a given culture?
- Is there some operation code or hidden format we are missing that actually drives the pattern of law?[194]

More specifically, the challenge is to reconcile the cultural and linguistic differences of the jurisdictions compared, which cannot be fully reconciled in this research. From time to time throughout the book, there is a reference to China when making a brief comparison with its intellectual property laws. This book compares China's respective laws with those of other jurisdictions only in regard to copyright and patent laws. No comments or recommendations are made regarding China's policies, legal developments or legal approach. The inclusion of China is to highlight the dissimilarities with the other economies compared.

192 Peter de Cruz. *Comparative Law in a Changing World,* Cavendish Publishing Limited (1991).

193 Edward Eberle, The Methodology of Comparative Law, *Roger Williams University Law Review*, *16* (1) (2011), 51–53.

194 Ibid.

1.5 Referencing, Terminology, and Research Limitations

Throughout the book, the referencing format does not follow convention due to the breadth and depth of law examined and compared. Where legislative texts, reports, and documents are used, a web link will be provided indicating the source of the reference. This is because in the substantive chapters where laws are examined, it becomes evident that the comparison of the laws of several countries/jurisdictions is a complex undertaking. Hence, referencing has been structured in such a way as to ensure the reader can clearly identify the legal or scholarly source.

1.5.1 Research Questions

This important research will guide and direct students, business communities, governments, and regulators on the current status of the regulation and law of tokens and digital finance. The research questions are:

- What is the current status of the national and international regulatory framework pertaining to digital finance and, specifically, to tokens?
- What are the gaps in the law pertaining to tax, IP, arbitration, amongst others that relate to tokens over a blockchain?
- How effective can international arbitration be in resolving commercial disputes arising from digital finance and the use of tokens?

In the final chapter of this book, these questions are answered based on the findings and the opinions of the author.

1.5.2 Research Limitations

The book analyses and compares Australia, the European Union, India, Indonesia, Japan, Singapore, the United Kingdom, and the United States. It also draws upon some of the work that has been undertaken in China. However, any reference to China in regard to its financial sector will be made in Chapter 6. No comment is made about policy matters related to China's economic activity, nor is there any recommendation that any of the countries undertake law reform. Switzerland and Liechtenstein are only compared in Chapter 2, and this is an area of further research. The purpose of the book is to highlight the gaps and differences in the laws of the economies that have been compared.

This book contains seven chapters. **Chapter 1** gives the background and history of digital finance. It highlights how tokens, while not a new concept, have been transformed significantly over the last decade. Today, they are being discussed as a new and emerging generator of wealth. This chapter highlights the developments in blockchain technology, and the complexity of understanding its application to tokens and various forms of digital finance.

Chapter 2 addresses the differences in the banking and financial regulations that economies are beginning to use to govern the use of tokens in particular. It demonstrates how this area of the law is moving rapidly, and that the jurisdictions compared are at different stages on the regulatory pathway. The chapter draws upon judicial decisions that address some of the recent issues, such as stolen [tokens] crypto assets and transactional mistakes. This chapter analyses all economies compared in this book, along with Switzerland and Liechtenstein, which are not compared in other areas of the law this book addresses.

Chapter 3 discusses tax as it relates to cryptocurrency and digital assets, as this is another area that is rapidly changing. This chapter calls for urgent research and work to be undertaken at the national and international levels to confirm or otherwise whether the current bilateral and/or multilateral tax arrangements that nation-states have in place can adequately address the gaps in cross-border taxing of this new financial activity. Notably, it has been determined that most nation-states are treating crypto-digital assets and tokens as property for taxation purposes. However, there are gaps that remain in relation to when a token is considered under national rules for value-added and goods and services tax.

Chapter 4 explores how blockchain insurance, distributed ledger, cryptography, and smart contracts have the potential to disrupt the insurance industry. On the other hand, the adoption of this technology will improve pricing, risk assessment, and efficiencies. Moreover, the chapter briefly demonstrates the importance of arbitration and the new developments in open insurance.

Chapter 5 is very significant as it discusses intellectual property – patent and copyright laws – and their application to tokens and, more broadly, digital finance. This is one of the most contested areas of the law that needs to be settled as a matter of urgency. A failure to settle patent law, in addition to the other areas of intellectual property law, has the potential to dilute property rights. The chapter also examines and compares the concepts and principles that underpin copyright law.

Arbitration is an important dispute resolution mechanism for commercial disputes.

Chapter 6 discusses the issues concerning the rules of evidence pertaining to blockchain technology. This chapter highlights the need to ensure that the arbitration agreement is clear regarding the application and use of evidence. However, it now needs to include and be specific about the use and adoption of technology (whatever that may be) for submission, adducing, and producing evidence. The arbitration agreement may play a more significant role in ensuring that parties are not forced into arbitration by the courts. The careful drafting of the arbitration agreement is becoming increasingly important, as it can minimise the costs incurred by the parties.

Chapter 7 concludes this book with the findings and the addressing of the research questions. It brings together the comparative analysis of the laws of banking-finance, tax, insurance, intellectual property [patents and copyright] and international commercial arbitration. It calls for more research. It makes the case for international cooperation and the need for legal practitioners and scholars to acquire some understanding of the new technology being applied in the financial sector of economies.

1.6 Conclusion

This book introduces the topic of digital finance and the law. It focuses specifically on tokens and the ensuing technology that will facilitate their development, use, and transaction/s. Chapter 1 has demonstrated that there is no consensus on the definition of this new area of the law. Furthermore, it is an area that needs to be reconciled at the international level.

This chapter has set the scene by discussing the sophisticated technology of blockchain and how it supports tokens. That is, on blockchain, an asset such as real estate is converted into a token that is given a value.

Based on the above, this converts the real estate to a token that can be used for transactions conducted on the blockchain. To date, four categories of tokens have emerged that provide the framework for a broad international consensus. These include fungible token, non-fungible token, security token, and utility token.

These categories can be used as starting points for the establishment of sector-based tokens such as infrastructure tokens, and energy tokens, real estate tokens, agriculture tokens, and fan tokens, amongst others. Furthermore, arbitration and cybersecurity will become very important direct and indirect areas of law and practice as a result of the development and implementation of digital financial products.

In addition to arbitration and cybersecurity, tax and insurance will also become significant issues in the token economy and digital finance in general. Individuals and entities are beginning to use blockchain technology. Thus, this new and fascinating area of the law will provide many opportunities and benefits to the economy and to the legal profession.

However, it will be just as challenging because many of the areas discussed in this book have not been fully accepted by governments. Hence, this area of the economy has the potential to become highly contested. The book proposes a way forward and identifies many areas of the law that need to be reconciled. It calls for urgent research to assist in the development of laws to regulate the token economy.

2 Finance and Banking

2.1 Introduction

The far-reaching potential changes resulting from the digital economy are still being considered, since the new digital economy may trigger a real disruption in the financial sector, with the emergence of new players, services, and ways of doing business. The extent to which this will occur is still unknown, but there are reasons for thinking that the digital revolution in the financial sector alone[1] has begun. For instance, the financial sector is now able to provide services to individuals and entities in different forms. Hence, 'the digital economy could lead to a very concentrated financial market, dominated by a handful of big techs, which could replace commercial banks in the provision of financial services (a world without banks is also visible on the horizon)'.[2] If fully realised, this will have significant implications for the national economies of nearly all countries.

Some countries and jurisdictions have based their regulatory framework on the traditional finance-banking sector that is heavily backed by government in times of economic shocks. However, decentralised finance is a rapidly rising phenomenon seeking to eliminate intermediaries in financial transactions, replacing them with software protocols. In these scenarios, 'financial regulation and supervision would become extremely difficult. Monetary policy could also blow away from state control and even financial sovereignty would be under threat'.[3] A similar situation has been evolving in the banking sector. That is, unlike any other time in history, people are now moving toward online banking, instead of physically going into a local branch.

That said, 'with the rapid development of the Internet and e-Commerce, the competitive advantage of Internet banking is becoming more noticeable, in particular, the effect of scale. More and more Internet users are ready to switch

1 Jose Laguna de Paz, Some Implications of the New Global Digital Economy for Financial Regulation and Supervision, *Journal of Banking Regulation*, *24* (2023), 146–148.
2 Ibid.
3 Ibid.

DOI: 10.4324/9781003511687-2

to online banking'.[4] This has provided more efficiencies for businesses, with clients not having to visit local branches to make transactions, and new services being offered. Consequently, an increase in 'electronic payment, electronic money, mobile payment, and e-wallet, has changed the services provided by the banking industry'.[5] These technological advances can potentially improve banks' efficiency, leading to better performance and, eventually, greater stability of the banking sector.

However, the development of financial technology can also create new risks that can have a negative effect on financial stability.[6] This does not apply only to the Western banking sector. For example:

> in relation to Islamic banking, the finding shows that there is no Granger Causality between digital payment and Islamic banking stability. This result implies that currently there is no causality between digitalisation and Islamic banking stability. It is argued that this result is primarily due to the relatively small size of Islamic banking in the whole banking industry in Indonesia.[7]

Nonetheless, the risk posed by this transformation across both the banking and finance sectors is only beginning to be realised. The European Union has identified that:

> digitalisation also poses significant non-financial risks, both for banks and for fintech and big tech companies. These risks stem from i) greater concentration on providing basic services, such as cloud computing; ii) broader use of AI in finance; iii) overly automated or IT-oriented services that may be more prone to cyberattacks; iv) trust in a leading technology that might suddenly turn obsolete; and v) a false sense of security from overleveraging insights from AI.[8]

4 Oleg Litvishko, Kamar Beketova, Bibigul Akimova, Assem Azhmukhamedova, Gulnara Islyam, Impact of the Digital Economy on the Banking Sector, *E3S Web of Conferences*, 159 (04033) (2020), 6. https://www.e3s-conferences.org/articles/e3sconf/pdf/2020/19/e3sconf_btses2020_04033.pdf

5 Rahmatina Awaliah Kasri, Muhammad Budi Prasetyo, Digital Payment and Banking Stability in Emerging Economy with Dual Banking System. *Heliyon*, *8* (11), e11198. https://doi.org/10.1016/j.heliyon.2022.e11198. PMID: 36339746; PMCID: PMC9626548. https://www.ncbi.nlm.nih.gov/pmc/articles/PMC9626548/

6 Ibid.

7 Ibid.

8 Thorsten Beck, Stephen Cecchetti, Magdalena Grothe, Malcolm Kemp, Loriana Pelizzon, Antonio Sánchez Serrano, Will Video Kill the Radio Star? – Digitalisation and the Future of Banking, *Reports of the Advisory Scientific Committee*, 12 (January 2022), 3. https://www.esrb.europa.eu/pub/pdf/asc/esrb.ascreport202201_digitalisationandthefutureofbanking~83f079b5c7.en.pdf

This chapter will address some of these issues and confirm or otherwise whether the current-day banking and financial laws are still relevant for the jurisdictions being compared. While there is risk in any change or transformation, there can also be many benefits. For instance, digital financial inclusion can have a positive, two-fold effect. It can:

> ensure banking stability, which sends out a message about the economic stability of any country and will consequently lead toward achieving the Sustainable Development Goals (SDGs) by 2030. To attain the SDGs, economic sustainability is a must that can be ensured through the banking sector along with other financial sectors. Attainment of the SDGs becomes impossible without filling a huge investment gap. There is a $2.5 trillion investment gap to achieve the SDGs by 2030, which can be reduced by the banking sector along with other financial institutions.[9]

Essentially, digital financial inclusion will give more people across the world access to online banking and financial services. It will require a greater level of digital literacy in those developing countries that are yet to give their people full access to the internet. In part, the digitisation of these services is not new: credit card payments have been widely used for decades. However, they have not been available to everyone in the same way as online banking services. The ensuing question is whether the laws will change to accommodate any new products. This book will examine this in light of today's banking and finance laws. In addition, when coupled with the development of a possible digital currency, there could be broader implications in the short term for the current banking sector. Todd Keister and Daniel Sanches make an important point:

> policymakers have expressed concern that, by providing a safe alternative to bank deposits, a digital currency could facilitate runs on the banking system in periods of financial stress. Digital currencies can also be held and used internationally much more easily than physical currency, which could potentially alter capital flows and interact with domestic monetary policy. Understanding these issues and how they relate to the

9 Hasanul Banna, Md Rabiul Alam, *Is Digital Financial Inclusion Good for Bank Stability and Sustainable Economic Development? Evidence from Emerging Asia*, Asian Development Bank (2022), p. 53. https://www.adb.org/sites/default/files/publication/761526/adbi-harnessing-digitalization-122421-web.pdf The authors refer to works undertaken by H Banna, MR Alam, R Ahmad, NM Sari, Does Financial Inclusion Drive the Islamic Banking Efficiency? A Post-,Financial Crisis Analysis *The Singapore Economic Review* (2020) https://doi.org/10.1142/ s0217590819420050. M Niculescu, *Impact Investment to Close the SDG Funding Gap*, United Nations Development Programme (blog) (13 July. 2017).

GER Wilson, *There's a $2.5 Trillion Development Investment Gap. Blended Finance Could Plug It.* World Economic Forum (2016). https_://www.weforum.org/agenda/2016/07/blended-finance-sustainable-development-goals/

> fundamental effects of a CBDC identified in our analysis is a promising area of ongoing research.[10]

Viewed this way, there are going to be many obstacles if, and when, a central bank digital currency (CBDC) is implemented. The impact on the traditional banking sector is not fully understood. The way that people in all countries will react is also not understood. More research is needed. Arguably, in 2024 cash is being used increasingly less in favour of online payments, and in banking and financial transactions.

2.1.1 Digital Currency

A digital currency could be significantly transformed over the coming decade, not only as a result of technology but also because of new forms of currency. For instance, 'two dozen central banks across emerging and advanced economies are expected to have digital currencies in circulation by the end of the decade', the Bank for International Settlements (BIS).[11] Central banks globally have been studying and working on digital versions of their currencies for retail use to avoid leaving digital payments to the private sector amid an accelerating decline of cash. Some are also looking at wholesale versions for transactions between financial institutions.[12] However, it has been reported that this new form of currency will give rise to much economic uncertainty. Subsequently, this could have significant impacts on trade, investment, and the digital economy.

The Bank for International Settlements notes that the key development is tokenisation – the process of representing claims digitally on a *programmable* platform.[13] This can be seen as the next logical step in digital recordkeeping and asset transfer. Tokenisation could dramatically improve the capabilities of the monetary and financial system by offering new ways for intermediaries to interact when serving end users, removing the traditional separation of messaging, reconciliation, and settlement. Tokenisation could unlock new types of economic arrangements that the frictions inherent in the current monetary system have hitherto made impractical.

In practice, cryptocurrency and stablecoins reside on the same platform as other crypto assets used as a means of payment. Therefore, 'the full

10 Todd Keister, Daniel Sanches, Should Central Banks Issue Digital Currency? *Review of Economic Studies* (2023), 429.

11 Karin Strohecker, *Twenty-Four Central Banks Will Have a Digital Currencies by 2023, Survey Shows* (July 2023). https://www.reuters.com/markets/currencies/twenty-four-central-banks-will-have-digital-currencies-by-2030-bis-survey-2023-07-10/

12 Ibid. The Bank for International Settlements notes that 'If widely used for payments, cryptoassets including stablecoins may constitute a threat to financial stability'.

13 Bank for International Settlements, *Annual Report* (2023), p. 85. https://www.bis.org/publ/arpdf/ar2023e3.pdf

development of a wholesale central bank digital currency (CBDC) is core to the functioning of a tokenised environment'.[14]

2.1.2 *Stablecoins*[15]

Stablecoins are an alternative form of private tokenised money; however, they have significant shortcomings. Unlike tokenised deposits, stablecoins represent a transferable claim on the issuer, akin to a digital bearer instrument. A payment using stablecoins transfers the issuer's liability from one holder to another. Imagine that John holds 1 stablecoin unit (SCU) issued by a stablecoin issuer. When John pays Paul SCU 1, John's claim on the stablecoin issuer is transferred to Paul, who did not have a claim on that issuer before the transfer. There is no need to update the stablecoin issuer's balance sheet, and there is no settlement on the central bank's balance sheet.

Whoever holds the instrument has a claim on the issuer and can transfer it without requiring the consent or involvement of the issuer. In this case, Paul is left with a claim on an issuer he may not trust. As stablecoins are tradable, their prices can deviate from par, thus undermining the singleness of money. Deviations from singleness can occur if there are differences in the liquidity of stablecoins or if variations in the quality of the backing or characteristics of the issuer lead to differences in the perceived creditworthiness of different issuers.

The above suggests that what the future holds for the CBDC is not yet fully understood. With a number of pilot programmes being implemented around the world, the impact of stablecoins on the digital economy will no doubt be highly transformative. It will come with a number of positives and negatives. Some of the latter are explained below:

> Digital money currently sits at the edges of communication networks, where it resides in siloed proprietary databases operated by banks and non-banks. External messaging systems are required to link these databases. The separation of messaging, reconciliation and settlement can lead to delays and means that participants often have an incomplete view of completed actions. Consequently, errors may go undetected for longer, leading to higher error resolution costs and increased operational risk. For these reasons, payment processes can be costly, cumbersome, slow and opaque. They can fall short of meeting users' changing demands. The complexity and lack of transparency in existing payment systems is evident even in a simple payment involving customers of two different banks. A transfer of funds from payer to payee involves a large number of

14 Ibid., para 90.

15 Ibid., p. 92. Note that there is little to no regulation of stablecoins at the time of writing this book, and without a regulatory platform or being backed by a level of liquidity, this will pose challenges.

> messages, internal checks and adjustments. Participants generally cannot track the progress of their payments in real time. In particular, the payee does not see when the process is initiated, and the payer does not know when it is completed.[16]

Hence, not only stablecoin tokens but, more broadly, digital money will require a high level of vigilance. The implications for the current commercial legal framework are far from being understood, and further research is needed. For instance, the digital economy has the potential to change the way tax law is implemented because people will be able to more easily identify and follow their transactions around the world. This may require different tax requirements because the platforms on which transactions are conducted have no definitive location in any nation-states, or it could be a simple matter of the transaction being taxed at the location where it is carried out.

At this early stage in the development of these new types of payment systems, they are likely to fall under national banking and financial regulations. At the time of writing, the IMF noted that up to 100 countries were either developing a digital currency or undertaking a pilot programme.[17] The work that has been undertaken is 'driven primarily by the desire to maintain and strengthen the institutional underpinnings of modern monetary systems in the digital age, to promote competition in the payment systems, and to facilitate tokenization of finance'.[18]

Moreover, 'CBDC exploration has taken place in almost 30 countries including the African region, Caribbean region, and in Asia Pacific countries, to address macro-financial implications; legal, technology, and interoperability issues; as well as country experiences and lessons'.[19] Problematic is that nation-states are tending to go it alone, are restricting any development on a regional basis, or are waiting for others to take the lead and then follow or adapt the already-established models.

In one of the first signs that governments are beginning to move quickly in this area, in late 2023 the Singapore government issued licences to 14 entities, one of which allows them to 'operate in the city-state without transaction thresholds'.[20] Operationally, the licence, granted by the Monetary Authority

16 Ibid., p. 98. See also Bilal Bagis. *The Rise of Central Bank Digital Currency* (August 2023). www.setav.org/en/the-rise-of-central-bank-digital-currency/

17 International Monetary Fund. *IMF Approach to Central Bank Digital Currency Capacity Development* (April 2023). https://www.imf.org/en/Publications/Policy-Papers/Issues/2023/04/12/IMF-Approach-to-Central-Bank-Digital-Currency-Capacity-Development-532177

18 Ibid., p. 6.

19 Ibid., p. 7.

20 Rae Wee, *Crypto Firm Ripple Secures Singapore Payments Licence* (2023.) https://www.reuters.com/business/finance/crypto-firm-ripple-secures-singapore-payments-licence-2023-10-04/

of Singapore (MAS), will allow Ripple (a blockchain-based digital payment network) to provide regulated digital payment token services.[21] This is a sign of the rapid change in the sector, and the fast pace at which governments are making decisions in order to be the first in this space.

This poses challenges for the legal order and may well shape any newly proposed world order. It is likely that the legal frameworks developed will be highly divergent and will require cross-border experts to navigate national laws. In the absence of any international legal framework, this has the potential to become a highly contested area.

On the other hand, stablecoins have been described as a:

> subcategory of crypto assets that specifically seek to address this problem, such as by linking or "pegging" their values to those of another, more stable, asset (such as the US dollar, precious metals, or even another crypto asset) or a pool of other assets (for example, a basket of commodities).[22]

In their recent (2023) work, Christophe Waerzeggers, Irving Aw, and Jess Cheng found that most 'stablecoins that are currently in circulation attempt to mitigate their price volatility through some pegging mechanism'.[23] These authors state:

> It is important to distinguish between the concepts of 'pegging' and 'backing', depending on the nature of the claim that a coin holder may have against the issuer of the coin. The former merely requires the value of a stablecoin to be linked to that of an underlying asset or pool of assets (for instance, a claim against the issuer for redemption at par in US dollars), whereas the latter also involves the stablecoin issuer (or a third party on its behalf) setting aside assets with the understanding that the coin has some claim to those underlying assets (for instance, the pledging or other use of a pool of short-term government securities), possibly as a means to buttress such pegging. This distinction is important because some stablecoins may be clearly pegged to the value of an identified asset or pool of assets but coin holders lack any clear, legally enforceable claim to any particular asset itself.[24]

In addition to the above:

21 Ibid.

22 Christophe Waerzeggers, Irving Aw, Jess Cheng *Taxing Stablecoins*, International Monetary Fund (2023), Note 2023/002, p. 1–5.

23 Ibid.

24 Ibid.

> stablecoins can be further distinguished based on the type of reference asset against which they are pegged, which can be both on chain (that is, another crypto asset) or off chain (such as traditional currencies or commodities), and a stablecoin can be backed by more than one type of asset.[25]

Currently, they are being viewed as a type of property in exchanges and transactions. This has generally been driven by tax purposes. Waerzeggers, Aw, and Cheng show how stablecoins are backed by on- and off-chain assets (recourse to asset–no recourse to asset), unbacked, and hybrid (recourse to asset–no recourse to asset).[26]

Given the above, the unbacked stablecoin poses the most risk of volatility to the market. The backed stablecoin and token could be backed by either a national currency or a commodity. Thus, the challenges arising in the area of tax alone need to be addressed. A greater problem is the inconsistent and incoherent approach being undertaken around the world to regulate stablecoins, along with the other crypto-digital assets discussed in this book. This approach will only lead to a highly contested and fragmented legal framework.

Nonetheless, Georgios Dimitropoulos, who references the G7 Group, notes that:

> The emerging Cornwall Consensus under the auspices of the G7 brings digital technologies and digital globalisation to the centre stage of the contemporary international order. Cornwall envisages a new social contract for digital technologies. It imagines a relationship between the law and the digital world that will be largely different from the relationship between law and economic globalization as was developed during the twentieth century. Cornwall does not envisage a universalist digital globalization. It aims instead at reclaiming digital naturalism through a process of devolution. International law is also to take a new shape in the digital sphere and beyond: that of plurilateralism.[27]

This important work reaffirms the current rules-based system that the world has become accustomed to and that it relies upon for trade and investment decisions and activities. Dimitropoulos further points out that:

> The Cornwall Consensus mimics in its title the Washington Consensus, the constitution of the neoliberal world order. Cornwall's goal is to achieve a new consensus and restore public trust in a rules-based, free, fair

25 Ibid.
26 Ibid., p. 6.
27 Georgios Dimitropoulos. *Law and Digital Globalisation*, *The University of Pennsylvania Journal of International Law*, *44* (1) (2022), 103.

> and open economic system. The Consensus builds on traditional notions of international ordering favouring a rules-based world order. Free trade should remain one of the main pillars of this order. Multilateralism—both multilateral agreements as well as multilateral dispute settlement, such as before the WTO—remain important in the new world envisaged by Cornwall.[28]

With such a commitment by this group of nations, which, despite the small size of some, are among the most developed and wealthy nations in the world, it can be argued that the current commercial legal frameworks will be, in part, suitable for the digital economy.

Arguably, the history of transnational trade and investment called for international and national commercial trade and investment law. That said, post-World War II, there has been a significant amount of work undertaken by the world community to develop an international legal framework that facilitates trade and protects all parties involved in trade and investment. Therefore, the next section will briefly explain the current transnational commercial and investment laws that are serving the digital economy.

2.1.3 The Transition

The banking and finance sector is, arguably, undergoing one of the most profound changes in modern history. For decades, the larger banking and finance entities have managed to corner the market. Technology has been described as the most disruption[29] that this sector has experienced in recent times. Artificial intelligence (AI) combined with machine learning (ML) can gather, mine, analyse, and exploit large quantities of data (big data). When integrated with quantum technology, the challenges posed to the legal frameworks of nation-states are far from being fully understood. The technology has the potential to resolve financial problems and is 'able to make calculations that can protect against competitors getting hold of customer information'.[30] It could serve to provide 'greater compliance, employing behavioural data to enhance customer engagement, and faster reaction to market volatility are some of the specific benefits we expect quantum computing to deliver'.[31]

28 Ibid., p. 104. *The History of the G7.* https://www.bundesregierung.de/breg-en/service/the-history-of-the-g7-397438

29 Organisation for Economic Cooperation and Development, *Digital Disruption in Banking and Its Impact on Competition* (2020), pp. 3–5. https://www.oecd.org/competition/digital-disruption-in-banking-and-its-impact-on-competition-2020.pdf

30 IBM, applying emerging quantum technology to financial problems. https://www.ibm.com/thought-leadership/institute-business-value/en-us/report/exploring-quantum-financial For health, see also Keshav Kaushik Adarsh Kumar. *Demystifying Quantum Blockchain for Healthcare.* https://arxiv.org/pdf/2210.03638.pdf

31 Ibid.

It could provide real-time calculations that may result in an improved ability to respond to financial-liquidity shocks.[32] This chapter examines judicial decisions that address issues such as transactions undertaken by mistake and transactions where crypto assets have been stolen; it also considers whether the current national laws adequately address digital payments, and examines the obligations of software developers when their software is used to facilitate crypto transactions, amongst others.

The vulnerability of the financial system cannot be underestimated, particularly when combined with the threat and impact of cybersecurity incursions. The Bank of International Settlements (BIS), in its 2023 report to the financial sector, reaffirmed the vulnerability of cybersecurity.[33] Most notable is that the BIS is calling for urgent action[34] to prepare the world for the technology once it becomes available for widespread implementation. In relation to the law, the BIS noted that the law of quantum theory is fundamental and applies to every physical object. In its view, the laws will be required to describe collective behaviour, globally.

However, this position is not new. Laws have been used for more than a century to control the thinking, behaviour, and attitudes of people in nearly every sector of society. The BIS goes on to say that the traditional laws of today that everyone has been accustomed to are now being exploited by the computer. However, the BIS is not referring to the law that is made by the judiciary or government. It is referring to the law of physics. Not only is the cybersecurity issue potentially significant, the BIS is asserting that:

> The stakes are high, given that data protection mechanisms for internet communications, digital signatures, passwords, contracts and other documents would become instantly obsolete as soon as a sufficiently powerful quantum computer became operational. Among other things, this would destroy the integrity of today's digitally signed contracts, as the validity of the signer's identity could no longer be ensured.[35]

Therefore, the potential vulnerabilities are far-reaching. The technology will have an enormous impact not only on smart contracts but also on contracts in general that provide a framework for governing trade and investment agreements. The 'other documents' referred to above could be related to personal health, education, or commercial transactions that contain sensitive IP information. Moreover, there are components of quantum-based technology that may be eligible for patent protection:

32 Bank of International Settlements. *Quantum-Proofing the Financial System* (2023). https://www.bis.org/publ/othp67.pdf

33 Ibid., p. 6.

34 Ibid.

35 Ibid., p. 17.

> The technology building blocks (qubits), quantum gates & multipliers, quantum integrated circuit chips, the various types of quantum processors such as spin qubits and superconducting transmon qubits, quantum interference devices, compiler engines (i.e. optimisers, translators, mappers), decoders, a simulator and an emulator, a circuit drawer, the microarchitecture (quantum execution block & quantum error block), the quantum-classical interface, the quantum instruction set architecture, quantum memory. The 'quantum computing process' can be protected by patent as well. The dilution refrigerator as a whole, including its individual cryoperm shield, quantum amplifiers, cryogenic isolators, a mixing chamber, superconducting coaxial lines, input microwave lines and a qubit signal amplifier component, are also eligible for patenting.[36]

In addition to the above, there are other areas that will fall under copyright, anti-trust, and trademark categories. In the case of AI hybrids that utilise machine learning to train datasets, the clearance of the 'input functionality and computer implemented inventions' can be made. Thus, with the uptake of AI and the collection of vast amounts of data, there are privacy concerns, along with uncertainty about ownership of data.[37] What Kop is saying is that today more than ever, technological developments demand that lawmakers acquire interdisciplinary competences.[38] The difficulty lies not only in the creation of a legal framework that fosters innovation but also in obtaining balance, protection, and security for governments and the private sector. This is because:

> quantum computing threatens blockchain protocols and networks because they utilise non-quantum resistant cryptographic algorithms. When quantum computers become robust enough to run Shor's algorithm on a large scale, the most commonly-used asymmetric algorithms, utilised for digital signatures and message encryption, will be no longer secure. Quantum computers will be able to break them within a short period of time.[39]

36 Mauritz Kop, Regulating Transformative Technology. In *The Quantum Age: Intellectual Property, Standardisation & Sustainable Innovation* (2020), p. 11.
https://law.stanford.edu/wp-content/uploads/2020/11/Mauritz-Kop_Regulating-Transformative-Technology-in-The-Quantum-Age_Intellectual-Property-Standardization-Sustainable-Innovation_Stanford.pdf

37 Ibid., p. 12.

38 Ibid., 15.

39 Marcos Allende, Diego León, S Cerón et al. Quantum-Resistance in Blockchain Networks. *Sci Rep, 13* (5664) (2023). https://doi.org/10.1038/s41598-023-32701-6 See also Joseph Kearney, Carlos Delgado, *Vulnerability of Blockchain Technologies to Quantum Attacks.* https://www.sciencedirect.com/science/article/pii/S2590005621000138
M. Edwards, A. Mashatan, S. Ghose, *A Review of Quantum and Hybrid Quantum/Classical Blockchain Protocols.* https://arxiv.org/pdf/1912.09280.pdf. Blockchain technology is

Should this be fully realised, the banking and finance sector, along with national security, defence, health, and law enforcement, amongst others, could very soon be subject to sophisticated intrusions that have never before been experienced. No law or legal framework will be able to prevent such breaches. National governments around the world would be extremely vulnerable should this ever eventuate. Such intrusions on blockchain will become possible, making everything that relies on it significantly open to the world.

More specifically, five key areas have been identified as being the most vulnerable in blockchain technology: 'digital signatures; communication over the Internet relies on protocols such as HTTP; block mining; reverting hashed data; and rewriting history'.[40] Digital signatures are important for smart contracts and IP applications. More importantly, communication over the HTTP protocols is probably more concerning as this is what is needed for a computer to communicate with the outside world. Thus, blockchain, which supports crypto assets and to some extent digital payments,[41] will be impacted by AI and quantum technologies. This chapter will address the current-day laws for crypto assets and digital payments. Essentially, what governments and regulators are considering is whether their respective banking and finance legal frameworks are applicable to these new types of payments.

Banking and finance law is a pivotal pillar of the economy. It is central to national and transnational markets and enables individuals and large entities to transact money on a daily basis. Over the last decade, new forms of finance have emerged that are outside the traditional banking system. Put another way, banking and finance law 'derives from market governance and possesses visible lineaments. It is an emergent order resulting from legal and institutional features that organise how contemporary markets work and that set the terms within which profit-seeking firms and individual households operate'.[42] It is a:

---

facing critical issues of scalability, efficiency, and sustainability. It is essential that these problems be solved if blockchain is to become a technology that can be used responsibly. Useful quantum computers could potentially be developed by the time that blockchain will be widely implemented for mission-critical work at financial and other institutions. Nivedita Dey, Mrityunjay Ghosh, Amlan Chakrabarti, *Quantum Solutions to Possible Challenges of Blockchain Technology* (2021). https://arxiv.org/pdf/2110.05321.pdf. See also Tanya Srivastava, Bharat Bhushan, Saurabh Bhatt, AKM Bhalul Haque, Integration of Quantum Computing and Blockchain Technology: A Cryptographic Perspective. In R Kuma, R Sharma, PK Pattnaik, *Multimedia Technologies in the Internet of Things Environment*, 3. *Studies in Big Data*, *108*, Springer Singapore (2022), pp. 197–201.

40 Ibid.

41 Mohammad Ahmed, Kandala Meenakshi, Mohammad Obaidat, Ruhul Amin, Pandi Vijayakmumar, Blockchain-Based Architecture and Solution for Secure Digital Payment System (2021). *IEEE*. 10.1109/ICC42927.2021.9500526

42 Bruce Carruthers, Law, Governance, and Finance: Introduction to the Theory and Society Special Issue, *Theory of Society*, *49* (2020), 152. https://doi.org/10.1007/s11186-020-09390-5

> mixture of historical contingencies, path dependencies, political interests, and institutional legacies: it is much more of a loose collection than a coherent system with a unitary architecture. It certainly is not a particularly efficient arrangement. Contemporary financial markets face the problem of legal pluralism: financial transactions often cross political borders and are subject to multiple and often inconsistent legal rules.[43]

The point raised by Carruthers in relation to cross-political borders can be applied to transnational borders. The financial markets today, while regulated nationally, are usually international at the transactional level. As an indication of the change in the market, in 2023 the International Monetary Fund released a report[44] stating that there had been a 'sustained level of financial inclusion, bolstered by the rise in digital financial services. Notably, microfinance institutions played a pivotal role in responding to the financial needs of the most vulnerable segments of society'.[45] Putting this into context, and as this book demonstrates, the digital economy is changing all areas of economic activity. Finance and banking are no different. The IMF makes the point that digital finance is expanding in every region of the world.

Diagram – IMF Digital financial services expand in most regions[46]

The figure above demonstrates the transition in the financial markets, as people increasingly engage in financial transactions via the internet. Arguably, the use of cash is in decline[47] and has been for some time. The turning point was the pandemic[48] in 2020–2022. On the other hand, the number of bank accounts continues to rise. The IMF further notes that:

43 Ibid.

44 International Monetary Fund, *IMF Releases the 2023 Financial Access Survey Results*, p. 2. https://www.imf.org/en/News/Articles/2023/10/03/pr23332-imf-releases-the-2023-financial-access-survey-results Also see, International Monetary Fund, *Financial Access Surveys*. https://data.imf.org/?sk=e5dcab7e-a5ca-4892-a6ea-598b5463a34c

45 Ibid.

46 Ibid. Mobile money is a digital medium of exchange and store of value using mobile money accounts, facilitated by a network of mobile money agents. A bank account is not required to use mobile services. Mobile and internet banking is the use of an application on a mobile or another electronic device to access banking services and execute banking activities.

47 Bruna Bruno, Marisa Faggini, The Cashless Man: Do Preferences Matter? *Journal of Evolutionary Economics* (2022), 1528. https://link.springer.com/article/10.1007/s00191-022-00775-6

48 Radoslaw Kotkowski, Michal Polasik, COVID-19 Pandemic Increases the Divide Between Cash and Cashless Payment Users in Europe, *PubMed Central* (2021). https://doi.org/10.1016/j.econlet.2021.110139 See example in Australia, Thuong Nguyen, Benjamin Watson, *Consumer Payment Behaviour in Australia* (2023), pp. 1–3. https://www.rba.gov.au/publications/bulletin/2023/jun/pdf/consumer-payment-behaviour-in-australia.pdf A similar pattern is emerging at different rates across all countries. There is a trend where cash is being used less.

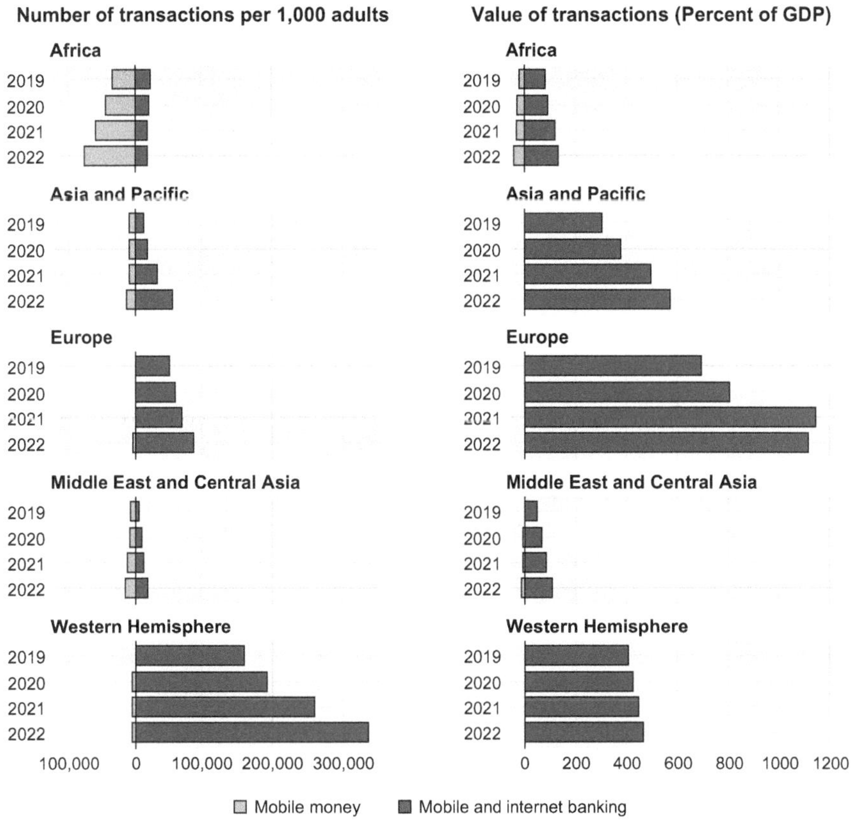

Figure 2.1 Number and value of transactions across the FinTech sector for 2020–2022.

between 2021 to 2022, the number of deposit accounts at commercial banks grew across all regions, with Asia having a significant increase compared to most other regions. In the Asia and Pacific region, the number of Pacific deposit accounts increased by 13 percent in 2022, mostly driven by China, Nepal, and Indonesia. In China, the increase may partly reflect households' seeking to maximise returns on deposits in Europe a falling interest rate environment given that depositors tend to be price sensitive.[49]

It was also highlighted that:

49 International Monetary Fund, *IMF Releases the 2023 Financial Access Survey Results*, p. 5. https://www.imf.org/en/News/Articles/2023/10/03/pr23332-imf-releases-the-2023-financial-access-survey-results

> in Nepal, the reported 15 percent increase in deposit accounts was driven by increasing interest rates, a greater Middle East inflow of remittances, and expansion in banking outreach, supported by a more extensive use of and Central and Central information technology.[50]

Significantly, the IMF points out that the:

> number of loan accounts at commercial banks has remained broadly stable across most regions during 2020–2022, except in Western Hemisphere, where the number of loan accounts has risen in countries such as Brazil and Hemisphere Paraguay, in part due to a carry-over effect from the measures introduced in 2020–2021 to support credit.[51]

On the one hand, in an indication that there could be a shift in the banking sector, 'the aggregate value of outstanding deposits and loans as a percentage of GDP decreased across all regions except for Asia and Pacific'.[52] This trend suggests that the Asia Pacific region is the fastest and strongest growing area[53] in the world. On the other hand, even though digital payments continue to rise, cash is far from being replaced.[54] Undoubtedly, this is one area where there is a significant shift taking place in the world economy. In the forthcoming decade, the likelihood that cash will be the predominant tool used for daily local, national, and international transactions will diminish to where it is no longer viable for countries to print cash. Subsequently, governments and regulators will have to change their current regulatory framework to accommodate these new activities.

2.2 International Law

The International Organisation of Securities Commissions (IOSCO)[55] is currently developing global standards. In May 2023, the IOSCO developed a set of principles-based and outcomes-focused recommendations to deal with:

50 Ibid.
51 Ibid.
52 Ibid., p. 6.
53 The World Bank, *East Asia and Pacific: Sustained Growth, Momentum Slowing* (2023). https://www.worldbank.org/en/news/press-release/2023/10/01/east-asia-and-pacific-sustained-growth-momentum-slowing
54 Marc Glowka, Anneke Kosse, Robert Szemere, Digital Payments Make Gains but Cash Remains, *CPMI Brief, 1*, Bank for International Settlements (2023), p. 1. https://www.bis.org/statistics/payment_stats/commentary2301.pdf
55 International Organisation of Securities Commissions, p. 3. https://www.iosco.org/library/pubdocs/pdf/IOSCOPD734.pdf, also, https://www.iosco.org/news/pdf/IOSCONEWS693.pdf

1) conflicts of interest arising from vertical integration of activities and functions;
2) market manipulation, insider trading and fraud;
3) cross-border risks and regulatory cooperation;
4) custody and client asset protection;
5) operational and technological risk; and
6) retail access, suitability, and distribution.[56]

The IOSCO is encouraging the industry to take 'a functional, economic approach to mitigate against the risks, rather than attempting to develop a one-size fits all prescriptive taxonomy'.[57] Accordingly, the IOSCO is developing an outcomes-focused, principles-based approach for each of the key areas listed above. This approach involves the mapping of IOSCO standards, principles, and relevant sectoral recommendations and guidelines to relevant elements of the infrastructure and to the activities of and services provided by participants. Standards are going to be an important component of the overall regulatory framework. On the other hand, the Bank for International Settlements has noted that the nature of crypto assets[58] lends itself to regulatory and supervisory arbitrage,[59] opting for more favourable and less stringent regulatory and supervisory environments given that their function and purpose are closely linked with cross-border financial transactions.[60] This work, undertaken at the international level, is more important now. On many occasions, the development of the law has come well after an economic activity or technology has been well established. International standards and legal mechanisms could be developed so as to create an environment of legal harmonisation.

2.3 National Laws

This section examines national laws and, in the case of the EU, the supranational law, if any, in relation to the above. Due to the rapidly changing legal landscape of banking and finance, this chapter examines only the law as of March 2024. Additionally, it does not examine the regulators that have been established in each jurisdiction because there are a number that deal with not only the regulation of the banking-finance entities themselves, but also the regulation of transnational transactions above a certain threshold, tax, and securities. The chapter addresses the legal landscape of tokens and makes

56 Ibid.
57 Ibid.
58 Bank for International Settlements, Financial Stability Risks from Crypto-Assets in Emerging Market Economies Consultative Group of Directors of Financial Stability, *BIS Papers, 138* (2023).
https://www.bis.org/publ/bppdf/bispap138.pdf
59 Ibid., p. 25.
60 Ibid., p. 38.

reference to them or stablecoins. In short, this is a rapidly developing area of the law which, over the next one to two years, will see significant changes.

2.3.1 Australia

Currently, digital payments are not regulated in Australia. Generally, the laws pertaining to banking and finance at the national level in Australia include the *Banking Act 1959*, the *Payment Systems (Regulation) Act 1998*, the *Financial Sector Collection of Data Act 2001*, the *Corporations Act 2001*, and the *Financial Sector (Shareholdings) Act 1998*, which places a threshold ownership of 20% in a financial sector company that does not need approval from the Treasurer. Generally, an Australian Financial Services Licence[61] must be obtained to operate in Australia, or an institution must be authorised to provide a product or service.[62] There is no need to compare the application process that must be undertaken by an applicant.

As recently as October 2023, Australia introduced a Bill[63] which will give the Reserve Bank of Australia (RBA) powers to respond to the growing area of digital payments, including stablecoins. It will provide a framework for new entrants into the market.[64] In a further recent development, in 2023, the 'AUDD was released, which is a company of Novatti's A$ backed stablecoin that is intended to facilitate transactions between entities and their customers. It can be used corporate-to-corporate, and is backed by the Australian currency'.[65] This is a significant development in the stablecoin market and token economy for Australia.

Nonetheless, there is an urgent need for reform as, increasingly, there are platforms being developed allowing people to obtain credit and undertake transactions online with ease, and the new entrants are not regulated in Australia. This is particularly the case for those registered and based in a third

61 Australian Securities and Investments Commission. https://asic.gov.au/for-finance-professionals/afs-licensees/

62 *Banking Act 1959*, section 2 defines banking to mean, a business that consists of banking within the meaning of paragraph 51(xiii) of the Constitution; or (b) a business that is carried on by a corporation to which paragraph 51(xx) of the Constitution applies and that consists, to any extent, of: (i) both taking money on deposit (otherwise than as part-payment for identified goods or services) and making advances of money; or (ii) other financial activities prescribed by the regulations for the purposes of this definition. Also see APRA. https://www.apra.gov.au/licensing-guidelines-for-authorised-deposit-taking-institutions

63 Australian Government, *Reforms to the Payment Systems (Regulation) Act 1998*, Explanatory Materials.
https://treasury.gov.au/sites/default/files/2023-10/c2023-452114-em.pdf Exposure Draft. https://treasury.gov.au/sites/default/files/2023-10/c2023-452114-ed.pdf The proposal aims to include stored-value facilities (SVFs) such as payment stablecoins. These are a subset of stablecoins.

64 Ibid., p. 5.

65 AUDD, *The Next Leap in Payments Innovation*. https://audd.digital

country. The proposal recognises the RBA as the only entity with the regulatory powers or functions to undertake this task for the current-day regulation of finance. Thus, the proposal will allow the RBA to:

> designate a payment system; impose an access regime on participants in a designated payment system; determine standards to be complied with by participants in a designated payment system; give directions to participants in designated payment systems to ensure compliance with an access regime or standard; and arbitrate disputes between participants in a designated payment system.[66]

Should this proposal be approved in its current form, it could be challenged by new entrants into the community, as they may view this as the imposition of another regulatory burden. However, and arguably, there is a need to implement these laws to protect consumers. Under the *Banking Act 1959*, a provider of a purchased payment facility (PPF provider) enables the development and availability to consumers of payment services. A PPF provider constitutes: a) a person providing a purchased payment facility that has been determined to be banking business under Regulation 3 of the *Banking Regulations 1966*; or b) a holder of stored value that falls within the *Payment Systems (Regulation) Act 1998* that makes payments (as mentioned in paragraph 9(1)(c) of that Act) in relation to a PPF that has been determined to be banking business under Regulation 3.[67] However, in Australia, digital payments are somewhat fragmented and also regulated by voluntary codes that have been established by the Australian Securities and Investment Commission (ASIC).[68] These types of codes are generally national in their scope. The evolving nature of the law in this area has not yet resulted in published court decisions specific to digital payments. However, there are historical cases that deal with issues such as wrongful payments (mistake) and the right to recover those digital payments (money). This is a problem that could easily occur nowadays, not unlike errors that could be made in the long-standing practice of issuing paper-based cheques. Nowadays, people could inadvertently click one too many times when making a purchase online. As a hypothetical example, a person has booked into a motel and, to purchase food, they have to do it online via a tablet or other device.

66 Australian Government, *Reforms to the Payment Systems (Regulation) Act 1998*, Explanatory Materials.
https://treasury.gov.au/sites/default/files/2023-10/c2023-452114-em.pdf
Exposure Draft. https://treasury.gov.au/sites/default/files/2023-10/c2023-452114-ed.pdf p. 6.

67 Australian Prudential Regulation Authority.
https://www.apra.gov.au/enabling-legislation outlines the extensive list of legislative instruments that govern the banking-finance sector in Australia.

68 Australia Investment Commission, *E/payments Code 2022*. https://download.asic.gov.au/media/lloeicwb/epayments-code-published-02-june-2022.pdf

Accidentally, the person makes a mistake and clicks multiple times on the same item, giving rise to the question: can they recover that cost after the food has already been prepared and delivered? In another example: if a person makes a mistake when purchasing airline tickets online, can they obtain a refund? Under normal circumstances, it may be very difficult to obtain a refund if the entities involved do not acknowledge a simple mistake.

The High Court in *ANZ Group Ltd v Westpac Banking Corporation*[69] clarified an important question about the right of recovery for money paid under a mistake of fact:

> There was an agreed overdraft limit of $70,000 but the branch manager had a discretion, which he was prepared to exercise, to allow further overdraft accommodation of $20,000 with the result that the effective overdraft limit was $90,000. After opening entries at the start of business on Tuesday 27 October 1981, the account showed a debit balance of $67,700.96. In the course of that day, the branch received for the credit of the account two cheques and a telegraphic transfer. The telegraphic transfer was of $114,158.20 made by ANZ's Martin Place branch, through its St. Albans branch, purportedly on behalf of one of its customers. It was effected by telephone communication between the two ANZ branches followed by the delivery of a written warrant by the St. Albans branch to Westpac's St. Albans branch. In fact, ANZ had been instructed by its customer to transfer $14,158.00 only. The extra $100,000 was transferred as the result of a clerical mistake made by one of its staff in the preparation of documents.[70]

Subsequently, the judgement stated that:

> receipt of a payment which has been made under a fundamental mistake is one of the categories of case in which the facts give rise to a prima facie obligation to make restitution, in the sense of compensation for the benefit of unjust enrichment, to the person who has sustained the countervailing detriment.[71]

Moreover, in relation to the recovery of money, the court asserted that:

> the grounds of the action for recovery are framed in the traditional words of trust or use and that contemporary legal principles of restitution or unjust enrichment can be equated with seminal equitable notions of

69 *ANZ Group Ltd v Westpac Banking Corporation* (1987) 164 CLR 662. https://jade.io/article/67417

70 Ibid., para 2.

71 Ibid., para 11.

> good conscience, the action itself is not for the enforcement of a trust or for tracing or the recovery of specific money or property. It is a common law action for recovery of the value of the unjust enrichment and the fact that specific money or property received can no longer be identified in the hands of the recipient or traced into other specific property which he holds does not of itself constitute an answer in a category of case in which the law imposes a prima facie liability to make restitution.[72]

As a further point regarding restitution, the court stated:

> The prima facie liability to make restitution is imposed by the law on the person who has been unjustly enriched. In the ordinary case of a payment of money, that person will be the payee. However, when the person to whom the payment is directly made receives it as an intermediary (e.g., as agent for a designated principal), there may be uncertainty about the identity of the actual recipient of the benefit at the moment of payment. If the circumstances are such that the intermediary is to be seen as being himself the initial recipient of the benefit, his prima facie liability will ordinarily be displaced when he has handed the money received on to the person for whom he received it.[73]

In giving the background of the facts in this case, the court noted that in addition to the above:

> the transfer of funds was expressly made by ANZ to the credit of Jakes' account at Westpac's St. Albans branch. The funds were received by Westpac solely in the capacity of intermediary for Jakes. It was submitted on behalf of ANZ that Westpac should not be seen as receiving the amount of the overpayment as agent for Jakes for the reason that it lacked Jakes' authority to receive that surplus amount. That submission must, however, be rejected. There is nothing at all in the evidence, in banking practice or in common sense to suggest that Westpac's authority, as between Jakes and itself, to receive payment to the credit of Jakes' account was limited to amounts which it could somehow ascertain in advance were in fact due and owing to Jakes. Be that as it may however, it is plain that, regardless of the theoretical limits of Westpac's authority as between itself and Jakes, the funds were received by it not on its own behalf as principal but as an intermediary: they were paid to it and received by it as Jakes' banker on the express basis that they were to be credited to Jakes' account and they were in fact so credited.[74]

72 Ibid.
73 Ibid., para 12.
74 Ibid., para 13.

This case demonstrates that payment-related mistakes are nothing new. The court determined that where there is an intermediary involved, there are questions pertaining to the role of that individual or entity in receiving a payment. Did that entity have an obligation to pass it on to another entity? A further accentuating question was whether the entity had clear instructions from the payee to deal with the money in a certain way. However, since the matter above has in part been addressed by the ASIC E/Payments Code 2022, the problematic aspect is that it is only voluntary. Nonetheless, a subscriber to the code must comply with it. Thus, sections 23–36 outline a clear process for dealing with mistaken payments. Therefore, the courts will consider not only the code and any other requirements formally put in place by the regulator but any previous judicial decisions made regarding mistaken online payments.

2.3.2 European Union (EU)

To regulate the banking and financial institutions of its members, the EU[75] has applied the Basel Framework.[76] Most notably, Regulation 2023/1114,[77] which is similar to Indian law, has been quick to provide a level of legal certainty in regulating crypto assets that are used in digital (non-currency/money) payments. The regulation states that 'crypto-assets are electronic surrogates for coins and banknotes and are likely to be used for making payments'.[78] This definition also extends to stablecoins:

> Where a crypto-asset falls within the definition of an asset-referenced token or e-money token, Title III or IV of this Regulation should apply, irrespective of how the issuer intends to design the crypto-asset, including the mechanism for maintaining a stable value of the crypto-asset. The same applies to so-called algorithmic 'stable coins' that aim to maintain a stable value in relation to an official currency, or in relation to one or several assets, via protocols, that provide for the increase or decrease in the supply of such crypto-assets in response to changes in demand. Offerors or persons seeking admission to trading of algorithmic

75 European Commission, *Financial Services Regulation*. https://finance.ec.europa.eu/regulation-and-supervision/financial-services-legislation/overview-financial-services-legislation_en

76 European Central Bank. https://www.bankingsupervision.europa.eu/legalframework/regulatory/html/index.en.html

77 Regulation 2023/1114 of the European Parliament and of the Council, of 31 May 2023 on Markets in Crypto-Assets, and Amending Regulations (EU) No 1093/2010 and (EU) No 1095/2010 and Directives 2013/36/EU and (EU) 2019/1937, *Official Journal of the European Union, L150/40.*

78 Ibid., Preamble 18. Those crypto assets should be defined in this Regulation as 'e-money tokens'. The second type of crypto assets concerns 'asset-referenced tokens', which aim to stabilise their value by referencing another value or right, or a combination thereof, including one or several official currencies. The third type consists of crypto assets other than asset-referenced tokens and e-money tokens, and covers a wide variety of crypto assets, including utility tokens.

> crypto-assets that do not aim to stabilise the value of the crypto-assets by referencing one or several assets should in any event comply with Title II of this Regulation.[79]

To reinforce the above, a crypto asset is 'a digital representation of a value or of a right that is able to be transferred and stored electronically using distributed ledger technology or similar technology'.[80] This was reaffirmed by a Greek court in 2022,[81] which stated that 'according to the Greek legal order, bitcoin is considered a "*digital asset*" and not a currency. In essence, it is a digital unit of value that can be exchanged electronically and has no physical form'.[82] In addition to the above, 'an electronic money token or e-money token is a type of crypto-asset that 'purports to maintain a stable value by referencing the value of one official currency'.[83] Although the EU is moving towards a central bank digital currency,[84] it is also revising its legal framework to allow digital payments.[85] The proposal is intended to increase:

> integration and provide a framework for the single euro payments area; to promote competition and innovation by improving the level playing field for payment service providers; to increase the safety, convenience and efficiency of payment services; and to provide a high level of consumer protection.[86]

Apart from the above, the main obligation of individuals and entities providing crypto assets is that they adhere to these stipulations:

- act honestly, fairly and professionally in their actual and potential clients' best interests;
- provide clients with fair, clear and non-misleading information;

79 Ibid., Preamble 41.
80 Ibid., Article 3.
81 No 88/2021 Decision of the Court of Appeal of Western Central Greece, Bitcoin and Public Policy In International Arbitration Enforcement, Market Screener. https://www.marketscreener.com/quote/stock/PUBLIC-POLICY-HOLDING-COM-130670778/news/Bitcoin-And-Public-Policy-In-International-Arbitration-Enforcement-40711447/
82 Ibid.
83 Regulation 2023/1114 of the European Parliament and of the Council, of 31 May 2023 on Markets in Crypto-Assets, and Amending Regulations (EU) No 1093/2010 and (EU) No 1095/2010 and Directives 2013/36/EU and (EU) 2019/1937, *Official Journal of the European Union, L150/40*, Article 3.
84 European Central Bank, *ECB Says It Can Compensate Banks if Dgital Euro Causes Deposit Flights* (2023). https://www.reuters.com/markets/europe/ecb-says-it-can-compensate-banks-if-digital-euro-causes-deposit-flight-2023-04-24/ See also, European Commission. https://ec.europa.eu/search/?QueryText=digital%20payments&swlang=en
85 Revision of Directive (EU) 2015/2366 on Payment Services (2023). https://www.europarl.europa.eu/RegData/etudes/BRIE/2023/747447/EPRS_BRI(2023)747447_EN.pdf
86 Ibid., p. 2.

- not deliberately or negligently mislead clients on the real or perceived advantages of crypto-assets, and warn them of the risks involved;
- make their pricing, costs, fee policies, and climate and environment-related impact of each cryptoasset prominently available on their website;
- have in place prudential safeguards at least equal to the higher of the following the permanent minimum capital requirements in Annex IV, or one quarter of the preceding year's fixed overheads;
- ensure members of the management body are of good repute and have the knowledge, experience, skills and time to perform their duties effectively;
- implement policies and procedures to prevent any money laundering, terrorist financing or other offences;
- keep clients' crypto-assets and funds separate from other assets and not use them on their own account;
- establish and maintain effective and transparent procedures to handle clients' complaints promptly, fairly and consistently;
- maintain and operate an effective policy to identify, prevent, manage and disclose conflicts of interest;
- take all reasonable steps to avoid any risk when outsourcing activities;
- devise a plan for an orderly wind-down of their activities if necessary.[87]

These stipulations can best be best described as laying the foundations and setting high-level principles for the way entities are to act towards their clients, ensuring they act honestly, fairly, and professionally. It forces entities to develop a self-regulatory framework to ensure that a number of financial and social goals of the EU are implemented. That is, entities will need to develop internal systems to ensure they fully understand the climatic and environmental impacts of their decisions. It calls for entities to be clear about their obligations regarding 'money laundering and terrorist financing'. The obligations extend to forcing entities to assess the risks to themselves and to the broader economic market in which they operate. There is a threshold for reporting certain transactions where the 'issuer infringes Article 22(1) by not reporting, for each significant asset-referenced token with an issue value that is higher than EUR 100,000,000, on a quarterly basis to EBA'.[88] The policy underpinning this reporting will be similar to that of cash transactions that are transferred transnationally. This is an area that governments and regulators should harmonise. More specifically, what this means for stablecoins is that most:

87 Ibid., also see European Union Law, *European Crypto-Assets Regulation*. https://eur-lex.europa.eu/EN/legal-content/summary/european-crypto-assets-regulation-mica.html

88 Regulation 2023/1114 of the European Parliament and of the Council, of 31 May 2023 on Markets in Crypto-Assets, and Amending Regulations (EU) No 1093/2010 and (EU) No 1095/2010 and Directives 2013/36/EU and (EU) 2019/1937, *Official Journal of the European Union, L150/40*, Annex V.

issuers will have to be incorporated in the form of a legal entity established and authorised in the EU in order to operate, and publish a crypto-asset white paper that explains what the product is and how they operate, approved by a competent authority. Similar requirements apply to issuers of EMTs within the meaning of Article 2(1) of Directive 2009/110.[89]

The developments of the EU legal framework are important to the overall legal landscape of digital payments. The EU has the opportunity, similar to that of the data laws[90] established in the 1980s, to drive and influence other countries to develop similar laws. There is no doubt that the EU is in a good position to influence the world's legal framework for digital payments through crypto assets facilitated by blockchain technology.

2.3.3 India

Generally, banking and finance law is broad and complex, no matter the jurisdiction. However, in the same way that the other jurisdictions compared in this book have been examined, this section deals only with digital payments. Essentially, for public and private sector banking and finance, the principal legislative instruments are the *Banking Regulation Act 1949*,[91] *Reserve Bank of India Act 1934*, *Recovery of Debts Due to Banks and Financial Institutions Act 1993*, and *Securitisation and Reconstruction of Financial Assets and Enforcement of Security Interest Act 2002*. Generally, these instruments authorise the operations of a bank or other financial institution.

As one of the most advanced jurisdictions in the regulation of digital payments, India, by means of the *Payment and Settlement Systems Act 2007* (PSA), provides for 'mobile wallets, prepaid cards, and online platforms'.[92] It covers payments, securities, settlements, and netting, all regulated by the Reserve Bank. In India, digital payments have evolved significantly over a short period of time, rapidly transforming the use of cash across the country, in a way similar to many other countries around the world. The PSA goes further by developing a more efficient and effective means for the large population of India to access payments online. A level of authorisation is required under section 5 of the PSA. This authorisation is in the form of a licence or permit. It is

89 European Parliament, *Non-EU Countries' Regulations on Crypto-Assets and Their Potential Implications for the EU*. https://www.europarl.europa.eu/RegData/etudes/BRIE/2023/753930/EPRS_BRI(2023)753930_EN.pdf

90 Graham Greenleaf, Global Data Privacy Laws 2021: Despite COVID Delays, 145 Laws Show GDPR Dominance, *Privacy Laws & Business International Report*, 169 (UNSW Law Research Paper 21–60).

91 Department of Financial Services. https://financialservices.gov.in/act-rule/Banking/Banking-Acts. Note the exhaustive list of in-country regulation.

92 *The Payment and Settlement Systems Act 2007*. https://www.indiacode.nic.in/bitstream/123456789/2082/1/A2007_51.pdf

the same or a similar format to that which is likely to be implemented by the jurisdictions compared. This chapter will not compare the application process or conditions that must be met by the applicant to obtain authorisation. This will differ from country to country and jurisdiction to jurisdiction according to local sovereign needs.

In the case of *Lotus Pay Solutions*[93] the court noted that *Lotus* made the case that Payment Aggregators (PAs), which are intermediaries, do not fall within the scope and ambit of the PSA. It was also highlighted that Lotus did not agree with clauses 3, 4, and 8 of the *Guidelines for the Regulation of Payment Aggregators and Payment Gateways* (Guidelines).[94]

Lotus is a company that is engaged in the business of providing 'recurring payment solutions' for businesses in India via an authorised payment system known as the National Automated Clearing House. The Union of India is the founder and Chief Executive Officer of petitioner no.1 company. Therefore, unless the context requires otherwise, they shall be collectively referred to as petitioners.[95] Lotus uses the following procedure highlighting how it:

> collects funds from customers on behalf of its clients i.e., merchant clients/e-commerce marketing companies. These funds are then placed in a special bank account, known as the 'nodal bank account. The nodal bank account is maintained in a designated Nodal Bank. The funds are remitted from the nodal bank account to petitioner no.1's merchant clients/e-commerce marketing companies, as per pre-agreed terms and conditions contained in the Nodal Account Agreement. In effect, a three-day settlement period is provided for transmission of funds from the nodal bank account to petitioner no.1's merchant clients/e-commerce marketing companies. Lotus, has been carrying on the business of facilitating safe and secure online recurring transactions since 2016, in consonance with the instructions contained in the document dated 24.11.2009, titled Directions for opening and operation of Accounts and settlement of payments for electronic payment transactions involving intermediaries.[96]

Further, in relation to the application of the PSA, the court noted that it:

> makes a clear distinction between 'payment system', 'system participant' and 'system provider'. Lotus only provides an intermediary tool, which is used by the payment system to facilitate the remittance of payments

93 *Lotus Pay Solutions Pvt Ltd & Anr v Union of India & Others*, W.P (C) 8215/2020, CM APPLs. 26623/2020& 34346/2021. https://www.livelaw.in/pdf_upload/ras15092022cw82152020173218-435603.pdf

94 Ibid., paras 1–5.

95 Ibid., paras 6–8.

96 Ibid., paras 11.1–11.3.

> received from the customers to the merchant clients/e-commerce marketing companies. The intermediary, thus, cannot be treated as a 'payment system'. The RBI, which is invested with the authority to regulate and supervise payment systems in the country, cannot regulate PAs, which act as intermediaries between merchant clients/e-commerce companies and banks. The PAs are, in effect, 'system participants', as defined in Section 2(1)(p) of the 2007 Act.[97]

Moreover, in applying the Guidelines, the court argued that by applying the test of proportionality:

> they mandate restrictive conditions for the operation of PAs, even though less invasive measures are available. The 2020 Guidelines fail to take into account, recommendations and suggestions made by various stakeholders on net worth requirements. The 2020 Guidelines will act as a disincentive for creating a digital payment environment in the country, as it fails to set up a regulatory framework which promotes competition and innovation, and at the same time protects the interests of the consumers.[98]

In coming to its decision, the court ruled that in 'any digital payment transaction, there is a payer and a beneficiary'.[99] Thus, the question was whether the PA being the intermediary had anything to do with facilitating the transaction. On that basis, the court was of the belief that:

> the interface is the PA, which ensures that the money is transferred to the designated nodal account, and after a gap of a stipulated timeframe, which the petitioners say is three days, a settlement takes place and funds are transmitted to the merchants account.[100]

The court ruled that the PAs fell within section 23 in regard to settlements. In its conclusion, the court stated that it applied the public interest[101] test provided for in section 23A. In the end, Lotus lost its claim. This case shows that the tests of proportionality and public interest have become important concepts that the court will consider when applying national law and any accompanying guidelines to determine whether the functions of digital payments

97 Ibid., para 11.9.
98 Ibid., paras 13.1–13.3.
99 Ibid., para 16.4.
100 Ibid.
101 Ibid., para 15. Section 23A of the PSA provides the Reserve Bank may, in the public interest or in the interest of the customers of designated payment systems, act to prevent the affairs of such designated payment systems from being conducted in a manner prejudicial to the interests of its customers.

fall within the PSA. Specifically, it concluded that technology which is used to facilitate digital payments does so. However, in regard to data in particular, the technology still has many vulnerabilities.

2.3.4 Indonesia

As mentioned earlier in this book, Indonesia has two financial systems: one under the traditional legal framework that has been inherited from civil law, and one under Islamic law. Indonesia has also moved quite quickly in this area, with the implementation of the following:

- Bappebti Regulation No. 8/2021 on Guidelines for Conducting Crypto Asset Physical Market Trading on Commodity Exchanges as amended by Bappebti Regulation No. 13 of 2022.
- Bappebti Regulation of the commodities trading supervisory agency number 4 of 2023 concerning amendment to the regulation of the commodities trading supervisory agency number 11 of 2022 concerning determination of list of crypto assets traded in the physical market of crypto assets.
- Law No. 4 of 2023 on the Development and Strengthening of the Financial Services Sector (the Financial Omnibus Law).[102]

Based on the above, and while the English version was not available at the time of writing, the industry will be regulated. It has been reported that the types of crypto-trading-related businesses that are recognised include:

- Futures exchanges. These are business entities that provide systems and/or facilities for buying and selling commodities based on futures contracts, sharia derivative contracts, and/or other derivative contracts.
- Crypto futures clearing houses. These provide systems and/or facilities for clearing and guaranteeing the settlement of futures trading transactions.
- Crypto-asset storage managers. These obtain approval from the Head of Bappebti to carry out storage, maintenance, supervision and/or delivery of crypto assets.
- Crypto-asset physical traders. These obtain approval from the Head of Bappebti to carry out transaction activities related to crypto assets.[103]

Therefore, the scope of crypto-asset physical trader activities should include:

- selling and/or purchasing crypto assets between crypto and rupiah currencies;
- exchanging one or more types of crypto assets;

102 Alyssa Abrams, *Crypto Regulation in Indonesia – All You Need to Know in 2023* (August 2023). Learn more about crypto regulations in Indonesia and how to stay compliant. https://sumsub.com/blog/crypto-regulations-indonesia/

103 Ibid.

- storage of crypto assets; and
- transfer of crypto assets between wallets.[104]

Importantly, and because Indonesia also utilises the Islamic banking system, what does this mean for the regulation of crypto assets? It has been asserted that under:

> Islamic finance, blockchain technology plays a crucial role. By simply allowing execution when the conditions (smart code in a blockchain smart contract) have been met through automatic validation and implementation, blockchain technology ensures strict shariah compliance. Additionally, blockchain smart contracts provide improved safety and scalability for a broader Muslim and non-Muslim market and operate as executable agreements or complex financing protocols for transactions in an Islamic economic environment.[105]

Hence, it is argued that the:

> growth and development of Islamic crypto assets (ICAs) contribute to the social economy. The potential exists for paying zakat using cryptocurrencies from investments in crypto assets in many countries, including Malaysia and Indonesia. Furthermore, ICAs are supported by finance and the halal industry. Therefore, by using blockchain technology in sukūk transactions increases transparency and is compatible with drafts on Islamic finance.[106]

On that basis, where the ICA itself provides for the 'security token and is used as an investment medium or securities, in part, it automatically applies Shariah principles. In addition, the ICAs are halal if they meet the following three criteria: 1) the cryptocurrency represents maal, wealth, or precious property; 2) the cryptocurrency has met the Shariah permissibility standard; and 3) the cryptocurrency fulfils the principle of Maqasid al-Shariah'.[107] Therefore, crypto assets will fall under Islamic law provided they meet the three criteria above. Both of the financial systems available in Indonesia will allow crypto

104 Ibid.

105 Jamal Wiwoho, Irwan Trinugroho, Dona Budi Kharisma, Pujiyono Suwadi, Islamic Crypto Assets and Regulatory Framework: Evidence from Indonesia and Global Approaches, *International Journal of Law and Management* (2023). https://www.emerald.com/insight/content/doi/10.1108/IJLMA-03-2023-0051/full/pdf?title=islamic-crypto-assets-and-regulatory-framework-evidence-from-indonesia-and-global-approache

106 Ibid.

107 Ibid. Note also Malaysia has an ICA called GOLDX. HelloGold, based in Malaysia, has gained shariah-compliant accreditation for its gold-backed cryptocurrency and intends to build an online gold platform.

transactions under its local licencing regime. What can be demonstrated is that Indonesia is applying Islamic law to this issue while at the same time applying its traditional national legal framework. There is a subtle but important overlap between the two legal regimes.

2.3.5 Japan

Japan was one of the early adopters of crypto regulation. In recognising the importance of the role that the crypto economy can play in the national economy, Japan has implemented the Payment Services Act (PSA).[108] All exchanges must be registered with the Financial Services Agency, although neither crypto assets nor digital assets have been defined. Rather, Japan has opted to define what constitutes a virtual currency. The PSA defines this as:

> property value (limited to that which is recorded on an electronic device or any other object by electronic means, and excluding the Japanese currency, foreign currencies, and Currency-Denominated Assets; the same applies in the following item) which can be used in relation to unspecified persons for the purpose of paying consideration for the purchase or leasing of goods or the receipt of provision of services and can also be purchased from and sold to unspecified persons acting as counterparties, and which can be transferred by means of an electronic data processing system.[109]

This definition is broad, so a crypto asset or digital asset could constitute a property value that is recorded by an electronic device or by electronic means. The question is whether blockchain technology constitutes an electronic means. Further, the term, Currency-Denominated Assets:

> used in this Act refers to assets which are denominated in the Japanese currency or a foreign currency, or for which performance of obligations, refund, or anything equivalent thereto (hereinafter referred to as 'performance of obligations, etc.' in this paragraph) is supposed to be made in the Japanese currency or a foreign currency. In this case, assets for which performance of obligations, etc. is supposed to be made by means of Currency-Denominated Assets are deemed to be Currency-Denominated Assets.[110]

108 *Payment Services Act* (PSA).
https://www.japaneselawtranslation.go.jp/en/laws/view/3078/en Note that in 1948, the Financial Instruments and Exchange Act regulated securities and applies to any financial institution that facilitates security trading, including banks.
109 Ibidl, Article 2(5).
110 Ibidl, Article 2(6).

However, neither definition can be applied to explain how crypto assets fall within the PAS. More specifically, the term 'Crypto Asset Exchange Services' (or CAES) means any of the following acts carried out as a business: i) purchase and sale of a virtual currency or exchange with another virtual currency; ii) intermediary, brokerage, or agency services for the act set forth in the preceding item; and iii) management of users' money or virtual currency, carried out by persons in connection with their acts set forth in the preceding two items.[111] Thus, stablecoins fall within this framework.

Another recent addition to the PSA is Article 63–64 that requires a Register of Virtual Currency Service Providers.[112] In effect, it provides a reporting process for the transactions of stablecoins and other crypto assets. The registration–register process is an important mechanism that enables the tracing of transactions. However, it may not solve the problem of the traceability of all transactions and identifying the person or entity who made the transaction. Hence, it would record only the initial purchase or payment. This is an area of concern because the identification of individuals and entities using this technology is going to be difficult due to the decentralised architecture of blockchain technology.

2.3.6 Singapore

In Singapore, banking and finance law is no different from that of many other states. The legal framework has been established to address compliance and regulation through a licence provided to entities undertaking financial activities. The legal landscape applies to the FinTech sector including, but not limited to, technology contracts (smart contracts), data, IP, and general financing. Beginning with the *Securities and Futures Act* (SFA),[113] it provides the platform for regulating capital markets services intermediaries, finance advisers[114] and fund managers that include crypto.[115] More specifically, the *Payment Services Act* (PS Act)[116] provides for the issuing of licences to carry on a payment service. It does not define digital assets, stablecoin, blockchain, or cryptocurrency. However, it does define digital payment token and e-money.[117] While there are no specific provisions for reporting on a cybersecurity

111 Ibid., Article 2(7).

112 Ibid., Article 63–64.

113 *Securities and Futures Act 2001. https://sso.agc.gov.sg/act/sfa2001*

114 Ibid., and see also *Financial Advisers Act* (FAA). *https://sso.agc.gov.sg/Act/FAA2001*

115 Ibid.

116 *Payment Services Act* (PS Act) (2019). *https://sso.agc.gov.sg/Acts-Supp/2-2019/Published/20190220?DocDate=20190220*

117 Ibid., section 2, 'digital payment token' means any digital representation of value (other than an excluded digital representation of value) that is expressed as a unit; is not denominated in any currency, and is not pegged by its issuer to any currency; is, or is intended to be, a medium of exchange accepted by the public, or a section of the public, as payment for goods or services or for the discharge of a debt; can be transferred, stored, or traded electronically;

intrusion or other technology failure, section 17 requires that periodic reports be submitted to the regulator. However, this is very broad and is at the request of the regulator. This pertains to section 16 that requires a licence holder to provide information on the operation of the licencee: pricing of, or any other form of consideration for, any payment service offered or provided by the licencee.

This broad framework for reporting is, arguably, a step in the right direction. It is argued that it should be more specific while not diluting its reach. That is, it should require specific reporting when personal and commercial financial data have been compromised by a cyber event or technology impact. Most notable are the auditing requirements that are established under the PS Act. This is an important point. The PS Act established a two-tiered system for auditing. Section 37 provides that a licencee must annually, and at their own expense, appoint an auditor. However, the regulator can appoint an auditor when required. The auditor's function is to audit accounts, monitor transactions, and ensure compliance with the PS Act. In addition to this audit process, section 68 requires an annual audit of 'operators and settlement institutions of designated payment systems'.[118] It is an institutional-based audit that examines the annual accounts and transactions made by the institution. Apart from the PS Act providing for the above, the licencing arrangements also ensure that there is a legal platform for regulating financial business in its entirety.

At a practical level, because this is a new area of the digital economy, Singapore has established Regulatory Sandbox[119] and Sandbox Express. The Regulatory Sandbox allows 'FinTech players to experiment with innovative financial products or services in a live environment but within a well-defined space and duration'.[120] On the other hand, Sandbox Express provides firms with a faster option to test certain innovative financial products and services in the market within 21 days of applying to the regulator.[121] This form of practical application allows an organisation to undertake an experiment to conform with the relevant legal requirements.

and satisfies such other characteristics as the Authority may prescribe. E-money means any electronically stored monetary value that is denominated in any currency, or pegged by its issuer to any currency, has been paid for in advance to enable the making of payment transactions through the use of a payment account, is accepted by a person other than its issuer, and represents a claim on its issuer.

118 Ibid., section 68.

119 Monetary Authority Singapore, *Overview of Regulatory Sandbox*. https://www.mas.gov.sg/development/fintech/regulatory-sandbox

120 Ibid.

121 Ibid. Note the Financial Industry API Register. https://www.mas.gov.sg/development/fintech/financial-industry-api-register

In the matter of *CLM*,[122] the Singapore High Court was required to deal with the question of whether 'stolen cryptocurrency assets be the subject of a proprietary injunction? Additionally, does the court have jurisdiction to grant interim orders against persons whose identities are presently unknown?'[123] The facts of this case were that the plaintiff CLM commenced an action to trace and recover 109.83 Bitcoin and 1497.54 Ethereum, which were collectively stolen by CLN (Cryptocurrency Assets) and allegedly misappropriated by unidentified persons.[124] Further, 'a portion of which has been traced to digital wallets that were controlled by cryptocurrency exchanges with operations in Singapore'.[125] What followed was a 'Summons No 2444 of 2021 ("SUM 2444")', which was heard on 8 June 2021. The plaintiff sought the following interlocutory relief via an *ex parte* application for a:

(a) proprietary injunction prohibiting the first defendants from dealing with, disposing of, or diminishing the value of the Stolen Cryptocurrency Assets.
(b) worldwide freezing injunction prohibiting the first defendants from dealing with, disposing of, or diminishing their assets up to the value of US$7,089,894.68, being the value of the Stolen Cryptocurrency Assets.
(c) Ancillary disclosure orders against the second and third defendants to assist in the tracing of the Stolen Cryptocurrency Assets and the identification of the first defendants.[126]

Furthermore, with Summons No. 4880 of 2021 ('SUM 4880'), the plaintiff sought 'leave to join persons as defendants to the action because they were either a) individuals believed to have participated in or assisted with the theft or b) entities who had received the Stolen Cryptocurrency Assets'.[127] Thus, to understand what actually occurred, the court was required to acquire knowledge of digital (public) wallets whereby:

> The wallets also provide some security. In other words, 'for security, BTC and ETH wallets employ one or more "private keys that should be known only to the wallet owner. The private key functions like a signature that confirms that any given transaction is authorised by the wallet owner. Private keys are represented by a string of 64 numbers and

122 *CLM v CLN and others* [2022] SGHC 46.
123 Ibid.
124 Ibid., para 2.
125 Ibid.
126 Ibid., para 3.
127 Ibid., para 4.

alphabets. Thus, anyone in possession of the private key can access the linked wallet and transfer BTC and ETH out'.[128] The loss of a private key would result in 'the funds held in the wallet and not being able to be accessed. There are more than a billion permutations for what a private key may be, it is virtually impossible for one to guess the private key of a digital wallet'.[129] Therefore, the private key provides a high level of security for the wallet owner-holder. In the lead-up to the alleged theft of the wallets, the Court stated that:

the Stolen Cryptocurrency Assets were accessible through two separate digital wallets, controlled by two software applications which were downloaded onto the plaintiff's mobile phone and marketed publicly as 'Exodus' and 'BRD'. BRD and Exodus wallets are decentralised 'hot' wallets (i.e., wallets that are connected to the Internet) that are accessible through a free mobile application that is locked by either a password or a biometric key. BRD and Exodus provide users with a public wallet address and allow the private key to be stored directly on the user's phone. BRD and Exodus wallets do not themselves hold cryptocurrencies but rather manage the private key through which a user can access those cryptocurrencies (which are maintained on the BTC or ETH blockchain). While the plaintiff had locked both his Exodus and BRD wallets with a password, both wallets employed recovery seeds that could be used to recover the passwords and could therefore allow him to gain access to the cryptocurrencies in the event that his mobile phone was lost or destroyed.[130]

Subsequently, on 8 January 2021, the plaintiff accessed his Exodus and BRD wallets and discovered that his BTC and ETH had been withdrawn without his knowledge or consent. As a consequence, in reviewing the transaction records, it was noted that:

> the BRD and Exodus applications showed that on 8 January 2021, the following transfers were made to three different wallet addresses that the plaintiff did not control or own: a) at 7.16pm, 59.38 BTC was transferred from the Exodus wallet to wallet address [address redacted]; b) at 7.17pm, 50.45 BTC was transferred from the BRD wallet to wallet address [address redacted]; and c) at 7.19pm, 1497.54 ETH was transferred from the Exodus wallet to wallet address [address redacted]. The plaintiff claimed that, since his mobile phone was with him when the above transactions took place, the defendant could not have effected the transfers using the BRD and Exodus applications on his mobile phone.[131]

128 Ibid., para 12.
129 Ibid.
130 Ibid., para 1–416.
131 Ibid., para 17–20.

Due to the nature of blockchain technology, the traceability of the transactions is relatively straightforward. However, any traceability will show only when the transactions took place, and not the person or entity who conducted them. What ensued was that the identity of the first defendant was unknown. The court granted both the SUM 2444 and SUM 4880. This was not before the court examined a number of cases from other jurisdictions, predominantly the UK, that dealt with an unknown person. By being able to categorise persons whose identities were not known, the court could refer to them as persons unknown,[132] and therefore the orders sought could be issued. While this case dealt with stolen cryptocurrency and the challenges of trying to identify an individual conducting transactions via the digital private wallet, it also provided a good insight into the operation of blockchain.

In a more recent case in relation to stablecoins more specifically, the Singapore High Court *Bybit Fintech Ltd*[133] noted that 'Tether (a stablecoin) was linked to a fiat currency, the United States Dollar'.[134] By way of background, Bybit Fintech Limited sought a:

> summary judgment against Ms Ho Kai Xin. At issue was that she was in breach of her employment contract, and had transferred a quantity of USDT to 'Addresses' secretly owned and controlled by her, as well as a quantity of fiat currency to her own bank account [the fiat currency on trust for Bybit]. Bybit accordingly sought an order for payment of a sum equivalent in value.[135]

More specifically, the broader issues the court was required to resolve included whether 'USDT is property capable of being held on trust; and whether Bybit is entitled to summary judgment'.[136] After a lengthy investigation, the court ruled that 'USDT may be transferred from one holder to another cryptographically without the assistance of the legal system, nonetheless are choses in action'.[137] A chose in action is common under trust, and the common law. They provide that a beneficiary is able to compel a trustee to retain the trust that is in the best interest of the beneficiary. The court further ruled that 'like any other thing in action, USDT is capable of being held on trust'.[138] On this basis, a stablecoin can be considered property that can be held on trust and falls within the parameters of being categorised as a chose in action. In the early stages of stablecoin regulation and the law, as it has not been regulated in many countries as of 2023, this case provides an insight into how the courts

132 Ibid., paras 23–36.
133 *ByBit Fintech Ltd v Ho Kai Xin and others* [2023] SGHC 199.
134 Ibid., para 2.
135 Ibid.
136 Ibid., para 28.
137 Ibid., para 4.
138 Ibid.

will view them as a financial tool. As far as a regulatory framework is concerned in relation to crypto assets, Singapore has certainly been one of the first to establish crypto assets within a licencing framework that replicates their current legal framework for regulating financial and banking services. However, as this chapter is quickly demonstrating, because countries are not taking a coordinated approach to developing the law for crypto assets, this will only lead to a highly fractured cross-border legal regime with which the world will have to grapple.

2.3.7 United Kingdom (UK)

The UK is no different from any other country. In 2022 and 2023 it has been examining what and how digital assets are seen as part of the digital economy. The UK is in the early stages of developing a legal framework and has begun this process with the *Financial Services and Markets Act 2000*[139] (FMA). The FMA has been developed to provide a high level of stability to the financial markets in the UK. The UK has for many decades seen itself as a financial hub. Following its exit from the EU, the UK has been reinforcing its position as a financial hub for the world. At the time of writing, the amendments to the FMA had not been finalised. Nonetheless, there are several important concepts that need to be understood as a starting point.

To begin with, funds constitute digital-settlement assets. In turn, a digital-settlement asset is a 'digital representation of value or rights, whether or not cryptographically secured that can be used for settlement of payment obligations, can be transferred, stored or traded electronically, and uses technology supporting the recording or storage of data'.[140] Moreover, a crypto asset is 'any cryptographically secured digital representation of value or contractual rights that can be transferred, stored or traded electronically, and that use technology supporting the recording or storage of data (which may include distributed ledger technology)'.[141] This is a broader definition compared to those of Singapore and the US. The US definition is more detailed and refers to 'digital assets' rather than 'crypto assets'. The UK does not mention stablecoin, whereas the US makes a clear distinction that stablecoin forms part of a digital asset. It is argued that stablecoin could also be defined as a digital-settlement asset. This is because the stablecoin 'technologies rely on proof-of-work consensus mechanisms to validate transactions, which involve so-called miners" competing to solve complex cryptographic problems'.[142]

139 *Financial Services and Markets Act 2000*. https://www.legislation.gov.uk/ukpga/2000/8/data.pdf. For the most recent amendments, see https://www.legislation.gov.uk/ukpga/2023/29/data.pdf

140 F*inancial Services and Markets Act 2023*, p. 167. https://www.legislation.gov.uk/ukpga/2023/29/data.pdf

141 Ibid., p. 95.

142 Mitsu Adachi, Pedro Bento Pereira Da Silva, Alexandra Born, Massimo Cappuccio, Stephanie Czák-Ludwig, Isabella Gschossmann, Georg Paula, Antonella Pellicani, Sarah-Maria

Adachi et al. make an important point that stablecoins do make a considerable contribution to liquidity. That is:

> they provide most of the liquidity in DeFi applications such as decentralised exchanges and lending protocols. Stablecoins provided around 45% of the liquidity in decentralised exchanges (DEXs) in May 2022 (Chart 1, panel b). About half of this amount was provided by collateralised stablecoins. However, for collateralised stablecoins like Tether and USD Coin, liquidity provision for decentralised trading or lending is relatively low compared to their total market capitalisation (less than 8%). This suggests they are still mainly used for other purposes in the crypto-asset ecosystem. By comparison, for algorithmic stablecoins like DAI (more than 30%) and TerraUSD (more than 75% before its crash), liquidity provision in DeFi represents a substantial share of their total market capitalisation. For these particular stablecoins, usage in DeFi is thus quite important.[143]

However, while the stablecoin is a new addition to the financial market, it has not come without a level of criticism. Adachi et al. further point out that they can 'fall short of what is required of practical means of payment for the real economy, when compared with the traditional payment systems that offer other benefits such as legal certainty, settlement finality and operational resilience'.[144] In my view, this could be a short-lived challenge. This is because as the market matures and the application of stablecoins expands, the market itself will naturally address this problem. In the UK, the gradual development of the stablecoin-token economy is being undertaken in phases. At the time of writing, the process had reached phase two, with the amendments to the FSMA Act.

Diagram – UK – Phased approach for regulating crypto assets[145]

State Figure 2.2 Approach to Regulating Cryto Assets.

The approach taken in the United Kingdom to regulating crypto assets.

Based on the above, when fully implemented, subject to ongoing review and reform, the approach will enable the UK to manage all levels of risk that these activities pose to the financial markets. Importantly, it will allow the UK

Philipps, Mirjam Plooij, Ines Rossteuscher, Pierfrancesco Zeoli, *'Stablecoins' Role in Crypto and Beyond: Functions, Risks and Policy*, ECB Macroprudential Bulletin, European Central Bank (2020). https://www.ecb.europa.eu//pub/financial-stability/macroprudential-bulletin/html/ecb.mpbu202207_2~836f682ed7.en.html

143 Ibid.

144 Ibid.

145 *Future Financial Services Regulatory Regime for Crypto Assets – Consultation and Call for Evidence* (February 2023), p. 12. https://assets.publishing.service.gov.uk/government/uploads/system/uploads/attachment_data/file/1133404/TR_Privacy_edits_Future_financial_services_regulatory_regime_for_cryptoassets_vP.pdf

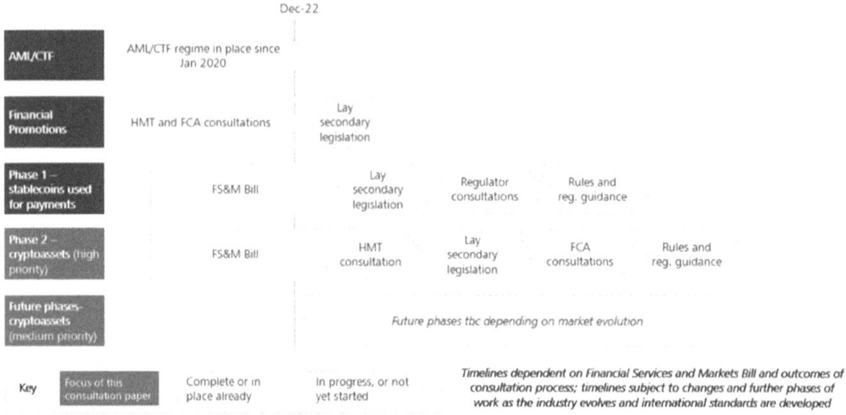

Figure 2.2 Approach to Regulating Cryto Assets

to determine the future risks that consumers will be exposed to, and address them as they arise. While the 2023 FMS Act does not state that the aforementioned activities require a licence, they fall within the 2000 FSM Act under section 22[146] as a regulated activity that requires authorisation from the regulator. The developing national legal frameworks are going to pose challenges in cross-border transactions given the way that these activities are being defined under the respective legal frameworks. While generally they are achieving the same thing, by categorising a crypto asset as a financial product and activity, the laws do diverge in terms of how they define the activity.

In the 2023 case of *Tulip*[147] the court was required to determine 'whether the developers who look after bitcoin may arguably owe fiduciary duties or duties in tort to an owner of that cryptocurrency'.[148] This matter was seeking leave from the court of Appeal to appeal in order to address a serious issue both at law and in public policy related to the governance of crypto assets (bitcoin). The background of this case was that Tulip claimed to be the:

> owner of some bitcoin with a very high total value ($4 billion). The bitcoin is held at two addresses on the blockchain called 1Feex and 12ib7. However, the private keys have been lost in a hack, likely stolen. Without

146 *Financial Services and Markets Act 2000.* https://www.legislation.gov.uk/ukpga/2000/8/data.pdf An activity is a regulated activity for the purposes of this Act if it is an activity of a specified kind which is carried on by way of business and (a) relates to an investment of a specified kind; or (b) in the case of an activity of a kind which is also specified for the purposes of this paragraph, is carried on in relation to property of any kind. 'Investment' includes any asset, right or interest (including where an asset, right or interest is, or comprises or represents, a crypto asset).

147 *Tulip v Van der Laan* [2023] EWCA Civ 83; [2023] 4 WLR 16. https://downloads.coindesk.com/cd3/Tulip+Trading+-v-+van+der+Laan.pdf

148 Ibid., para 1.

> its private keys Tulip cannot access its assets or move them to safety. However, Tulip contends, the developers named as defendants in this case control and run the four relevant bitcoin networks, and it would be a simple matter for them to secure Tulip's assets, e.g., by moving them to another address which Tulip can control. Tulip contends that the role the developers have undertaken in relation to Tulip's property (the bitcoin) and the power this role gives them, and all the circumstances (discussed below), mean that the developers should be recognised as a new *ad hoc* class of fiduciary, owing fiduciary duties to the true owners of bitcoin cryptocurrency, including in this case Tulip as true owner of the bitcoin at 1Feex and 12ib7. The fiduciary duties owed should extend to implementing the necessary software patch to solve Tulip's problem and safeguard Tulip's assets from the thieves.[149]

In reconciling the above, the court asserted that there were four relevant grounds for appeal:

> **1:** this is a developing, complex and uncertain area of law; **2:** the conclusions are in error because they are based on findings impermissibly assumed against Tulip; **3:** Taking into account the Law Commission project was an error; **4:** The judge was wrong to hold that Tulip has no real prospect of establishing that the claimed fiduciary duties exist.[150]

The point to note is that the court is highlighting the complexity and uncertainty in the law pertaining to crypto assets. While important in confirming what, if any, fiduciary duties exist, the case demonstrates the significant challenges that lie ahead in reconciling the many different types of disputes that can arise. It will require deep and specialised knowledge of the operation of the technology, and how that technology falls within the law.

Further to the above, the court undertook to explain the entities responsible for facilitating the operations of the technology:

> A feature of the present case is that literally all there is, is software. A physical coin has properties which exist outside the minds of people who use it and in that sense is tangible. Bitcoin is similar. It also has properties which exist outside the minds of individuals, but those properties only exist inside computers as a consequence of the bitcoin software. There is nothing else. And crucially, asserts Tulip, it is the developers who control this software. In Tulip's case, that control is very significant. In a bank, the software developers as individuals will be tasked with maintaining the source code for the bank's accounts and payment systems, but they are subject to ultimate control by the board (and subject to regulation).

149 Ibid., para 2.
150 Ibid., para 67.

> The bank's developers have nothing like the control over the customer's assets which Tulip alleges the bitcoin developers have over bitcoin. These allegations are heavily contested by the developers in this case, who advance their case on decentralisation, but that cannot be resolved on this application or appeal.[151]

Above, the court is also comparing the operation of the software for crypto assets with that of a standard bank and how current-day banks manage software to enable transactions to be undertaken. Noteworthy too was the court's expansion of its analysis of the above:

> Focussing on a software bug, if a third party identifies such a problem and the developers agree it should be fixed, then the developers will no doubt act to introduce a change in the source code in the relevant GitHub account, and computers on the network will update the software they are running (absent a fork, which again can only be a matter for trial). The fulfilment role of developers involves taking active steps to update the code.[152]

Viewed this way, the court made the point that such an activity constitutes a level of authority exercised by developers, because they are given 'control to access the source code, and it is a decision-making role, in effect making decisions on behalf of all the participants in the relevant bitcoin network, including miners and also including the owners of the bitcoin'.[153] The court further stated that:

> when acting in the role of developers – they should be held to owe a duty in law to bitcoin owners not to compromise the owners' security in that way. It would be a duty which involves abnegation of the developer's self-interest.[154]

Nevertheless, given the above, the court in applying a common principle that is used in investor–state arbitration – legitimate expectations –, made the point that:

> it is realistic to say that bitcoin owners have a legitimate expectation that the developers will not exercise their authority in their own self-interest to the detriment of owners, and that they will act in good faith to use their skills to fix bugs in the software drawn to their attention.[155]

151 Ibid., para 72.
152 Ibid., para 73.
153 Ibid., para 74.
154 Ibid., para 75.
155 Ibid., para 79.

Thus, in applying this principle, the court was reinforcing that a level of responsibility did arise in relation to the security of the software. Finally, in applying the above, the court stated:

> the duty is said to arise when it is established (e.g., by a court of competent jurisdiction) that the true owner of the bitcoin at a certain address is unable to access it because their private key has been stolen by thieves. The true owner's property is vulnerable because the thieves might be able to extract the private key from what they have stolen and transfer the owner's bitcoin for themselves. The duty which is said to arise in these circumstances is to introduce a code update which will transfer that bitcoin into a safe account controlled by the true owner or which will safeguard that bitcoin in some other way.[156]

This case demonstrates that in cases of fraud that have resulted in the theft of a crypto asset, the UK courts are likely to look at the role of the software developer to understand their level of maintenance obligations in determining the extent of this obligation. That is, how the obligation contributed to or otherwise the fraudulent activity.

2.3.8 United States (US)

The US legal framework for crypto assets and digital payments is similar to that of the other jurisdictions compared. This section will focus only on the federal laws, even though work is being undertaken by a number of states to establish their own legal frameworks. In 2022, the first Executive Order[157] was handed down that has set the policy direction for digital assets:

> advances in digital and distributed ledger technology for financial services have led to dramatic growth in markets for digital assets, with profound implications for the protection of consumers, investors, and businesses, including data privacy and security; financial stability and systemic risk; crime; national security; the ability to exercise human rights; financial inclusion and equity; and energy demand and climate change.[158]

By 2021, in the US, 'non-state issued digital assets reached a combined market capitalisation of USD $3 trillion, up from approximately USD $14 billion in early November 2016'.[159] This significant increase in capitalisation alone

156 Ibid., para 81.

157 *Executive Order on Ensuring Responsible Development of Digital Assets.* https://www.whitehouse.gov/briefing-room/presidential-actions/2022/03/09/executive-order-on-ensuring-responsible-development-of-digital-assets/

158 Ibid.

159 Ibid.

highlights the pace at which the sector is advancing. However, similar to the other jurisdictions compared, the regulation and law on crypto assets in the US are continuing to evolve and are far from settled.

The *Executive Order* (EC), when setting the policy direction for crypto assets, emphasises consumer protection. This, it is argued, is a common theme in US federal legislation pertaining to the digital economy. In reinforcing this point, the EC goes on to say in relation to digital assets that not only consumers, but also investors and businesses across the US, must be protected.[160] It further indicates the interconnectedness of the entire digital economy that is supported by digital assets. That is:

> the unique and varied features of digital assets can pose significant financial risks to consumers, investors, and businesses if appropriate protections are not in place. In the absence of sufficient oversight and standards, firms providing digital asset services may provide inadequate protections for sensitive financial data, custodial and other arrangements relating to customer assets and funds, or disclosures of risks associated with investment.[161]

Moreover, significantly, 'cybersecurity and market failures at major digital asset exchanges and trading platforms have resulted in billions of dollars in losses'.[162] What this tells us is that the multi-layered approach to the digital economy not only has a human rights and consumer protection element because it pervades the economy more broadly.

Most notably, the United States' outward-facing influence and direction in controlling the world economy are to be protected. Doing so will provide greater financial and investment stability than the world has experienced (even though there have been shocks along the way) since the 1950s. Therefore, through the Executive Order, it is recognised that the US has a major role to protect 'global financial stability and mitigate systemic risk'.[163] However, the complexity of digital assets has yet to be fully understood in the US or the global community.

In recognition of this complexity, the Executive Order stated that 'digital asset trading platforms and service providers have grown rapidly in size and complexity and may not be subject to or in compliance with appropriate regulations or supervision'.[164] Further, it calls for the coordination of a number

160 Ibid.
161 Ibid.
162 Ibid.
163 Ibid.
164 Ibid. Digital asset issuers, exchanges and trading platforms, and intermediaries whose activities may increase risks to financial stability should, as appropriate, be subject to and in compliance with regulatory and supervisory standards that govern traditional market infrastructures and financial firms, in line with the general principle of 'same business, same risks,

of different federal government portfolios, which is also extended to international coordination. Over the coming year, 120, 180, and 210 days from the establishment of the Executive Order, certain milestones need to be reached, which will be used to inform and develop the next steps in this area of policy and the law.

At the time of writing, there were about another 100 days remaining for the outcomes to be tabled. Nonetheless, in establishing the foundation for defining specific terms in any new laws, the Executive Order provisions include blockchain, central bank digital currency, cryptocurrencies, digital assets, and stablecoins. Thus, section 9 of the Executive Order states:

(a) The term '**blockchain**' refers to distributed ledger technologies where data is shared across a network that creates a digital ledger of verified transactions or information among network participants and the data are typically linked using cryptography to maintain the integrity of the ledger and execute other functions, including transfer of ownership or value.
(b) The term 'central bank digital currency' or 'CBDC' refers to a form of digital money or monetary value, denominated in the national unit of account, that is a direct liability of the central bank.
(c) The term '**cryptocurrencies**' refers to a digital asset, which may be a medium of exchange, for which generation or ownership records are supported through a distributed ledger technology that relies on cryptography, such as a blockchain.
(d) The term '**digital assets**' refers to all CBDCs, regardless of the technology used, and to other representations of value, financial assets and instruments, or claims that are used to make payments or investments, or to transmit or exchange funds or the equivalent thereof, that are issued or represented in digital form through the use of distributed ledger technology. For example, digital assets include cryptocurrencies, stablecoins, and CBDCs. Regardless of the label used, a digital asset may be, among other things, a security, a commodity, a derivative, or other financial product. Digital assets may be exchanged across digital asset trading platforms, including centralised and decentralised finance platforms, or through peer-to-peer technologies.
(e) The term '**stablecoins**' refers to a category of cryptocurrencies with mechanisms that are aimed at maintaining a stable value, such as by pegging the value of the coin to a specific currency, asset, or pool of assets or by algorithmically controlling supply in response to changes in demand in order to stabilise value.[165]

---

same rules'. The new and unique uses and functions that digital assets can facilitate may create additional economic and financial risks requiring an evolution to a regulatory approach that adequately addresses those risks.

165 Ibid.

Viewed this way, and most specifically, the definition of digital assets is all-encompassing. It includes the technology that is used to protect, facilitate, and generate economic activity throughout the economy. This includes all areas of trade and investment across financial markets that will use smart contracts and provides for IP, tax, mergers, and acquisitions, amongst other areas of the law. Importantly, it includes the blockchain technology that is used to underpin most, if not all, of the new crypto assets such as stablecoin.

Blockchain uses an algorithm to enable the control of supply and demand in order to stabilise value. It is a form of financial stability acquired by minimising price volatility. In making the case for greater harmonisation at an international level, the above definitions could and should be used to create and establish an international treaty, convention, model law, codes of practice, and standards. The urgency of this proposal cannot be underestimated.

There are many regional and international forums that can benefit from utilising the work the US has already undertaken. Four important forums that include the jurisdictions compared in this book are: the EU, ASEAN [Association of Southeast Asian Nations], APEC [Asia-Pacific Economic Cooperation], and the CS [Commonwealth Secretariat]. Apart from the EU, which has already done considerable work in this area, the other institutions have the opportunity to develop model laws and other instruments that can guide and direct their members. In addition to the above, and while outside the scope of this book, the African Union should be consulted along with international organisations such as UNCITRAL and UNIDROIT.

Against the backdrop of the above, the developments in the law in the US began with the *Securities Act 1933*.[166] In 2017, the US Securities and Exchange Commission (SEC) undertook a comprehensive investigation into a DAO [Decentralised Autonomous Organisation].[167] The DAO is a term used to describe a 'virtual' organisation embodied in computer code and executed on a distributed ledger or blockchain.[168] As mentioned earlier in this book, blockchain technology can be used for smart contracts and supports crypto-asset transactions. The background for the use and application of the DAO is:

> The DAO was created by Slock.it and Slock.it's co-founders, with the objective of operating as a for-profit entity that would create and hold a corpus of assets through the sale of DAO Tokens to investors, which assets would then be used to fund 'projects'. The holders of DAO Tokens stood to share in the anticipated earnings from these projects as a return

166 *Securities Act 1933*. https://www.govinfo.gov/content/pkg/COMPS-1884/pdf/COMPS-1884.pdf

167 Report of Investigation Pursuant to Section 21(a) of the Securities Exchange Act of 1934: The DAO, Release No. 81207/25 July 2017. https://www.sec.gov/files/litigation/investreport/34-81207.pdf

168 Ibid., p. 1.

> on their investment in DAO Tokens. In addition, DAO Token holders could monetise their investments in DAO Tokens by re-selling DAO Tokens on a number of web-based platforms ('Platforms') that supported secondary trading in the DAO Tokens. After DAO Tokens were sold, but before The DAO was able to commence funding projects, an attacker used a flaw in The DAO's code to steal approximately one-third of The DAO's assets. Slock.it's co-founders and others responded by creating a work-around whereby DAO Token holders could opt to have their investment returned to them, as described in more detail below.[169]

From the above operation, at issue was whether the US federal 'securities laws to the offer and sale of DAO Tokens, including the threshold question of whether DAO Tokens themselves are securities'.[170] The outcome of this investigation was a test of the US laws. In fact, it was found that the 'DAO Tokens did constitute securities according to the Securities Act of 1933 (SA) and the Securities Exchange Act of 1934'. More specifically, it determined that according to section 21 (a) of the Exchange Act 'those who use DAOs or other distributed ledger including blockchain-enabled means for capital raising, are to take appropriate steps to ensure compliance with the US federal securities laws'.[171] Subsequently, between:

> 30 April 2016 through to 28 May 2016, the DAO offered and sold approximately 1.15 billion DAO Tokens in exchange for a total of approximately 12 million Ether ('ETH'), a virtual currency used on the Ethereum Blockchain. As of the time the offering closed, the total ETH raised by the DAO was valued in US dollars ('USD') at approximately $150 million.[172]

As a result, in determining the application of the SA, the report noted that an 'investment contract exists, the investment of "money" need not take the form of cash'.[173] Most noteworthy was the reference to the Howey test[174] which focused on the investment contract itself. In other words:

> an investment contract is an investment of money in a common enterprise with a reasonable expectation of profits to be derived from the entrepreneurial or managerial efforts of others. An investment contract 'is the presence of an investment in a common venture premised on a reasonable

169 Ibid., p. 1.
170 Ibid., p. 1.
171 Ibid.
172 Ibid., p. 2.
173 Ibid., p. 11.
174 Ibid. Also see *SEC v W.J. Howey Co., 328 U.S. 293 (1946)*. https://supreme.justia.com/cases/federal/us/328/293/

> expectation of profits to be derived from the entrepreneurial or managerial efforts of others. This definition embodies a '*flexible rather than a static principle*, one that is capable of adaptation to meet the countless and variable schemes devised by those who seek the use of the money of others on the promise of profits'. Further, 'investment of money', it is well established that cash is not the only form of contribution or investment that will create an investment contract. Such investment is the type of contribution of value that can create an investment contract.[175]

On that basis, and according to the law of the US, 'investors in The DAO used ETH to make their investments, and DAO Tokens were received in exchange for ETH'.[176] The resulting effect of this investigation was not to punish the individuals involved, but rather to provide a level of advice and legal certainty to future investors. Therefore, those individuals and entities engaged in this type of investment activity will need to comply with US Securities law.

In addition to the above developments, there have been other developments in the law. For example, the Lummis-Gillibrand Bill 2022 was reintroduced in 2023 and, if approved, will combat 'the use of crypto assets in illicit finance, imposes new penalties for wilfully violating money laundering laws, and will require stablecoins to be issued by depository institutions'.[177] The Stabenow Bill of 2023 was also reintroduced in 2023, now referred to as the *Digital Commodities Consumer Protection Act*.[178] It

> defines 'digital commodity', which includes Bitcoin and Ether and excludes certain financial instruments including securities; amends the definition of 'commodity' in the Commodity Exchange Act ('Act') to include 'digital commodity'. And, introduces new categories of registration including 'digital commodity broker', 'digital commodity custodian', 'digital commodity dealer', 'digital commodity trading facility' (collectively, 'digital commodity platforms') and associated persons of digital commodity brokers and digital commodity dealers. Mining activity, alone, is not sufficient to trigger registration as a digital commodity platform.[179]

175 Ibid., p. 11.

176 Ibid. These requirements apply to those who offer and sell securities in the United States, regardless of whether the issuing entity is a traditional company or a decentralised autonomous organisation, regardless of whether those securities are purchased using US dollars or virtual currencies, and regardless of whether they are distributed in certificated form or through distributed ledger technology.

177 United States Congress (2023). https://www.lummis.senate.gov/wp-content/uploads/Lummis-Gillibrand-2023.pdf

178 *Digital Commodities Consumer Protection Act 2022.* https://www.agriculture.senate.gov/imo/media/doc/crypto_bill_section_by_section1.pdf

179 Ibid., p. 1.

The ensuing legal framework in the US will be multi-layered, making it difficult for businesses to understand and navigate. In 2022, the US also introduced the *Tornado Cash Bill*[180] to strengthen its ability to investigate and deal with money laundering matters that arise from transactions using crypto assets. Arguably, the US has the beginnings of a solid legal framework for crypto assets. The above definitions provide a pathway forward to clearly understanding what constitutes a digital asset.

Since the investigation above of the DAO, there have been a number of decisions handed down by the SEC in relation to the unregistered offerings of crypto assets. In 2023, the SEC charged 'Stoner Cats 2 LLC (SC2) with conducting an unregistered offering of crypto asset securities in the form of purported non-fungible tokens (NFTs) that raised approximately $8 million from investors to finance an animated web series called Stoner Cats'.[181] That is, 'on July 27, 2021, SC2 offered and sold to investors more than 10,000 NFTs for approximately $800 each, selling out in 35 minutes'.[182] Further, the SEC Order found that:

> before and after Stoner Cats NFTs were sold to the public, SC2's marketing campaign highlighted specific benefits of owning them, including the option for owners to resell their NFTs on the secondary market. In addition, the order finds that, as part of the marketing campaign, the SC2 team emphasised its expertise as Hollywood producers, its knowledge of crypto projects, and the well-known actors involved in the web series, leading investors to expect profits because a successful web series could cause the resale value of the Stoner Cats NFTs in the secondary market to rise. Further, the order finds that SC2 configured the Stoner Cats NFTs to provide SC2 a 2.5 percent royalty for each secondary market transaction in the NFTs and it encouraged individuals to buy and sell the NFTs, leading purchasers to spend more than $20 million in at least 10,000 transactions.[183]

In reaffirming the position taken by the SEC in the DAO investigation, it found that 'according to the SEC's order, SC2 violated the Securities Act of 1933 by offering and selling these crypto-asset securities to the public in an unregistered offering that was not exempt from registration'.[184] This is one example of many, and it is likely to increase as this area of the digital economy

180 Cindy Cohn, *An Update on Tornado Cash.* https://www.eff.org/deeplinks/2023/04/update-tornado-cash
181 *SEC Charges Creator of Stoner Cats Web Series for Unregistered Offering of NFTs.* https://www.sec.gov/news/press-release/2023-178?utm_medium=email&utm_source=govdelivery
182 Ibid.
183 Ibid.
184 Ibid.

continues to expand. It highlights the importance for individuals and entities to ensure they are registered under the *Securities Act 1933*.

A further clarification was determined by the court in 2023, whereby the Securities and Exchange Commission sought to affirm the securities law status of XRP, Ripple's[185] native token XRP offerings. The SEC bought action against Ripple Labs, Inc. (Ripple), alleging they had engaged in the unlawful offer and sale of securities in violation of section 5 of the *Securities Act 1933*, 15 U.S.C. section 77e(a) and (c). Am. Compl.[186] Dating back to 2011 and 2012, a source code for a:

> cryptographically secured ledger, or a blockchain, which is now known as the XRP Ledger was developed. The aim was to create a faster, cheaper, and more energy-efficient alternative to the bitcoin blockchain, the first blockchain ledger which was introduced in 2009. When the XRP Ledger launched in 2012, its source code generated a fixed supply of 100 billion XRP. XRP is the native digital token of the XRP Ledger, and the XRP Ledger requires XRP to operate. Each unit of XRP is divisible into one million 'drops', and each unit or drop of XRP is fungible with any other unit or drop.[187]

The court determined that Ripple, through wholly owned subsidiaries:

> sold XRP directly to certain counterparties (primarily institutional buyers, hedge funds, and ODL customers) pursuant to written contracts (Institutional Sales). The SEC alleges that Ripple sold approximately $728.9 million of XRP in these Institutional Sales. Second, Ripple sold XRP via digital asset exchanges 'programmatically', or through the use of trading algorithms. Ripple's XRP sales on these digital asset exchanges were blind bid/ask transactions. Ripple did not know who was buying the XRP, and the purchasers did not know who was selling it. The SEC alleges that Ripple sold approximately $757.6 million of XRP in Programmatic Sales used the proceeds from the Institutional and Programmatic Sales to fund its operations.[188]

Most noteworthy is that the court noted that:

> Ripple also distributed XRP as a form of payment for services. For instance, Ripple distributed XRP to its employees as a form of employee

185 *Securities and Exchange Commission v Ripple Labs.* https://www.nysd.uscourts.gov/sites/default/files/2023-07/SEC%20vs%20Ripple%207-13-23.pdf
186 Ibid.
187 Ibid., I.
188 Ibid.

> compensation. Ripple also distributed XRP in conjunction with its Xpring initiative to fund third parties that would develop new applications for XRP and the XRP Ledger. The SEC alleges that Ripple recognised revenue of $609 million from its distributions of XRP to individuals and entities in exchange for services. Ripple did not file a registration statement as to any offers or sales of XRP. Ripple did not publicly file any financial statements or other periodic reports, nor did it make any EDGAR filings with the SEC for Ripple or XRP, such as a Form 10-Q, Form 10-K, or Form 8-K relating to XRP.[189]

Against the backdrop of the above, it was alleged that 'in 2013 Ripple began extensive, years-long marketing efforts representing they would search for purported "use" and "value" for XRP—and casting XRP as an opportunity to invest in those efforts'.[190] By adopting the following approach, the SEC was of the view that Ripple had not complied with the relevant laws pertaining to the offering of securities. The court further noted that a 'range of statements, including informational brochures, internal talking points, public blog posts, statements on social media, videos, interviews with various Ripple employees' with Ripple employees.[191] The offerings were also made via social media and other platforms. Nonetheless, Ripple sought legal:

> memorandum which analyses, the legal risks associated with selling XRP. It stated that '[i]f sold to [i]nvestors, [XRP tokens] are likely to be securities', and "[t]o the extent that [the founders"] issuance of [XRP] does not involve an investment of money', there is a low risk that [XRP] will be considered an investment contract.[192]

In applying the Howey test, the court referred to section 5 of the *Securities Act on Liability*. According to section 5, it is:

> unlawful for any person, directly or indirectly … to offer to sell, offer to buy or purchase[,] or sell' a 'security' unless a registration statement is in effect or has been filed with the SEC as to the offer and sale of such security to the public (15 U.S.C. section 77e(a), (c), (e)).[193]

However, for this to be proved, the court made the point that the SEC must show that Ripple had '(1) no registration statement was filed or in effect as to the transaction, and (2) that the defendant directly or indirectly offered to sell

189 Ibid.
190 Ibid.
191 Ibid
192 Ibid.
193 Ibid.

or sold the securities (3) through interstate commerce'.[194] In further applying Howey, the court asserted that:

> The plain words of *Howey* make clear that 'an investment contract for purposes of the Securities Act means a *contract, transaction* [,] *or scheme*'. 328 U.S. at 298–99 (emphasis added). But the subject of a contract, transaction, or scheme is not necessarily a security on its face. Under *Howey*, the Court analyzes the economic reality and totality of circumstances surrounding the offers and sales of the underlying asset. *Howey* and its progeny have held that a variety of tangible and intangible assets can serve as the subject of an investment contract.[195]

In addition to the above, on the point of programmatic sales, the court concluded that they were not the offer of the sale of investment contracts. In applying the above, amongst other tests, the court ruled that the Summary Judge, which is non-binding, found that Ripple had not contravened the securities law. It further concluded that the programmatic sales and institutional sales were also denied. The securities law requires that the entity creating the digital asset and/or blockchain be directly involved for the sale of these assets to constitute securities. It is another example of how blockchain technology is being considered when creating and providing the digital asset, and how it can be offered as a security under national law. However, the Howey test may not be fully accepted.

Apart from the requirements to comply with the securities laws, the courts are also requiring arbitration. In *Donnovan*[196] the court in the state of California noted that:

> Coinbase operates a currency exchange, which allows users to buy and trade various forms of cryptocurrency. Coinbase's Mot. 2; Decl. of Suellen Black ('Black Decl.'). Cryptocurrency is a decentralised, digital representation of value secured through cryptography. Currency exchange platforms like Coinbase facilitate investment by allowing account holders to store their cryptocurrency in digital wallets. Coinbase's Mot. 2; Black Decl. ¶ 2. To use its 'services and make cryptocurrency transactions, prospective users are first required to create an account and accept the Coinbase User Agreement'. Coinbase's Mot. 2; Black Decl.[197]

194 Ibid.

195 Ibid.

196 *Kenneth Donovan et al., Plaintiffs v COINBASE GLOBAL, INC., et al.*, Case No. 22-cv-02826-TLT. https://storage.courtlistener.com/recap/gov.uscourts.cand.395530/gov.uscourts.cand.395530.78.0.pdf

197 Ibid.

Importantly, the User Agreement contains an arbitration agreement. Coinbase's Mot. 4; Black Decl., Ex. F, Appendix 5. Specifically, section 1.1 of the arbitration agreement states:

> Subject to the terms of this Arbitration Agreement, you and Coinbase agree that any dispute, claim, disagreements arising out of or relating in any way to your access to or use of the Services or of the Coinbase Site, any Communications you receive, any product sold or distributed through the Coinbase Site, the Services, or the User Agreement and prior versions of the User Agreement, including claims and disputes that arose between us before the effective date of these Terms (each, a 'Dispute') will be resolved by binding arbitration, rather than in court ... (*Id.* at section 1.1).[198]

Based on this, the defendant Coinbase put forward that the:

> User Agreement expressly delegates "gateway" arbitration questions to the arbitrator—including questions about the enforceability, scope, and interpretation of the arbitration agreement itself—this Court need not evaluate the agreement's validity or whether its arbitration clause encompasses [the Coinbase] Plaintiffs' claims against Coinbase.[199]

Therefore, and in response, the court automatically referred to the *Federal Arbitration Act* (FAA), which governs the motion to compel arbitration (9 U.S.C. section 1 *et seq.*). The court highlighted how, according to the FAA, a district court determines (1) whether a valid agreement to arbitrate exists and, if it does, (2) whether the agreement encompasses the dispute at issue. To evaluate the validity of an arbitration agreement, federal courts should apply ordinary state-law principles that govern the formation of contracts. If the court is satisfied 'that the making of the arbitration agreement or the failure to comply with the agreement is not in issue, the court shall make an order directing the parties to proceed to arbitration in accordance with the terms of the agreement' (9 U.S.C. section 4). 'Any doubts concerning the scope of arbitrable issues should be resolved in favour of arbitration'.[200] By applying the FAA, the concept of unmistakability and unconscionability, the court compelled the parties to arbitration. This case demonstrates that when the arbitration agreement is clear and cannot be mistaken for anything but arbitration, the courts will force the parties to arbitrate. It also clearly demonstrates the burgeoning area of arbitration in the crypto asset area of the economy.

198 Ibid., p. 2.
199 Ibid., p. 3.
200 Ibid.

2.3.9 *Switzerland*

Switzerland has been one of the first countries that have established specific blockchain regulations. In 2021, the:

> Federal Act on the Adaptation of Federal Law to Developments in Distributed Electronic Register Technology (DLT) and the associated blanket ordinance came into force.[201] Among other things, this legislation improves the conditions for companies using blockchain in Switzerland (introduction of security rights registered on a blockchain), increases legal certainty in the event of bankruptcy (segregation of cryptoassets), creates a new licence category for DLT/blockchain-based trading systems within the framework of financial market supervision, and provides a proportionate response to the risks identified in the area of money laundering and terrorist financing.[202]

The Switzerland Financial Market Supervisory Authority (FINMA) supervises the implementation of financial market regulation by financial intermediaries.[203] The legal certainty provided by the above-mentioned regulations also enabled it to grant a banking licence to financial service providers specialising in DLT/blockchain in 2019 and to approve the first Swiss crypto fund in 2021.[204]

The Federal Act on the Adaptation of Federal Law to Developments in Distributed Electronic Register Technology (DLT),[205] and in one of the first countries to do so, from:

> 1 August 2021 is a licence for DLT [distributed ledger] trading facilities, i.e. financial market infrastructures for DLT securities that can admit other companies and persons to trading in addition to financial intermediaries. Legal certainty will be increased in insolvency law by explicitly regulating the segregation of crypto-based assets in the event of bankruptcy.[206]

201 State Secretariat for International Finance, *Fact Sheet*. https://www.sif.admin.ch/sif/en/home/finanzmarktpolitik/digit_finanzsektor/blockchain.html
202 Ibid., *Fact Sheet*, p. 2.
203 Financial Market Supervisory Authority. https://www.finma.ch/en/
204 State Secretariat for International Finance, *Fact Sheet*, pp. 2–3. https://www.sif.admin.ch/sif/en/home/finanzmarktpolitik/digit_finanzsektor/blockchain.html
205 *Federal Act on the Adaptation of Federal Law to Developments in Distributed Electronic Register Technology* (DLT). https://www.newsd.admin.ch/newsd/message/attachments/67575.pdf
206 Financial Market Supervisory Authority. https://www.admin.ch/gov/en/start/documentation/media-releases.msg-id-84035.html

The DLT[207] while not defining a blockchain, does, however, define a DLT trading facility as operating commercially if it:

1. thereby generates gross earnings of more than CHF 50,000 per calendar year;
2. per calendar year, has a business relationship with more than 20 participants in accordance with Article 73c paragraph 1 letter e of the FinMIA (private participants) or with at least one participant in accordance with Article 73c paragraph 1 letters a to d of the FinMIA; or
3. has unlimited power of disposal over third-party DLT securities that exceed CHF 5 million at any given time.[208]

Importantly, 'if a threshold under paragraph 1 is exceeded, the DLT trading facility must report this to FINMA within 10 days. It must submit an application for authorisation as provided for in the FinMIA to FINMA within 60 days'.[209] The new laws focus on the DL technology itself, providing a platform for a trading facility. It does not define or mention tokens, but rather refers to securities and derivatives.[210] Yet, the DLT could be used to facilitate token transactions. A security is a tradable asset, which could be tokenised. Similarly, derivatives already come in the form of tokens.

Nevertheless, the laws have required a level of disclosure and information to be provided, whereby, 'the DLT trading facility shall monitor all transactions conducted on its systems with admitted DLT securities. It shall disclose this data free of charge to all approved DLT trading facilities'.[211] The DLT 'trading facilities with private participants shall provide them with the associated prospectus or key information document for each DLT security admitted to the DLT trading facility'.[212] On the other hand:

> cryptobased assets within the meaning of Article 1*b* paragraph 1 of the BankA [Bank Act]are assets in accordance with Article 16 number 1 letter b of the BankA (cryptobased assets in collective custody) which are actually used or intended by the organiser issuer to be largely used as a means of payment for acquiring goods or services or as a means of money or value transfer.[213]

207 *Federal Act on the Adaptation of Federal Law to Developments in Distributed Electronic Register Technology* (DLT). https://www.newsd.admin.ch/newsd/message/attachments/67575.pdf
208 Ibid., p. 14.
209 Ibid.
210 Ibid., p. 15.
211 Ibid., p. 16.
212 Ibid.
213 Ibid., p. 6.

Significantly though, what is not a crypto-based asset in accordance with paragraph 1:

> assets in the form of non-interest-bearing credit balances which solely serve the purpose of settling client transactions and are held on client accounts of precious metal traders, portfolio managers or similar firms, provided settlement takes place within 60 days, or securities firms or DLT trading facilities; assets from domestic and foreign banks or other companies subject to state supervision; assets from institutional investors with professional treasury operations.[214]

Moreover, what will constitute a commercial activity under the BankA is where there are more than 20 public deposits or crypto-based assets in collective custody over the long term or publicly advertises that it accepts public deposits or crypto-based assets in collective custody, even if fewer than 20 public deposits or crypto-based assets are received as a result. Any party that accepts more than '20 public deposits or crypto-based assets in collective custody over the long term or that publicly advertises that it does so shall not be deemed to be engaging in commercial activity within the meaning of the BankA if it accepts public deposits or crypto-based assets in collective custody amounting to a maximum of CHF 1 million'.[215] Noteworthy too, is that the law does not categorise the DLT to be public or private, but rather specifies where certain activities fall within the private or public (participants) domain.

For smaller DLTs, trading facilities are subject to the following thresholds in relation to DLT securities: 'annual trading volume: CHF 250 million; custody volume: CHF 100 million; and annual settlement volume: CHF 250 million'.[216] In addition, if a threshold is reached or exceeded, the 'DLT trading facility must report this to FINMA within ten days. It must submit a modified application for authorisation as provided for in the FinMIA to FINMA within 90 days'.[217] From the brief discussion on Switzerland's new laws, it is clear that they have addressed the DLT trading facility within the current-day financial and banking legal framework, requiring a level of licencing. There are different levels of thresholds for both smaller and larger trading facilities. A token is not defined, but rather a crypto asset is afforded a level of definition. Most importantly, while a token is not mentioned or defined, they arguably form part of the crypto assets, derivatives, and securities referred to under the laws that can be transacted across the DLT trading facility. Switzerland has one of the most comprehensive laws on DLT. However, it must be noted that the law is not specifically regulating the DLT itself, but rather, regulating

214 Ibid., p. 7.
215 Ibid.
216 Ibid., p. 17.
217 Ibid.

DLT as a trading facility. It is the trading facility that enables the facilitation of token transactions.

2.3.10 Liechtenstein

The *Liechtenstein Blockchain Act* (the Act) took effect on 1 January 2020.[218] The new blockchain law in Liechtenstein enables the tokenisation of all types of assets and rights without the need to circumvent the law and improves the country's capacity to host digital tokens legally.[219] The FMA requires companies to register and obtain a licence before operating.[220] In addition, applicants need to meet the minimum capital requirement and pay supervisory fees.[221] Importantly, the new law 'does not regulate the technology itself or individual applications of it. The law provides a broad, technology-neutral approach to regulating the entire token economy'.[222]

Significantly, it defines the minimum requirements for these activities on blockchain systems and requires them to be registered with the Liechtenstein Financial Market Authority (FMA).[223] Most noteworthy is that the 'Act defines the term "token" as a new construct to enable the transformation of the "real" world to blockchain systems while ensuring legal certainty, thereby opening up the full application potential of the so-called token economy'.[224] The government of Liechtenstein notes:

> The introduction of the legal construct of the 'token' requires that the legal consequences – such as ownership, possession, and transfer – must also be legally defined. Due to the great potential of the token economy for large parts of the economy, the newly adopted legislation aims at strengthening legal certainty for users and service providers in order to support the positive development of the token economy in Liechtenstein. The new law is a response to the need of market participants for greater legal certainty in connection with blockchain systems.[225]

218 Guneet Kaur, *An Overview of the Liechtenstein Blockchain Act.* https://cointelegraph.com/learn/an-overview-of-the-liechtenstein-blockchain-act#:~:text=The%20foundation%20of%20the%20Liechtenstein,%22loaded%22%20into%20the%20container
219 Ibid.
220 Ibid.
221 Ibid.
222 Liechtenstein. https://www.liechtenstein-business.li/en/economic-area/blockchain-liechtenstein/das-tvtg/grundlegendes
223 *Liechtenstein's Parliament Approves Blockchain Act Unanimously.* https://www.liechtensteinusa.org/article/liechtensteins-parliament-approves-blockchain-act-unanimously see also, *Law of 3 October 2019 on Tokens and TT Service Providers (Token and TT Service Provider Act; TVTG).* https://www.regierung.li/text/16318/law#section14480
224 Ibid.
225 Ibid.

More specifically, in relation to blockchain technology itself, it has been outlined that:

> The applications of blockchain technology are therefore not restricted to simple transactions of coins or tokens with an exchangeable value between private individuals. Rather, they provide the option for a large range of economic services, as assets or rights can also be recorded in blockchain systems in general. This provides the possibility to create a digital recording of means of payment or assets and the possibility to conduct transactions with no direct intermediary being responsible for the execution of such transaction. Thus, companies offering financial services on blockchain systems use generally available digital infrastructure to provide their services.[226]

The specific definition of a token is 'a piece of information on a TT System which 'can represent claims or rights of memberships against a person, rights to property or other absolute or relative rights; and is assigned to one or more TT Identifiers'.[227] Of importance, Article 19a states:

> The following service providers that have already been issued a licence under financial market legislation and intend to provide TT Services in Liechtenstein must be entered into the TT Service Provider Register under a simplified registration procedure in accordance with article 19b before providing the service for the first time:
>
> a) banks with a licence under the Banking Act for activities referred to in article 2(1) letters k to y;
> b) electronic money institutions with a licence under the Electronic Money Act for activities referred to in article 2(1) letters k to n and y;
> c) central securities depositories with a licence under Regulation (EU) No 909/201453 for activities referred to in article 2(1) letters n, r to t, and y;
> d) investment firms with a licence under the Banking Act for activities referred to in article
> e) letters k to n, q, r to t, and w to y;
> f) asset management companies with a licence under the Asset Management Act for activities referred to in article 2(1) letters m, r to t, and x; management companies with a licence under the Law concerning Specific Undertakings for Collective Investment in Transferable Securities or the Law concerning Alternative Investment Fund Managers for activities referred to in article 2(1) letters m, r to t, and x.[228]

226 Ibid.
227 *Law of 3 October 2019 on Tokens and TT Service Providers (Token and TT Service Provider Act; TVTG)*, Article 2. https://www.regierung.li/text/16318/law#section14480
228 Ibid., Article 19.

Viewed this way, the law enables an entity who has been afforded a licence under the abovementioned laws to undertake TT Services in Liechtenstein, provided they are registered on the TT Service Provider Register. This enables the entity to engage in the facilitation of token transactions. Moreover, Article 30 sets out how a token can be issued, whereby the Token Issuers must prepare basic information according to the following provisions; publish the basic information in an easily accessible way; and report the Token Issuance to the Financial Management Authority.[229] Article 31, goes further providing exceptions to Article 30 where the token offerings are for the public, and the offer is geared towards fewer than 150 users; or the sale price of the total issue does not exceed 5 million Francs or the corresponding equivalent in another currency; or there is already an obligation to publish qualified information about the public offering of tokens according to other laws.[230] This legislation is the most comprehensive law in the world specifically related to tokens. Unlike the law of Switzerland, there is no mention of a ledger or blockchain. Yet, the laws do not preclude this technology from being used to facilitate token transactions. It requires a level of licencing. Further analysis is required of Liechtenstein's token laws.

2.4 Conclusion

The laws pertaining to tokens [crypto assets\stablecoins] is evolving at a rapid rate. That being the case, by the time this book is published, there may well be further additions and changes to the above. It is an area of high vigilance.

Nonetheless, what is likely to emerge is that the current banking and financial system will be challenged significantly over the coming decade. The current large banks that exist may no longer exist in the new world of digital assets. The ensuing challenge for regulators and governments will be to balance the innovation in this new area of the economy while ensuring that there is an adequate level of protection and controls in place to ensure trade and investment continue with a high level of certainty. Conversely, nation states may well direct the token economy to fall within the current day banking and financial regulatory framework. If os, this would exclude many from the new digital activity, because they would not meet the threshold requirements such as equity and captial requirements to obtain a licence.

It is argued that the groundwork has begun to be put in place by the jurisdictions compared. However, what this chapter has highlighted is that there will be significant divergences in approach. In other words, while there is likely to be a standard response by governments to licence the sector, the underlying law and licencing framework and their ensuing obligations will differ significantly.

This chapter has demonstrated that most jurisdictions have established national laws, not specifically to govern token transactions, but to allow for the activity, in part, to fall within the current banking and financial legal framework

229 Ibid., Article 30.
230 Ibid., Article 31.

(or are working towards this framework). The exception is Australia and the US. The laws are very quickly diverging from each other, and while there appears to be a consensus that this financial activity will be authorised through a licence or some other mechanism, it has been defined very differently. In my view, the definition(s) provided by the US 2022 Executive Order are the most specific, direct, and coherent. Collectively, blockchain, cryptocurrencies, digital assets, and stablecoins are all defined separately, but on analysis, they are connected through the technology of blockchain. They constitute a digital asset. Yet the token itself is not mentioned.

In addition to the above, there is a general theme emerging of licencing as the preferred regulatory model. As an extension of the current US model, the Switzerland model has gone further, requiring a level of licencing. Switzerland is not specifically regulating the DLT itself, but rather, regulating DLT as a trading facility. It is the trading facility that enables the facilitation of token transactions. On the other hand, of the jurisdictions compared, Liechtenstein is the first state to establish token-specific laws. It is argued that more specific token based laws are required.

This chapter has called urgently, both regionally and internationally, to develop a model law, high-level principles, and concepts that can guide and direct other nation-states in the development of this area of law. In a similar way to data laws having high-level principles set by the OECD in the early 1980s which have found their way into most, if not all, national laws, this will minimise legal divergence.

There is a need for greater collaboration internationally and regionally through the many organisations and institutions that already exist. For instance, ASEAN, APEC, and the Commonwealth Secretariat could be very important to the development of the law. Additionally, the African Union should be consulted along with UNCITRAL and UNIDROIT. Doing so, will strengthen the rules-based system and rule of law across this new financial sector of the digital economy. The chapter has also demonstrated how the judiciary is beginning to resolve complex matters in this area of the economy.

This chapter has not explored the self-regulatory frameworks that are also are beginning to emerge, such as the work done by the International Standardisation Organisation (ISO) and other national standards organisations such as Standards Australia. This is an area requiring urgent research and is an important means of providing certainty, consistency, and interoperability across nation-states.

Finally, one of the challenges for the judiciary is understanding the operation of the technology behind crypto exchanges and transactions. This will require new skills and capacities to be developed across the legal profession. The chapter demonstrated how the judiciary had to address issues such as transactions undertaken by mistake, transactions where crypto assets have been stolen, and whether the current national laws address digital payments, along with obligations of software developers where that software is used to facilitate crypto transactions, amongst others. This will require ongoing research as the cases evolve and become more complex.

3 Taxation

3.1 Introduction

Over the past decade, the 'digital economy is increasingly becoming the centre of economy activity itself. That said, it would be difficult, if not impossible, to ring-fence the digital economy from the rest of the economy for tax purposes'.[1] Governments are likely to be challenged when raising tax revenue because traditional forms of taxation may be diluted or reduced by technology replacing humans. This chapter does not compare the jurisdictional laws on tax. Rather, it looks at what has been evolving in the area of the digital economy.

Nonetheless, it is in a 'continuous state of evolution and possible future developments need to be monitored to evaluate their impact on tax systems'.[2] The new developing 'business models present some key features which are potentially relevant from a tax perspective'.[3] These features include 'mobility (with respect to intangibles, users, and business functions), reliance on data, network effects, the spread of multi-sided business models, tendency toward monopoly or oligopoly, and volatility due to lower barriers to entry into markets and rapidly evolving technology'.[4] Importantly, it 'has also accelerated the spread of global value chains in which multinational enterprises integrate their worldwide operations'.[5] The question arises: could this provide governments with new forms of taxes, so as to raise the necessary revenues that, provide health, education, roads, and the many other public services that people have enjoyed for many decades in the developed nations?

A further significant question is: given the possibility that humans may be replaced by technology such as AI and quantum in robotics, what impact

1 Organisation for Economic Cooperation and Development. *OECD/G20 Base Erosion and Profit Shifting Project Addressing the Tax Challenges of the Digital Economy Action 1: 2014 Deliverable*, p. 157. https://www.oecd-ilibrary.org/docserver/9789264218789-en.pdf?expires=1692073482&id=id&accname=ocid42013661&checksum=F42C21232DF50EF53802A0C1D996C4C4

2 Ibid.

3 Ibid.

4 Ibid.

5 Ibid.

DOI: 10.4324/9781003511687-3

could this have on the current-day tax base and the laws that underpin it? Robots are being used with a high level of effectiveness to debate, perform surgery, play chess, and effect policing and security, and the AI that supports it is rapidly diffusing across both civil and criminal regulatory domains.[6] As noted by David Horton, robots have been used to experiment with judicial decisions in some countries, and this may be extended to arbitration as the technology develops. This chapter will demonstrate the need for further research that is urgently required by all nation-states, both nationally and internationally, to address these possible developments.

Notwithstanding the above, Kevin Körner, Marc Schattenberg, and Eric Heymann highlighted in 2018 that 'it would be possible to tax a corporation's cost savings/profit gains due to the substitution of human labour'.[7] The authors proposed a new tax because of the potential shift in human labour requirements as the economy increasingly becomes more automated. However, and while it is inevitable that there will be elements of the economy which will be permanently automated, governments do have the power to step in and restrict or slow the progress of this technology. Doing so will enable a more measured transition across the economy, from humans retaining most of their current-day tasks. It would also allow people to reskill and transition into new jobs across the digital economy.

Nevertheless, the proposed new tax espoused by Körner et al. 'could make up for the (potential) loss in any labour income taxation and publicly collected social security contributions and help mitigate/offset the social costs caused by automation's displacement effects in the labour market'.[8] Effectively, Körner and others are making the case for a possible robot tax. They note that such a tax:

> would also change the relative prices between the input factors of labour and capital (e.g., robots and machines), thus making the employment of human labour more attractive. However, a robot tax would generally punish firms that aim to become more cost-efficient. It could deter capital investment and, in the worst case, any further innovation. Without some international framework, it could lead to intensified regulatory competition between nations, protectionism and the migration of capital towards more attractive jurisdictions.[9]

Should this be fully realised, it would go some way to compensate for the structural changes caused by the loss of employment across the economy. Körner and others went further in referring to note that the Nobel Prize Laureate

6 David Horton, Forced Robot Arbitration, *Cornell Law Review*, 109 (2023), 4.

7 Kevin Körner, Marc Schattenberg, Eric Heymann, *Digital Economics: How AI and Robotics are Changing our Work and our Lives*, Deutsche Bank (2018), p. 13. https://d-nb.info/1237663954/34

8 Ibid.

9 Ibid.

Milton Friedman, in his book 'Capitalism and Freedom' of 1962 proposed a universal basic income (UBI). It could replace most current social spending items (such as public expenses on health insurance or housing allowances).[10] The authors make a further point that governments should:

> aim to restore their fiscal space by moving towards greater taxation of capital income, wealth (on financial or real estate assets), value creation and/or consumption of such items as luxury goods. Still, in order to be successful, governments around the globe would likely need to secure a high level of tax coordination and cooperation amongst themselves, as wealthy individuals and multinational corporations might try shifting income to low-tax destinations.[11]

Whatever way one looks at the above proposal, it is complex, daunting, challenging, and is unlikely to be achieved. This is because countries around the world are at very different stages of the economic cycle. The developed world is far more advanced than the developing world and Third World nation-states. Some of the developing countries have had a rapid rise in the past five decades. Others are just about to turn the corner. For example, India, has a population of more than 1 billion people, and the average age of its population is younger[12] than that of most nations around the world.

However, smaller nation-states such as Singapore could be in a vulnerable position as the digital economy takes hold. This is because it has a small geographical landmass, small population, no natural resources, and a very low tax base to attract foreign investment. Therefore, one way to ensure a level of conformity is to have an international tax regime that evenly distributes the revenue on a per-capita basis.

On the backdrop of the above, the 2023 G20 Group of Nations issued a very important statement indicating the direction of tax in the digital economy. The G20 Group noted that:

> progress has been made on delivery of a text of a Multilateral Convention (MC), and work on the framework for simplified and streamlined application of the arm's length principle to in-country baseline marketing and distribution activities, as well as the completion of the work on the development of the Subject to Tax Rule.[13]

The MC was concluded in 2016 by more than 100 jurisdictions to enable the implementation of a series of tax treaty measures to update international

10 Ibid.
11 Ibid.
12 UN population and demographic figures for India …
13 G20 Group, *One Earth, One Family, One Future* (2023), p. 24. https://www.g20.org/content/dam/gtwenty/gtwenty_new/document/G20-New-Delhi-Leaders-Declaration.pdf

tax rules.[14] At the core of this project has been the rationale to minimise and control the ability of individuals and entities to exploit base erosion and profit shifting. These measures will also transfer from the traditional economy to the digital economy. However, further research is needed to better understand their impact on the ability to shift profits from one jurisdiction to the others across the digital economy.

In addition to the above, the G20 Group went on to say that the 'swift implementation of the Crypto Asset Reporting Framework is important to commence exchanges between countries by 2027 and to report to our future meetings on the progress of its work'.[15] In other words, it is this new form of finance technology that has the potential to cause the most disruption to the current national tax base. Put another way:

> The Crypto-Asset market, including both the Crypto-Assets offered, as well as the intermediaries and other service providers involved, poses a significant risk that recent gains in global tax transparency will be gradually eroded. In particular, the Crypto-Asset market is characterised by a shift away from traditional financial intermediaries, the typical information providers in third-party tax reporting regimes, such as the Common Reporting Standard, to a new set of intermediaries and other service providers which only recently became subject to financial regulation and are frequently not yet subject to tax reporting requirements with respect to their users. Furthermore, the ability of individuals to hold Relevant Crypto-Assets in wallets unaffiliated with any service provider and transfer such Relevant Crypto-Assets across jurisdictions, presents the risk that Relevant Crypto-Assets are used for illicit activities or to evade tax obligations. Overall, the characteristics of the Crypto-Asset sector have reduced tax administrations' visibility on tax-relevant activities carried out within the sector, increasing the difficulty of verifying whether associated tax liabilities are appropriately reported and assessed.[16]

14 *Multilateral Convention to Implement Tax Treaty Related Measures to Prevent BEPS.* https://www.oecd.org/tax/treaties/multilateral-convention-to-implement-tax-treaty-related-measures-to-prevent-beps.htm

15 G20 Group, *One Earth, One Family, One Future* (2023), p. 24. https://www.g20.org/content/dam/gtwenty/gtwenty_new/document/G20-New-Delhi-Leaders-Declaration.pdf

16 Organisation for Economic Cooperation and Development, *International Standards for Automatic Exchange for Information in Tax Matters* (2023), p. 11. https://www.oecd-ilibrary.org/docserver/6cb9f288-en.pdf?expires=1695780990&id=id&accname=guest&checksum=1381D138460078930EE2997781EB5966 Crypto-Asset exchanges and wallet providers, which may currently only be subject to limited regulatory oversight. Crypto-Asset exchanges typically facilitate the purchase, sale and exchange of Crypto-Assets for other Crypto-Assets or Fiat Currencies. Wallet providers offer digital 'wallets', which individuals can use to store their Crypto-Assets via authorisation through public and private keys. These services may either be provided in online (i.e. 'hot') wallets, or via service providers offering products allowing

On that basis, it has been proposed that a reporting framework is to be developed that will provide for three types of transactions:

> 1) exchanges between Relevant Crypto-Assets and Fiat Currencies; 2) exchanges between one or more forms of Relevant Crypto-Assets; and 3) transfers (including Reportable Retail Payment Transactions) of Relevant Crypto-Assets. This means that transactions will be reported on an aggregate basis by type of Relevant Crypto-Asset and distinguishing outward and inward transactions in order to improve the usability of the data for tax administrations.[17]

Moreover, the proposed reporting framework:

> for Crypto-Asset-to-Fiat Currency transactions [provide for] the fiat amount paid or received is reported as the acquisition amount or gross proceeds. For Crypto-Asset-to-Crypto-Asset transactions the value of the Crypto-Asset (at acquisition) and the gross proceeds (upon disposal) must (also) be reported in Fiat Currency. [A] transaction is split into two reportable elements, i.e.: (i) a disposal of Crypto-Asset A (the reportable gross proceeds based on the market value at the time of disposal); and (ii) an acquisition of Crypto-Asset B (the reportable acquisition value based on the market value at the time of acquisition). [The] taxpayers' holdings and transfers of Relevant Crypto-Assets outside the scope of Reporting Crypto-Asset Service Providers subject to reporting are also relevant to tax authorities. In order to increase visibility on these, it requires reporting of the number of units and the total value of Transfers of Relevant Crypto-Assets effectuated by a Reporting Crypto-Asset Service Provider, on behalf of a Crypto-Asset User, to wallets not associated with a virtual asset service provider or a financial institution. In case this information gives rise to compliance concerns, tax administrations could then request more detailed information on the wallet addresses.[18]

However, at the time of writing, no national government had implemented this reporting framework, let alone established a level of specific taxes related to these transactions. Thus, there is no tax on these transactions such as capital gains tax, for example, in Singapore. On the other hand, in Australia, this activity gives rise to a capital gains tax event that constitutes selling an asset; trading, exchanging, or swapping assets; loss or destruction of an asset or

individuals to store their Crypto-Assets offline on downloaded (i.e. 'cold') wallets. Both types of products are relevant for tax authorities.

17 Ibid., p. 14.

18 Ibid.

creating contractual or other rights (this is known as an involuntary disposal).[19] Therefore, in Australia there is a tax on the capital gain derived from the sale or trade of the asset. Noteworthy is that any capital gains tax can derive a discount of 50% if the asset has been owned for a period of 12 months or more, resulting in only half the tax having to be paid on the sale or transaction of the asset.

At the lower end, Indonesia charges only 0.1% on the sale of crypto assets under its value-added tax.[20] India has, to date, developed the most comprehensive tax laws in this area. As of October 2023, trading in crypto will be taxed at 30% (plus 4% excess).[21] Additionally, section 194S levies a 1% tax deduction at the source of the transfer of a crypto asset where the transaction exceeds 50,000 in the same financial year.

The EU has adopted the reporting approach set out by the Organisation for Economic Cooperation and Development (OECD) under a regulation[22] that still remains a proposal to improve the tax framework for crypto assets. It does adopt the reporting process as outlined earlier in the chapter. However, taxes remain the responsibility of each member state. That includes current and future crypto assets to be taxed. This book does not compare the member states' tax approaches to crypto transactions.

On the one hand, and similar to Australia, the UK has adopted the approach that crypto assets will incur a level of tax. That is, if a person is resident and domiciled in the UK, tax will be incurred on any income received from anywhere in the world.[23] If a person is resident and domiciled in another country, any foreign income is likely to be excluded from tax. For gains, crypto assets will be calculated in the same way as shares of a company. In the UK, there is a discount rate for any fees associated with the transaction(s); however, the more transactions, the greater the complexity. However, if a person has received crypto assets as a form of reward, then they will usually be taxable.

On the other hand, where crypto assets are received as an unrequested gift without the recipient having to do anything in return, then they will generally not be taxed as income.[24] More specifically, the general rule for tax is that

19 Australian Taxation Office (2023). https://www.ato.gov.au/individuals/capital-gains-tax/cgt-events/

20 *VAT and Income Tax on Crypto Asset Transaction in Indonesia, Regulation No. 68/PMK.03/2022 (MoF-68)*. https://indonesia.acclime.com/news/vat-income-tax-crypto-asset-transaction/

21 *Taxation on Cryptocurrency: Guide to Crypto Taxes in India* (2023). https://cleartax.in/s/cryptocurrency-taxation-guide

22 *Regulation of the European Parliament and of the Council on Markets in Crypto-assets, and Amending Directive (EU) 2019/1937*. https://eur-lex.europa.eu/resource.html?uri=cellar:f69f89bb-fe54-11ea-b44f-01aa75ed71a1.0001.02/DOC_1&format=PDF

23 *Crypto Assets and Tax*. https://www.litrg.org.uk/tax-guides/savers-property-owners-and-other-tax-issues/cryptoassets-and-tax

24 Ibid.

a person be domiciled in a nation-state for 183 days[25] of the calendar year. However, this may vary slightly from state to state, and people would need to confirm the local rules. For instances, in 2022, Singapore specified a number of professions that would be subject to paying double tax. A lecturer who was stranded in Singapore during the pandemic in 2021 and 2022, and derived income from Australia (paying income tax in Australia), was required to also pay income tax on that salary in Singapore under the rule of the place where the service was rendered.[26] Put another way, as people become more transient, they may have their place of residence in the UK, for example, and be paid by an employer within the UK although the individuals have been staying in the US. The tax authorities could increasingly look to other factors to determine residency/domicile. This could include, but should not be limited to, where bank accounts are located, in addition to homes, flats, apartments rented or remaining vacant, name on the utility bills, superannuation, amongst other factors. Thus, what has emerged is how a person is connected to a nation-state.

In the Australian case of *ZKBN*,[27] the Court was required to clarify the meaning of 'resident'. Essentially the Court was required to consider the domicile test for residence. The Court noted that:

> The Commissioner of Taxation ('the Commissioner') has determined that the applicant was an 'Australian resident' in the years ending 30 June 2007 and 30 June 2008 ('the relevant tax years') in accordance with the provisions of the Income Tax Assessment Act 1997 (Cth) ('ITAA 1997') and the Income Tax Assessment Act *1936* (Cth) ('ITAA 1936'). On 2 June 2011, the Commissioner issued notices of assessment in which the applicant's income was identified as $116,744 and $168,635, respectively, for the relevant tax years. In an application dated 20 February 2012, the applicant objected to those assessments. The Commissioner disallowed the objection in relation to the 2007 tax year but allowed, in part, the objection to the 2008 tax year on the basis that part of the applicant's foreign income earned in the United Kingdom ('UK') in May and June 2008 was exempt under s23AG of the ITAA 1936. Accordingly, an amended assessment for the 2008 tax year was issued on 7 December 2012 on the basis of the applicant's income of $161,282. The applicant seeks review of the Commissioner's objection decisions

25 Australian Tax Office, *183 Day Rule*. https://www.ato.gov.au/Individuals/Coming-to-Australia-or-going-overseas/Residency-tests/Residency---the-183-day-test/#:~:text=or%20do%20next-,What%20is%20the%20183%2Dday%20test,to%20take%20up%20residence%20here.

26 Note, that this was the actual case for the author of this book. Also see *Tax Act 1947*, sections 7 to 9. This rule can apply to a number of different professions such as Kings Counse; however, the list is rarely made public and need to consult the Inland Revenue Office to clarify the current-day rules.

27 *ZKBN and Commission of Taxation* [2013] AATA 604 (27 August 2013). http://www8.austlii.edu.au/cgi-bin/viewdoc/au/cases/cth/aat/2013/604.html

> which were based upon the applicant being a resident of Australia in the relevant tax years.[28]

In looking to the legislation, the Court made the point that an 'Australian resident' means a person who is a resident of Australia for the purposes of the ITAA 1936. A 'resident of Australia' is defined in s6(1) of the ITAA 1936 to mean (a) a person, other than a company, who resides in Australia and includes a person i) whose domicile is in Australia, unless the Commissioner is satisfied that the person's permanent place of abode is outside Australia; ii) who has actually been in Australia, continuously or intermittently, during more than one half of the year of income, unless the Commissioner is satisfied that the person's usual place of abode is outside Australia and that the person does not intend to take up residence in Australia; or iii) who is: a member of the superannuation scheme established by deed under the Superannuation Act 1990; or an eligible employee for the purposes of the Superannuation Act 1976; or the spouse, or a child under 16).[29]

Importantly, the 'applicant bears the onus of proof in this matter or that the standard of proof is on the balance of probabilities'.[30] The Court examined a number of issues to determine whether the applicant was resident in Australia. These included, but were not limited to:

- Entry and exits at immigration points in Australia;
- Immigration declaration card where a person is required to declare where they will be resident in the coming 12 months;
- Contracts of rental properties for example in the UK;
- Paid tax outside of Australia;
- Intended address in Australia;
- Intention to live in Australia for next 12 months;
- Resident returning to Australia;
- Length of stay outside of Australia;
- Country where most time spent outside of Australia.[31]

Based on these tests applied by the Court, it found that the applicant was resident in Australia, according to section 6(1) of the ITAA 1936. While this case pertains to the Australian tax law, further analysis is needed of the other jurisdictions compared to confirm whether they have a similar test. In other nation-states, there may be similar rules that apply, and people will need to be vigilant when conducting business in the way that is enabled by the digital economy.

28 Ibid., para 1.
29 Ibid., para 3.
30 Ibid., para 25.
31 Ibid., paras 20–25.

The US has adopted a slightly different approach to the other jurisdictions compared. They have aggregated up crypto assets to also include digital assets, which include, but are not limited to, convertible virtual currency and cryptocurrency, stablecoins, and non-fungible tokens.[32] At this early juncture of imposing tax on digital assets, in the US, unlike the other jurisdictions compared, the rules have been expanded to include:

- Sale of a digital asset for fiat;
- Exchange of a digital asset for property, goods, or services;
- Exchange or trade of one digital asset for another digital asset;
- Receipt of a digital asset as payment for goods or services;
- Receipt of a new digital asset as a result of a hard fork;
- Receipt of a new digital asset as a result of mining or staking activities;
- Receipt of a digital asset as a result of an airdrop;
- Any other disposition of a financial interest in a digital asset.[33]

This expanded set of rules in the US could well be transposed to other jurisdictions as they consider what and how they can be used to enhance a state's revenue base. This will certainly be an area to watch in future and, in my view, will likely lead to further taxes being introduced as more commercial transactions are undertaken online. Japan has taken the position that earnings that exceed 200,000 JPY are miscellaneous income; thus, the rate of tax can be up to 55%.[34] This is higher than the standard 20% tax rate for shares. A non-permanent resident in Japan will pay 20% rate on all income earned in the country.[35] The variations in tax rates and tax types for digital assets and/or crypto assets is significant, across the jurisdictions compared. Generally, tax is a nation-state's own decision to ensure it meets its own sovereign needs. The ensuing challenge will be whether nation-states can overcome their differences and find a balance by imposing the same or similar tax so that there is a global approach. The next section examines the tax on digital tokens.

3.1.1 Digital Tokens

Digital tokens are different from crypto assets. However, across the jurisdictions compared there may be a level of cross-over between these tokens and crypto assets. For instance, Singapore has categorised these tokens into three

32 Inland Revenue Service. https://www.irs.gov/businesses/small-businesses-self-employed/digital-assets
33 Ibid.
34 Zac McClure, *The Essential Guide to Crypto Tax in Japan* (2023). https://tokentax.co/blog/crypto-taxes-in-japan
35 Ibid.

areas: Payment, Utility, and Security.[36] To begin with, the tax authority has developed guidelines to encourage the recording of the operation of tokens by individuals and entities, these include:

- Date of transaction;
- Number of units of digital tokens received or sold;
- Value of digital token at the time of the transaction;
- Exchange rate used;
- Purpose of the transaction;
- Details of customers/suppliers (for buy-sell transactions);
- Details of the ICO;
- Receipts/invoices of business expenses.[37]

In applying the example of tax rationale to a payment token, Singapore treated this as a barter trade. Therefore,

> the recipient of the payment tokens would be taxed on the value of the underlying goods provided/services performed. The taxable income in this case is the value of the one unit of payment token at the time that the income accrues to the business.[38]

On the other hand, a

> company is generally set-up with a profit-seeking motive, a company engaging in mining activities will be regarded as carrying on a business of mining and general tax rules will apply. It will be allowed to claim deduction on its mining expenses on an 'incurred' basis from the date of commencement of business. This refers to the date that the business has established its profit-making structure and started its first commercial activity. Indications that a mining business has commenced include mining equipment purchased and/or sale of mined digital tokens.[39]

36 Inland Revenue Authority Singapore, *IRAS e-Tax Guide Income Tax Treatment of Digital Tokens.* https://www.iras.gov.sg/media/docs/default-source/e-tax/etaxguide_cit_income-tax-treatment-of-digital-tokens_091020.pdf?sfvrsn=91dbe1f7_17. Payment tokens constitute payment token is regarded as an intangible property. Consequently, transactions involving the use of payment tokens as payment for goods or services are viewed as barter trade and the value of goods or services transferred should be determined at the point of transaction. Utility token is the use of a utility token to exchange for goods or services is unlikely to create an income subject to tax on the user at the point of exchange. It may, on the other hand, give rise to a deductible expense subject to usual deduction rules. Security Token is the taxability of the return derived from a security token depends on the nature of the return, for example, whether it is in the form of interest, dividend or other distributions.

37 Ibid., p 7.

38 Ibid., p 9.

39 Ibid., p 11.

On this basis, the tax rates will be those that are applicable to normal company and individual/personal tax rates.

In Australia, tokens are considered to be crypto assets. However, under the rules, there is a different category known as the 'non-fungible token (NFT) that involves similar digital technology as other crypto assets. A non-fungible token is not interchangeable in the same way as crypto coins or tokens'.[40] They will be subject to capital gains tax, revenue account as trading stock, as part of a business, and as a profit-making scheme.[41] Apart from the tax-related issues that will arise from NFTs, they also come with a level of copyright and intellectual property[42] attached.

Nonetheless, NFTs also exist in the US,[43] which is currently developing a tax rate for them. To date, they have been categorised as a collectable[44] that will incur a capital gains tax of 28%.[45] However, at the time of writing, a final determination had not been handed down by the US national government. In the UK, there are multiple ways by which NFTs can be taxed through capital gains of between 10–20%,[46] income tax 20 to 45%,[47] inheritance tax 40%[48] and VAT 20%. Moreover, at the time of writing, Japan, released its guidelines[49] on taxing NFTs, although these are not available in English. Therefore, further research can be conducted only after a translated version of the guidelines becomes available obtain so as to better understand them. This is a new and evolving area of taxation which is likely to change significantly over the coming decades. It will vary from jurisdiction to jurisdiction. In the EU, there are likely to be many differences between member states, since taxation remains the responsibility of each member state.

40 Australian Tax Office, *Non-Fungible Tokens.* https://www.ato.gov.au/individuals/investments-and-assets/crypto-asset-investments/transactions---acquiring-and-disposing-of-crypto-assets/non-fungible-tokens/

41 Ibid.

42 Jacob, Gallagher, NFTs Are the Biggest Internet Craze: Do they Work for Sneaker? *The Wall Street Journal* (2021). https://www.wsj.com/articles/nfts-and-fashion-collectors-pay-big-money-for-virtual-sneakers-11615829266. Also see Josie Thaddeus-Johns, What are NFTs Anyway? One Just Sold for $69 Million, *The New York Times.* https://www.nytimes.com/2021/03/11/arts/design/what-is-an-nft.html

43 *IRS Treatment of Certain Nonfungible Tokens as Collectibles, Notice 2023–2027.* https://www.irs.gov/pub/irs-drop/n-23-27.pdf

44 Ibid.

45 Ibid., p 2.

46 *NFT Taxes UK: Complete HMRC Info + Instructions* [2023]. https://blockpit.io/en/blog/uk-nft-tax/. Also see Gary Ashwood, *UK Tax Authority Seizes NFTS – What Does This Mean for Crypto Investors?* https://news.bloombergtax.com/daily-tax-report-international/u-k-tax-authority-seizes-nfts-what-does-this-mean-for-crypto-investors

47 Ibid.

48 Ibid.

49 Jerry Christopher, *Japan Issue Guidelines on NFT Transaction Taxation* (2023). https://www.todaynftnews.com/japan-issues-guidelines-on-nft-transaction-taxation/

Notwithstanding the above, the technology that has been developed to support and facilitate this new form of transaction is difficult to understand because crypto assets also make use of a DLT-based infrastructure (distributed ledger technologies).[50] Markus Heckel and Franz Waldenberger make the point that:

> assets and their infrastructures can be used for transactions and as a store of value. However, despite their impressive diffusion and valuation, they are not recognised as legal tender. Their use is limited to economic entities who explicitly agreed to participate by investing money or real assets in the respective schemes. The infrastructural implications of crypto assets depend on how far they are able to take over or support core functions of the financial system. The answer to this question remains unclear as there are still fundamental problems stemming not only from the high price volatility, but also from regulatory and security issues.[51]

Therefore, taxation systems and frameworks are having to change so as to accommodate the new payments systems and infrastructure that have been developed. This will include both online and mobile payments and transactions. Heckel and Waldenberger reinforce this point by stating that

> cashless mobile or online payments were made possible by the internet, mobile networks, smartphones, and the development and diffusion of application programming interfaces (APIs). In contrast to DLTs, they rely on the existing banking infrastructure. Although they have important implications for the design level of business models, from an infrastructural perspective, they simply add what is essentially an additional digital layer.[52]

Consequently, two technology systems have emerged to support and facilitate different payment methods. Arguably, the DTLS system is likely to be more mature than the APIs and is, therefore, more widely used by the banking sector. It is argued that the banking sector are leaders in securing and facilitating cross-border transactions internationally, and have done so for decades.

Despite the above, Peter Mullins highlights that challenges and complexities will arise due, in part, to the high level of cross-border transactions. In 2022, Mullins noted that the:

50 Markus Heckel, Franz Waldenberger, *The Future of Financial Systems in the Digital Age Perspectives from Europe and Japan*, Springer (2022), p. 33.

51 Ibid.

52 Ibid.

> mismatch between the tax rules and the operation of the digital economy limits the ability of countries to collect taxes from cross-border digital transactions, and also creates opportunities for tax planning, at the expense of government revenues. Multinational enterprises are especially adroit at exploiting the tax planning opportunities to significantly reduce their tax liabilities. Tax issues can also arise with domestic transactions in the digital economy, especially for online peer-to-peer transactions, because of a lack of clarity on how these transactions should be treated under domestic tax laws.[53]

Furthermore, in reinforcing the above, Mullins expands on the challenges posed by cross-border taxation of the digital economy, stating that:

> Many of the challenges in taxing the digital economy relate to cross-border tax issues and weaknesses in the existing international tax framework, but there are also domestic tax issues. Much of the discussion in this section focuses on the challenges relating to international tax rules, given their recent prominence. However, there is also discussion on domestic tax issues relating to the digital economy, such as the taxation of the sharing economy. These are discussed briefly subsection III.B, and also in more detail in section IV on the VAT.[54]

This international weakness has been evident globally, with countries failing to collaborate and coherently develop an international model for tax. At no other time in history is there an opportunity for the world community to work together to develop a single tax approach for the digital economy.

While this chapter is not intended to provide a solution to the possible revenue taxation shortfalls through an economic analysis, it nevertheless argues that the Tobin tax, which was proposed in 1972 by James Tobin, could go some way to addressing the international divergence. The Tobin tax[55] could be applied to all spot conversions from one currency to another, proportional to the size of the transaction. By applying a 1% tax, this would result in an eight-point differential in annual treasury yields of a currency. Many decades later, elements of the Tobin proposal are only now starting to be adopted and applied.

For instance, the European Commission in 2023, 'tabled a proposal for a minimum 0.1% tax rate for transactions in all types of financial instruments,

53 Peter Mullins, *Taxing Developing Asia's Digital Economy* (2023), p. 2. https://www.adb.org/sites/default/files/institutional-document/782851/ado2022bp-taxing-developing-asia-digital-economy.pdf

54 Ibid., p 7.

55 James Tobin, *A Proposal for International Monetary Reform*, Yale University (1972), p. 155. file:///Users/macbookair/Desktop/V4N3_4P153_159.pdf

except derivatives which would be subject to a minimum of 0.01% tax rate'.[56] Nonetheless, one could be excused for thinking that this is a novel idea. It is far from the truth. Financial and banking entities have been issuing credit and debit cards to customers for decades. When so doing, the customer incurs a small charge for the use of the card, which varies depending on the jurisdiction. For example, in Australia, the Australian Competition and Consumer Commission reported that the general charge for the use of these cards by institutions ranged between 0.05 to 1.5%.[57] While it is outside the scope of this book to examine whether each of the jurisdictions applies the same or similar charge, in the future, this charge could be turned into a tax for all online national and international transactions.

Even though this chapter has not dealt with the tax issue comprehensively and further research on tax in a digital economy is needed, the author is not an accountant and has provided only a basic overview of the challenges that lie ahead. That said, as Mullins has highlighted, there are a number of nation-states that have been addressing this issue through income, capital gains, inheritance, and other forms of taxation. However, to date, there has been no coherent approach to the issue of taxation in a digital economy, and some nation-states do not fully support the current international approach to taxation.[58] As nations become more competitive in terms of investment in the digital economy, pressure will be on national governments to provide tax incentives. This, in and of itself, will further challenge the current tax rules and rates.

Mullins is calling for all countries to provide a consistent 'definition of "permanent establishment" in domestic laws to include digital services provided in the country, even if there is no physical presence, is a measure all countries can adopt'.[59] Any developments need to be considered in light of the developing United Nations Model on Double Taxation Convention.[60] The

56 European Parliament. *Legislative Train Schedule, Financial Transaction Tax* (2023). https://www.europarl.europa.eu/legislative-train/theme-an-economy-that-works-for-people/file-financial-transaction-tax

57 Australian Competition and Consumer Commission. https://www.accc.gov.au/consumers/pricing/card-surcharges#:~:text=As%20a%20guide%2C%20the%20Reserve,between%201%25%20and%201.5%25.

58 Peter Mullins, *Taxing Developing Asia's Digital Economy* (2023), pp. 32–34. https://www.adb.org/sites/default/files/institutional-document/782851/ado2022bp-taxing-developing-asia-digital-economy.pdf

59 Ibid., p 32.

60 United National Model Double Taxation Convention. https://www.un.org/esa/ffd/wp-content/uploads/2018/05/MDT_2017.pdf, The United Nations Model Convention generally favours retention of greater so called 'source country' taxing rights under a tax treaty – the taxation rights of the host country of investment – as compared to those of the 'residence country' of the investor. This has long been regarded as an issue of special significance for developing countries, although it is a position that some developed countries also seek in their bilateral treaties. Guidance in applying transfer pricing rules can be found in *OECD Transfer*

transformation of the tax regime will continue to be debated, and it is estimated that annually there will be upwards of 250 USD[61] billion in tax revenue. As Mullins concludes:

> The rise of the digital economy has challenged the traditional tax systems. The international tax rules have proved inadequate in dealing with cross-border transactions, with larger multi-national entities exploiting the weaknesses in existing national tax frameworks. The challenges with the taxation of the digital economy have led to tax reform initiatives that could significantly reform the current tax systems and enhance the taxation of the digital economy. However, the response has been mixed, with the more developed countries likely to adopt the reforms. Any tax reform strategy for addressing the taxation of the digital economy will depend on the country's circumstances (e.g., economic development, size of the digital economy, need for revenue, and tax administration capacity), so careful analysis should be undertaken before adopting the new global initiatives.[62]

Viewed this way, could new technologies such as AI and quantum technology provide the answer to taxation within the digital economy? Arguably, technology may provide the answer because it can be used to exploit current tax systems in order to facilitate laundering activities. Nevertheless, in one of the most recent major reforms, more than 130 countries[63] agreed to a number of changes. Since then, nation-states have been reviewing their positions, and corporate tax rates have been changing. For instance, in the US alone, the corporate tax rate in 2022 was scheduled to come down to 15%.[64] As mentioned earlier in this chapter, Australia has followed suit with a reduction to 25%.[65]

Essentially, what is becoming increasingly evident is that technology could be used to transform the tax system within a digital economy. For example, quantum technology has transformed the speed and accuracy with

Pricing Guidelines for Multinational Enterprises and Tax Administrations (2017) and the *UN Practical Manual on Transfer Pricing for Developing Countries* (2017).

61 Ibid., pp. 33–34.

62 Ibid., pp. 36–38.

63 Organisation for Economic Cooperation and Development, *International Community Strikes a Ground Breaking Tax Deal for the Digital Age*. https://web-archive.oecd.org/2021-10-20/612898-international-community-strikes-a-ground-breaking-tax-deal-for-the-digital-age.htm

64 J D Hamilton et al., *Inflation Reduction Act include 15% Corporate Minimum Tax on Book Income* (2022).
https://www.thetaxadviser.com/issues/2023/jan/inflation-reduction-act-includes-15-percent-corporate-minimum-tax-on-book-income.html#:~:text=On%20Aug.,tax%20based%20on%20book%20income

65 Ibid.

which people deal with many different areas of the economy. This is no different in the area of taxation. It is predicted that the technology will be able to analyse legislation and data to detect evasion and report on tax matters that, under the current computing framework, take decades.[66] However, although technology will resolve a number of structural issues, it will not address them all.

3.2 Additional Tax Considerations

While the above has focused on the broader issues related to tax of tokens and crypto assets, this section will briefly identify the emerging trends regarding tax for stablecoins. As highlighted above most crypto-digital assets will be treated as property for the purposes of tax 'when used as a means of payment'.[67] This will generally come down to how each jurisdiction will define these types of class assets. The dilemma will be where states treat them differently under the tax rules, when compared to how they are treated in exchanges and transactions. For instance, the Australian Tax Office in 2023, issued a note that stated a 'stablecoin that is pegged to the value of some other asset (such as a commodity or fiat currency) is not a digital currency. The supply of a stablecoin is an input-taxed financial supply unless it is GST-free'.[68] On the other hand, the US, 'treat federal income tax purposes all crypto assets as property and so all transactions involving crypto assets are regarded as barter transactions'.[69] However, the UK takes a different approach since it does not 'consider any of the current types of crypto assets to be money or currency' and that 'any Corporation Tax legislation, which relates solely to money or currency, does not apply to exchange tokens or other types of crypto asset'.[70] While this variation can be challenging to navigate, the stability of stablecoins in the market does provide some certainty. Christophe Waerzeggers, Irving Aw, and Jess Cheng reinforce this notion, taking the view that:

> The treatment of stablecoins as property for income taxation purposes means that each payment made using stablecoins constitutes a realization event – resulting from a barter transaction – that triggers tax

66 Carrie Brandon Elliott. *Quantum Computing Can Revolutionise Tax Administration* (2022). https://www.forbes.com/sites/taxnotes/2022/12/15/quantum-computing-can-revolutionize-tax-administration/?sh=31038caf16c3

67 Christophe Waerzeggers, Irving Aw, Jess Cheng, *Taxing Stablecoins*, International Monetary Fund (2023), p. 14.

68 Australian Tax Office, https://www.ato.gov.au/Business/GST/In-detail/Your-industry/GST-and-crypto-assets/GST-and-digital-currency/

69 Christophe Waerzeggers, Irving Aw, Jess Cheng, *Taxing Stablecoins*, International Monetary Fund (2023), p. 14.

70 Ibid., p. 15.

> consequences. This is likely to substantially increase the tax compliance burden for taxpayers that choose to make payment using stablecoins rather than traditional currencies in the context of tax systems that generally tax capital gains. This is because income tax rules generally allow for foreign exchange gains or losses to be computed at the end of a tax period instead of on a per-transaction basis, as is typically the case for gains (or losses) arising from property transactions. In addition to increasing relative compliance burdens, this difference in treatment could also lead to different income tax burdens relative to transactions in traditional currencies. Although stablecoins are at least in theory less susceptible to price fluctuations than other crypto assets, their price stability nevertheless is tied to the value of the assets or currencies to which they are pegged.[71]

Problematic though, is that as of 2023, so few nation-states have regulated stablecoins and classed them as an asset that can comprise part of the financial services market. It will come down to what will back them and how this will be done. Put another way, and drawing on the work of Waerzeggers, Aw, and Cheng, stablecoin has two functions: a 'means of payment, or, a negotiable promissory note that is payable to its bearer on demand'.[72] Therefore, it can be a form of money. On the other hand, it can be a promise that has no bearing or note related to a money-currency transaction because the person is holding the stablecoin (redeemable stablecoin by contract). Moreover, the authors note that

> prefiat (that is, gold standard) link between currency and gold or silver, it could be argued that few differences exist between redeemable stablecoins and currency, apart from the sovereign status of the issuer. The stablecoin is an electronic representation of the underlying asset and therefore is appropriately treated as property.[73]

For instance, a recent stablecoin that was issued in Australia[74] has been backed by the sovereign currency. To overcome some of the emerging challenges associated with stablecoins, Waerzeggers, Aw, and Cheng have proposed the following for national governments and regulators to consider:

71 Ibid.
72 Ibid.
73 Ibid.
74 AUUD. https://audd.digital

The international aspects of the direct taxation of transactions involving stablecoins. In particular, challenges may arise in the context where jurisdictions adopt different tax positions in relation to the classification of stablecoins. Consider an example where A in country A exchanges stablecoins with B in country B for traditional currency. Suppose that country A treats the stablecoins as property – that is, any gains on realization are subject to capital gains – whereas country B treats the transaction as a provision of exchange services. Assume further that A has sufficient nexus in country B such that the latter has taxing rights over some of the A's income arising from the transaction. This would potentially result in double taxation of A's gains arising from exchanging stablecoins with B.

Double nontaxation could equally arise from a different tax classification of stablecoin gains by jurisdictions. For instance, country A may consider the gains from the exchange of stablecoins as business profit with a sufficient nexus in country B – and therefore taxing rights rest with country B – whereas country B classifies the stablecoins as property and therefore primary taxing rights in respect of the gains belong to country A.

Moreover, for country A to properly apply and administer residence-based taxation of capital gains, proper exchange of information between country A's tax administration and the tax administration of the jurisdiction in which the issuer of the stablecoin resides would be a prerequisite, assuming that the stablecoin is not decentralised. Reliance on third-party information – which is the traditional response of the international tax system to compliance challenges – may not be feasible or effective where the stablecoin is decentralised and private peer-to-peer transactions are not recorded by centralised authorities or intermediaries.[75]

I agree with the authors who are calling for more

> international coordination and cooperation will also be needed both in relation to substantive tax treatment to avoid cross-border tax arbitrage and to tax administration and enforcement to provide tax authorities with the necessary tools to ensure compliance with domestic tax obligations. A greater level of consistency in regulatory treatment of stablecoins could offer a common language and reference framework to inform the discussion between tax policymakers and administrators on their tax treatment and compliance frameworks.[76]

This will comprise the entire cycle of taxation that should include national and cross-border arrangements. Double-tax treaties may need to be revised to accommodate this new financial activity, and this is another area that requires urgent research. This has been reinforced by the OECD, which is calling for a reporting framework that can be used to inform and reform the current and future development

> of bilateral or multilateral competent authority agreements or arrangements for the automatic exchange of information collected under the

75 Ibid., p. 17.
76 Ibid.

> CARF with jurisdiction(s) of residence of the Crypto-Asset Users, based on relevant tax treaties, tax information exchange agreements, or the Convention on Mutual Administrative Assistance in Tax Matters.[77]

Such a framework will help to provide a level of transparency.

3.3 Arbitration

With the likelihood that there will be tax disputes as a result of the complex rules pertaining to tax, arbitration is a potential beneficiary. Arbitration as a means of resolving tax disputes can apply to both investor-state and commercial matters. The data that was collated back in 2018 demonstrated this trend:

> disputes are particularly prevalent in the extractive sectors (oil and gas, and mining), but fiscal measures are also being challenged in numerous other contexts. These cases concern matters as wide-ranging as retroactive profits taxes, corporation tax, VAT/GST, capital gains tax, transfer pricing, tax stabilisation mechanisms, taxation of income trusts, tax procedures, tax audits and investigations or the removal of tax incentives. They may give rise both to commercial arbitrations in respect of disputed contractual tax obligations and to investor-state arbitrations, as may arise under bilateral or multilateral investment treaties (BITs and MITs)[78]

Thus, for both arbitration and litigation practitioners, the highly fragmented approach of national legal frameworks and tax rates poses a challenging pathway forward. Furthermore, the above are generally related to the non-digital economy. As the digital economy derives new taxes from both individuals and entities, there is likely to be an increase in the number of disputes.

3.4 Technology Challenges and Advancements

The development of quantum technology has been, and continues to be, addressed by many technology, legal, and policy scholars. However, the blockchain that supports and facilitates the transactions involving crypto assets, including stablecoin, currently provides a high level of security. However,

77 Organisation for Economic Cooperation and Development, *Crypto-Assets Reporting Framework and Amendments to the Common Reporting Standard, OECD* (Paris, 2023). https://www.oecd.org/tax/exchange-of-tax-information/crypto-asset-reporting-framework-and-amendments-to-the-common-reporting-standard.pdf

78 *Arbitrating International Tax Disputes* (2018), p. 19. http://www.iberglobal.com/files/2018-2/arbitration_trends_freshfields.pdf. See also Michael Lang, Jeffery Owens, *International Arbitration in Tax Matters* (2015), p. 122. https://www.ibfd.org/sites/default/files/2021-12/15_075_International-Arbitration-Tax-Matters_final_web.pdf

quantum technology could threaten this. Hence, it poses one of the greatest challenges to the stability of the digital economy, as mentioned earlier in this book.

Given the potential disruption that could be caused by quantum technology, work is being undertaken to develop 'quantum-resistant blockchains, whereby, the cryptographic processes will be resistant to attacks via quantum computers'.[79] Such is the concern that Allende et al. stress that when

> running some quantum algorithms on full-scale quantum computers will necessitate the protection of internet and telecommunication information exchanges for widely used cryptography protocols. Most notably, some entities are currently running a post-quantum cryptography competition for standardisation to replace existing cryptographic algorithms that are susceptible to breakage using quantum computers.[80]

Nevertheless, the continuing development and implementation of 'symmetric standards are believed to provide adequate security against quantum adversaries'.[81] However, there is no absolute certainty in the technology sector that blockchain will not be compromised by quantum technology when fully implemented. In more recent research completed in 2023, it was concluded that the security of blockchain will be undermined after the implementation of quantum technology.[82] More specifically, and while not adding to the governance of blockchain, the research made the point that by adding the National Institute of Standards and Technology to:

> post-quantum signatures Dilithium, FALCON, and *SPHINCS+* to the blockchain and analysed their performance compared with the widely used ECDSA. The Falcon and Dilithium-based systems are recommended for applications that prioritise strong performance in key generation, signing, and verification times, especially when utilizing the suggested IPFS for managing large keys. If the IPFS is not preferred, then Falcon is a suitable choice. Block capacity as well as the issue of quantum attack are both resolved in this manner.[83]

79 Omega John Unogwu, Ruchi Doshi, Kamal Kant Hiran, Maad Mijwil, *Introduction to Quantum Resistant Blockchain*, IGI Global Publishing (2022). https://www.igi-global.com/chapter/introduction-to-quantum-resistant-blockchain/311206

80 Marcos, Allende et al., *Quantum Resistance in Blockchain Networks*, Inter-American Development Bank (2021). https://publications.iadb.org/en/quantum-resistance-blockchain-networks

81 Ibid., p. 4.

82 P. Thanalakshmi, A. Rishikhesh, Joel Marion Marceline, Gyanendra Prasad Joshi, Woong Cho, A Quantum-Resistant Blockchain System: A Comparative Analysis, *Mathematics, 11* (2023), 3947. https://doi.org/ 10.3390/math11183947

83 Ibid.

The authors go on to say:

> It is worth emphasising that these quantum-resistant algorithms could be extended to various other blockchain models, including those employed by Ethereum, Polygon, Cosmos, and similar platforms, but mention applicability to Ethereum, Polygon, and similar platforms. While Bitcoin systems primarily facilitate transactions, Ethereum and related systems allow users to include data other than transactions in the blockchain. This key distinction introduces variability in block sizes, thus rendering the problem more intricate.[84]

Based on the above, an extensive amount of research needs to be undertaken to address the vulnerabilities of blockchain created by quantum technology. This will be important to governments and regulators because as the aforementioned market continues to grow, unless these issues are addressed, the new tax base will be significantly compromised. This is why, in terms of the digital economy that has sectors and segments, the integration of technology will be like no other time in history. The technology that is vulnerable to data breaches will pose serious economic, social, environmental, and national security threats. It is no longer enough to think of these elements of society in a singular context. Because of these technological developments, it has been demonstrated in this book that all areas examined, from arbitration, smart contracts, CISG contracts, IP, tax, mergers/acquisitions to insurance, that use blockchain technology will be facing challenges. Therefore, potentially, this has enormous implications for taxation systems. If the issue is not addressed as a matter of urgency, the subsequent effect on national budgets will be highly problematic.

3.5 Conclusion

The digital economy is changing, and this is challenging governments, regulators, and industry in every sector of the economy, including taxation. The changing economic landscape is forcing a rethink of the current rules and rates of tax to be applied. New regulatory frameworks are being developed, while at the same time, the existing rules are being utilised to capture elements of the digital economy that can be taxed, such as capital gains, inheritance, and income.

Undoubtedly, the collection, use, and sale of personal data can produce substantial economic benefit. Therefore, future taxation could include 'digital advertising services, sale of user data, online sales of goods and services, data processing and storage, subscription-based media'.[85] The problem globally with taxation systems in general is the volume and type of cross-border

84 Ibid.
85 *Digital Service Taxes and Other Unilateral Measures Roadmap* (2022). https://assets.bbhub.io/bna/sites/9/2022/11/Digital-Service-Taxes-and-Other-Unilateral-Measures-Road-

transactions, in the first instance. The second problem is the nature of the transaction frameworks, ownership, value, the nature of consideration: the various aspects explored earlier in this chapter.

Another challenge that has emerged for the general consumer is that due to online facilities, transactions are no longer being restricted by borders of single nation-states. Banks and financial institutions have been undertaking trans-border commerce for decades. However, in terms of individuals, this is a relatively recent phenomenon. For instance, an Australian citizen who is resident in Australia, but happens to be located in Singapore, can get online and make a bank transfer of funds from their Australian bank (located in Australia) to a bank in Singapore without having to use the services of a bank. Two decades ago, consumers would not have thought this possible. Via the Internet and other technological developments, people can now conduct transactions daily and with ease, between and across national borders.

To briefly return to Chapter 1, it is problematic that the current digital economy has not been specifically defined. It is open to interpretation, and for good reason. This, in and of itself, poses a significant dilemma, in that it has generally been categorised into section/sectors. Thus, the application of new tax rules and rates will lack cohesion. Generally, nation-states are currently applying their already-established tax rules and rates to the digital economy, rather than taking a strategic approach to developing what is needed to address possible shortfalls in future revenue sources.

Generally, what has emerged is that for tax purposes, crypto-digital assets and stablecoin are being considered as property. On the one side, there are a number of challenges that lie ahead. There is an opportunity and need for a review of current double-tax treaties and other bilateral and multilateral instruments to ensure they take into account this new economic activity. On the other side, those nation-states that have a business-friendly tax base could be the winners in this new economy. This is because there will likely be a competition between nations to provide tax incentives to ensure they attract business and investment to the country.

The new digital economy will be no different from the industrial-based economy, and will be subject to financial and other international disruptions that will affect the exchanges and transactions involving these new forms of assets. On the one hand, crypto-digital assets do provide a stronger level of stability, because of the encryption that is currently available and being used. On the other hand, the volatility of pricing was evident for all to see between 2020 and 2023. The provision of these financial mechanisms that need to be backed, as in the case of most stablecoins, goes some way to minimising volatility.

---

map_10-14-22.pdf See report for country by country that pick up the elements discussed, amongst others.

The developments in online trade have enabled personal and business transactions to be undertaken with ease nationally and internationally. This has resulted in new economic activity which, in part, has not attracted any direct tax. For more than a decade, international organisations have been investigating the challenges of taxation in the digital economy. In 2014, the OECD noted the challenge ensuing from the development of the digital economy:

> reliance on intangible assets, the massive use of data (notably personal data), the widespread adoption of multi-sided business models capturing value from externalities generated by free products, and the difficulty of determining the jurisdiction in which value creation occurs. This raises fundamental questions as to how enterprises in the digital economy add value and make their profits, and how the digital economy relates to the concepts of source and residence or the characterisation of income for tax purposes.[86]

Therefore, this book also discusses the most recent developments and examines today's tax laws in the jurisdictions being compared. The new business model, which took off at the height of the COVID-19 pandemic, demonstrated the rapidity with which people turned to technology to undertake trade. The OECD reinforced this point, highlighting that 'new ways of doing business may result in a relocation of core business functions and, consequently, a different distribution of taxing rights which may lead to low taxation is not *per se* an indicator of defects in the existing system'.[87] Second, the fundamental principles of taxation and taxation law have been well settled and agreed upon by many countries. They include:

- Neutrality;[88]
- Efficiency;[89]

86 Organisation for Economic Cooperation and Development, *OECD/G20 Base Erosion and Profit Shifting Project Addressing the Tax Challenges of the Digital Economy Action 1: 2014 Deliverable*, p. 24. https://www.oecd-ilibrary.org/docserver/9789264218789-en.pdf?expires=1692072177&id=id&accname=ocid42013661&checksum=C1933C59EF5356760B15F44536CE81E0

87 Ibid.

88 Ibid., pp. 30–31. Taxation should seek to be neutral and equitable between forms of business activities. A neutral tax will contribute to efficiency by ensuring that optimal allocation of the means of production is achieved. A distortion, and the corresponding deadweight loss, will occur when changes in price trigger different changes in supply and demand than would occur in the absence of tax. In this sense, neutrality also entails that the tax system raises revenue while minimising discrimination in favour of, or against, any particular economic choice. This implies that the same principles of taxation should apply to all forms of business, while addressing specific features that may otherwise undermine an equal and neutral application of those principles.

89 Ibid. Compliance costs to business and administration costs for governments should be minimised as far as possible

- Certainty and simplicity[90]
- Effectiveness and fairness;[91]
- Flexibility.[92]

Most notably, the developments in regard to taxation within the digital economy not only meet the agreed principles above, but also the current-day national laws that apply. Third, the OECD makes an important point in relation to the fragmented taxation rules across the world, generally. They argue that:

> Domestic tax rules for the taxation of cross-border income generally address two situations: the taxation of outbound investments of resident companies, and the taxation of inbound investments of non-resident companies. With respect to the former category, the definition of residence is a key notion. Some countries determine the residence of a corporation based on formal criteria such as place of incorporation. In other countries, the residence of a corporation is determined by reference factual criteria such as place of effective management or similar concepts. Some countries have mixed systems, where there is both a place of incorporation test and a place of effective management test.[93]

Against the backdrop of the above, 2021 was a pivotal moment in the world economy because 137 out of the 141 countries in the OECD/G20 Inclusive Framework on Base Erosion and Profit Shifting reached a landmark agreement on a two-pillar solution to reform the international tax framework in response

90 Ibid. Tax rules should be clear and simple to understand, so that taxpayers know where they stand. A simple tax system makes it easier for individuals and businesses to understand their obligations and entitlements. As a result, businesses are more likely to make optimal decisions and respond to intended policy choices. Complexity also favours aggressive tax planning, which may trigger deadweight losses for the economy.

91 Ibid. Taxation should produce the right amount of tax at the right time, while avoiding both double taxation and unintentional non-taxation. In addition, the potential for evasion and avoidance should be minimised. Prior discussions in the Technical Advisory Groups (TAGs) considered that if there is a class of taxpayers that are technically subject to a tax, but are never required to pay the tax due to inability to enforce it, then the tax-paying public may view the tax as unfair and ineffective. As a result, the practical enforceability of tax rules is an important consideration for policy makers. In addition, because it influences the collectability and the administrability of taxes, enforceability is crucial to ensure efficiency of the tax system

92 Ibid. Taxation systems should be flexible and dynamic enough to ensure they keep pace with technological and commercial developments. It is important that a tax system is dynamic and flexible enough to meet the current revenue needs of governments while adapting to changing needs on an ongoing basis. This means that the structural features of the system should be durable in a changing policy context, yet flexible and dynamic enough to allow governments to respond as required to keep pace with technological and commercial developments, taking into account that future developments will often be difficult to predict.

93 Ibid., p. 34.

to the challenges relating to taxation of the digital economy.[94] The OECD had been coordinating the multilateral consensus approach, with the framework designed to ensure that multinational enterprises pay a fair share of tax where they operate and that they pay a minimum corporate tax.[95] The two pillars are explained below.

- Pillar One will ensure a fairer distribution of profits and taxing rights among countries with respect to the largest and most profitable multinational enterprises (MNE) by re-allocating some taxing rights over MNEs from their home countries to the markets where they have business activities and earn profits, regardless of whether the MNE concerned has a physical presence in the market. MNEs that will be covered by the rules are those with global sales exceeding EUR 20 billion and profitability above 10%, with 25% of the profits exceeding the 10% threshold reallocated to market jurisdictions.[96]
- Pillar Two will introduce Global Anti-Base Erosion (GLoBE) rules to ensure MNEs with consolidated annual revenues exceeding EUR 750 million pay a minimum (15%) level of tax on the income they derive from each jurisdiction in which they operate. Where the effective tax rate of an in-scope MNE in any of these jurisdictions is below the 15% minimum rate, it will have to pay a 'top-up' tax to account for the difference. Generally, this will be paid to the jurisdiction of the MNE's ultimate parent, though there is a back-stop rule that would give taxing rights to the jurisdictions in which the constituent entities of the MNE group operate. Finally, outside the GLoBE rules, Pillar Two provides for a Subject to Tax Rule that could override existing tax treaty rules benefiting payments that are not subject to a minimum level of tax in the recipient's jurisdiction.[97]

Hence, any changes in the legal and policy framework for taxation within the digital economy will be challenging and is likely to reduce the profits[98] of organisations. Most challenging is that this will need to be weighed against the sovereign financial needs of the respective jurisdictions. This is because larger nation-states derive their tax from a tax base that is different from that of smaller nation-states. For example, Singapore, which has no natural resources to boost its economy, relies largely on foreign investment and a local base to raise its revenue.

94 Organisation for Economic Cooperation and Development. https://www.oecd.org/tax/beps/inclusive-framework-on-beps-composition.pdf See also BDO Global. https://www.bdo.global/en-gb/services/tax/taxation-of-the-digital-economy

95 Ibid.

96 Ibid.

97 Ibid.

98 Daniel Klein, Christopher Ludwig, Christopher Spengel, Taxing the Digital Economy: Investor Reaction to the European Commission's Digital Tax Proposals, *National Tax Journal* (2022), 86.

Thus, the issues that currently exist and are evident in taxing the digital economy are: 1) double taxation of digital suppliers; 2) revenue recognition arising from the need to monetise value; 3) tax impact of legal structures; 4) monetisation strategies used by digital business models; and 5) the double revenue threshold mechanism.[99] This will be an important component of the digital economy where entities are establishing offices throughout the countries examined. In other words, a FinTech company with its central office in Sydney Australia, and with satellite offices in Singapore and India, will be subject to different tax laws at the national level.

A greater dilemma for national governments and regulators that move forward to open up this market activity, is the emergence of quantum technology. As highlighted earlier in this book, once quantum technology is available and combined with AI and blockchain technology, the security of crypto-digital assets and stablecoin will be significantly vulnerable. Therefore, urgent work is required to address this potential vulnerability, or the entire system-framework will be exposed to state and non-state actors who may have malicious intent.

Finally, international organisations and the programmes that have been developed, will become increasingly important to cross-border compliance. The OECD's[100]

> International Compliance Assurance Programme (ICAP) is a voluntary programme for a multilateral co-operative risk assessment and assurance process. It is designed to be an efficient, effective and co-ordinated approach to provide multinational enterprise groups willing to engage actively, openly and in a fully transparent manner with increased tax certainty with respect to certain of their activities and transactions.[101]

Importantly, it provides a level of standardisation and should be embraced to ensure that certainty and stability are maintained as these new taxation systems are developed for the digital economy.

99 Cristan Oliver Lucas-Mas, Raul Felix Junquera-Varela. *Economic and Legal Issues of Taxing the Digital Economy*. https://doi.org/10.1596/978-1-4648-1654-3_ch4

100 Organisation for Economic Cooperation and Development (2021). https://www.oecd.org/tax/forum-on-tax-administration/publications-and-products/international-compliance-assurance-programme-handbook-for-tax-administrations-and-mne-groups.pdf

101 Ibid., p. 7.

4 Insurance

4.1 Introduction

The transformation of the digital economy requires that business models be revised and restructured. As mentioned briefly in Chapter 1, data and cybersecurity laws are recent additions to the legal framework. They have been established by governments in response to the concerns that individuals and entities alike have in relation to the vulnerability of their personal and commercial data transmitted over the internet. Subsequently, there has been the emergence of additional economic activity in the insurance sector, where insurance has had to be rethought. It has been argued that 'traditional insurance companies are operated according to certain key features'.[1] First, insurers sign many insurance contracts with customers, allowing insurers to pool risk from various insureds in return for a cash premium. In doing so, insurers can provide insurance coverage for a range of customers who may be exposed to varying degrees of risk, although, to some extent, low-risk customers subsidise high-risk ones.[2] Second, they generate more income by relying on collected premiums.[3] Thus, insurers are generally exposed to a variety of risk factors including the underlying insurance risk, investment risk, and concentration risk. Third, retail or business customers are generally limited to off-the-shelf policies offered by insurance companies, with the exception of bespoke insurance policies negotiated individually (at a price) with a broker or insurer.[4]

What has emerged is the concept of InsurTech, which can be applied throughout the life cycle of an insurance product, from product development, underwriting, and distribution of platforms to administration and claims processing.[5] It is a platform that can help to facilitate insurance (smart) contracts.

1 Lin Lin, Christopher Chen, The Promise and Perils of InsurTech, *NUS Law Working Paper, 2019/021; NUS Centre for Banking & Finance Law Working Paper, 19/03*, p. 5. https://law.nus.edu.sg/cbfl/wp-content/uploads/sites/5/2020/04/021_2019_Lin-Lin.pdf

2 Ibid.

3 Ibid.

4 Ibid.

5 Ibid., p. 9.

DOI: 10.4324/9781003511687-4

Since the establishment of this technology, others have arrived on the open market and, as the sector matures, more products will be available to streamline the contractual components of insurance contracts.

Notwithstanding the above, one of the growth areas in the insurance sector as a whole is the collection, use, storage, and trading of personal data. It has been noted that:

> Data protection is an area that will require closer examination by regulators, as the volume of personal data handled by insurers increases, whether consensus was gained for the intended use becomes blurred. Data aggregation brings forth the possibility of certain segment of the population becoming uninsurable, so how data is harnessed should be closely considered. The treatment of algorithms is also an area for further discussion to ensure that the assumptions built in are appropriate and unintended consequences are avoided in so far as possible, and regulators have a means of engaging in this assessment. These could have implications on the ongoing monitoring of operational risk and internal control of insurers.[6]

Such is the evolution of the insurance sector in the digital economy that transformations are occurring annually. As this book has demonstrated, there are many features of the technology age that are reshaping nearly every sector. This can be seen from smart contracts to the use of AI and robots. The OECD (Organisation for Economic Cooperation and Development) has provided the following descriptions of various technologies being implemented today:

Algorithms are part of AI, where there is a set of steps for a computer programme to achieve a task under certain conditions. In the financial sector, algorithmic trading, such as high frequency trading, is wide spread, with pre-programmed trading instructions to execute large trading orders. The algorithm would follow a set of conditional instructions for placing a trade order at a speed and frequency that is not posssible for a human trader.

Robo-advice, or automated advice, is becoming prominent particularly for online investment and savings platforms. It can cover a broad spectrum of services, but is essentially an 'on-line automated advice model that ha[s] the ability to deliver advice in a more cost-efficient way'. Robo-advice is being developed for investment management and is now being increasingly used for quotes with automated advice and

6 Organisation for Economic Cooperation and Development, Technology and Innovation in the Insurance Sector (2017), p. 7. http.s://www.oecd.org/pensions/Technology-and-innovation-in-the-insurance-sector.pdf

offerings calculated through algorithms. Instead of or combined with face-to-face advice, robo-advice can provide automated guidance and execution on various financial decisions. Automated advice could assist pockets of population that do not have access to financial advice to gain input in a more cost-efficient way than a human advisor. However, depending on how the algorithm to provide advice is structured, it could also lead to inappropriate advice being made inadvertently.

Smart contract refers to any contract which is capable of executing or enforcing itself. They are written as programming code which can be run on a computer or a network of computers rather than in legal language on a printed document. This code can define strict rules and consequences that emulate a traditional legal document, stating the obligations, benefits and penalties due to either party being in various circumstances. Smart contracts often run on blockchains or distributed ledger technology.

Blockchain or distributed ledger technology is a protocol for the exchange of values or data over the internet which does not require an intermediary. The protocol of blockchain technology is to create a shared, encrypted database of transactions and other information. The technology is to establish an ever-lengthening chain of blocks of data. Each block has compact record of validated transaction by participants in the blockchain, and the premise of blockchain is that the information in the blocks is true. Once the transaction is validated and recorded, the stored record is irreversible. Blockchain originally referred to the database where all Bitcoin transactions are recorded and stored.[7]

The technologies described above are more than five years old, and technology advancements are so rapid that these developments are likely to have evolved into something even more efficient. There are also other distributed ledgers available that are not a blockchain. The point is that sophisticated technology is here to stay, and will be improved to provide even greater efficiencies. The OECD also states:

> While innovations are generally a positive development, there are a number of potential policy and regulatory ramifications which can create some uncertainty and certain limitations in business developments. In terms of competition policy, the potential to have new entrants to the market through the application of innovations and new technologies could bring greater consumer utility. The rationale for competition law or policy is to improve the consumers' welfare and the efficiency in production

7 Ibid., p. 12.

> and supply, which would lead to lower prices and wider choice. The possibility of new entrants in the form of start-ups and greater choice as a result of innovation and technology could bring a number of positive developments to competition in the insurance market.[8]

The challenge for the digital economy is that those players that arrived at the onset of the new economic activities have generally captured the market. Some view this as a level of anti-competition. However, should entities or individuals be penalised because they were first? In short, they should not. However, over time, the community will naturally demand that more people be able to access the market to create more choice and competition. More generally:

> innovations are a positive development, there are a number of potential policy and regulatory ramifications which can create some uncertainty and certain limitations in business developments. In terms of competition policy, the potential to have new entrants to the market through the application of innovations and new technologies could bring greater consumer utility. The rationale for competition law or policy is to improve the consumers' welfare and the efficiency in production and supply, which would lead to lower prices and wider choice. The possibility of new entrants in the form of start-ups and greater choice as a result of innovation and technology could bring a number of positive developments to competition in the insurance market.[9]

A further challenge is how to fully reconcile where and how data is now being dispersed:

- Paper document delivery provisions
- Medical examinations (absence of Telehealth)
- Insurance distribution regulation: Documents required for claim processing
- Data protection, data localisation, privacy regulation
- Wet signatures and other signature requirements
- Inability to enter into an insurance contract digitally
- Restrictions on how and where insurers can transact with their clients
- Prescriptive sales and marketing requirements
- Anti-money laundering and combating the financing of terrorism (AML/CFT)
- Provisions around electronic premium payments Insurance not listed as 'essential service' by government authorities

8 Ibid., p. 29.

9 Pawan Kumar, Sanjay Taneja, Mukul, Ercan Özen, *Digital Transformation of the Insurance Industry – A Case of the Indian Insurance Sector* (14 July 2023). https://doi.org/10.1002/9781394167944.ch6

- Know your customer (KYC) requirements
- Provisions for electronic claims payments[10]

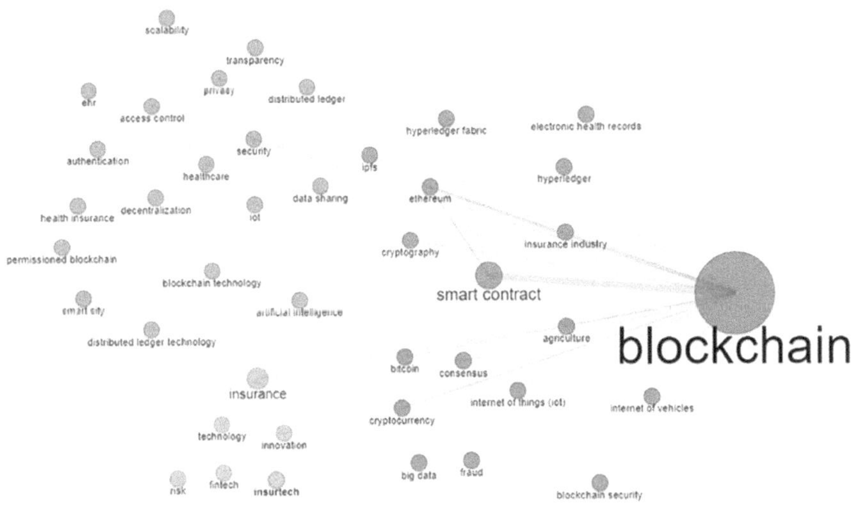

Figure 4.1 Data Captures by Insurance Sector

Data will be used by AI, quantum computing, and robots. It will have a transformative influence on the insurance sector. It has the ability to be aggregated and provide new products. For instance, the extent to which data is being applied across the insurance sector and, more specifically, blockchain is depicted below.[11]

The reach of blockchain is enormous. The diagram above indicates that the technology of blockchain is central to smart contracts (marked by the thick red line) and the insurance sector. In relation to insurance, blockchain has a two-fold application. First, a smart contract established on blockchain can be used to govern the insurance product between the insurance entity and the customer. Second, blockchain technology provides opportunities for different and new forms of insurance products to be created. However, there are several problems in this regard:

10 Dennis Noordhoek, *The Geneva Association, Regulatory Considerations for Digital Insurance Business Models* (2021), p. 12. https://www.genevaassociation.org/sites/default/files/digitalinsurance_web.pdf

11 Ankitha Shetty, Adithya D Shetty, Rashmi Yogesh Pai, Rohini R Rao, Rakshith Bhandary, Jyothi Shetty, Santosh Nayak, Tantri Keerthi Dinesh, Komal Jenifer Dsouza, Block Chain Application in Insurance Services: A Systematic Review of the Evidence, *Sage Open*, *12* (1) (2022). https://doi.org/10.1177/21582440221079877

> The insurance market is an asymmetric information market in which the customer and the insurer each have their own set of information that they do not want to share about each other. Insurance firms often try to gather sufficient information about the health of the insured when the insured buys life insurance, while the customer often wishes to mask those health conditions. To achieve the full exchange of knowledge and information on medical insurance and other forms of insurance, a broad consensus on the creation of blockchain must be established by the entire society. Achieving total sharing of information through industry-wide adoption of blockchain is difficult. Secondly, insurance products have distinct business structures or models that function differently, from life insurance and property insurance. The operating earnings of insurance institutions would be influenced by each of these variables. Whether a particular insurance policy is acceptable for the implementation of blockchain technology needs to be independently demonstrated, but the insurance companies' research on this aspect is just beginning.[12]

Viewed this way, and two years on, it is argued that the second point mentioned above is far from settled. More research needs to be undertaken on the insurance sector to fully understand the impact and adoption of blockchain technology. Furthermore, what has not been fully appraised is the impact on the legal and regulatory regime that is supported by many insurance products. For instance, an insurance product for technology and cybersecurity is very different from that of shipping. Hence, an insurance policy has to address different risks and impacts depending on a particular sector's characteristics and requirements. On the other hand, the very different legal frameworks for the smart contracts that will be used by the insurance sector will come with significant benefits, while also posing a level of challenges. In their study, Ankitha Shetty et al. found that:

> Blockchain insurance, distributed ledger, cryptography, and smart contract has the potential to generate disruption in the insurance industry it incorporates in triggered smart contracts, envisages better pricing and risk assessment and increases the back-end efficiency. A bright focus on designing an efficient approach for the processing of insurance related transactions that is based on a blockchain-enabled platform is the need of the hour in the service industry. In order to realise the actual potential of blockchain, insurers should incorporate other technologies in tandem, that includes advanced analytics, internet of things and artificial intelligence. The use of blockchain and blockchain based smart contracts by the insurance industry can bring about more transparency that benefits a

12 Ibid., pp. 5–11.

> company through making it more trustworthy, since data entered in the blockchain cannot be tampered with.[13]

Against the backdrop of the above, the insurance sector is another area that is likely to be significantly transformed over the next five years. It will most probably adopt blockchain technology and smart contracts to facilitate the sale and governance of insurance products, whether it be for data, cybersecurity, AI, and, possibly, quantum technology. The point is that as the insurance sector evolves by adopting new technology, it will also be required to determine the products that should be available to protect the business community. This section will examine the current-day *Insurance Contract Act* of Australia, Singapore,[14] the UK[15] and the US.[16] This section will discuss only Australia as an example and does not compare the statutes of other states. It illustrates how the concept of good faith is an important feature of insurance contracts.

Australia adopted the *Insurance Contracts* Act (ICA)[17] in 1984. In section 9, the application of this Act extends to contracts of insurance and proposed contracts of insurance, the proper law of which is or would be the law of a state or the law of a territory in which this Act applies or to which this Act extends.[18] Section 9 specifies exemptions for the health sector and pleasure craft used in the marine sector. Importantly, section 13 provides an overarching obligation to act in good faith.[19] The concept of good faith is not new to contract law. This also includes contracts for insurance that relate to consumers. The background of the *Carter* case was as follows:

> Governor Carter had charge of Fort Marlborough, a still-standing British-built fort on the island of Sumatra, in what is now Indonesia. He decided that there was a danger of the fort being attacked. He therefore wrote to a brother in England and asked him to arrange for the fort to be insured for a year. Thereafter, the brother liaised with Mr Boehm who eventually agreed to ensure the fort, the contingency being 'whether

13 Ankitha Shetty, Adithya D Shetty, Rashmi Yogesh Pai, Rohini R Rao, Rakshith Bhandary, Jyothi Shetty, Santosh Nayak, Tantri Keerthi Dinesh, Komal Jenifer Dsouza, Block Chain Application in Insurance Services: A Systematic Review of the Evidence *Artificial Intelligence for Smart Society – Literature Review* (2022), 13–14.

14 *Insurance Act 1966*. https://sso.agc.gov.sg/Act/IA1966

15 *Insurance Act 2015*, section 1 deals with contracts. https://www.legislation.gov.uk/ukpga/2015/4/enacted/data.pdf

16 Insurance, National Banks. https://uscode.house.gov/view.xhtml?path=/prelim@title15/chapter93&edition=prelim Also see *McCarran-Ferguson Act 1945*. https://www.govinfo.gov/content/pkg/COMPS-12153/pdf/COMPS-12153.pdf Note – each US state and territory has its own insurance laws and administration of insurance contracts.

17 *Insurance Contract Act 1984*. https://www.legislation.gov.au/Details/C2021C00108

18 Ibid., section 8 and 9.

19 Ibid., section 13.

> Fort Marlborough was or would be taken, by a European enemy, between October 1758, and October 1760'. The policy was signed in May 1760. As matters turned out, Fort Marlborough had been captured in April 1760 by French troops headed by the Comte d'Estaing, a notably successful 18 century French general and admiral who, despite his services to the French nation and his initial sympathies for the French Revolution, was ultimately guillotined during the Reign of Terror. A claim under the insurance policy followed on, court proceedings ensued in London, the matter was tried by Lord Mansfield before a special jury of merchants in April 1766, and a verdict was returned for Governor Carter. Thereafter, an unsuccessful application was made for a re-trial on the basis that the circumstances by reference to which the insurance was effected had not been sufficiently disclosed to the insurer. It was this application for re-trial that yielded Lord Mansfield's renowned judgment. At the heart of the application was the insurer's contention that the insurance had been obtained by way of fraud, specifically through the concealment of circumstances that ought to have been disclosed, viz. the weakness of the fort and the probability of its being attacked by the French, factors which, it was proved, had been disclosed by Governor Carter in a couple of letters, one to his brother and another to the East India Company.[20]

While this case was heard over a century ago, it has been influential in establishing a platform for the application of the concept in the modern-day contracts of most common law countries. In the case of Carter, it was established by the court that the governing principle is applicable to all 'contracts and dealings'; good faith forbids either party, by concealing what he privately knows, to draw the other into a bargain from his ignorance of that fact, and his believing the contrary; either party may be innocently silent, as to grounds open to both, to exercise their judgment upon'; and it is a mutual duty. The problem of unfairness and how to resolve it was an issue shouldered by both parties, not one thrust unreservedly by the law onto the shoulders of an insured party'.[21] In the common law countries examined in this chapter (Australia, the UK,[22] Singapore,[23] and the US[24]), the concept of good faith is well-entrenched in both statutory and case law.

20 *Carter v Boehm* (n 143) 1164 [1910]. https://www.ijsj.ie/assets/uploads/documents/pdfs/2020-Edition-01/6.%20Max%20Barrett%20.pdf

21 Ibid.

22 *Carter v Boehm* (n 143) 1164 [1910]. https://www.ijsj.ie/assets/uploads/documents/pdfs/2020-Edition-01/6.%20Max%20Barrett%20.pdf

23 Colin Liew, A Leap of Good Faith in Singapore Contract Law, *Singapore Journal of Legal Studies* (December 2012), 416–440

24 *Carter v Boehm* (n 143) 1164 [1910]. https://www.ijsj.ie/assets/uploads/documents/pdfs/2020-Edition-01/6.%20Max%20Barrett%20.pdf

Problematic is the way that blockchain technology operates in relation to smart contracts. It has been recently asserted that the 'concrete nature of smart contracts can eliminate the "good faith" or "reasonableness" subjectivity that often exists in traditional contracts'.[25] Put another way, under smart contracts, the concepts of 'good faith and negligence are also very difficult to encode'.[26] In further support of this view, it has been argued that:

> In addition to good faith, standard legal agreements also include representations and warranties which cannot be programmed by reference solely to data stored or managed on a blockchain-based network. In the case of warranties, complexity is an issue insofar as the test for determining what is a warranty and not a condition of the agreement is defined in relation to the 'general nature of the contract'.[27]

In support of the above, Edward McDonald asserted that smart contracts themselves:

> Being self-executing and written in code leads to a second feature, they are inherently unambiguous. A smart contract can rely only on its code and the available data, and based on that data it will either execute or not. This makes it unambiguous in that anyone who has the expertise to read a contract's code will be able to know ***ex ante*** the outcome it prescribes for any set of circumstances. This makes it (nearly) impossible to insert clauses that rely on qualitative judgements calls. There are benefits and drawbacks to having a contract that is inherently unambiguous. A lack of ambiguity can reduce the possibility of litigation and can lead to quicker execution. On the other hand, there are clauses and default rules that do not work within smart contracts, like good faith clauses.[28]

A further important issue that has arisen is that:

> smart contracts, and their attempt to circumvent state intervention, illustrate how singularly protecting freedom of contract (and the principles such as good faith that underpin contract development and

25 Armand Zottala, Channing Gatewood, Smart Contracts: A Brief Overview. *Tech Contract Quick Bytes* (2023). https://www.lexology.com/library/detail.aspx?g=f366313d-d947-4f87-aa2d-12050a0eb5ed

26 *A Beginner's Guide to Smart Contracts.* https://www.tamimi.com/pdflawupdate/?pageID=7364

27 William Brown, Limitations of Code in Contracts: What We Can Learn from The Plain English Movement, *Victoria University Law and Justice Journal* (2019), 66–67. https://vulj.vu.edu.au/index.php/vulj/article/view/1148/1768

28 Edward McDonald, Smart Contracts, *Columbia Business Law Review* (2021). https://journals.library.columbia.edu/index.php/CBLR/announcement/view/445

> implementation) is practically unfeasible and likely to lead to an imbalance between parties and resultantly unfavourable outcomes which are contrary to perceived notions of fairness and justice. This cements the proposition that English law ***requires*** a guiding doctrine of good faith, as a companion to its manifest propagation of freedom of contract.[29]
>
> [emphasis added]

Viewed this way, and unless blockchain technology can be updated so that these principles can be formally accepted and form part of the smart contract itself, this will raise complex issues for the interpretation of contracts under the law. This is one of several problems and challenges that the judiciary will face in the future. It could change the structure of long-held doctrines for contract law and, over time, they may become no longer relevant. In recent work, the UK Law Commission[30] made the point that

> some parties will transact on the blind faith that the code works as they expect it to, some will read the code to make sure they understand it and some will undertake verification and/or audit procedures to provide them with external assurances as to the potential outcomes of the code.[31]

Importantly, it was highlighted that applying the concept of 'good faith on the basis that they are not expressed fully, clearly, and legibly, and serve to take advantage of the consumer's lack of familiarity with code'[32] is problematic. On the one hand, it creates a lack of transparency in contract dealings and could be considered by the courts as not meeting the criteria for good faith and fairness. On the other hand, it is outside the scope of this book to deal with fairness in this chapter. In an example of good faith and the application of an order of rectification, the Law Commission noted that:

> The court may order rectification on the basis that it would be contrary to good faith for a party to enforce a contract which it knew was inconsistent with the bargain that the other party believed was being made at the time of entry into the contract. Alice could send the code to Bob for review, stating that she has received assurances from her coder that the code reflects the terms of the document. Bob's coder notices that the pricing formula is inaccurately recorded, and informs Bob. Bob, however, realising that the erroneous pricing formula works to his advantage,

29 Ipsa Yadav, *Are Smart Contracts* **Smart** *Enough? An Analysis through, and of, Good Faith and Freedom of Contract* (2022). https://blog.lselawreview.com/2022/04/smart-contracts-smart-enough-analysis-through-of-good-faith-freedom-contract

30 United Kingdom Law Commission, 5.47. https://s3-eu-west-2.amazonaws.com/lawcom-prod-storage-11jsxou24uy7q/uploads/2021/11/Smart-legal-contracts-accessible.pdf

31 Ibid.

32 Ibid., p. 160.

> does not tell Alice. In principle, Alice may have a claim to rectification in this scenario on the basis that she was mistaken about the terms of the code, and Bob knew this at the time the contract was made.[33]

Therefore, the Law Commission took the view that 'a court could make an order for rectification to amend the coded terms of a smart legal contract in a variety of circumstances'.[34] Although this would be the optimal outcome, it is also noted that the court may not be able to order that the code be modified as this is a difficult task in practice.[35] However, some have argued that to address the above, the 'issuing of a new code'[36] could reconcile this problem. The other problem that will arise is: when the code has already been used, amending it and addressing the above will be all but impossible. The ensuing question is whether rectification can be applied to address the above and the other errors in smart contracts. These will be more difficult to overcome. In part, this will depend on the platform that is being used and whether the smart [insurance] contract is fully coded or partially coded. The Law Commission noted that:

> Suppose Alice deploys a computer program on a cryptocurrency exchange platform. The program is coded to purchase bitcoin on Alice's behalf at the best available price on the platform. Bob also deploys a computer program on the platform, which is designed to sell bitcoin. Bob's program is coded so that, if there are no other offers to sell bitcoin on the platform, the program is to offer bitcoin at a highly inflated price. A system error occurs on the platform, which dramatically reduces the number of offers to sell bitcoin on the platform. As a result, Bob's program automatically offers bitcoin at the highly inflated price, and Alice's program automatically accepts that offer, it being the best available price for bitcoin on the platform. A contract for the sale of bitcoin is formed and the transaction is performed by the parties' programs. Alice, realising what has happened, claims that the contract is void for unilateral mistake. She says she believed, mistakenly, that bitcoin transactions on the platform would be concluded at prices approximating market rates, and Bob took advantage of this mistake by embedding a highly inflated price in his program.[37]

To reconcile the above, the Law Commission looked to Singapore and the case of *Quoine Pte Ltd v B2C2 Ltd ('Quoine')*.[38] In that case:

33 Ibid., 5.12, p. 106.
34 Ibid., 5.14, p. 106.
35 Ibid., p. 107.
36 Ibid., p. 108.
37 Ibid., p. 118.
38 Ibid., p. 118. [2020] SGCA(I) 02 (*Quoine*).

> the majority rejected the argument that the contract was void for unilateral mistake. The Court reasoned that there was no mistake as to the terms of the contract (namely, the price of the bitcoin), because the parties' computer programs had operated exactly as designed. The purchaser of the bitcoin had merely made a mistake as to how the programs would behave in the event of a system failure on the platform. This was not sufficient for a unilateral mistake. In any event, even if this were a relevant mistake, the seller did not have knowledge of it.[39]

Additionally, in relation to computer programs, the Law Commission made the point that:

> As the contract was made by deterministic computer programs, meaning that they were always going to operate within the parameters set by the programmer, the relevant enquiry was whether the programmer had designed its program to take advantage of the type of system failure that occurred.[40]

On that basis, the Law Commission again drew upon *Quoine*, noting that:

> The majority framed the enquiry as follows: when programming the algorithm, was the programmer doing so with actual or constructive knowledge of the fact that the relevant offer would only ever be accepted by a party operating under a mistake, and was the programmer acting to take advantage of such a mistake? The evidence in *Quoine* fell short of establishing that the programmer had this state of mind when designing the program.[41]

This only briefly touched on the issues that can arise for smart contracts that will facilitate and govern insurance products and, more broadly, consumer contracts. In proceeding with the use of smart contracts for insurance products, the Law Commission adopted a ten-point plan specifying that:

1. Before entering into a smart legal contract, parties should consider engaging in a rigorous planning phase to understand business requirements, and the objectives of the smart legal contract.
2. Parties should give thought as to the form the smart legal contract will take, and whether the form will vary between individual obligations.

39 Ibid.
40 Ibid.
41 Ibid.

3. Parties would be well advised to make clear the role of the code in their smart legal contract and, in particular, to specify if the code is intended both to define contractual obligations as well as to perform them, or only to perform them.
4. Parties should consider the relationship between any natural language and coded terms. In particular, where the same term is expressed in both natural language and in code, parties would be well advised to make clear which term takes precedence in the event of a conflict.
5. Smart legal contracts and associated technologies require parties to consider a broader range of factors before contracting than they would otherwise consider before concluding a traditional contract. Parties would be well advised to allocate risk in relation to, and to provide for (amongst other things): a) a malfunctioning oracle or inaccurate data inputs; b) external events beyond the parties' control which may affect performance of the code, such as system upgrades; c) bugs and coding errors in the code; and d) any potential mistakes that may arise due to the parties holding certain beliefs or assumptions about how the code will perform.
6. Parties would be well advised to make clear the role of any non-executable comments in the code and, in particular, if such comments constitute contractual terms.
7. Where the smart legal contract contains coded terms, parties would be well advised to provide a natural language explanation of the workings of the code, and to make clear that such explanation forms part of their contract. An understanding of the parties' intentions will be relevant in the event that the code performs in a way not expected by the parties.
8. Parties who intend their transactions on a distributed ledger system or other smart contract platform to create legal relations would be well advised to make this clear in natural language, either in a separate agreement or by way of comments in the code.
9. Parties would be well advised to consider designing the coded element of their smart legal contract such that performance of the code can be terminated if necessary. Thought will have to be given as to how best to structure this functionality so as to avoid any associated risks of abuse by one of the parties. Similarly, to avoid a scenario where the code performs pending the outcome of a dispute, parties would be well advised to provide a mechanism for suspension of performance of the code in their smart legal contract.
10. Parties would be well advised to include choice of court and choice of law clauses in their smart legal contract, either in a separate natural language agreement, or by way of comments in the code.[42]

42 Ibid., pp. 211–212.

Given the above, it appears that a lawyer's role will become more complex as the use of smart contracts increases. This will depend on the program used to engage the software and smart contract. It will further depend on whether the smart contract is going to be fully coded, or only part thereof. The smart contracts could be significantly compromised if the system program is compromised and stops during the phase of contractual development. Furthermore, choice of court and choice of law clauses should be established. In taking this further, dispute resolution clauses should also be established so that arbitration can be utilised. While the above was developed and proposed in 2019–2020, the question arises whether, over time, the technology can be improved to reconcile the aforementioned issues. Finally, the application of long-standing doctrines in contract law, such as good faith, amongst others, is going to be challenged under the new framework of smart contracts. It will take some work by both the technology and judiciary to address this issue. The judiciary cannot rely solely on any statutory provisions for the doctrines themselves when they have not been included in the contract clauses specifically. This inclusion could be just a simple reference framed to ensure that the doctrine of good faith does apply to the development and implementation of this contract. That could allow the judiciary to circumvent the subjective nature of the application of these doctrines because they are not generally referred to in contracts.

The question arises as to whether a smart contract falls within the meaning of the insurance laws and statutory provisions of the respective countries. First, and without an in-depth analysis, it is argued that smart contracts apply to the respective insurance statutory laws. Second, smart contracts apply the general contractual legal concepts of contract law, including offer, acceptance, and a level of consideration. During the traditional formation of a contract, the negotiations between individuals are generally both expressed and implied. Thus, this will fall within the respective insurance legislative provisions for contracts. Third, if there is no person-to-person contact specified within the contractual negotiations, this could become a challenge and a dilemma that the judiciary may have to reconcile. This is because the traditional notions of pre-contractual and contractual negotiations diverge and are undertaken solely through technology/computer programs that remove any person-to-person contact. The judiciary will need to determine the type of negotiations that were undertaken through blockchain technology, if any. The question that would need to be addressed is twofold. First, is the person inputting the information liable? Second, is the owner of the computer program responsible? These are issues for the courts to resolve. In my view, provided the computer program has not been tampered with by the user and is a standard program that can be used by anyone, it should be the person inputting this information who has responsibility. The Law Commission in the UK is of the view that interactions taking place only via the digitalised ledger and not in person can still constitute an offer and acceptance.[43] Should this become accepted

43 Ibid., p. 40.

practice, it is likely that courts from other jurisdictions outside the UK will follow. However, the business community will never fully know until such a dispute is decided upon in and by the courts.

Despite the above, some clarity can be found in the UK case of *Software Solutions*[44] where software systems were used by insurers to develop products. At issue was Software Solutions Partners Limited (SSP) against Her Majesty's Commissioners for Customs and Excise (now merged into HM Revenue and Customs) (Customs), and the systems used constituted an offer. That is,

> SSP designs, supplies, installs and maintains certain computer software, and provides ancillary computer hardware, for the insurance industry. The SSP software enables those insurance brokers who have access to it to carry out certain insurance transactions with those insurers with whom SSP has made previous arrangements and whose electronic communication systems are linked through SSP to the brokers.[45]

At the time, the UK was a member of the European Union. Nevertheless, the court, in regards to the formation of the contract by electronic means, stated that 'all the information necessary for electronic contract formation has been preprogrammed, according to strict parameters laid down by the insurer, in the SSP computer software. The relevant data is, therefore, processed automatically by electronic means through the computer software, and the transactions are self-executing within the specified parameters predetermined in the program.[46] The court went further to point out that the process undertaken by the parties to establish the contract was, in fact, automated, and the relevant insurers, expressly or impliedly, invited brokers who had access to the appropriate SSP software to use the computer programme in order to undertake contract formation and that the insurers undertook that, if the brokers followed the pre-programmed procedures, they would be bound by the automatically generated result.[47] Notwithstanding the above, in relying on *Thornton v Shoe Lane Parking [1971] 2 QB 163*, the court held that a ticket-vending machine constituted an offer, and *insurers hold out the SSP software as the automatic medium for contract formation*.[48] This case involved parties inputting information into a system that, in turn, generated a contract. The long-standing principles of formation of a contract had been established, just in a different way from the traditional means. Below are two recent cases that indicate the extent of the vulnerability of data in the new digital economy.

44 *Software Solutions Partners Ltd, R (on the application of) v HM Customs & Excise [2007] EWHC 971*. https://www.casemine.com/judgement/uk/5a8ff7b060d03e7f57eb13ec
45 Ibid., para 2.
46 Ibid., para 20
47 Ibid., para 65.
48 Ibid., paras 66–67.

While not specifically related to insurance contracts, they highlight the interconnectedness of the technology when data is being utilised, and the question is whether, over time, insurance products can be developed to manage these matters. Doing so would, to some extent, allow the issues to be dealt with outside of court.

4.2 Data – Cybersecurity

In the Singapore case, *Razer*[49] 2022, a 'dispute arose over the misconfiguration of a server file, which in turn led to a leak of Razer's non-public customer data (personal data). The plaintiff brings claims in contract and negligence against the defendant, its information technology consultant'.[50] Essentially, the claim went against the contractual terms between the parties. From a negligence perspective, 'on or about 15 June 2020, Mr Pradeep Annaiah (Pradeep), a Project Manager employed by Razer at the material time, was unable to log into and access the Kibana server and/or its application (Login Problem)'.[51] The case demonstrates just how complex data and cybersecurity matters have become. When combined with AI and quantum technology, those complexities could increase. There was a complex transformation-integration of Cloud-based technology to be undertaken. An important question is whether these types of issues could be resolved through AI and quantum technology implemented in the insurance sector in the future.

Razer engaged WSL for the MuleSoft integration as the latter was voted top MuleSoft solution partner of the year. Razer and WSL entered the CSA (consulting services agreement) on 1 March 2019. It is undisputed that the CSA acted as a sort of master agreement, and contained statements of work (SOW) detailing the services required at different stages of the MuleSoft project.[52] CSAs have become a common tool used by parties when undertaking contractual work. In this case, the

> CSA was entered into between Razer and WSL and became effective on 1 March 2019. Under cls 1.1 and 1.2 of the CSA, Razer retained WSL to perform consulting services. These consulting services and any additional services would be detailed in subsequent SOWs, which would be subject to terms and conditions set out in the CSA.[53]

More specifically, the court identified that according to cl 3(ii), WSL guaranteed that its services to Razer would be performed. It stated:

49 *Razer (Asia-Pacific) Pte Ltd v Capgemini Singapore Pte Ltd* [2022] SGHC 310
50 Ibid., para 1.
51 Ibid., para 19.
52 Ibid., para 1–3.
53 Ibid., paras 8–9.

(a) in a professional and timely manner and shall be of an appropriate proficiency, nature and quality, but in any case no less than the proficiency, nature, skill and care expected of an international firm or service provider providing similar services; (b) using personnel with the appropriate and adequate skill, qualifications and experience; (c) using reasonable methods and due care to protect against adware, viruses, worms, malware and any harmful code that might disrupt, disable, harm or otherwise impede the operation or performance of the Services (or [Razer]'s computer and other systems or network); (d) in compliance with all applicable laws (including data privacy and personal data protection laws) and such reasonable instructions and policies as [Razer] may prescribe from time to time; and (e) in compliance with any applicable service levels, KPIs, standards, warranties or other requirements set out in the corresponding Statement of Work or Exhibit. In addition, and without prejudice to any other rights of [Razer], [Razer] shall be entitled to require [WSL] to promptly, at [Razer]'s election, remedy or re-perform any Services which do not comply with the requirements of this Agreement or any Statement of Work / Exhibit, or provide a refund of any amounts paid for such Services.[54]

The importance of this contractual term cannot be underestimated. It called for the WSL to be proficient, have the required skills, qualifications, and experience when using methods to protect Razer's systems from adware, viruses, worms, malware, and any harmful code. It also required that WSL comply with relevant data laws and standards and take relevant action when non-compliance had been identified. The conditions went further, stating that where WSL could not address the issue, they were to refund Razer for that particular work. Throughout the life of the project, there were a number of SOWs agreed upon to access customer data, deploy the MuleSoft platform for a period of 12 months, and provide resources such as technical support between February and April 2020.[55] These came after the 2019 Data Processing Addendum (DPA), highlighting WSL's obligations in regard to the management of personal data.[56] Thus, unlike the traditional trade in goods and services under contract, the technology sector is very different. What has emerged is a number of contractual tools and/or agreements that have been developed either as single instruments or as attachments to a wider contract. Therefore, such an instrument is outside of the current legislation on, for example, data or cyber laws. They themselves do not specify how a contract would be formed and what it would constitute. An example under data laws is the Data Impact Assessment, which is an obligation specified by the data laws of many countries

54 Ibid., 10–14.
55 Ibid.
56 Ibid., para 15.

to ensure there is a similar level of protection of personal data when sharing or trading it with an entity in a third country.

Specifically, Razer sought declaratory relief according to cl 12 of the CSA and cl 12 of the DPA, because part of cl 12 of the CSA states that:

> Each party shall indemnify and hold harmless the other party and, at either party's request, defend the other party, its subsidiaries and affiliates from and against all claims, liabilities, damages, losses and expenses, including, but not limited to reasonable legal fees and costs of suit ... arising out of or in connection with any negligent, malicious or wilful act or any negligent, malicious or wilful omission of the other party, its employees, agents, suppliers or subcontractors, including but not limited to, liability arising from any injury or death to persons or loss of or injury to property resulting from the other party's failure to fulfil any obligation under this Agreement.[57]

On the other hand, cl 12 of the DPA provided:

> [Capgemini] shall, at all times during and after the term of the Agreement, indemnify [Razer] and its Affiliates against losses, damages, costs or expenses and other liabilities (including legal fees) incurred by [Razer] and its Affiliates arising out of or in connection with any (a) breach of [Capgemini's] obligations under this DPA, (b) [Capgemini's] negligence or wilful misconduct or (c) any Security Incident.[58]

Hence, the court ruled that based on clause 12 of the CSA and DPA, Capgemini had breached its obligations. Thus, the CSA and DPA were treated as a type of contract because of the obligations they imposed on the parties. Further, the court ruled that there was a level of negligence by Capgemini because of the login problem. Could an insurance contract/product adequately deal with the above? The short answer is that products are being developed for the new digital economy and, therefore, appropriate ones could be developed in the future to address the above.

In the case of *Reed*,[59] an appeal was upheld by the court in relation to the loss or damage according to section 32(1) of the Personal Data Protection Act 2012 (Act 26 of 2012) (PDPA).[60] The PDPA is the principal legislation in Singapore that regulates the collection, use, and storage of personal data. It was established over a decade ago and has been instrumental in influencing data laws throughout South East Asia. Section 32(1) confers the:

57 *Razer (Asia-Pacific) Pte Ltd v Capgemini Singapore Pte Ltd* [2022] SGHC 310, para 157.
58 Ibid., para 158.
59 *Reed, Michael v Bellingham, Alex* [2022] SGCA 60
60 Ibid., para 1.

> right of private action on any person who suffers loss or damage directly as a result of the contravention of any provision in Part IV, V or VI of the PDPA. It is the appellant's case that his emotional distress and the loss of control of his personal data fall within the meaning of 'loss or damage', and that he is therefore entitled to claim injunctive relief under s 32.[61]

This provision is quite powerful. Section 32 states the right of private action:

> 32.— (1) Any person who suffers loss or damage directly as a result of a contravention of any provision in Part IV, V or VI by an organisation shall have a right of action for relief in civil proceedings in a court.
>
> (2) If the Commission has made a decision under this Act in respect of a contravention specified in subsection (1), no action accruing under subsection (1) may be brought in respect of that contravention until after the decision has become final as a result of there being no further right of appeal.
>
> (3) The court may grant to the plaintiff in an action under subsection (1) all or any of the following: (*a*) relief by way of injunction or declaration; (*b*) damages; (*c*) such other relief as the court thinks fit.[62]

Against the backdrop of the above, the court stated that the issues to be determined were:

(a) whether section 4(1)(*b*) of the PDPA exempts the respondent from liability for breaching ss 13 and 18 of the PDPA;
(b) whether 'loss or damage' in section 32(1) includes emotional distress or loss of control of personal data; and
(c) whether the appellant suffered emotional distress or loss of control of personal data.[63]

In relation to the first point, section 4(1)(*b*) of the PDPA, the court noted that:

> we regard s 4(1) as being a defence that a party who is accused of breaching the PDPA may invoke to avoid liability for the putative breach. The corollary of this is that the burden of proof lies on the defendant to establish, on the balance of probabilities, the requirement(s) of the particular limb in s 4(1) on which reliance is placed. In the respondent's case, he must prove that he was 'acting in the course of his employment with an organisation' when the breaches of ss 13 and 18 PDPA

61 Ibid.
62 Ibid., para 3.
63 Ibid., para 35.

> occurred. Construing s 4(1) as a defence is consistent with principles of statutory construction. Treating s 4(1)(*b*) of the PDPA as a defence also promotes consistency with other parts of the PDPA. While s 48(1) does not expressly reference s 4(1)(*b*), it is in substance an application of the rule in s 4(1)(*b*). We see no reason for the burden of proof under ss 4(1)(*b*) and 48(1) to differ simply because the latter is a defence to a criminal charge rather than to a civil claim. Therefore, whenever an employee seeks to rely on s 4(1)(*b*) to avoid liability, he or she bears the legal burden of bringing himself or herself within the sub-section.[64]

Further, the court stated that:

> the PDPA supports reading s 4(1)(*b*) as a defence. The PDPA aims to strike a balance between 'the right of individuals to protect their personal data and the need of organisations to collect, use or disclose personal data for purposes that a reasonable person would consider appropriate in the circumstances. The respondent cannot now rely on s 4(1)(*b*) of the PDPA to exempt him from liability for breaching ss 13 and 18 of the PDPA by misusing the appellant's personal data'.[65]

The second point concerned whether the appellant was entitled to bring a section 32 action against him and apply for the injunctive relief provided for under section 32(3).[66] Thus, the court was required to differentiate between a statutory tort and a common law tort. The court argued that:

> For statutory torts, as the statute expressly creates the right of private action, the scope of that right of action is to be determined first and foremost by the principles of statutory construction. Common law principles are relevant only in so far as the rules of statutory construction permit. Conversely, for the tort of breach of statutory duty, the scope of the right of action and its attendant requirements are determined by the common law. The statute only provides the content of the duty which is alleged to have been breached.[67]

Thus, in taking the purposive approach to statutory interpretation, the court made the point that a reference to the level of emotional distress (loss-damage) can be found in section 32(1).[68] In drawing on earlier common law, the court ruled that:

64 Ibid., paras 42–43.
65 Ibid., paras 44 & 55.
66 Ibid., para 57.
67 Ibid., para 65.
68 Ibid., para 68.

> 'loss or damage' must have been suffered '***directly*** as a result of a contravention' [emphasis added] of identified provisions in the PDPA. Secondly, even if emotional distress is an actionable head of loss, there is no reason for the principle that there is no legal recourse for minimal loss (see *Rothwell v Chemical & Insulating Co Ltd and another and other suits* [2008] 1 AC 281 at [8]) not to apply. Thus, trivial annoyance or negative emotions which form part of the vicissitudes of life will not be actionable.[69]

The court concluded, after a lengthy analysis of section 32 and the direct or indirect impact that caused a level of loss or damage, that:

> the appellant indeed suffered 'loss or damage' within the meaning of s 32(1) directly resulting from the respondent's breaches of ss 13 and 18. He thereby obtained a right of private action under s 32(1).[70]

On that basis, the court upheld the injunction – appeal. This is another example where an insurance product could address the level of loss incurred by the parties involved, rather than proceeding to court. More specifically, in the US case of *P.F. Chang's v Federal Insurance Co.* that involved an insurance policy and a contract exclusion,[71] the court noted that:

> Pending before the Court is Defendant Federal Insurance Company's ('Federal') Motion for Summary Judgment. (Doc. 22.) P.F. Chang's China Bistro, Inc. ('Chang's') has responded and the matter is fully briefed. (Docs. 36, 38.) The Court heard Oral Arguments on the motion on April 19, 2016. (Doc. 41.) In essence, the main issue before the Court is whether coverage exists under the insurance policy between Chang's and Federal for the credit card association assessments that arose from the data breach Chang's suffered in 2013. The Court now issues following ruling.[72]

The data- and cyber-related issues were stated as follows:

> Record includes 'any information concerning a natural person that is defined as: (i) private personal information; (ii) personally identifiable information … pursuant to any federal, state … statute or regulation … where such information is held by an Insured Organization or on the Insured Organization's behalf by a Third Party Service Provider' or

69 Ibid., para 93.
70 Ibid., para 133.
71 *P.F. Chang's v Federal Insurance Co.* 2016 U.S. Dist. LEXIS 70749 (D. Ariz. 26 May 2016). https://casetext.com/case/pf-changs-china-bistro-inc-v-fed-ins-co
72 Ibid.

> 'an organization's non- public information that is ... in an Insured's or Third Party Service Provider's care, custody, or control' (Id.). 'Third Party Service Provider means an entity that performs the following services for, or on behalf of, an Insured Organization pursuant to a written agreement: (A) processing, holding or storing information; (B) providing data backup, data storage or data processing services'.[73]

In regard to the cybersecurity insurance policy, the court pointed out that:

> Federal sold a CyberSecurity by Chubb Policy ('Policy') to Chang's corporate parent, Wok Holdco LLC, with effective dates from January 1, 2014 to January 1, 2015. (Doc. 8-1 at 2.) On its website, Federal marketed the Policy as 'a flexible insurance solution designed by cyber risk experts to address the full breadth of risks associated with doing business in today's technology-dependent world' that '[c]overs direct loss, legal liability, and consequential loss resulting from cyber security breaches. Specific provisions of the Policy will be defined and discussed in greater detail below'.[74]

As part of the process to establish the insurance policy, the following emerged:

> During the underwriting processes, Federal classified Chang's as a high risk, PCI Level 1, client because Chang's conducts more than 6 million transactions per year. Further, because of the large number of Chang's transactions conducted with customer credit cards, Federal noted there was high exposure to potential customer identity theft. In 2014, Chang's paid an annual premium of $134,052.00 for the Policy.[75]

What followed was that after the insurance policy and contractual arrangements had been established,

> on June 10, 2014, Chang's learnt that computer hackers had obtained and posted on the Internet approximately 60,000 credit card numbers belonging to its customers (the 'security compromise' or 'data breach'). Chang's notified Federal of the data breach that very same day.[76]

Following the data breach on 2 March 2015, MasterCard issued:

> an 'ADC Operational Reimbursement/Fraud Recovery Final Acquirer Financial Responsibility Report' to BAMS. This MasterCard Report

73 Ibid., para 9.
74 Ibid., paras 2–4.
75 Ibid.
76 Ibid., paras 3–5.

> imposed three Assessments on BAMS, a Fraud Recovery Assessment of $1,716,798.85, an Operational Reimbursement Assessment of $163,122.72 for Chang's data breach, and a Case Management Fee of $50,000. The Fraud Recovery Assessment reflects costs, as calculated by MasterCard, associated with fraudulent charges that may have arisen from, or may be related to, the security compromise. The Operational Reimbursement Assessment reflects costs to notify cardholders affected by the security compromise and to reissue and deliver payment cards, new account numbers, and security codes to those cardholders.[77]

In regard to the contractual arrangements, the court noted that:

> The traditional view of the law of contracts is that a written agreement adopted by the parties will be viewed as an integrated contract which binds those parties to the terms expressed within the four corners of the agreement. However, the usual insurance policy is a special kind of contract, in part because it is not arrived at by negotiation between the parties. Instead, [i]t is largely adhesive; some terms are bargained for, but most terms consist of boilerplate, not bargained for, neither read nor understood by the buyer, and often not even fully understood by the selling agent. Moreover, [t]he adhesive terms generally are self-protective; their major purpose and effect often is to ensure that the drafting party will prevail if a dispute goes to court.[78]

However, the court emphasised that, regarding the interpretation of an insurance policy, it is a question of law. The court went further, stating that:

> Provisions of insurance policies are to be construed in a manner according to their plain and ordinary meaning, but if a clause is reasonably susceptible to different interpretations given the facts of the case, the clause is to be construed by examining the language of the clause, public policy considerations, and the purpose of the transaction as a whole, the policy may not be interpreted so as to defeat the reasonable expectations of the insured. Under this doctrine, a contract term is not enforced if one party has reason to believe that the other would not have assented to the contract if it had known of that term.[79]

Thus, the court made the important point that for cyber- and data-related claims, an insurance policy will be construed, in the US, as a contract. The court will examine closely the clauses of the contract and policy alike. It will

77 Ibid., paras 2–5.
78 Ibid., paras 3–6.
79 Ibid., paras 6–7.

also look at the public policy considerations, since data breaches and cybersecurity intrusions are on the rise and have the potential to significantly impact the economy and national security. Therefore, where an insurance policy contains exclusions and functions, the court noted in para 14 that such exclusions are the same in that they bar coverage for contractual obligations an insured assumes with a third party outside of the policy. Further, the doctrine of reasonable expectations will be applied since the insured's expectation of coverage must be objectively reasonable. Additionally, the insurer must have had reason to believe that the insured party would have purchased the policy if they had known that it included the complained provision.[80] Even though the case did not involve smart electronic contracts, it demonstrated how an insurance policy that makes specific reference to exclusion clauses will be treated as a contract. However, because other jurisdictions might not treat these provisions in the same way, further research is needed. At issue will be where in the US these provisions are viewed this way and, in cross-border issues, for instance, in Australia, whether they are viewed differently. In that situation, it will come down to the choice of law clause, provided such a clause is included. In addition, this approach is likely to also interpret the statutory provisions of the relevant insurance legislation of the state. Thus, the ensuing question is: Can arbitration deal effectively with these issues? In short, yes.

More recently in Australia, the Federal Court in *Chubb*[81] had to determine the construction of electronic and computer policy in relation to the level of a direct financial loss resulting from a ransomware attack.[82] Another issue was the relationship between the electronic policy and the insurance contract. Thus, the court asserted that:

> the expression 'directly caused by' in an insurance contract is, subject to the terms of the policy, to be construed as referring to the concept of proximate cause' and did not exclude all claims involving a 'step between the cause and the consequence.[83]

This meant that the court took the approach of determining how the policy, rather than any contractual arrangements, would apply. In doing so, the court noted that:

> Agreement 2: Computer Virus (IA2): Cover for 'Direct Financial Loss by reason of the loss resulting directly from the damage or destruction of Electronic Data, Electronic Media or Electronic Instruction owned by

80 Ibid., para 16.

81 *Australia Limited v Chubb Insurance Australia Limited* [2022] FCA 883. https://www.austlii.edu.au/cgi-bin/viewdoc/au/cases/cth/FCA/2022/883.html

82 Ibid.

83 Ibid., para 39.

> the Insured or for which the Insured is legally liable while stored within a Computer System covered under Insuring Agreement 1'.[84]
>
> Insuring Agreement 3: Electronic Data, Electronic Media, Electronic Instruction (IA3): Cover for 'Direct Financial Loss resulting directly from: (a) the fraudulent modification of Electronic Data, Electronic Media or Electronic Instruction being stored within or being run within any system covered under Insuring Agreement 1, (b) robbery, burglary, larceny or theft of Electronic Data, Electronic Media or Electronic Instruction, or (c) the acts of a hacker causing damage or destruction of Electronic Data, Electronic Media or Electronic Instruction owned by the Insured or for which the Insured is legally liable while stored within a Computer System covered under Insuring Agreement 1'.[85]

Notwithstanding the above, the court, by examining the wording closely, noted that the

> words 'in case of loss of, or damage to, Electronic Data (etc)' in general condition 4(i) in respect of Electronic Data (etc) as meaning 'in the event of' or 'if there is' such loss or damage. That is, the words 'in the case of' are a condition precedent to the operation of general condition 4(i) in respect of Electronic Data (etc).[86]

Importantly, this was part of the process to determine the level of liability. However, a further step was established by the court by examining the policy for liability of costs. The court noted that:

> the words in general condition 4(i): 'Chubb shall be liable under this Policy only if … and then *for not more than* …' On Inchcape's approach in the case of loss of, or damage to, Electronic Data (etc) Chubb shall be liable under the policy not 'only if … and then for not more than …' as specified. On its approach Inchcape could suffer loss of Electronic Data (etc). It could decide not to reproduce that data. It could then seek to claim some financial loss as a Direct Financial Loss resulting directly from the loss of the Electronic Data (etc). Leaving aside the requirement of directness and the exclusion of indirect or consequential loss of any nature in cl 3, this outcome seems incongruous. It fails to give effect to the fact that: (a) all potential events covered by IA 2 and IA 3 involve the loss of or damage to Electronic Data (etc) as referred to in the general condition, and (b) the words 'Chubb shall be liable under this Policy only if … and then for not more than …'

84 Ibid.
85 Ibid.
86 Ibid., para 24.

The use of the phrase 'words not more than' is specific and applies only to what the policy is setting out to achieve. Arguably, it cannot be more than what Chubb established in the policy. This indicates the challenges that the insurance sector will face regarding contractual and policy arrangements with parties. The construction of the respective contractual and policy clauses needs to be undertaken with much care. They need to determine where there is a cost to the party responsible for the software to ensure those costs are either direct, indirect, or not relevant to the claim. Put another way, where there is a general requirement by the software provider to upgrade software systems and those requirements are stipulated in the contract or policy, they must be followed to ascertain who is responsible for that cost. This will require the courts to make a determination that, based on the above, will be limited by the policy-contractual arrangements. Therefore, the use and the test of directness and its requirements could reduce the extent of cover for a party's loss.

A central theme throughout this book concerns the emerging new areas of law and economic activity. For instance, digital insurance, InsurTech, cyber insurance, and data insurance, amongst others, have been cited as signalling a new frontier in insurance. In order to adapt to the fast-changing environment of the digital economy, 'insurers will have to put a considerable focus on diversity, flexibility, and technology'.[87] A new skill set and in-depth knowledge will be required to deal with FinTech, autonomous vehicles, blockchain, AI, and quantum technology.

The OECD states that the 'rationale for insurance regulation is, generally speaking, to ensure that the interests of policyholders are protected, the stability and robustness of the insurance market are promoted, and inappropriate behaviour by (re)insurers and affiliated service providers is avoided'.[88] The cost of insurance is immense and is estimated to rise exponentially during the next decade. It was reported that in

> 2020, the global insurance industry spent approximately $194 billion on its IT, and that globally, long-term IT spending in insurance will grow at 6.4% to $271 billion in 2025, driven by IT services and software growing at 7.9% and 11.2%, respectively.[89]

This is an added expenditure or investment. What is certain is that as technology becomes more advanced, and the ability of individuals and entities to disrupt the digital activity of both the government and the private sector becomes

87 HDI Global SE, *The Role of an Insurer in the Digital World.* https://www.hdi.global/infocenter/insights/2022/digital-economy/

88 Organisation for Economic Cooperation and Development, *The Institutional Structure of Insurance Regulation and Supervision* (2018), p. 11. https://www.oecd.org/finance/The-Institutional-Structure-of-Insurance-Regulation-and-Supervision.pdf

89 Damion Philippon, *Why Data and IT Leaders Favor Zelros.* https://www.zelros.com/2023/05/16/why-data-and-it-leaders-favor-zelros/

more sophisticated, the cost of insurance is likely to climb significantly. The growing reliance on new insurance products in the digital economy is only beginning to be fully realised.

In a small but important study undertaken in 2021 by the Geneva Association, the findings[90] indicated the emerging challenges faced by digital insurance. On the one hand, insurance products are being developed as a protective measure against data loss and cybersecurity intrusions. On the other hand, technology has been developed to manage new insurance products. That said, the broad findings are:

1. Insurance regulatory frameworks are perceived to be much less conducive to digitalisation than macro-level factors, such as government policies, digital infrastructure and local culture.[91]
2. The three most commonly cited regulatory barriers are paper document delivery provisions, insurance distribution regulation, and a lack of telehealth provisions for medical exam procedures.[92]
3. Regulatory barriers to digitalisation resulted in additional costs for 60% of insurers.[93]

To overcome these issues, Nordhoek believes that 'regulators should adopt a technology-agnostic framework ready to accommodate future technological developments'.[94] Nordhoek further asserts that

> many jurisdictions have requirements in place that prevent one or multiple stages of the process being conducted electronically, including the need for wet signatures, paper information provision and the issuance of paper policies. Examples of obstacles to digitalisation include the European Union Insurance Distribution Directive (IDD), which includes a default paper requirement. In a similar vein, the European Packaged Retail and Insurance-based Investment Products regulation includes a provision on paper document issuance.[95]

When examining the insurance sector, one of the challenges is the varied and different products and regulatory frameworks currently in place. For instance,

90 Dennis Nordhoek, *Regulatory Considerations for Digital Insurance Business Models,* The Geneva Association (2021), pp. 4–6.
https://www.genevaassociation.org/sites/default/files/digitalinsurance_web.pdf
91 Ibid.
92 Ibid.
93 Ibid.
94 Ibid.
95 Ibid. See also Directive (EU) 2016/97 of the European Parliament and of the Council of 20 January 2016 on Insurance Distribution (Recast) Text with EEA Relevance, *OJ L, 26* (2 February 2016), 19–59.

nations such as the US have state- and national-based insurance laws. In this book, only the national insurance laws are discussed.

In reconciling the above, Callan Johns notes that arbitration clauses have become entrenched within almost every employment and consumer contract and are used as a vehicle to resolve a vast array of tort law ranging from personal injury to sexual harassment and discrimination in the work place.[96] Today, as Johns puts it, arbitration is a widely accepted dispute resolution tool utilised by the insurance sector. Johns further notes that the maritime sector has embraced arbitration within its insurance contracts. Thus, not only is arbitration widely accepted throughout the commercial world; it is being used effectively in tort, criminal, and private law. On the one hand, marine insurance is defined as insurance against the losses 'incident to the marine adventure'.[97] On the other hand, marine insurance is generally comprised of three elements:

1) a contract of indemnity against loss;
2) the indemnity is triggered by an accident or fortuity; and
3) the 'adventure' or peril insured against must be specifically maritime in character.[98]

Based on the above, there are likely to be similarities that are not mutually exclusive to the insurance disputes within the marine industry. This is because the core components of the digital economy related to data, cybersecurity, AI, and quantum will pervade the marine industry.

4.3 Arbitration

Arbitration is also increasingly being used and applied to disputes involving insurance contracts and policies. In *Enka*[99] the court had to reconcile the 'system of national law governs the validity and scope of the arbitration agreement when the law applicable to the contract containing it differs from the law of the seat of the arbitration'.[100] The issue that led to the dispute began on 1 February 2016 when a 'power plant situated at Berezovskaya in Russia was severely damaged by fire. The appellant (Chubb Russia) is a Russian insurance company which had insured the owner of the power plant, a company now named PJSC Unipro (Unipro), against such damage'.[101] The contract between

96 Callan J Johns, The Rising Tide of Arbitration Clauses Claims Maritime Insurance as Its Next Victim, *Loyola Maritime Law Journal, 18* (1) (2019), 77–78.
97 Ibid.
98 Ibid.
99 *Enka Insaat Ve Sanayi AS v OOO Insurance Company Chubb* [2020] EWCA 574. https://www.supremecourt.uk/cases/docs/uksc-2020-0091-judgment.pdf
100 Ibid., para 2.
101 Ibid., para 7.

Energoproekt and Enka dated 27 June 2012 contained the dispute resolution clause from Article 50. It stated:

> The Parties undertake to make in good faith every reasonable effort to resolve any dispute or disagreement arising from or in connection with this Agreement (including disputes regarding validity of this agreement and the fact of its conclusion (hereinafter – 'Dispute') by means of negotiations between themselves. In the event of the failure to resolve any Dispute pursuant to this article within 10 (ten) days from the date that either Party sends a Notification to the opposite Party containing an indication of the given Dispute (the given period may be extended by mutual consent of the Parties) any Party may, by giving written notice, cause the matter to be referred to a meeting between the senior managements of the Contractor and Customer (in the case of the Contractor senior management shall be understood as a member of the executive board or above, in the case of Customer, senior management shall be understood as general directors of their respective companies). The parties may invite the End Customer to such Senior Management Meeting. Such meeting shall be held within fourteen (14) calendar days following the giving of a notice. If the matter is not resolved within twenty (20) calendar days after the date of the notice referring the matter to appropriate higher management or such later date as may be unanimously agreed upon, the Dispute shall be referred to international arbitration as follows: the Dispute shall be finally settled under the Rules of Arbitration of the International Chamber of Commerce (ICC), the Dispute shall be settled by three arbitrators appointed in accordance with these Rules, the arbitration shall be conducted in the English language, and the place of arbitration shall be London, England.[102]

Based on the above, the dispute was to be settled according to the institutional rules of the ICC, whereby three arbitrators make up the panel, and England was the place of arbitration. The court noted that 'unless there has been an express choice of the law that is to govern the arbitration agreement, the general rule should be that the arbitration agreement is governed by the law of the seat, as a matter of implied choice'.[103] In this case, there was no express choice of law within Article 50. Hence, arbitration clauses should be drafted clearly to prevent or minimise further dispute and the potential need for a court to make such a determination. The risk of not doing so can result in complications for the enforcement of the arbitration agreement. The above, in part, was reinforced in the 2021 case of *Kabab*,[104] although the difference was that the party

102 Ibid., paras 9–10.
103 Ibid., para 4.
104 *Kabab-Ji SAL (Lebanon) v Kout Food Group (Kuwait)* [2021] UKSC 48.

was not part of the arbitration agreement. The point is that arbitration clauses need to be drafted with care and accuracy.

Against the backdrop of the above, arbitration has been used extensively for more than a decade to resolve insurance contract disputes. For instance, below is a current example of an arbitration clause for cyber data and other technology-related matters. The arbitration clause constitutes:

> We and the policyholder shall submit any dispute or controversy arising out of or relating to this Policy to arbitration, whether arising during or after the period of this Policy. Unless otherwise agreed by the parties, such arbitration shall be administered by an arbitration tribunal (the Tribunal) consisting of three arbitrators, one to be appointed by the policyholder, one to be appointed by us and the third to be appointed by the two appointed arbitrators (the 'Third Arbitrator'). The Third Arbitrator shall be appointed as soon as practicable (and no later than thirty (30) days) after the appointment of the two party-appointed arbitrators. The Tribunal shall be constituted upon the appointment of the Third Arbitrator. The arbitrators shall be persons (including those who have retired) with not less than ten years' experience of insurance or reinsurance within the industry or as lawyers or other professional advisers serving the industry. All costs of the arbitration shall be at the discretion of the Tribunal who may direct to and by whom and in what manner they shall be paid. The parties to the arbitration shall share equally the fees and expenses of the Third Arbitrator as well as other common expenses of the arbitration process. The dispute or controversy submitted to the Tribunal shall be settled by arbitration in accordance with the UNCITRAL Arbitration Rules as at present in force when notice of arbitration is submitted.[105]

Importantly, the clause provides for the default that the arbitration will be undertaken according to the UNCITRAL Arbitration Rules. This clause is a good starting point for any organisation that is taking out an insurance policy. This calls for specialist arbitration practitioners to be included in the panel of three that will make up the arbitration tribunal.

4.4 Conclusion

The insurance sector is undergoing a profound change due to the implementation of blockchain technology. This chapter has demonstrated that the insurance sector, while relying on historical legal concepts and principles, is in

105 Zurich Australia, *Cyber, Security and Privacy Protection Insurance Policy Wording*, p. 24. https://brokers.zurich.com.au/content/dam/au-documents/business-insurance/financial-lines/security-and-privacy-protection/security-and-privacy-protection-insurance-policy.pdf See p. 24, for the full arbitration clause.

a state of rapid transition to the digital economy. That is, in the common law countries examined in this chapter, Australia, the UK, Singapore, and the US, the concept of good faith is well-entrenched in both statutory and case law.

However, an evolving dilemma concerns the way that blockchain technology operates in relation to smart contracts. This is because the nature of smart contracts can eliminate the subjective *good faith* or *reasonableness* that often exists in traditional contracts. For common law countries, this will be difficult to reconcile, and the judiciary may need to address this at some point. Moreover, when using a smart contract, the concept of 'good faith' must be encoded. The ensuing issues and impacts on insurance contracts resulting from technology are the same as those highlighted in earlier chapters, particularly in regard to smart contracts.

The chapter drew upon a number of judicial decisions that demonstrate the challenges facing data and cybersecurity related to insurance products and contracts. The judiciary further indicated how an insurance policy that makes specific reference to exclusion clauses will be treated as a contract. However, not all states that have adopted the common law may take this approach, and further research is needed. Importantly, the chapter demonstrated that care will need to be taken in relation to the drafting of contractual and insurance policy clauses.

There is a need for vigilance as blockchain technology is adopted by the sector to ensure that contractual and policy clauses are clear concerning economic and other losses. In addition, as the judiciary has to grapple with new challenges, the direct and indirect losses will need to be specified so that they are unambiguous.

While not discussed in this chapter, open insurance is the next transition for the sector. It has been described as:

> covering, accessing and sharing insurance-related personal and non-personal data usually via APIs. Open insurance is the practice of insurers sharing and consuming data and services in order to create more appealing value propositions and new revenue streams. These data and services are exchanged with third parties both within and beyond the insurance industry and are made externally accessible and openly consumable by means of APIs. Where relevant, customers authorise their service providers to make their data accessible, in return for which they expect better, more personalised services and experiences.[106]

106 Willem Standaert, Steve Muylle. *Framework for Open Insurance Strategy: Insights from a European Study*, Springer Nature (2022), pp. 643–688. https://www.ncbi.nlm.nih.gov/pmc/articles/PMC8807377/ See also Open Insurance. https://openinsurance.io/tech-lab/how-insurance-leaders-are-embracing-open-insurance/ European Insurance and Occupational Pensions Authority. https://www.eiopa.europa.eu/browse/digitalisation-and-financial-innovation/open-insurance_en

The above is far from settled, and the authors highlight the need for urgent research to be undertaken. It is a potential game changer for the sector and will have far-reaching implications for data protection, data flows, and cyber security. It will likely rely on AI and quantum technology, and is yet another area that will challenge the law, particularly in relation to contract and insurance policy requirements. This is because the data and information acquired will be more available to third parties.

To date, the judiciary has not had to contend with this issue. Hence, it will need to create new business models that provide customers with a greater level of control over their insurance products. Arbitration has played a long-standing role in resolving disputes in relation to insurance contracts across the industrial economy and may become increasingly relied upon. However, with the use of smart contracts in insurance, further legal challenges will arise, and arbitration will have a role to play in resolving commercial disputes. Contractual clauses for arbitration agreements and insurance policies need to be prepared with care to ensure that the clauses reflect the choice of law and seat of arbitration.

5 Intellectual Property Law [Patent and Copyright]

5.1 Introduction

In recent times, intellectual property (IP) has, arguably, become one of the most contested areas of the law. This is because a design or other form of property considered as IP can be uploaded[1] to a blockchain or distributed ledger. Birgit Clark states that 'blockchain solutions can hold, execute and monitor contractual codes, such as smart contract performance they could be of interest for digital rights management and other IP transactions'.[2] Clark explains that, even back in 2018,

> smart contracts could be used to establish and enforce IP agreements such as licenses and allow the transmission of payments in real time to IP owners; smart information about IP rights in protected content, a song or an image, for example, could be encoded in digital form.[3]

Therefore, tokens can form part of smart contracts, and they can be established on a blockchain, to be transacted outside of a smart contract. Put another way, IP law itself that includes trademarks, copyright and patents can be represented[4] on a blockchain token.

On the one hand, the IP issue is far from settled and comes with many challenges, such as the enforceability, interoperability, and standardisation of blockchains.[5] To understand the legal implications of this issue, one needs to understand the operation (the mechanics) of blockchain itself. Hence, tokenisation has a role to play in the establishment of efficiencies to govern IP rights;

1 Birgit Clark, Blockchain and IP Law: A Match made in Crypto Heaven? *WIPO Magazine* (2028). https://www.wipo.int/wipo_magazine/en/2018/01/article_0005.html
2 Ibid.
3 Ibid.
4 Blockapps, *Legal Aspects of intellectual Property Tokens* (2024). https://blockapps.net/blog/legal-aspects-of-intellectual-property-tokens/
5 *The Road to Tokenisation* (2023). https://flagship.fyi/outposts/real-world-assets/understanding-tokenized-ip-intellectual-property-rights-copyright/#

DOI: 10.4324/9781003511687-5

that is, the process of tokenisation can 'ease the process of transferring IP rights'.[6] Further, it does not require intermediaries to be involved in the process; rather, the entire process can be executed via the smart contract (on the blockchain).[7] The benefit to the consumer is a more cost-efficient way of selling or transferring IP rights, and can reduce the need for comprehensive negotiations and agreements.[8] This is another potential benefit of tokenising IP rights.

On the other hand, two questions regarding tokens have emerged. The first is: how can tokens be used to provide an IP right either partially or in its entirety? Noteworthy is how a token can be applied to a partial IP right. Second, and just as important: what are the international and national laws that enable and facilitate the protection of IP rights via patents and copyright? Another question that arises is: does the blockchain itself have an IP attached? However, this question is neither relevant nor a potential factor to be considered in regard to IP rights that could potentially attached to a token. This is because whoever uses the blockchain technology does so as an individual or entity and uses it to input a code to develop and govern a smart contract and/or tokenise an IP right.

Also important is the White Paper released in 2022 by the World Intellectual Property Organisation (WIPO),[9] which dealt specifically with blockchain. WIPO noted that the technology of blockchain:

- can help with proof of generation and record keeping of IP assets, by proving the date and ownership of preparatory documentation that may lead to the filing of an application for a patent, utility model or any other industrial property right;
- can be used to provide tamper-proof and solid evidence during the life cycle of the application, including examination, opposition and cancellation stages;
- allows right holders to streamline registered rights that can be autonomously managed by their owners and use smart contracts for the licencing and assignment of registered IP rights. Tokenisation can also help the right holder to securitise their IP assets or to use them as collaterals; and
- facilitates interoperability and collaboration among IP offices to streamline the administration of international IP systems.[10]

This chapter examines and compares the patent and copyright laws of Australia, the United Kingdom, India, Singapore, and the United States. First,

6 Ibid.
7 Ibid.
8 Ibid.
9 World Intellectual Property Organisation, *Blockchain Technologies and IP Ecosystems: A WIPO White Paper* (2022), p. 4. https://www.wipo.int/export/sites/www/cws/en/pdf/blockchain-for-ip-ecosystem-whitepaper.pdf
10 Ibid., p. 4.

it examines the patent law for tokens.[11] In reinforcing the above, Bamakan and others note that NFTs tokens provide the opportunity to:

> accelerate this process with considerable confidence and assurance about protecting the ownership of an IP. NFTs can offer IP protection while an applicant waits for the government to grant his/her more formal protection. It is cause for excitement that people who believe NFTs and Blockchain would make buying and selling patents easier, offering new opportunities for companies, universities, and inventors to make money off their innovations.[12]

This would result in the patent itself being tokenised. Therefore, with blockchain technology, patent holders will have the ability to 'tokenise' their patents. Because every transaction would be logged on a blockchain, it will be much easier to trace any changes in patent ownership.[13] Furthermore, this process benefits IP holders 'by embedding automatic royalty collecting methods inside inventors' works, providing them with financial benefits any time their innovation is licensed'.[14] In practice, an 'inventor's patent would be minted as an NFT, and the NFTs would be joined together to form a commercial IP portfolio and minted as a compounded NFT'.[15] Most noteworthy is how 'unlike industrial property rights require registration to achieve protection (patents, trademarks and industrial designs, for instance), creative works are protected under copyright from their creation according to the provisions in international treaties that no formalities for copyright protection are required'.[16] In the next section, the national laws for patents will be compared, and the key features of the international legal framework will be outlined.

5.2 Patents

The international law for patents constitutes the International Patent System[17] that falls within the Patent Cooperation Treaty (PCT).[18] The PCT is of great

11 Seyed Mojtaba Hosseini Bamakan, Nasim Nezhadsistani, Omid Bodaghi, Qiang Qu, Patents and Intellectual Property Assets as Non-Fungible Tokens; Key Technologies and Challenges. *Sci Rep, 12* (2178) (2022). https://doi.org/10.1038/s41598-022-05920-6 Note the authors offer a token NFT framework for patents.

12 Ibid.

13 Ibid.

14 Ibid.

15 Ibid.

16 World Intellectual Property Organisation. *Blockchain Technologies and IP Ecosystems: A WIPO White Paper* (2022), p. 40. https://www.wipo.int/export/sites/www/cws/en/pdf/blockchain-for-ip-ecosystem-whitepaper.pdf

17 World Intellectual Property Organisation, *The International Patent System.* https://www.wipo.int/pct/en/

18 *Patent Cooperation Treaty 2001.* https://www.wipo.int/pct/en/texts/articles/atoc.html. World Intellectual Property Organisation, *The PCT Now has 157 Contracting States.* https://www.wipo.int/pct/en/pct_contracting_states.html

importance today. It allows an individual or entity to file an application that will apply not only in their home state-jurisdiction, but also in others that are signatories to the Treaty. Lionel Bently, Brad Sherman, and Dev Gangjee make the 'point that patent law is unique because it does not provide the extensive time limits of protection such as copyright and trademark, however, the protections are more extensive'.[19] The justification for such protection is generally based on the natural rights of inventors to the products of their mental labour,[20] or the contribution is to be recognised by a grant reward. Moreover, the public interest test can be applied in some economies to protect the individual or entity who introduced a technology. This implies that the technology might not have been developed or invented by the individual or entity who introduced it into the market.[21] This section will draw upon selected cases from the jurisdictions compared. It will not provide a comprehensive comparative analysis of the way the courts have approached the various issues raised. This chapter will highlight the importance of the principles and concepts of prior art, novelty, invention, specification requirements, breach of confidence, enablement, written description, non-obvious, opposition, and purposive approach. These principles and concepts will be specific to certain states, and might not be applicable in all jurisdictions. Importantly, the adoption and application of these principles and concepts will vary across the states compared, and vigilance is required, particularly in relation to how the respective courts have applied them. This chapter does not explore or examine patents related to manufacture; rather, it focuses on technology and the theme of the book: blockchain and tokens.

Importantly, 'all PCT Contracting States are bound by Chapter II of the PCT relating to the international preliminary examination',[22] and this enables an international application can be filed[23] in any contracting state. More specifically, Article 3(4) provides that an 'international application shall i) be in a prescribed language; ii) comply with the prescribed physical requirements; iii) comply with the prescribed requirement of unity of invention; iv) be subject to the payment of the prescribed fees'.[24] Article 4 sets out the initial requirements of the international application, being the designated state; the name of and other prescribed data concerning the applicant and the agent (if any);

19 Lionel Bently, Brad Sherman, Dev Gangjee, *Intellectual Property Law*, Oxford University Press (2022), p. 409.

20 Ibid., p. 413, referring to Fritz Machlup, Edith Penrose, The Patent Controversy in the Nineteenth Century, Cambridge University Press, *The Journal of Economic History, 10*(1), (1950), 11–17.

21 Ibid., p. 414.

22 World Intellectual Property Organisation. *The PCT Now has 157 Contracting States.* https://www.wipo.int/pct/en/pct_contracting_states.html

23 P*atent Cooperation Treaty 2001*, Article 3. https://www.wipo.int/pct/en/texts/articles/atoc.html

24 Ibid., Article 3(4).

the title of the invention; the name of and other prescribed data concerning the inventor where the national law of at least one of the designated States. Of importance are Articles 43 and 44 that provide the relevant protections. Article 43, in part, states that

> in respect of any designated or elected State whose law provides for the grant of inventors' certificates, utility certificates, utility models, patents or certificates of addition, inventors' certificates of addition, or utility certificates of addition, the applicant may indicate, as prescribed in the Regulations.[25]

What this means is that the elected state national laws that are used to make the application according to the PCT are to provide for certificates.

Further to the above, the important elements of the PCT are Articles 9 to 23. Also of importance to the national laws is Chapter III, Articles 31 to 41, which deal with international examination. To start with, Article 9 provides that 'any resident or national of a Contracting State may file an international application'.[26] Article 9(3), is also significant as it addresses the concept of residence and nationality when there are several applicants from different contracting states. Article 10 ensures that an application is filed in the relevant office. That is, a patent application for the UK will be filed with the UK office. Moreover, Article 11 specifies certain requirements[27] for the receiving office; it must record the date of receipt of the international application, prescribed language such as the English language, the contracting state, name of the applicant, and description of the proposed patent being claimed. Article 12 requires that one copy of the international application be forwarded to the WIPO's International Bureau. On the other hand, according to Article 13, a designated office can be requested from the International Bureau to transmit to it a copy of the international application prior to the communication provided for in Article 20.[28]

The obligation placed on the receiving office to check that the application has been signed, does not contain the prescribed indications, title, or abstract; and the regulations would not conform with Article 14.[29] Therefore, an international search according to Article 15[30] becomes highly important. The Article essentially operates to confirm or otherwise whether a similar

25 Ibid., Article 43.
26 Ibid., Article 9.
27 Ibid., Article 11(3) Subject to Article 64(4), any international application fulfilling the requirements listed in items (i) to (iii) of paragraph (1) and accorded an international filing date shall have the effect of a regular national application in each designated State as of the international filing date, which date shall be considered to be the actual filing date in each designated State.
28 Ibid., Article 20 provides for communication to designated offices.
29 Ibid., Article 14.
30 Ibid., Article 15.

application or patent exists. According to Article 16, this search is undertaken by the International Searching Authority, which may be either a national office or an intergovernmental organisation such as the International Patent Institute.[31] The confirmation of whether a patent exists or there is an application in process is a fundamental feature of the international patent framework. This minimises the likelihood of any duplication, and the exclusive protection rights allow the first person or entity to secure the IP right. Articles 17 and 18[32] set out the procedure for the search and require a report to be prepared, while Article 19[33] allows for an amendment to the application. It provides for a prescribed time, although that is generally left up to the institution where the application is submitted. To clarify, the PCT does not prescribe a time period under Article 19. Articles 20 to Article 30 are by and large administrative, and therefore irrelevant to the purposes of this book. Further to the above and of importance are Articles 31 to 42 in Chapter II. Article 31 provides for an application to demand an international preliminary examination. However, procedurally, Article 31(3) requires that the 'international preliminary examination shall be made separately from the international application'.[34] This requires specifying the 'Contracting State or States in which the applicant intends to use the results of the international preliminary examination, and is to be accompanied by the appropriate fee'.[35] Article 32 requires that the International Preliminary Examining Authority is to carry out the examination, and Article 31(2)(a) and Article 31(2)(b) require that careful consideration be given to the examination itself, in addition to applying 'Article 16(3) *mutatis mutandis* (making necessary alterations while not affecting the main point of the application itself), in respect of International Preliminary Examining Authorities'.[36]

Article 33 is also highly significant because any 'international preliminary examination is a preliminary and non-binding opinion on the questions whether the claimed invention appears to be novel, to involve an inventive step (to be non-obvious), and to be industrially applicable'.[37] The point is that this step is only an opinion, and therefore is non-binding. It only addresses whether the invention is novel or otherwise. Most significant is the procedure guiding the international preliminary examination. Article 34 provides this

31 Ibid., Article 16,
32 Ibid., Articles 17–18.
33 Ibid., Article 19.
34 Ibid., Article 31(3).
35 Ibid., Article 31(4).
36 Ibid., Article 32.
37 Ibid., Article 33. For industrial application, the international preliminary examination, a claimed invention shall be considered industrially applicable if, according to its nature, it can be made or used (in the technological sense) in any kind of industry. 'Industry' shall be understood in its broadest sense, as in the Paris Convention for the Protection of Industrial Property.

process, whereby, the International Preliminary Examining Authority shall grant the applicant a right to:

> communicate orally and in writing with the International Preliminary Examining Authority. The applicant shall have a right to amend the claims, the [written] description, and the drawings, in the prescribed manner and within the prescribed time limit, before the international preliminary examination report is established. The amendment shall not go beyond the disclosure in the international application as filed.[38]

The applicant shall receive at least one written opinion from the International Preliminary Examining Authority unless such Authority considers that all of the following conditions are fulfilled:

(i) the invention satisfies the criteria set forth in Article 33(1),
(ii) the international application complies with the requirements of this Treaty and the Regulations in so far as checked by that Authority,
(iii) no observations are intended to be made under Article 35(2), last sentence. (d) The applicant may respond to the written opinion.[39]

Where the application is considered to not comply with the requirements of unity of invention as set forth in the regulations, the applicant can be advised to amend the application so that it does comply. This flexible approach does go some way to assisting the applicant to ensure that they meet the requirements for assessment. However, the national laws of the state where the application has been lodged would need to be consulted so that

> those parts of the international application which, as a consequence of the restriction, are not to be the subject of international preliminary examination shall, as far as effects in that State are concerned, be considered withdrawn unless a special fee is paid by the applicant to the national Office of that State.[40]

On the other hand, if the applicant has not complied with the prescribed time limits, the 'International Preliminary Examining Authority shall establish an international preliminary examination report on those parts of the international application which relate to what appears to be the main invention'. It is important to also consult the national laws to ensure that those parts of the 'international application which do not relate to the main invention shall, as far as effects in that State are concerned, be considered withdrawn. That is,

38 Ibid., Article 34.
39 Ibid., Article 34.
40 Ibid.

unless a special fee is paid by the applicant to that Office'.[41] Therefore, the International Preliminary Examining Authority considers:

(i) that the international application relates to a subject matter on which the International Preliminary Examining Authority is not required, under the Regulations, to carry out an international preliminary examination, and in the particular case decides not to carry out such examination, or
(ii) that the description, the claims, or the drawings, are so unclear, or the claims are so inadequately supported by the description, that no meaningful opinion can be formed on the novelty, inventive step (non-obviousness), or industrial applicability, of the claimed invention, the said Authority shall not go into the questions referred to in Article 33(1) and shall inform the applicant of this opinion and the reasons.[42]

It is important that the applicant ensures that any claim appropriately justifies what and why the application has been made and that it describes the steps taken to produce the invention or creation. A failure to demonstrate this in the application may leave the Authority no choice but to decline the application. Articles 35 and 36 provide for the report and communication of the report. Article 37 allows the applicant to withdraw the application. Article 38 is important because it provides for a high level of confidentiality attached to the application and applicant, unless authorised by the applicant to release certain information.[43] The remaining Articles 39 to 42 are generally procedural and deal with translation, fees, processing, amendments to claims, and result of national examination. Arguably, this applies the purposive approach because it requires that a certain procedure be followed.

While the procedural steps above explain how the applicant and application will be examined, this is also done by considering Chapter III, Articles 43 to 49, which provide specific protections. Article 43 sets out certain kinds of protection, although, a protection will only apply where there are national laws in place 'for the grant of inventors' certificates, utility certificates, utility models, patents or certificates of addition, inventors' certificates of addition, or utility certificates of addition'.[44] The governance of such protections is the choice of the applicant. More specifically, Article 44 expands on Article 43, offering two kinds of protection. This is applicable where a designated national law allows for more than one (two kinds) of protection to the applicant. Articles 45, 46, and 47 relate to regional treaties, incorrect translations, and time limits. Of most importance are the time limits that are established

41 Ibid.
42 Ibid.
43 Ibid., Articles 36, 37, 38.
44 Ibid., Article 43.

by the regulations,[45] which specify a number of different time limits that apply to, but are not limited to, international searches, amendments, payment of fees under the PCT, including drawings and furnishing indications. The regulations set out the rules under each of the PCT chapters. They have been designed to establish additional specific information that has not been otherwise accounted for in the PCT. This further layer of regulation specifies the details of, for example, the criteria and/or contents of an application request. While it is outside the scope of this book to critically analyse the regulations and rules pertaining to the PCT, it is argued that they have become an essential tool for patent-related applications. Chapter IV of the PCT provides for information services, requirements, and technical assistance from The International Bureau,[46] Assembly,[47] and relations with other Treaties.[48] Chapter V, Article 53 regulates the Assembly, Executive Committee,[49] International Bureau,[50] Committee for Technical Cooperation,[51] and Finance in Article 57. The international framework has been developed to protect inventors. The patent itself serves as powerful protection for inventors, ensuring that they receive credit for the IP and invention.[52] Challenging though, in the current transition to the digital economy, the application and recognition of technological innovations, such as artificial intelligence (AI), as a patent ensuring IP rights are challenging. This is particularly important given the significance of blockchain technology and tokens. A court in South Africa was one of the first to grant a patent[53] for AI. This is an important step forward. However, as noted by Jessica Smith, the UK, Australia, and the US have yet to grant a patent for AI. However, applications for a patent for a particular token are emerging. For instance, in the US, there have been applications for patents to be attached to dynamic tokens.[54] In a broader search,

45 Ibid., Article 58. World Intellectual Property, *Regulations and Administrative Instructions.* https://www.wipo.int/pct/en/texts/index.html. See also the *Regulations Under the Patent Cooperation Treaty 2022.* https://www.wipo.int/export/sites/www/pct/en/docs/texts/pct-regs.pdf

46 *Patent Cooperation Treaty 2001*, Article 50. https://www.wipo.int/pct/en/texts/articles/atoc.html

47 Ibid., Article 51.

48 Ibid., Article 52.

49 Ibid., Article 54.

50 Ibid., Article 55.

51 Ibid., Article 56.

52 Jessica Smith, Let Me Get My Human for That: The Struggles of a Broken Patent System for AI Inventors, 29 SW. *Journal of International Law, 160* (2023), 162.

53 Ibid., pp. 163–164. *Referring to Quartz Africa: In a World First, South Africa grants a Patent to an Artificial Intelligence System* (accessed 26 June 2024). https://qz.com/africa/2044477/south-africa- grants-patent-to-an-ai-system-known-as-dabus/

54 Patent Number: US 10,719,819B2. https://patentimages.storage.googleapis.com/06/3e/bf/1115204d4501b5/US10719819.pdf A method assigns token requirements to service subscriptions in a service platform, such as a service platform containing entities or a database containing a plurality of said entities. The operator of the service platform establishes cus-

the extent of patents being granted[55] indicates a significant number in 2023 and 2024 alone. For instance, two recent applications that have been successful are Patent Number: 11991160 and Patent Number 11985124. The first, granted in 2024, was in relation to:

> Systems and methods for providing one or more secure services are disclosed. One method can comprise authenticating and/or authorizing a user device to receive a security token.[56]

Specifically, it was not the token itself that constituted the patent, but rather, the systems and methods for providing the security service. Second, and more significantly, Patent Number 11985124 relates to the secure tokenisation of an NFT through multifactor authentication. The common denominator of these two patents is not the tokens themselves, but the security mechanisms created to protect them from being intruded upon.

Most noteworthy is Patent Number: 11915235.[57] This was granted for the systems and methods used to communicate token attributes with a token vault. It relates to the operation of the token itself, whereby the systems and methods for interoperable network token processing are available through third-party wallets, e-commerce merchants, payment enablers, and service providers.[58] Importantly, the token vault that constitutes part of the patent is essentially a registry that extends to token generation and token issuance.[59] Thus, patent applications are evolving to include tokens and the systems and methods that they rely upon to operate, particularly their security. There are also patents that have been granted for possession,[60] along with data management and token transactions.[61] These are just four examples of where and how a patent will be afforded to a token itself or the system supporting its use. Arguably, there will be other reasons for patent applications to either support token application and/or the systems supporting them. Furthermore, the number of such applications is likely to increase as the world transitions to a token-based economy.

Moreover, and noteworthy in relation to this book, South Africa, although it has not been chosen for comparison, has afforded a patent to blockchain. It relates to a blockchain-based exchange with tokenisation[62] that secures a

---

tomisation factors and maintains records reserving data services associated with token requirements for delivery to entities.

55 Justia Patents. https://patents.justia.com/patents-by-us-classification/713/172
56 Ibid., Patent Number: 11991160.
57 Ibid.
58 Ibid.
59 Ibid.
60 Ibid., Patent Number: 11838284.
61 Ibid., Patent Number: 11829996.
62 *Blockchain-Based Exchange with Tokenisation*, ZA201805033B. https://patents.google.com/patent/ZA201805033B/en

'method for exchanging entities via a blockchain. The invention incorporates tokenisation techniques, and also techniques for embedding metadata in a redeem script of a blockchain transaction'.[63] This is a demonstrates the interface of patent law with tokens and blockchain technology. There are two elements in the above: first, security; and second, the incorporation of tokenisation technology for embedding metadata. Problematic though is the security of the token itself, which would arguably also include cybersecurity.

In addition to the above, the World Intellectual Property Organisation Patent Law Treaty (PLT) was completed in 2000.[64] The PLT was developed to streamline formal procedures in respect of national and regional patent applications.[65] Specifically, the PLT standardises the filing date, form, and content of applications, model international forms, reduced costs, avoidance of unintentional loss of substantive rights, and ensuring the co-existence of both paper and electronic communications.[66] These harmonisation measures have been very effective for patent applications no matter the state where one is located. The next section discusses patent law in Australia, the United Kingdom, the United States, the European Union, and India.

5.2.1 Australia

The Patent Act 1990 (PA), and in particular section 29, provides for the application for a patent under the PCT.[67] Schedule 1 of the PA defines PCT.[68] This section will not discuss all the administrative components; it outlines only what the PA recognises as the requirements for a patent application. A key feature of the PA is section 7, which covers the concepts of novelty, inventive step, and innovative step. First, novelty applies

> when compared with the prior art base unless it is not novel in the light of any one of the following kinds of information, prior art information made publicly available in a single document or through a single act, or, prior art information through doing 2 or more related acts, if the relationship between the documents or acts is such that a person skilled in the relevant art would treat them as a single source of that information.[69]

63 Ibid.
64 Lionel Bently, Brad Sherman, Dev Gangjee, *Intellectual Property Law*, Oxford University Press (2022), p. 432. See also *Patent Law Treaty*. https://www.wipo.int/treaties/en/ip/plt/
65 Ibid.
66 Ibid.
67 *Patent Act 1990*, section 29A. https://www.legislation.gov.au/C2004A04014/latest/text
68 Ibid., Schedule 1, PCT means the Patent Cooperation Treaty signed at Washington on 19 June 1970, as that treaty is in force for Australia from time to time, together with the regulations annexed to that treaty, as those regulations are in force for Australia from time to time.
69 Ibid., section 7.

These criteria are to be assessed separately. Second, an inventive step is clearly separated from an innovative step and applies again to prior art information, where there is a 'prior art base unless the invention would have been obvious to a person skilled'.[70] Three, an innovative step extends to a 'person skilled in the relevant art, in light of the common general knowledge as it existed (whether in or out of the patent area) before the priority date of the relevant claim'.[71] Importantly, all three concepts are restricted to prior art information. Section 9 provides for the secret use of an invention in an area eligible for a patent.

Most notably, and in addition to section 29 above, section 10 provides for 'certain international applications to be taken to have been given an international filing date'.[72] It directly references the PCT, stating that where: a)

> an international application specifies Australia as a designated State under Article 4(1)(ii) of the PCT; and b) the receiving Office does not give the application an international filing date; and c) the Commissioner is satisfied, on the balance of probabilities, that the application should, under Article 25(2)(a) of the PCT, be treated as if it had been given an international filing date; the application is to be taken, for the purposes of this Act, to have been given an international filing date under Article 11 of the PCT.[73]

The applicability of this section is subject to English language requirements.

In 2022, the Federal Court of Australia in *Thaler*[74] reaffirmed the application of the PCT in Australia and that it has been given effect by the PA. The case was on appeal, and the

> respondent, Stephen Thaler, is the applicant for patent application No. 2019363177 titled 'Food container and devices and methods for attracting enhanced attention' which was filed on 17 September 2019 under the terms of the Patent Cooperation Treaty (Washington, 19 June 1970) (PCT).[75]

The brief background to this case was that Thaler:

> entered the national phase of processing on 9 September 2020, and, shortly after that date, IP Australia wrote to Dr Thaler's patent

70 Ibid.
71 Ibid.
72 Ibid., section 10.
73 Ibid.
74 *Commissioner of Patents v Thaler* (2022) 289 (FCR) 45. See also, Adam Liberman, One Small Step for 'Artificial Intelligence' and a Giant Leap for the Australian Patent System? The Federal Court Decision in *Thaler v Commissioner of Patents*. *Journal of Intellectual Property Law & Practice*, *17*(2) (February 2022), 164–178. https://doi.org/10.1093/jiplp/jpab181
75 Ibid., para 2.

> attorneys stating that the application did not comply with reg 3.2C of the *Regulations* because it failed to identify a natural person as the inventor. IP Australia invited Dr Thaler to supply the name of one or more natural persons as the inventors, or provide submissions explaining how DABUS could be recorded as an inventor, failing the acceptance of which the application would lapse.[76]

Hence, two fundamental and important elements of an application for a patent are: 1) the applicant's correct personal details must be provided; and 2) the relevant office must provide the relevant details within the required time frame. The further question for the court was

> considered by Dr S D Barker, the Deputy Commissioner of Patents, who determined that the terms of the *Patents Act* and *Regulations* were inconsistent with an artificial intelligence being treated as an inventor: *Stephen L. Thaler* [2021] APO 5. The consequence was that the application lapsed.[77]

Furthermore, and as a central consideration of the court, Chapter 2, section 15 of the PA is important as it specifies who may be granted a patent. In addition, and more specifically, the court confirmed that section 29A of the PA and the *Patent Regulations 1991* provides for patent applications that fall within the scope of the PCT.[78] The appeal was successful. The PCT is operational in Australia. Applicants must follow the processes stipulated by the national laws that give effect to the PCT. Another important thing to consider in this case is that

> [although] His Honour, Beach J is prepared to say that an artificial intelligence system can be an inventor for the purposes of the Act, he is not prepared to define 'artificial intelligence', but rather is prepared for the moment to equate DABUS with artificial intelligence if it operates in the fashion that Dr Thaler has represented.[79]

To date, artificial intelligence does not have a universally agreed-upon definition. Instead, nation-states are beginning to define the concept within their respective national laws to suit a particular purpose.

76 Ibid., para 3.
77 Ibid., para 4.
78 Ibid., paras 18, 19, 20.
79 Adam Liberman, One Small Step for 'Artificial Intelligence' and a Giant Leap for the Australian Patent System? The Federal Court Decision in *Thaler v Commissioner of Patents, Journal of Intellectual Property Law & Practice, 17*(2) (February 2022), 165.

Sections 15, 16, and 17 of Chapter 2 deal with ownership by a single individual or co-ownership. Section 15 is specific in the sense that a patent will be granted only to a person who is the inventor, to be assigned to a person, derives title to the invention, or is a legal representative of a deceased person who was the inventor.[80] There is no requirement that a person making the application for a patent be an Australian citizen. Co-ownership can occur and will be equally shared unless there is a formal agreement or contract in place. In some circumstances, there will be more than two owners, and therefore, section 17 allows the Commissioner to provide directions on the share of the patent, such as the level of interest or licences granted under the patent.

However, there is a 14-day time limit for parties who need to complete certain tasks if the Commissioner has directed them to do so. Otherwise, a patentee could be directed to do what the other patentee was supposed to undertake as part of the direction. However, the Commissioner is restricted in providing any such directions and cannot infringe the rights or obligations of a trustee or legal representative of a deceased person.[81] Part 3 deals with the validity of a patent. Section 18 describes what can be patented. Notably, Section 18 outlines what cannot be patented: 'plants and animals, and the biological processes for the generation of plants and animals, are not patentable inventions'.[82] Sections 19, 20, and 21 further deal with validity and direct the court to do certain things where a certificate is to be issued certifying a patent claim or otherwise. The remaining sections of Part 3 deal with validation requirements.

Notwithstanding the above, the most significant sections of the PA are sections 29 and 29A. Section 29 sets out the general rules for making a patent application. Section 29A sets out the rules for making an application according to the PCT. Also, section 29 requires that an application be prepared in a prescribed form, be in English, and outline any specification. There are provisional application and complete application processes. The complete application process needs to consider section 229, which affords the Commissioner the flexibility to specify the formality requirements.[83] Furthermore, for international applications under the PCT, section 29A is important. Notably, this section considers these international applications to be the same as those under the PA. Section 29A pertains to drawings, graphics, photographs, and claims contained in a PCT application, stating that these are to be treated as a complete specification filed in respect of the application. This type of application

> is to be taken to comply with the prescribed requirements of this Act that relate to applications for standard patents, but is not to be taken, merely because of subsection (1) or (2), to comply with any other requirements of this Act.[84]

80 *Patent Act 1990*, section 15. https://www.legislation.gov.au/C2004A04014/latest/text
81 Ibid., section 17.
82 Ibid., section 18.
83 Ibid., section 29.
84 Ibid., section 29A.

If the application is written in a foreign language, it is to be translated into English and the required fee is to be attached.

The Australian Patent Office has issued a *Patent Manual of Practice and Procedure* (PMPP).[85] Its purpose is to provide the general 'principles and legal standards patent examiners are to apply during examination'.[86] However, a closer examination of this *Manual* is outside the scope of this book. Moreover, section 29B of the *Australian Patent Regulations* allows for Convention applications, which generally means that a person can apply to a third country that has been proscribed by the *Patent Regulations 1991*[87] that also proscribes the procedural components and forms of an application. Sections 30 to 33 of the PA provide for joint applications, disputes, filing dates, and opposition of an application. Specifically, section 33 allows a person to oppose a patent application, and allows the Commissioner to oppose an innovation or person. The Commissioner has the ability to revoke an application under section 35. Also pertinent, section 36 explains what constitutes an eligible person. The court in *Factor Finance*[88] was required to give directions in relation to a matter under section 36 of the *Patents Act*, and to give direction for the filing of details of the case of each party – a statement regarding particulars.[89] In dealing with section 36 specifically, the court noted that 'disputes under section 36 are not covered by the procedures in Chapter 5 of the *Regulations*. Rather, such disputes are governed by the powers conferred on the Commissioner by regulations 22.22 and 22.24'.[90] The court went further and noted that 22.22 specifically provides:

(1) The Commissioner must give a person an opportunity to be heard before exercising a discretionary power under the Act or these Regulations adversely to the person.
(2) The Commissioner must give the person an opportunity to be heard by:
    (a) asking the person for written submissions; or
    (b) notifying the person that, on request to the Commissioner, the person may be heard by way of an oral hearing on a date, and at a time and place, determined by the Commissioner; or
    (c) notifying the person of the date, time and place of an oral hearing.
(3) The Commissioner may exercise the discretionary power if the person:
    (a) notifies the Commissioner that the person does not want to be heard; or

85 Australian Patent Office, *Patent Manual of Practice and Procedure*. https://manuals.ipaustralia.gov.au/patent/8.16.1

86 Ibid.

87 *Patent Regulations 1991*. https://www.legislation.gov.au/F1996B02697/latest/versions

88 *Factor Financial Analytics Pty Ltd v Xero Ltd* (2021) 162 IPR 374. http://www.austlii.edu.au/cgi-bin/viewdoc/au/cases/cth/APO//2021/2.html

89 Ibid.

90 Ibid., paras 6–7.

(b) does not file written submissions if requested under sub regulation 22.23(1); or
(c) does not attend an oral hearing if notified under sub regulation 22.23(2).

(4) If the Commissioner exercises discretionary power in any of the circumstances mentioned in sub regulation (3), the Commissioner must notify the person of the Commissioner's decision.[91]

In relation to 22.24, the court states that the practice and procedure other than for opposition proceedings are:

(1) Subject to these Regulations:
(a) if the Act or these Regulations authorise the Commissioner to hear and decide an application or matter that is not an opposition; or
(b) in a matter being decided on the motion of the Commissioner;
the practice and procedure to be followed for the purposes of enabling the application or matter to be decided is to be determined by him or her.

(2) A person to be heard at a hearing may apply to the Commissioner in respect of the practice and procedure in relation to the hearing to be determined by the Commissioner.[92]

By understanding the above, the court was able to determine the level of discretion and mandatory obligations that are to be applied in providing any level of direction. Thus, in this case, the court ruled that directions can apply to a statement of particulars. Arguably, what the court was implementing here is the purposive approach to the interaction between the substantive Act and regulations. They support each other in relation to the concept of opposition.

Sections 40, 41, and 42 deal with specifications in general related to microorganisms. More importantly, section 43 provides for another specific requirement related to patent applications: the priority date. The section does not specify the number of days or actual dates; rather, it states that the priority date is the 'date of the filing of the specification'.[93] Therefore, the priority date begins on the day the application has been filed. Section 43AA deals with disclosure requirements. Section 43A also becomes important as it relates to searches and opinions. This procedural step allows the Commissioner to undertake a preliminary search and provide an opinion on the application. Sections 44 and 45 allow for the request for examination and the examination itself, which become very relevant because they allow the Commissioner to decline or otherwise approve the application. For PCT examinations, the Commissioner, according

91 Ibid.
92 Ibid.
93 *Patent Act 1990*, section 43. https://www.legislation.gov.au/C2004A04014/latest/text

to section 45(1), where the prescribed requirements have not been met, can decline the examination in full and request further specification. Sections 49, 49A, 50, and 50A all place obligations on the Commissioner to act according to the PA when accepting an application for a patent. Section 51 provides a general provision for appeal to the Federal Court.

Distinctively from the general application for a patent, an innovation application under section 52 requires a level of formal checks to be undertaken by the Commissioner. While the PA itself does not specify the categories of checks, the test for the balance of probabilities is applied by the Commissioner. This threshold test provides a high level of flexibility in meeting the relevant requirements set out by the law. The balance of probabilities test in common law countries, particularly Australia, is applied to civil matters and is a lower test than that of criminal matters requiring such matters to be proved beyond reasonable doubt.

Sections 53 to 58 deal with the requirements around the publication of applications, including those under the PCT. Of importance, though, is also section 59, which allows any person and a Minister to oppose [opposition] the granting of a standard patent. However, this is restricted to a nominated person, and the invention is not patentable. The point is that the major reason for opposing the patent is that the invention does not meet the threshold test to warrant being protected by a patent.

In the case of *Inter Aqua Advance*[94] the court was required to reconcile the opposition to the grant of a patent under section 59 of the PA. The court ruled that the opposition was unsuccessful.[95] Specifically, paragraph 13 states that regulation 5.23 allows the Commissioner to consult documents:

> (1) For the purposes of deciding an opposition, the Commissioner may consult a document that: (a) is relevant to the opposition; and (b) has not been filed under this Chapter; and (c) is available in the Patent Office. (2) If the Commissioner proposes to rely on the document, the Commissioner must give the parties: (a) notice of the Commissioner's intention to do so; and (b) a copy of, or access to, the document; and (c) an opportunity to give evidence or make representations about the document.[96]

Most noteworthy is that the court refers to the 2015 case of *Merial Limited*[97] where it was stated that 'If the new information is not likely to change the outcome of the opposition in a significant way, there is little advantage gained

94 *Inter Aqua Advance A/S v Bent Urup Holding APS* (2018) 142 IPR 344. https://jade.io/article/599753 See also *Phoenix Contact GmbH & Co KG v Pivot Electronics Pty Ltd* (2020) 158 IPR 379 regarding opposition. https://jade.io/article/762750

95 Ibid., para 213.

96 Ibid., para 13.

97 Ibid., para 16, *Merial Limited v Bayer Intellectual Property GmbH* [2015] APO 16

by bringing it into the opposition'.[98] Therefore, it can be concluded that for an opposition to be successful, there needs to be new information presented that will question the application for a patent. The granting of a patent falls under sections 61 to 63.

Arguably, two of the most important provisions of the Australian PA apply to the period of time a patent will be afforded to an individual. Thus, section 67 provides a 20-year period for a standard patent, while under section 68, the term of an innovation patent is eight years.[99] Most notable is that the periods apply to the two forms of patents available: the standard and the innovation patent. Section 70 applies only to pharmaceutical products and allows an applicant to apply for an extension of the standard period of 20 years for the patent. Chapter 6 deals with divisional patents and therefore is irrelevant to the scope of this book. Chapter 7 deals with a standard patent, with sections 80 and 81[100] onwards allowing for a patent addition in cases where there has been an improvement on the original product. Section 83 stipulates the same period for the patent unless it has required an extension. Further to this, a re-examination of the patent application is to be undertaken by the Commissioner,[101] where the patentee or another person has made such a request. This examination of Australian laws demonstrates that it has established a process whereby patent applications are governed, examined, and granted. A similar re-examination process, and opposing of an innovation patent, is set out in Chapter 9. Amendments to an application can be made but do not apply to a complete specification where the claim or disclosed matter extends beyond particular documents.[102] Further to this, a court can direct that certain amendments be made according to section 105, and the Commissioner can do so under section 106. Section 117 deals with the infringement of a patent, where

> the use of a product by a person would infringe a patent, the supply of that product by one person to another is an infringement of the patent by the supplier unless the supplier is the patentee or licensee of the patent.[103]

However, an exemption applies if

> immediately before the priority date of the relevant claim the person was exploiting the product, method or process in the patent area; or had taken definite steps (contractually or otherwise) to exploit the product, method or process in the patent area.[104]

98 Ibid.
99 *Patent Act 1990*, sections 67, 68. https://www.legislation.gov.au/C2004A04014/latest/text
100 Ibid., sections 80, 81.
101 Ibid., section 97.
102 Ibid., section 102.
103 Ibid., section 117.
104 Ibid., section 119.

Specific exemptions apply to pharmaceuticals under section 119A,[105] although this will not be examined in depth. Most importantly, in order for any infringement to apply, any such proceeding must commence '3 years from the day on which the relevant patent is granted; or 6 years from the day on which the infringing act was done whichever period ends later'.[106]

Furthermore, section 121[107] is important because it places the burden of proof on the defendant who needs to prove otherwise. However, this applies only to the process for obtaining a product. Of note is that this section steps outside the traditional rules of evidence in Australia because it stipulates the way that a defendant is to adduce under these circumstances and places an obligation on the court to consider the 'defendant's legitimate interests in having business and manufacturing secrets protected'.[108] In assessing the level of infringement and whether there should be relief provided to a party, the court is restricted to 'granting (either) an infringement or injunction'.[109]

When awarding any damages, the court will be required to also consider

> the flagrancy of the infringement; the need to deter similar infringements of patents; the conduct of the party that infringed the patent that occurred after the act constituting the infringement; or after that party was informed that it had allegedly infringed the patent.[110]

Additionally, the court would also need to consider 'any benefit shown to have accrued to that party because of the infringement; and all other relevant matters'.[111] The court has the discretion to consider all other relevant matters pertaining to elements of an infringement that are not described by the PA or its regulations.

In conclusion, the court has the power to grant licences,[112] including licences for pharmaceutical inventions. The point is that the court can grant a general licence and a compulsory licence. The impact of this is that the general time limit of protection can be reduced. The remainder of the PA deals with the surrender of a patent and other administrative functions. Arguably, Australia has integrated the international patent framework into its national legal regime. Ultimately, this is of great significance and benefit to Australia and its innovators and inventors as it provides a secure and certain platform for inventors to do what they do best – invent.

105 Ibid., section 119A.
106 Ibid., section 120.
107 Ibid., section 121.
108 Ibid., section 121.
109 Ibid., section 122.
110 Ibid.
111 Ibid.
112 Ibid., Chapter 12. Sections 132A, 132B, 133.

5.2.2 European Union (EU) and United Kingdom (UK)

The EU and UK have, by and large, the same legal framework for patent applications. Therefore, it has been decided to combine both jurisdictions in this section. While the UK is no longer a member of the EU, they have largely retained[113] many of the commercial laws, particularly intellectual property. It can be argued that the UK did leave the EU club; however, they will never be able to leave entirely. This is due to a number of economic and social factors that are outside the scope of this book to address.

Importantly, the UK extended the application of the PCT to the Isle of Man, with effect from 2 October 1993, the territory of Gibraltar from 2021, and Bailiwick of Guernsey in March 2021.[114] The *Patent Act 1977*[115] provides the framework for the application and granting of a patent in the UK under the PCT and European Patent Convention[116] (EPC). The European Patent Office (EPO) is located in Munich, Germany, according to Article 6 of the EPC. The European Patent is given effect under section 77[117] onwards of the PA. The UK approach to applications for and granting of a patent generally follows the European approach. This includes, but is not limited to[118] novelty,[119] patentable inventions,[120] non-prejudicial disclosures,[121] inventive step,[122] industrial application,[123] entitlement,[124] multiple applications,[125] right to a European Patent,[126] right of inventor,[127] and term of the patent, which is 20 years,[128]

113 United Kingdom Government, *Retained EU Law for Intellectual Property*. https://www.gov.uk/government/publications/intellectual-property-and-retained-european-union-law-the-facts/retained-eu-law-for-intellectual-property See also Lionel Bently, Brad Sherman, Dev Gangjee, *Intellectual Property Law*, Oxford University Press (2022), Chapters 14 and 15.

114 World Intellectual Property Organisation, *The PCT Now has 157 Contracting States*. https://www.wipo.int/pct/en/pct_contracting_states.html

115 *The Patent Act 1977*. https://www.gov.uk/government/publications/the-patents-act-1977#:~:text=The%20Patents%20Act%201977%20sets,the%20Patent%20Co%2Doperation%20Treaty. Also see *The Patent Rules 2007* and *Patents (Fees) Rules 2007*. https://www.gov.uk/government/publications/the-patents-rules-2007-and-patents-fees-rules-2007

116 *European Patent Convention*, as at 2024. https://link.epo.org/web/EPC_17th_edition_2020_en.pdf

117 *The Patent Act 1977*, section 77.

118 *European Patent Convention*, as at 2024 Article 53. https://link.epo.org/web/EPC_17th_edition_2020_en.pdf

119 Ibid., Article 54.

120 Ibid., Article 52.

121 Ibid., Article 55.

122 Ibid., Article 56.

123 Ibid., Article 57.

124 Ibid., Article 58.

125 Ibid., Article 59.

126 Ibid., Article 60.

127 Ibid., Article 62.

128 Ibid., Article 63,

revocation,[129] and general rights.[130] Article 64 is important as it provides for the general rights of a patent granted under the EPC, placing this responsibility on the contracting state. Therefore, where there is an infringement of the rights under national laws, it is the national laws of Member States that will provide relief or otherwise. While out of scope to compare all the differences between the EU and Member States' legal regimes, Article 131 fosters a high level of administrative and legal cooperation. In fact, the provision establishes a platform for the European Patent Office and the courts or authorities of contracting states to, on request, give assistance to each other by communicating information or opening files for inspection.[131] The interrelationship of the EU and national legal frameworks is paramount to ensuring there is an effective and robust framework in place for inventors to obtain a patent. It confirms the policy of the single market of the EU for which many commercial laws have been harmonised. Relevant to this section and book is the appeal decision of T 0767/21[132] whereby the EPO is required to determine whether, in fact, there is an inventive step according to Article 56.[133] The decisions involved

> features were also known from D1 ('White Paper. Ethereum/wiki Wiki. GitHub' [actually titled 'A Next-Generation Smart Contract and Decentralized Application Platform'], Internet citation published on 11 June 2015) and D2 (F. Tschorsch and B. Scheuermann: 'Bitcoin and Beyond: A Technical Survey on Decentralized Digital Currencies' published on 15 May 2015).[134]

Notably, it is the smart contract and Ethereum that use blockchain technology to operate. Importantly, the matter involved a 'blockchain consensus protocol that alternates between two parameters: proof of stake and the number of counterparties a miner has transacted with (no inventive step – not technical), and how the invention concerns the problem of preventing malicious agents from taking control of a blockchain storing digital currency, thereby being able to falsify transactions, such as spending the same coin twice – double spending'.[135] Even though the appeal was dismissed, it demonstrated the challenges of obtaining patents for blockchain technology and the technology that supports its application. This appeal relied solely on the provisions of the EPC, and not national law. This demonstrates the importance of an application being able to demonstrate that there is a real inventive step.

129 Ibid., Article 101.
130 Ibid., Article 64.
131 Ibid., Article 131. Also see Article 135.
132 T0767/21 (Blockchain Generation Method/Nippon) (10-10-2023.) https://www.epo.org/en/boards-of-appeal/decisions/t210767eu1
133 Ibid., para 1.
134 Ibid., para 2.
135 Ibid., Reasons for Decision, para 2.1.

It is noted, however, that there are a number of specific areas in the European approach that differ from the UK framework, such as making and using evidence.[136] This is likely to be because, at a national level, there are specific evidence laws. In addition to the above is the London Agreement,[137] one of the major benefits of which is that

> parties to it undertake to waive, entirely or largely, the requirement for translations of European patents to be filed in their national language. This means in practice that European patent proprietors will no longer have to file a translation of the specification for patents granted for an EPC contracting state party to the London Agreement and having one of the three EPO languages as an official language.[138]

Additionally,

> where this is not the case, they will be required to submit a full translation of the specification in the national language only if the patent is not available in the EPO language designated by the country concerned. For more details, see Articles 1 and 2 of the agreement. This breakthrough on the language issue will significantly reduce the cost of European patents.[139]

This is, arguably, one of the most efficient reforms undertaken by the EU and its Member States. The ensuing benefit is that it is unlike all other commercial laws that have to be fully translated into all member state languages, which is a costly exercise. The Unified Patent Court (UPC)[140] is specific to EU Member States. The UK is not a party to the UPC and relies on the judiciary.

Under the PA, section 1 is specific in allowing for a patent to be granted where the invention is new and involves an inventive step, along with being capable of industrial application.[141] Section 1(2) explains that an invention is not considered to be patentable under the PA if it is a

> discovery, scientific theory or mathematical method, a literary, dramatic, musical or artistic work or any other aesthetic creation whatsoever, a scheme, rule or method for performing a mental act, playing a game or doing business, or a program for a computer or the presentation of information.[142]

136 Ibid., Article 117.
137 World Intellectual Property Organisation, *London Agreement*. https://www.wipo.int/wipolex/en/text/589366
138 Ibid.
139 Ibid.
140 Unified Patent Court. https://www.unified-patent-court.org/en
141 *The Patent Act 1977*, section 1.
142 Ibid.

Notwithstanding the above, the patent application of *Nextivia Inc*[143] demonstrates how a decision to grant a patent utilises the PCT and UK frameworks. The UK Intellectual Property Office (UIPO) was required to address concerns regarding patent application GB2118756.2, (the application), entitled *System and Method of Creating and Organizing Private Chat Messages* in the name of Nextiva Inc.[144] At issue was 'whether the invention as claimed in this application is excluded from patentability under section 1(2)(c) of the Patents Act 1977 (hereafter "the Act") as a program for a computer'.[145] By way of background, there were:

> rounds of correspondence concerning substantive examination under section 18(3) of the Act focussed upon inventive step, however the examiner also warned the applicant that they would need to consider whether the application concerned excluded matter once the issue of inventive step had been resolved. Subsequently, the examiner has raised an objection that the invention, as claimed, relates to a program for a computer which is excluded under section 1(2)(c) of the Act. This objection was maintained over successive amendment rounds, and having reached an impasse, the applicant was offered a hearing.[146]

The invention itself concerned the 'organisation of chat-based communication systems which enable the establishment of private chat threads, or conversations, between a range of devices, such as computers, tablets and smart phones'.[147] The UIPO, focusing on the issue of section 1, made the point that section 1(2) of the Act reads as follows:

> It is hereby declared that the following (among other things) are not inventions for the purposes of this Act, that is to say, anything which consists of –
>
> (a) ...;
> (b) ...;
> (c) *a scheme, rule or method for performing a mental act, playing a game or doing business, or a program for a computer;*
> (d) *the presentation of information; but the foregoing provision shall prevent anything from being treated as an invention for the purposes of this Act only to the extent that a patent or application for a patent relates to that thing as such.*[148]

143 *Nexticvia Inc*, BL O/0189/24. https://www.ipo.gov.uk/p-challenge-decision-results/o018924.pdf
144 Ibid., para 1.
145 Ibid., para 2.
146 Ibid., para 4.
147 Ibid., para 6.
148 Ibid., para 12.

In reconciling the above, by drawing on the common law, the court made the point that section 1(2) is governed by the judgment of the Court of Appeal in '*Aerotel/Macrossan*, as further interpreted by that court in *Symbian*'. In *Aerotel/Macrossan*, the court reviewed the case law on the interpretation of Section 1(2) and established a four-step test to decide whether a claimed invention is patentable. These steps are:

(1) Properly construe the claim;
(2) Identify the actual contribution;
(3) Ask whether it falls solely within the excluded matter;
(4) Check whether the contribution is actually technical in nature.[149]

Importantly, the point was that this test was not considered a departure from domestic law, but a reaffirmation of the common law. In part, it applies the purposive approach to legislative implementation. Therefore, and in applying this test, the UIPO ruled that the 'invention as claimed in patent application GB2118756.2 does not provide a technical contribution and defines subject matter that is excluded from patentability by section 1(2)(c) of the Act as a computer program as such'.[150] This is one instance where the UIPO had to address the interpretation of the national laws to confirm or otherwise the granting of a patent. In this case, based on section 18 of the Patent Act on which the UIPO relied, the application was refused. Those practitioners applying for a patent on behalf of a client need to ensure that they fully understand the provisions of the national laws. They are complex. Although there are similarities between patent law and immigration law, they are both very procedural. The legal framework for both has been established to provide a clear process for applying for and being granted an immigration visa or a patent.

Section 2 provides for a novel invention, provided it does not form part of the state of the art. Section 3 mentions an inventive step where it is not obvious to a person skilled in the art. In the case of *Rockwool*,[151] paragraph 21 makes a point regarding the words 'not obvious' in section 3. The court stated, 'the word "obvious" is an ordinary word of English usage, and the courts have resisted attempts to re-articulate the statutory requirement'.[152] The court went further by referring to the case of *Medimmune Ltd v Novartis Pharmaceuticals*[153] in which Kitchin LJ noted:

149 Ibid., para 13. *Aerotel Ltd vs Telco Holdings Ltd & Macrossan's Patent Application [2007] RPC 7 Symbian Ltd's Application [2009] RPC 1.* See also BL O/0874/23. https://www.ipo.gov.uk/p-challenge-decision-results/o087423.pdf that also decided on whether the application meets section 1.

150 Ibid., para 39.

151 *Rockwool International A/S v Knauf Insulation Ltd* [2020] EWHC 1068 (Pat)

152 Ibid., para 21.

153 Ibid., para 21 [2012] EWCA Civ 1234.

> One of the matters which it may be appropriate to take into account is whether it was obvious to try a particular route to an improved product or process. There may be no certainty of success but the skilled person might nevertheless assess the prospects of success as being sufficient to warrant a trial. In some circumstances, this may be sufficient to render an invention obvious. On the other hand, there are areas of technology such as pharmaceuticals and biotechnology which are heavily dependent on research, and where workers are faced with many possible avenues to explore, but have little idea if any one of them will prove fruitful. Nevertheless, they do pursue them in the hope that they will find new and useful products. They plainly would not carry out this work if the prospects of success were so low as not to make them worthwhile. But denial of patent protection in all such cases would act as a significant deterrent to research.[154]

Thus, in this case, the strict interpretation of section 3 has not been applied, and the judiciary sought to ensure there was a degree of common sense allowed so as not to place a high-level threshold on the words 'not obvious'.

Notably, the UK and India are both similar to and different from Australia in providing for a standard or innovative patent. Moreover, the section clearly states that a patent will not be granted for 'a method of treatment of the human or animal body by surgery or therapy, or a method of diagnosis practised on the human or animal body'.[155] Under section 4, an exemption is applied to pharmaceutics. Single or joint applications for a patent can be made that will result in a single owner or co-owner[156] of a patent grant.

A person or entity can obtain a right in a patent under section 33 by claiming that an earlier transaction, instrument, or event was not registered, not published, or that they did not know of the earlier transaction, instrument, or event.[157] The life or term of a patent is generally consistent among jurisdictions, with the UK, according to section 25, providing for a 'period of 20 years beginning with the date of filing the application for the patent or with such other date as may be prescribed'.[158]

One of the most important features of the UK legal framework is the priority date, because it provides the actual date of filing,[159] [whereby the clock begins, so to speak]. Industrial inventions including agricultural applications also exist according to section 4. Arguably, section 7 is highly significant as it provides for the right to apply for a patent by an inventor or joint inventors, or the

154 Ibid.
155 *The Patent Act 1977*, section 4.
156 Ibid., section 36.
157 Ibid., section 33.
158 Ibid., section 25(1).
159 Ibid., section 5.

successor or successors in title of any person or persons who have applied.[160] While there are procedural steps in place for joint applications, amongst others, essentially, the application process is similar to that of Australia and the other states compared.

Section 14 sets out the process for making the application on the appropriate form that has been prepared by the Patent Office. Section 14(5) requires that a claim define the matter for protection, be clear and concise, and provide a description of the invention.[161] The date of filing, preliminary examination, publication, and search[162] are generally evident in the other jurisdictions.

A further and more comprehensive examination that will result in the granting or refusal of the application for a patent is provided for under section 18. The comptroller presiding over the application has specific obligations when making the assessment to grant or refuse the application, which will not be discussed in this section as they are procedural.

Regarding a failed application for a patent, section 20 specifies the procedure to follow after the expiry of the appeals period in section 97. That is, an appeal lies with the Patents Court after any decision made by the comptroller.[163] Section 20A allows for an application to be reinstated 'where an application for a patent is refused, or is treated as having been refused or withdrawn, as a direct consequence of a failure by the applicant to comply with a requirement of this Act or rules'.[164] Notably, UK residents are restricted from making patent applications to the UK from a third country.[165] Also similar to the other states, section 24[166] requires the comptroller to publish the grant after the granting of a patent. However, a specification can be amended.[167]

Importantly for the UK, a patent can apply to Scotland[168] according to section 31. Sections 37, 38, and 39 provide for various additional rights for employees. Licences of a right, or otherwise compulsory licences, are available under section 46. All states have similar licencing requirements. In addition to this, section 48 provides for general compulsory licences, and section 48B[169] these types of licences[170] for other specific circumstances where there is no World Trade Organisation proprietor. Unlike the other states compared, the UK and EU, according to sections 50 and 51, can take into consideration competition issues across the market and, to a large extent, minimise the opportunity for monopolies to be established.

160 Ibid., section 7.
161 Ibid., section 14(5).
162 Ibid., sections 15, 16, 17.
163 Ibid., section 97.
164 Ibid., section 20A.
165 Ibid., section 23.
166 Ibid., section 24.
167 Ibid., section 27.
168 Ibid., section 131A.
169 Ibid., section 48, 48B.
170 Ibid. Also see section 128A for compulsory pharmaceutical licences.

An individual can oppose[171] an application under section 51. Furthermore, sections 72 and 75 of the PA allow for a patent to be revoked and amended. This was reaffirmed in the matter of BL O/088/23, where the UK Intellectual Property Office stated that 'in accordance with section 72(4) of the Act, I ordered that patent GB2468976 be revoked unless it is amended under section 75 to the satisfaction of the comptroller'.[172] This matter referred to a number of court decisions that had interpreted the operation of these provisions. The point is that an applicant needs to follow every procedural step set out in the national laws. It is further incumbent on applicants to follow the recommendations or directions given by the IPO [Intellectual Property Office]. This position can be applied in any nation-state.

Against the backdrop of the above, and under the European Patent Convention, Article 99 states that 'within nine months of the publication of the mention of the grant of the European patent in the European Patent Bulletin, any person may give notice to the European Patent Office of opposition to that patent'.[173] Arbitration[174] is a key feature of the UK legal framework, and it can be used as an effective tool to resolve different disputes, such as licences granted to use a patent. However, arbitration does not apply to a matter under the control of the comptroller.[175] Moreover, a patent can be revoked by a comptroller.[176] In the matter of Cairnstores,[177] on 6 March 2002, Laddie J handed down his judgment in the conjoined actions for revocation of Aktiebolaget Hässle's European Patents (UK) Numbers 0247983 and 0496437. The claimants seeking revocation were Cairnstores Ltd and Generics (UK) Limited.[178] This case demonstrates that any person can make an application for a patent to be revoked, and this includes anyone who has no interest[179] in the patent itself. Thus, under the PCT framework, a patent application can be obtained in two ways. One is through the UK, otherwise referred to as the 'national phase' according to section 89 pertaining to international applications; and the other is through the European[180] regional office. It is acknowledged that further research is needed across all of these jurisdictions because this book has only touched the surface in relation to the legal requirements. The next section will discuss the state of India. This is logical because India generally follows the UK legal system.

171 Ibid., section 52.
172 BL O/0088/23. https://www.ipo.gov.uk/p-challenge-decision-results/o008823.pdf
173 *European Patent Convention*, as at 2024 Article 99. https://link.epo.org/web/EPC_17th_edition_2020_en.pdf. See Article 100 for grounds to oppose.
174 *The Patent Act 1977*, section 52.
175 Ibid., section 128B.
176 Ibid., section 72.
177 *Cairnstores Ltd v Akteibolaget Hassle (Application for Revocation)*, 2002, [2002] EWCA Civ 1504. https://vlex.co.uk/vid/cairnstores-ltd-v-aktiebolaget-792782425
178 Ibid., para 1.
179 Lionel Bently, Brad Sherman, Dev Gangjee, *Intellectual Property Law*, Oxford University Press (2022), p. 459.
180 Ibid., p. 410.

5.2.3 India

The *Patent Act 1970*[181] is more than 60 years old. As a member nation of the World Trade Organisation, and similar to other common law jurisdictions, patents in India are considered property. In India,

> there is a positive constitutional entitlement to the scientific temper and prescribes a duty to *develop* the spirit of inquiry and reform. Constitution of India mandates that no one shall be deprived of 'property' except with the authority of law. grant and recognition of patents.[182]

Notably, and not surprisingly, 'India inherited its patent regime from the British, and the Indian Patents and Designs Act, came into effect in 1911'.[183] After the implementation of the *Patent Act* in 1970 (PA),[184] India undertook further reform when it

> signed and acceded to the PCT in September 1998, which entered into force in India in December 1998. The provisions relating to applications under the PCT were incorporated under the Patents (Amendment) Act, 2002. Under the Patents Act, 1970, an 'international application' in accordance with Article 6 of the TRIPS Agreement. The principle of was defined as an application made as per the provisions of the PCT.[185]

In section 2, '"Patent Cooperation Treaty" means the Patent Cooperation Treaty done at Washington on the 19th day of June, 1970'.[186] Thus, the PCT was formally integrated into Indian national law. Section 3, similar to Australia's law, stipulates what is not patentable: an invention where the primary or intended use is commercial exploitation, a mere discovery of a scientific principle or the formulation of an abstract theory or discovery, or the mere discovery of a new form of a known substance which does not result in enhancement.[187] Also, elements of agriculture, plants, micro-organisms, animals, and atomic energy are excluded under this section and section 4.

181 *Patent Act 1970*, India. https://ipindia.gov.in/writereaddata/Portal/ev/sections-index.html
182 Justice Madan B Lokur, Justice Gautam Patel, Justice Prathiba M Singh, Justice Manmohan Singh, *An International Guide to Patent Case Management for Judges*, World Intellectual Property Organisation. https://www.wipo.int/patent-judicial-guide/en/full-guide/india
183 Ibid. See also as the authors refer to the primary source, the *Patents Act, 1970*, section 2(1)(ia). This was inserted by the *Patents (Amendment) Act*, 2002.
184 *India Patent Act 1970*. https://ipindia.gov.in/writereaddata/Portal/IPOAct/1_31_1_patent-act-1970-11march2015.pdf
185 Ibid.
186 Ibid., section 2.
187 Ibid., section 3.

Similar to other national laws, the PA establishes the procedure to follow when applying for a patent. Section 6 provides that a person can apply for a patent if they are the first inventor of the invention, an assignee of the person claiming to be the true and first inventor, or the legal representative of any deceased person who immediately before his death was entitled to make such an application.[188] This is predicated on section 134; however, this restricts section 6, which does not provide for reciprocal rights to apply for a patent in another country. Section 7 describes the form of an application, stipulating the procedural steps to follow. Moreover, it requires that every 'application for a patent shall be for one invention only and shall be made in the prescribed form and filed in the patent office'.[189]

In addition to this, every 'international application under the Patent Cooperation Treaty for a patent, as may be filed designating India shall be deemed to be an application under this Act, if a corresponding application has also been filed before the Controller in India'.[190] Whether a local or PCT application, section 7 requires that all applications state 'the person claiming to be the true and first inventor'.[191] The actual process and information to be provided as part of the patent application will vary slightly from, but are generally the same as, those of other nation-states depending on whether it is a national or PCT application. This is because a patent application is for an invention, which is an agreed universal concept.

Foreign applications can be made in India by a single person or jointly by more than one person.[192] Specific procedures must be followed by the applicant, such as ensuring they inform the Indian Controller of the application and any other similar inventions. Unlike the Australian framework (standard and innovative), India does not differentiate between patent applications. However, similar to Australia, India deals separately with elements of pharmaceuticals. For instance, section 92A specifies that a compulsory licence for the export of patented pharmaceutical products can be granted in certain exceptional circumstances.[193]

More generally, under section 91, licences can also be issued at any time after the sealing of the patent. Thus, licencing is another common theme that enables the governance of patents and further economic activity. For example, it may be in the public interest for a licence to be issued so the rapid production of a product can go ahead in response to a national or international crisis (such as COVID-19). The point is that there are both general and compulsory[194] licences.

188 Ibid., section 6.
189 Ibid., section 7.
190 Ibid., section 7(1A).
191 Ibid., section 7(3).
192 Ibid., section 8.
193 Ibid., section 92.
194 Ibid., see sections 82, 83, 84, 85, 86, 87, 88, 89, 90, 91, 92.

Given the above, the ability of a person or entity to oppose a patent application is somewhat limited. Section 87 requires that any application made according to sections 84 and 85 allows the Controller to

> direct the applicant to serve copies of the application upon the patentee and any other person appearing from the register to be interested in the patent in respect of which the application is made, and shall publish the application in the official journal.[195]

Therefore, a

> patentee or any other person desiring to oppose [opposition[196]] the application may, within such time as may be prescribed or within such further time as the Controller may on application allow, give to the Controller notice of opposition. Any such notice of opposition shall contain a statement setting out the grounds on which the application is opposed.[197]

In the case of *Anaghaya Million Pharma LLP*[198] the court noted that the

> Petitioner (ANAGHAYA MILLION PHARMA LLP) has filed the above revocation petition before this Hon'ble Board for Revocation of our Patent No. 280086. The Respondent No. 1 has corresponding granted patents in the USA, EP, Japan, China, and South Korea. Neither a pre-grant opposition nor a post-grant opposition was filed against the IN 280086. The said Patent covers a 'METHOD FOR PRODUCING DICHLOROPYRAZINE DERIVATIVE' and was granted on 14 January 2010.[199]

The court, in applying and interpreting section 25, stated:

> The Act, therefore, makes a distinction between an opposer at the stage of pre-grant opposition, who could be 'any' person, and the opposer at the post-grant stage, who could only be a 'person interested'. The legislative intent is that the right to file a post-grant opposition under Section 25 (2) is restricted to any person interested. The fact that the restriction of the time to file a pre-grant which results from the interpretation

195 Ibid., sections 87, 85, 84. Section 84 deals with compulsory licences, and section 85 deals with the revocation of a patent.

196 Ibid., section 25, sets out a number of grounds for filing a pre-grant opposition.

197 Ibid., sections 87, 85, 84.

198 *Anaghaya Million Pharma LLP v Nippon Soda Co. Ltd*, MANU/IC/0074/2020. https://www.courtkutchehry.com/Judgement/Search/t/1901111-anaghaya-million-pharma-llp-vs

199 Ibid., para 7.3.

> given by this court may impact the two classes of pre-grant opposers differently.[200]

This is the pre- and post-grant opposition process that is specific to India. The court also went on to say that:

> While restricting the time period for filing a pre-grant opposition to the time when such patent is granted may inconvenience 'any person' who wishes to file a pre-grant opposition, it is certainly not going to inconvenience a 'person interested'. Even if such 'interested' person misses the bus at the pre-grant stage, the right of such person to oppose at the post-grant stage is preserved under Section 25 (2) of the Act. Therefore, the interpretation placed by this Court certainly cannot prejudice a person interested in opposing the grant of patent. As regards any person, other than a person interested, the legislative intent appears to restrict the scope of such person confined to the stage of pre-grant. It would be necessary, therefore, for such person (who may not be an 'interested' person) to be vigilant and to watch out for the date of advertisement of the complete specification and understand that the limitation for filing a pre-grant opposition begins to run from that date onwards.[201]

Viewed this way, the pre- and post-grant opposition under section 25 provides a two-step process, whereby the person making the opposition can do so if they miss the pre-grant opposition, and can still submit an opposition after the granting of the patent. Arguably, the court in this case has been careful to not interpret section 25 in a narrow context. The court was applying the purposive approach to the interpretation of section 25. It was pointing to the right of a person and, to do so, the court would have to construe this in the wider context of the Act's purpose, which is to provide for the application and granting of a patent.

Importantly, a patent exists for 20 years from the date of filing the application, and this includes PCT patents.[202] Where a compulsory licence is being applied for, this can only be granted three years after the grant of a patent.[203] Thus, there is limited protection of a patent for three years. However, occasionally there may be exemptions to this rule that a licence is to be granted in the national interest, for instance, a pandemic. The time period of 20 years is consistent across all jurisdictions compared. It provides for the protection of confidential information pertaining to the invention. The confidentiality exists

200 Ibid., para 60.
201 Ibid., para 61.
202 *Patent Act 1970*, section 53. https://ipindia.gov.in/writereaddata/Portal/IPOAct/1_31_1_patent-act-1970-11march2015.pdf
203 Ibid.

throughout the entire cycle of application, examination[204] and grant of a patent. In the case of *Rochem*,[205] the issue involved the submission of affidavits for a civil matter, in relation to a patent being granted in the US, crossing over into copyright law.[206] Moreover, there was the question of whether the execution of the ex-parte ad-interim order resulted in material now being available to the court to verify the extent of the breach of confidentiality on the part of the defendants, particularly defendants No. 2 and 3.[207] In making the case for this breach of confidentiality, the court made a clear 'distinction between public and private information. It stated that 'confidential information' – that which is not in the public domain – must be accurately and specifically identified, and protection must be sought only in respect of that'.[208] However, confidential information must be clearly identified, together with proprietary and any contractual obligations.[209] Thus, in any application for a patent, confidential information has to be clearly indicated.

The rights of the patentee are important. Section 48 provides that upon being granted a patent, the patentee has the 'exclusive right to prevent third parties, who do not have his consent, from the act of making, using, offering for sale, selling or importing for those purposes that product in India'.[210] This right also prevents third parties, who do not have consent, from offering for sale, selling or importing for those purposes the product obtained directly by that process in India.[211] Similar to other jurisdictions, there can be co-owners of a patent.[212] Significant too, an important feature of the Indian law is that residents of India[213] cannot apply for a patent outside of the state unless they have approval to do so.

Finally, if an infringement of an issued patent has occurred, under section 151, the court has the ability to deal with such matters. Thus, the court can provide relief and damages for the breach of a patent.[214] Moreover, the concept of purposive construction[215] is central to the claims of patent applications

204 Ibid., section 144.
205 *Rochem Separation Systems (India) Pvt. Ltd v Nirtech Private Limited & Ors*, 2023:BHC-OS:2172. https://www.livelaw.in/pdf_upload/rochem-v-nirtech-467958.pdf
206 Ibid., para 4.
207 Ibid., para 3.
208 Ibid., paras 15, 16, 17, 18.
209 Ibid.
210 Patent Act 1970, section 48. https://ipindia.gov.in/writereaddata/Portal/IPOAct/1_31_1_patent-act-1970-11march2015.pdf
211 Ibid.
212 Ibid., section 50.
213 Ibid., section 39.
214 Ibid., section 106.
215 *F Hoffmann-La Roche Ltd v Cipla Ltd* MIPR 2016 (1) 1, which followed the United Kingdom case of *Catnic Components Ltd v Hill and Smith Ltd* (1982) RPC 183. Note that the United Kingdom has revised this approach, and the current standard in the UK requires a court to adopt a 'normal interpretation' approach. For further explanation, see *An Interna-*

in India. The same approach[216] was adopted in Australia, and the UK approach has been included in the practice management manual.[217] There are, however, minor but important exemptions to these rules. The concepts are applied to assist with the interpretation and application of national laws and the patent application itself. Without such rules being agreed upon by the judiciary, there would be a high level of ambiguity and uncertainty, creating too much flexibility when construing the application and the law. In addition to the PA, the Patent Rules[218] are another general addition to the legal frameworks of the jurisdictions compared. Their name and title will vary, along with the rules themselves, to take into account the local national requirements.

The general theme thus far is that the common law countries are effectively following each other. This is arguably one of the most harmonised international approaches to law, outside of contract law, in the world. This brief outline of the Indian law has confirmed its alignment with the other jurisdictions compared. The next section provides a brief comparison of the United States' patent laws.

5.2.4 United States (US)

The US Patent and Trademark Office[219] has a similar role to those of Australia, the UK, the EU, and other national and regional IP offices. Similar to the other jurisdictions compared, the laws[220] clearly stipulate the procedures to be followed when applying for and being granted a patent in the US. This section concerns only the application for a patent, what constitutes a patent, examination, opposition, revocation, co-ownership, and infringement. An invention that can become patentable has been defined according to section 101 to be a 'new and useful process, machine, manufacture, or composition of matter, or any new and useful improvement thereof, may obtain a patent therefor, subject to the conditions and requirements of this title'.[221] Novelty has become a key term used in the states compared. Section 102 defines conditions for patentability; novelty where the 'claimed invention was patented, described in

tional Guide to Patent Case Management for Judges, World Intellectual Property Organisation, p. 266. https://www.wipo.int/patent-judicial-guide/en/full-guide/india

216 Michael Pendleton, The Purposive Approach to Patent Construction: A Divergence in Anglo-Australian Judicial Interpretation, *Melbourne Law Review*, *14* (1983), 73–74.

217 Australian Government, *Patent Manual of Practice and Procedure*, 5.5.4.7. https://manuals.ipaustralia.gov.au/patent/5.5.4.7-for-use-in-when-used-and-similar-wording-in-claims

218 India, *Patent Amendment Rules*. https://ipindia.gov.in/rules-patents.htm

219 United States Patent and Trademark Office. https://www.uspto.gov/patents/laws

220 *Consolidated Patent Laws*, United States Code Title 35 – Patents. https://www.uspto.gov/web/offices/pac/mpep/consolidated_laws.pdf

221 United States Code Title 35 – Patents, section101. https://www.uspto.gov/web/offices/pac/mpep/consolidated_laws.pdf Also see *Patent Rules*, https://www.uspto.gov/web/offices/pac/mpep/consolidated_rules.pdf

a printed publication, or in public use, on sale, or otherwise available to the public before the effective filing date of the claimed invention'.[222]

Thus, for a patent to be utilised by a person, the invention had to be 'known or used by others in this country, or patented or described in a printed publication in this or a foreign country, before the invention thereof by the applicant for patent'.[223] Section 103 states that a patent cannot be claimed if the features of the proposed application are identical to those of other patents that have been granted or to other products on the market. What this is saying is that there has to be a clear, new element in whatever is being claimed to be a patent. There has to be a demonstrable difference between the proposed application and that of any product already on the market.

Expressed affirmatively, sections 111 to 120 set out the process for making an application. Of importance, as each office will have its own procedures and forms,

> the specification shall contain a written description of the invention, and of the manner and process of making and using it, in such full, clear, concise, and exact terms as to enable any person skilled in the art to which it pertains, or with which it is most nearly connected, to make and use the same, and shall set forth the best mode contemplated by the inventor or joint inventor of carrying out the invention.[224]

Significantly, the principle of enablement is important and has been the focus of judicial decisions as recently as 2023. On 18 May 2023, the US Supreme Court handed down its decision in *Amgen v Sanofi*,[225] the most recent instalment of the global battle between Amgen and Sanofi over the cholesterol-lowering drug, Praluent. The court upheld the decision of the Federal Circuit Court of Appeals, finding two of Amgen's patents (US 8829165 and US 8859741) lacked enablement. The court noted that Congress has left this 'enablement' obligation largely intact, and the courts have addressed the enablement requirement many times.[226] Importantly, the court noted that where the 'patent's specification must enable a person skilled in the art to make and use the entire class, only one statutory enablement standard exists'.[227] Further, the court stated that,

> just as in 1790, the law secures for the public its benefit of the patent bargain by ensuring that, 'upon the expiration of [the patent], the

222 Ibid., section 102.
223 Ibid., section 102.
224 Ibid., section 112.
225 *Amgen v Sanofi*, No. 21–757. Argued March 27, 2023 – Decided 18 May 2023 https://www.supremecourt.gov/opinions/22pdf/21-757_k5g1.pdf
226 Ibid., p. 2.
227 Ibid.

> knowledge of the invention [i]njures to the people, who are thus enabled without restriction to practice'.[228]

The cautionary note provided by the court stated that

> if a patent claims an entire class of processes, machines, manufactures, or compositions of matter, the patent's specification must enable a person skilled in the art to make and use the entire class. In other words, the specification must enable the full scope of the invention as defined by its claims. The more one claims, the more one must enable.[229]

This approach differs from the UK approach. In December 2023, the Supreme Court of Appeal in *Fibrogen*[230] was withdrawn. However, two years earlier, in 2021, *Fibrogen*[231] stated that the 'patentee must enable the invention to be performed in respect of each of them'.[232] In addition, the court stated that a patent is

> sufficiently enabled if one can reasonably expect the invention to work with anything which falls within the general term, and reference to a requirement of 'connecting means' is enabled if the invention can reasonably be expected to work with any means of connection. The patentee does not have to have experimented with all of them.[233]

Thus, the test by the UK court focused on the scope of the patent being claimed, whether the invention works, and whether it was predetermined that the patent will operate as described. That is, the functionality of the proposed patent. However, the US court looked to the described methodology, and not the functionality of the compounds. More importantly, the courts of the two jurisdictions considered the experiments that had been conducted, before concluding that the party had a workable new invention. The court examined the time and effort put into the development of the compound, the different components of the end product, and the experiments conducted on the final product. In relation to the concept of enablement, this is an important feature differentiating the two states.

Notwithstanding the above, there can be one or more specifications, and they can be written 'independent or, if the nature of the case admits, in dependent

228 Ibid., p. 8.
229 Ibid., p. 13.
230 *Fibrogen v Akebia* [2021] EXCA Civ 1279. https://www.bristows.com/app/uploads/2024/03/Review-of-Patent-Cases-in-the-English-Courts-2023.pdf Note the appeal was withdrawn.
231 *Fibrogen v Akebia* [2021] EXCA Civ 1279. https://www.bailii.org/ew/cases/EWCA/Civ/2021/1279.html
232 Ibid., para 51.
233 Ibid.

or multiple dependent form'.[234] Drawings are dealt with separately under section 113, along with model specimens provided for in section 114, allowing the director to request a specimen. Unlike the laws of the other states compared, section 115 requires an inventor to provide an Oath or Declaration. While this is provided for under the laws in the US, and without examining the other states' procedures, it is likely that there would be a form of declaration when completing and signing off on the relevant form. Section 116 provides for more than one inventor, and section 117 provides for the death of an inventor.[235] The application for a patent does not necessarily need to be filed by the inventor. A third party, such as a legal practitioner, can undertake this process on the inventor's behalf.[236]Importantly, the right or priority[237] enables the 'first in, best dressed' to file an application. This protects the rights of the first applicant, particularly if the application is filed in the United States.[238] The other laws compared in this book do not necessarily provide these protections. Nonetheless, the remaining sections pertain to the administrative processes and the courts within the US that have a level of oversight for appeals of patent decisions.

After a patent has been granted, the inventor is afforded certain rights. Chapter 14, section 154, stipulates several provisional rights. Chapter 18[239] provides for an additional set of rights where a patent has been granted with US Federal assistance in the form of financial or other assistance. A review of a decision can be undertaken by the courts, and there is a formal process for this to be implemented in Chapter 13. This will not be discussed in this section. A patent will be granted[240] upon meeting all of the obligations set out by this law and the requirements of the Patent Office.

Thus, a decision has to be made within three years of the application being filed.[241] Standard provisional rights upon being granted a patent include, but are not limited to, obtaining a reasonable royalty, and the date of publication of the application, and ending on the date the patent is issued

> makes, uses, offers for sale, or sells in the United States the invention or imports into the United States products made by that process as claimed in the published patent application; and published in a language other than English, had a translation of the international application into the English language.[242]

234 United States Code Title 35 – Patents, section 112. https://www.uspto.gov/web/offices/pac/mpep/consolidated_laws.pdf,
235 United States Code Title 35 – Patents, sections 116 and 117. https://www.uspto.gov/web/offices/pac/mpep/consolidated_laws.pdf,
236 Ibid., section118.
237 Ibid., section119.
238 Ibid., section120.
239 Ibid., Chapter 18.
240 Ibid., sections 151, 152, 153.
241 Ibid., section 154.
242 Ibid.

On that basis, the rights to a patent also align with the ownership, whether jointly[243] or otherwise. Therefore, an interest in a patent is a fundamental principle at law. It is no different from other areas of the law such as personal or commercial property. In fact, a patent provides a proprietary right and interest to an individual or group of individuals. What is clear throughout the patent laws of the US are the provisions pertaining to the interest, development, and application of a patent with the government. The other jurisdictions' patent laws are not as detailed as those of the US.

Moreover, there is an additional set of rights regarding limitations on royalties and amendments/adjustments that need to be made along the way. Any changes are likely a likely step in the process of application and examination due to the complex issues involved. It also provides for the rights pertaining to the PCT,[244] which has been given effect under section 351. Sections 361 to 368 set out the process for an international application under the PCT, specifically for examination, designation of the US office, the procedure itself, right of priority, withdrawal, and secrecy. Generally, they replicate the national application approach. There are also specific rights set out in Chapter 18 for federal assistance, which will not be addressed in this section. For the practitioner, to understand the legal regime in the US and other states is to clearly discern between the public and private elements of patent law.

Nonetheless, before the above has been determined and a patent has been granted, the process of examination is conducted as set out in Chapter 12. Section 154 directs the Director of the IPO to establish a process for the examination of the application and the 'alleged new invention'.[245] In addition, the term of a patent (20 years) is consistent with those of the other states compared.[246] The term can be adjusted, and there are priority considerations that will be taken into account.[247] Interestingly, under the US laws, no formal process is stipulated for any person to oppose the patent. Rather, under section 141, a review can be undertaken.

In relation to relief and damages, the infringement of a patent has to be protected at all costs. This is because, if there is no protection, there will be a significant dilution of certainty for innovators and inventors. Section 271 deals with the infringement of a patent, and the liability rests solely with the infringer 'who without authority makes, uses, offers to sell, or sells any patented invention, within the United States, or imports into the United States any patented invention during the term of the patent therefor, infringes the patent'.[248] On the other hand, and unlike its counterpart law in the UK,

243 Ibid., section 261.
244 Ibid., section 351. Treaty means the *Patent Cooperation Treaty* done at Washington, on 19 June 1970.
245 Ibid., section 131, 132.
246 Ibid., section 154.
247 Ibid., priority, see sections 119, 365(a), 365(b), 386(a), or 386(b).
248 Ibid., section 271.

Matthew Wilkerson[249] is of the view that when examining the US and UK, 'the United States will only hold a party liable for infringement if the infringing act occurs in the United States per 35 U.S.C'. Section 271.11 and section 271(a) states,

> except as otherwise provided in this title, whoever without authority makes, uses, offers to sell, or sells any patented invention, within the United States or imports into the United States any patented invention during the term of the patent therefor, infringes the patent.

Wilkerson goes on to say that the 'statute and the US courts have identified instances in which the patent may not be literally infringed in the United States, yet the law will still consider the actions infringing'.[250] According to Wilkerson, the major difference between the two common law countries is that the United Kingdom typically:

> does not find liability in international and cross-border infringement due to their statutory language. This, however, does not prevent courts in the United Kingdom from finding indirect infringement in cross-border schemes. The British courts have achieved this through [UK] Patents Act section 60(2), which they have determined requires finding (1) who uses the infringing item and (2) where is it used. Disharmony is not efficient, but the clarity with which the United States, Germany, and the United Kingdom treated extraterritorial patent infringement historically limited legal uncertainty, which mitigates risk and keeps transactional costs minimal. This legal uncertainty is no longer limited.[251]

However, the extraterritorial response to transnational infringements is problematic. Wilkerson, in referring to the case of *WesternGeco LLC v ION Geophysical Corp*,[252] states that the issue was whether a party could recover lost profits and compared this matter with a previous matter of whether the component being exported was comprised of components that were causing the infringement, unlike the component infringing on the territory of the US. In the case of *WesternGeco*, the court held that a patent owner who proves infringement under section 271(f)(2) is entitled to foreign lost profits under section 284.6.[253] This established a new approach to handling extraterritorial infringements. There is

249 Matthew T. Wilkerson, *International [Dis]Harmony: Solving Legal Uncertainty in Extraterritorial Patent Infringement Suits.* Transnational Law & Contemporary Problems, *29* (2020), 377.

250 Ibid.

251 Ibid.

252 Ibid., p. 378, *WesternGeco LLC v ION Geophysical Corp. https://www.supremecourt.gov/opinions/17pdf/16-1011_6j37.pdf*

253 Ibid., p. 384.

no doubt that this issue is also relevant for the other states compared. However, this is an area requiring further research. This new development in the case overturned a previous decision whereby 'the Federal Circuit had previously held that section 271(a), the general infringement provision, does not allow patent owners to recover for lost foreign sales'.[254] This demonstrated highlights that the interpretation of national laws evolves and is shaped by societal change. On the other hand, as these matters find their way into the higher courts, the interpretation of the legislation will be subject to greater scrutiny.

Where an infringement of the laws has been proven, damages can be awarded by the courts and are measured so as 'adequately to compensate for the infringement but in no event less than a reasonable royalty'.[255] Hence, the amount of compensation is to be no less than a royalty payment, whatever that amount is. This will vary from patent to patent. However, a claim for damages expires after six[256] years prior to the filing. An important feature of the US legal regime is the secrecy provisions. Of note are sections 181 to 188. In particular, section 184 prevents a patent from being 'filed in a third country without a licence prior to six months after filing the application'.[257] It is not clear whether this provision has been established to protect US interests and is a way of managing and controlling the invention via a licence. Despite this, the licencing requirements identified earlier in the other states are different from those of the US. A licence is required only under the secrecy provisions of Chapter 17 above and, according to section 185, it requires that a patent could be excluded from filing without a licence.

However, this is specific to cases where a patent would not be required

> if that person, or his successors, assigns, or legal representatives shall, without procuring the license prescribed in section 184, have made, or consented to or assisted another's making, application in a foreign country for a patent or for the registration of a utility model, industrial design, or model in respect of the invention.[258]

What it does do is provide some oversight for filings for patents in third countries. Arguably, this would assist in tracking and governing the invention. The case of *Kingston*,[259] involved an appeal from a decision of the Patent Trial and

254 *WesternGeco LLC v ION Geophysical Corp. https://www.supremecourt.gov/opinions/17pdf/16-1011_6j37.pdf* In *Power Integrations, Inc. v Fairchild Semiconductor Int'l, Inc.*, 711 F. 3d 1348 (CA Fed. 2013) at 1350–1351.

255 United States Code Title 35 – Patents, section 284. https://www.uspto.gov/web/offices/pac/mpep/consolidated_laws.pdf

256 Ibid., section 286.

257 Ibid., section 184.

258 Ibid.

259 *Kingston Technology Company, Inc v SPEX Technologies*, Inc, Case: 19-1342. https://fedcircuitblog.com/wp-content/uploads/2019/09/Kingston-opinion.pdf

Appeal Board rejecting a petition to institute an inter partes review (IPR) and request to join a related IPR. It also diverged from the Board's decision that terminated the related IPR after all the parties to that case had reached a settlement agreement.[260] Significantly, Chapter 31[261] provides for a review of the decision for a patent following a petition.

In *Kingston*, the court stated that 'there has been a resistance to limiting section 314(d)'s bar on appellate review to the denial of a petition for failure to establish a reasonable likelihood of success'.[262] In noting where the power to appeal resides, the court stated:

> right to appeal, if any, comes from 35 U.S.C. § 141(c), which states that '[a] *party* to an inter partes review ... who is dissatisfied with the final written decision of the Patent Trial and Appeal Board under section 318(a) ... may appeal the Board's decision only to the United States Court of Appeals for the Federal Circuit' (emphasis added); *see also* 35 U.S.C. § 319 ('A party dissatisfied with the final written decision ... may appeal the decision pursuant to [§ 141]'.).[263]

This begs the question: Who are the parties to the patent application? The court concluded that 'Kingston is absolutely not a party under section 141, it has no right to appeal'.[264] Subsequently, the appeal was dismissed, and Kingston was awarded costs. Thus, a cautionary take from this case is that the claimant must be a party to the patent. Finally, while not stated by the judiciary or within US patent law, the purposive approach to statutory interpretation is evident. At the heart of this doctrine is the interpretation of legislation for its real and actual purpose. Therefore, the patent laws would arguably fall into this category. As noted by Kevin Stack:

> the purposive account of agency statutory interpretation conceives of the relationship between law and politics differently. To be sure, one function of law and legal considerations is to identify the scope of the agency's powers. But, on the purposive view of interpretation, there is necessarily a continuing role for legal considerations within the zone of those actions that are within the agency's powers. Purposive reasoning has a teleological form in the sense that it obliges the agency to carry forward the ends established by statute. As a result, on a purposive account,

260 Ibid.

261 United States Code Title 35 – Patents, sections 311 to 319. https://www.uspto.gov/web/offices/pac/mpep/consolidated_laws.pdf

262 *Kingston Technology Company, Inc v SPEX Technologies*, Inc, Case: 19-1342, p. 4. https://fedcircuitblog.com/wp-content/uploads/2019/09/Kingston-opinion.pdf

263 Ibid., p. 6.

264 Ibid.

'law' has just as much to say about decision making within a zone of authorised actions as it does about how to identify that zone.[265]

Arguably, the adoption of this approach offers a high level of consistency and certainty to patent decisions across the US. The purposive approach takes the decision maker back to what the legislation establishes. In this case, it provides a legal framework for the application, and the granting and governance of patents in all the jurisdictions compared. Generally, from the brief comparison given above, the respective legal regimes have similar processes for patents in terms of applying, granting, examining, reviewing, appealing, infringing, and obtaining relief. Any differences are due to the specific laws framed according to each state's own sovereign needs. The EU framework has been harmonised to account for all Member States, although the general process has been left to the national laws of each state. All states have adopted and apply the international PCT. This level of acceptance signifies a high level of agreed harmonisation pertaining to patents across the world. What is evident are the emerging challenges posed to patent law, particularly in regard to whether a technological development or innovation is considered to be an invention. For instance, courts have been reluctant to provide a definition of AI. The technology pertaining to the application and operation of tokens has emerged in patent applications. This has the potential to increase over the coming years, particularly if tokens are widely accepted and adopted. Copyright has also developed into an important area of law that has similarities to but also differences from that of patent law.

5.2.5 China

This section will briefly discuss China's laws and approach to patent law. According to Article 42, the duration of an invention is 20 years and a design patent right will be afforded ten years protection.[266] Most notably, China has generally linked invention with creation. That is, a patent under China law is very similar to that of other civil and common law countries. Article 4 describes an invention as a creation that will not be afforded any protection where it violates the law or social ethics, or harm public interests under Article 5.[267] Article 6 states that for an employment invention-creation, the employer has the right to apply for a patent.[268] After such application is granted, the employer shall be the patentee. Thus, it is likely that the employer and not an employee would

265 Kevin Stack, *Purposivism in the Executive Branch: How Agencies Interpret Statutes*, 109 (4) (2015), 928–930.

266 World Intellectual Property Organisation, *Patent Law of the People's Republic of China 2008*, Article 42. https://www.wipo.int/wipolex/en/legislation/details/5484

267 Ibid., Article 5.

268 Ibid., Article 6.

be afforded any patent right. That is, unless there is a contractual arrangement. Nonetheless, a patent right can be transferred to another entity.

Of note, in 2020, the *Patent Law* was amended, and accordingly Article 71(1) of the Chinese *Patent Law 2020* was amended to include

> serious intentional patent infringement, the amount of compensation for damage should be one to five times the amount of 'the actual loss suffered by the right holder due to the infringement' or 'benefits obtained by the infringer from the infringement' or a reasonable multiple of the royalty for the patent.[269]

Additionally, under Article 71(2), the 'statutory compensation was also increased from RMB 10,000 to 1 million Yuan to RMB 30,000 to 5 million Yuan'.[270] In strengthening the burden of proof, Article 71(4) was also changed to provide that, in order to determine the amount of compensation for the damage, the court may order an infringer to provide the account books and materials related to the infringement, which are mainly in the possession of the infringer if the rights holder has already made an effort to adduce evidence.[271] This amendment places a greater level of obligation on the alleged infringer to submit any relevant evidence. Further important additions were also made to improve employees' access to patent rights, by allowing an employee to transfer the right to an employee.[272] The reasoning for this change is explained as:

> Articles 6 and 15 of the newly amended Patent Law 2020 clearly entitle the patentees of employees' inventions (such as universities and research institutes, etc.) to dispose of the property rights of patents for employees' inventions. Because the lawmakers believed that inventors are the most important persons to promote and realize the implementation of patented technologies, sharing the patent right of the employees' inventions with inventors, universities and research institutes etc. could encourage inventors to devote themselves to promoting the implementation of patented technologies. According to the author's opinion, however, it should be more important to cultivate and encourage experts to perform patent licensing and technology transfer. This is because most inventors are actually weak at marketing and managing.[273]

Also, for pharmaceuticals, the patent duration was extended to five years.[274] There was also a further delegation of enforcement responsibility to localised

269 Ling Feng, Xiang Yu, The Fourth Amendment of Chinese Patent Law and Discussion on its Practical Effects *European Review*, *31* (2) (2022),196–199.
270 Ibid.
271 Ibid.
272 Ibid., p. 198.
273 Ibid., p. 207.
274 Ibid., p. 199.

authorities, and the introduction of an open licence that can be provided to 'any entity or individual exploiting his/its patent technology with a certain royalty and the payment method and standard'.[275] Another change specified domestic priority. To render

> Article 2(4) of the Patent Law 2020 more feasible, domestic priority right for design of six months for design is added into Article 29(2) accordingly. This amendment balances the content of the rights of a patentee for a design patent with that of a patent for an invention.[276]

Of note was the change to Article 42(1) of Patent Law 2020, where 'the protection duration of a design patent is extended from 10 years to 15 years'.[277] In addition, the amount of patent infringement damages was increased significantly, with the proportion of judged cases with damages more than RMB30,000 yuan increasing from 36.5% to 93%.[278] Arguably, the 2020 amendments to China's laws have enhanced its adoption of TRIPS, with many of the laws being similar to those of the states compared, with only some minor differences. This section, while very brief, was included to provide an overview of the patent laws of China; no comments or recommendations on policy or changes to the law are made. The next section will compare the national laws for copyright. It will also outline key features of the international legal framework pertaining to copyright.

5.3 Copyright

Similar to patent law, copyright has been recognised internationally. This section will briefly compare the copyright laws of Australia, the EU, the UK, India, and the US.

The World Intellectual Property Copyright Treaty (the Treaty) came into effect in 1996.[279] The Treaty, according to the WIPO, is a special agreement that falls under the Berne Convention 1979.[280] This section will identify the core principles and concepts of copyright law that include, but are not limited to, acknowledgement, creative and intellectual works, original [originality] works of authorship, the time period of a copyright (unlike patents, copyright protection extends well past 20 years), and public versus privately produced works.

275 Ibid., p. 200.
276 Ibid., p. 201.
277 Ibid.
278 Ibid.
279 World Intellectual Property. https://www.wipo.int/treaties/en/ip/wct/
280 World Intellectual Property Organisation, *Berne Convention 1979*. https://www.wipo.int/treaties/en/ip/berne/

Unlike patents, copyright does not necessarily stop another person from producing a work. The notable difference is that a patent is given for an invention that can, under a licence, or upon expiry of the 20-year term, be utilised by others. Copyright does not pertain to an invention and can be utilised provided that the user acknowledges the person or entity who produced the original work. However, there is some overlap between the two protections. Generally, they pertain to works of literature, art and computer software.

The Treaty deals with computer programs and compilations of data or other material, with Article 4 describing a computer program as: 'whatever may be the mode or form of their expression'.[281] In 2022, the WIPO stated that blockchain used for the purpose of copyright can assist in providing:

- trustable information of ownership, licensing and tracking the use of digital content; and
- increased transparency and better rights data management; and
- through time-stamping, the ability for creators and authors proof of ownership and establish the actual *dies a quo* of the corresponding protection attributed to a specific work; and
- who is using the work.[282]

The importance of the above cannot be underestimated. It can also be used to develop and govern contracts and agreements that are used to facilitate token exchanges and transactions. The potential efficiencies in protecting copyright for creators can only be of benefit economically to many. In relation to NFTs and copyright established on blockchain, it can be a:

- tool to attribute authorship, ownership and authenticity to digital works; and
- unique identifier of a digital asset (e.g. a work of art in digital format); and
- unique digital item(s), indicating that a digital work is unique, original and no other item will bear such characteristics or attributes.[283]

Thus, the relationship between the above and smart contracts allows for specific conditions to be established throughout the life-cycle of the NFT that is

281 World Intellectual Property Organisation, *Copyright Treaty 1996*. https://www.wipo.int/wipolex/en/text/295157 See Article 2 of the Berne Convention for the Protection of Literary and Artistic Works this applies to [*Protected Works:* 1. 'Literary and artistic works'; 2. Possible requirement of fixation; 3. Derivative works; 4. Official texts; 5. Collections; 6. Obligation to protect; beneficiaries of protection; 7. Works of applied art and industrial designs; 8. News]

282 World Intellectual Property Organisation, *Blockchain Technologies and IP Ecosystems: A WIPO White Paper* (2022), p. 40. https://www.wipo.int/export/sites/www/cws/en/pdf/blockchain-for-ip-ecosystem-whitepaper.pdf

283 Ibid., p. 40.

assigned to the specific digital asset. Arguably, this is what makes the application and use of blockchain more credible as a means of providing a higher level of transparency and traceability. The next section will examine the copyright laws of Australia.

5.3.1 Australia

The *Copyright Act 1968*[284] (CRA) is the principal legislation that protects original literary works, dramatic, musical and artistic works, and subject matter other than works. Essentially, the works must be original. The laws do not protect information, names or titles. For the purposes of this section and book, copyright information, and original works will be referred to as 'materials'. Section 10 defines 'copy' as the reproduction, recording or copying of certain material. From an international perspective, the CRA follows the transnational framework such as the

> Berne Convention for the Protection of Literary and Artistic Works 1886 (Berne Convention)[285] and the Agreement on Trade-Related Aspects of Intellectual Property Rights 1994 (TRIPS Agreement).[286] These conventions define minimum periods and levels of protection for copyright in member States, and provide for limitations and exceptions to copyright in certain circumstances.[287]

Also pertinent to this book is the definition of a computer to mean 'a set of statements or instructions to be used directly or indirectly in a computer in order to bring about a certain result',[288] as it pertains to copyright law. This definition would cover blockchain technology and the technology that supports tokens. However, as this section demonstrates, the limitations of the copyright laws generally do not extend to the technology itself, that is, the blockchain. By and large, the laws apply to what has been produced by means of the technology. This is different from patent law that focuses on the invention itself, such as a technological artefact.

Notably also,

284 *Copyright Act 1968*. https://www.legislation.gov.au/C1968A00063/2019-01-01/text. See also supporting instruments of *Copyright Regulations 2017* and the *Copyright (International Protection) Regulations 1969*

285 Ibid., section 10.

286 Ibid., section 10.

287 Australian Law Reform Commission, *Copyright Law 2010*. https://www.alrc.gov.au/publication/genes-and-ingenuity-gene-patenting-and-human-health-alrc-report-99/28-copyright-and-databases/copyright-law/

288 *Copyright Act 1968*, section 10.

> access control technological protection measure: means a device, product, technology or component (including a computer program) that is used in Australia or a qualifying country by, with the permission of, or on behalf of, the owner or the exclusive licensee of the copyright in a work or other subject-matter, but, does not include such a device, product, technology or component related to cinematograph film.[289]

Additionally, other terms that have also been defined include 'electronic rights management information',[290] 'technological protection measure',[291] and 'Copyright Tribunal' (CT).[292] The CT[293] is specific to Australia and not well understood. It makes decisions in relation to licencing and whether there has been a copyright breach of a licence. Nonetheless, this section will be limited to original works, licence, rights owners[294] and exclusive licence holders,[295] moral right,[296] electronic rights,[297] protections, fair dealing/use,[298] and infringement.

In light of the developments in the digital economy, in 2014, the Australia Law Reform Commission released its report[299] on copyright and noted that, today, this is the standard economic model of copyright law, whereby 'copyright provides an economic incentive for the creation and distribution of original works of authorship'.[300] There are also specific provisions pertaining to a non-infringement copy of a computer program that relates to a qualifying country.[301] A qualifying country is one of the states that are party to the international Convention mentioned earlier in this section.

Importantly, in regard to the reproduction of computer programs, section 21 deals with a work where the

> code version of the program is derived from the program in source code by any process, including compilation; or a source code version of the program is derived from the program in object code by any process, including de-compilation and any such version is taken to be a reproduction of the program.[302]

289 Ibid., section 10.
290 Ibid.
291 Ibid.
292 Ibid.
293 Copyright Tribunal. https://www.copyrighttribunal.gov.au/decisions
294 *Copyright Act 1968*, section 116.
295 Ibid., section 119.
296 Ibid., sections 190–192.
297 Ibid., Subdivision 3.
298 Ibid., section 40.
299 Australian Law Reform Commission, *Copyright and the Digital Economy*. https://www.alrc.gov.au/wp-content/uploads/2019/08/final_report_alrc_122_2nd_december_2013_.pdf
300 Ibid., p. 44, footnote 22.
301 *Copyright Act 1968*, section 10AB.
302 Ibid., section 21.

Arguably, this will relate to smart contracts that deal with tokens as they rely on code based on blockchain technology. It will also include software technology that is used to authenticate token use.

Therefore, where an entity develops and uses blockchain technology and smart contracts for the administration of tokens, and that technology is reproduced without authority, this would be a breach of the law. Section 31 provides for copyright of original works that can include a computer program under a commercial rental arrangement.[303] However, this does not apply where such an arrangement was entered into before the

> commencement of Part 2 of the Copyright (World Trade Organization Amendments) Act 1994; the commercial rental arrangement is entered into in the ordinary course of a business conducted by the program owner; and the program owner was conducting the same business, or another business that consisted of, or included, the making of commercial rental arrangements in respect of computer programs, when the copy was purchased.[304]

What this means is that there are exemptions to whether a computer program will constitute 'original works'.

The principle of original works is fundamental to the application and operation of copyright law. The principle was discussed by the Federal Court of Australia in the case of ...[305] in relation to the possible infringement of copyright in a cloud-based real estate marketing software.[306] The court went into some detail when explaining that section 32 of the CRA pertains to the principle of original works and whether an infringement has occurred. In referring to earlier case law, the court stated that the 'exclusive rights comprised in the copyright in an original work subsist by reason of the relevant fixation of the original work of the author in a material form'.[307] Generally, rather than focusing on the principles, the courts have tended to focus on the words 'original' or 'originality' and applied this concept to the works.

For instance, the court stated that the work originated with an author, and that it was not merely copied from another work(s).[308] Significantly,

> the assessment of originality is done by reference to the whole of the identified work, and not identifiable elements within it, although there may be a separate issue as to whether identifiable elements within a larger work are themselves an original work.[309]

303 Ibid., section 31.
304 Ibid.
305 Ibid.
306 *Campaigntrack Pty Ltd v Real Estate Tool Box Pty Ltd* [2021] FCA 809. https://jade.io/article/824275
307 Ibid., paras 176–177.
308 Ibid., para 178.
309 Ibid., para 131, referring to *Coogi Australia Pty Ltd v Hysport International Pty Ltd* (1998) 86 FCR 154 at 172.

Moreover in relation to specific or exclusive rights, the court pointed to section 31 of the CRA stating that 'copyright in relation to a "work" is the exclusive right to do certain acts in relation to that work, including the right to reproduce it in a material form and to communicate the work to the public'.[310] That right extends to material form. The court went on to say that the

term 'material form' includes 'any form' (whether visible or not) of storage of the work, or a substantial part of the work or adaptation, (whether or not the work or adaptation, or a substantial part of the work or adaptation, can be reproduced).[311]

In relation to rights, the court will consider what has been provided by the CRA, and what if any, agreement or contract has been developed to afford a certain right to parties.

In addition to the above, this case also touched on the test for infringement under section 36. The court stated that section 36

> provides for two causes of action: 'primary infringement', namely direct infringement by the 'doing [of] … any act comprised in the copyright'; and 'secondary infringement', namely the authorisation of the doing of the act or acts comprised in the copyright constituting the primary infringement.[312]

By reconciling authorisation without a licence under section 36, the court took into account three important factors: 1) a person's power to prevent the act, 2) the relationship between the person/s-parties, and 3) whether reasonable steps were taken to avoid any breach.[313] On that basis, the court concluded that 'authorise' has its ordinary meaning of 'sanction, approve, countenance'.[314] Therefore, when determining those rights that have been breached without authority such as an agreement, contract, licence or some other binding obligation, the court will look at the power of the person, the relationship (formal or otherwise) and the steps, if any, taken to minimise the breach.

The above case, heard in 2021, covered many areas of the CRA and the tests undertaken to reconcile the application of the legislation. It provides steps to understanding elements of technology and how copyright will be afforded or otherwise under the CRA.

Pertinent too, is the developing concept of a moral right[315] under the CRA. In Australia, this concept does not extend to computer technology including artificial intelligence. This cannot be afforded through a licence, contract or other binding agreement. In 2012, the Federal Court handed down a decision

310 Ibid., para 182.
311 Ibid., para 183.
312 Ibid., para 268.
313 Ibid., para 269.
314 Ibid., para 170.
315 *Copyright Act 1968*, section 190.

in *Perez*[316] whereby a party 'combined the Audio Drop with the MP3 Copy, using and audio editing software program'.[317] The court had to determine whether the infringement constituted a breach of moral rights. The court stated that moral rights 'have independent existence from the bundle of "economic" rights protected by copyright, are inalienable to the author, and give protection to the investment of the author's personality in their creation'. Furthermore, 'moral rights draw their jurisprudential force from civil law traditions and a number of international copyright and human rights conventions'.[318] At issue was the

> infringement of copyright and moral rights claimed by the applicants (Mr Perez, an international recording artist known as 'Pitbull' and two corporate entities associated with him) in a sound recording and musical work known as *Bon, Bon*. The infringements involved the respondent (Mr Fernandez, a disc jockey and music promoter in Perth) distorting the *Bon, Bon* work in a way which was said to be harmful to its author's reputation, and then streaming that distorted version of the song from a website owned and operated by Mr Fernandez.[319]

Software programs were used to help facilitate this infringement of copyright. Finally, the court declared that the respondent had infringed the moral rights of the first applicant regarding the literary and musical works that had been compromised.[320] This is an area requiring vigilance. Why? Because as software becomes more sophisticated and code or other advanced technology is used increasingly to breach these copyrights, moral rights could one day be considered as rights pertaining to the copying of works on a blockchain. However, it must be noted that it is unlikely that the technology will ever be afforded copyright. Having said that, there may be a time when technology is being used to reproduce original works without authorisation or a licence, thereby infringing a copyright.

Another key feature of the CRA is that it enables material to be used and copied under licence.[321] The CRA provides for statutory and voluntary licences,[322]

316 *Perez v Fernandez* (2012) 260 FLR 1; [2012] FMCA 2. http://www8.austlii.edu.au/cgi-bin/viewdoc/au/cases/cth/FMCA/2012/2.html This followed the 2006 case of *Meskenas v ACP Publishing Ltd* [2006] FMCA 1136, regarding moral rights provisions of the *Copyright Act 1968* (Cth).

317 Ibid., para 31.

318 Ibid., para 81.

319 Ibid., para 1.

320 Ibid., para 3. See also Jani McCutcheon, *Perez v Fernandez:* Australia's First Decision on the Moral Right of Integrity, University of *Western Australia, Faculty of Law Research Paper, 2013-32.* https://api.research-repository.uwa.edu.au/ws/portalfiles/portal/9217539/SSRN_id2297191_Perez_v_Fernandez.pdf

321 *Copyright Act 1968*, sections 15, 29, 44A, 55, 59, 61, 70, 91, 100AF, 107, 112A, 113C and 113T.

322 Ibid., Division Part IVA Division 4, section 113T,

and an exclusive licence.[323] These provide certain rights in relation to the use of original works to protect copyright. These are important when licence agreements have been established between entities for the use of technology and software, including code that is used to develop the agreement-contract to govern tokens. This is another emerging area that has been recognised by the WIPO as there are many forms of technology-related agreements established for data, cybersecurity, artificial intelligence, software amongst others that are commonplace in the digital commercial world.

In Australia, there are a number of situations where a licence can be granted for the use of materials. The Copyright Tribunal in *DLA Group*[324] had to determine whether section 167(3) of the *CRA* requires a party to produce certain documents. The matter related to a sub-licence and arrangements between entities for the use of software. While not related directly to blockchain and tokens, where there are licence agreements between entities for the use of software that supports tokens, when a dispute arises, documents may be required for disclosure as part of evidence. Of note, the Tribunal can decide on matters of evidence that is outside the reference to the standard rules of evidence in the Commonwealth and state-based evidence[325] legislation.

Also of importance is the matter of use or dealing. Section 40 onwards in the CRA provides for fair dealing; however, in other states it is referred to as 'fair use of a copyright'. In Australia, this is based on a percentage of the use. For example, copyright still applies, albeit with a small amount of flexibility, to lecture notes provided by universities. Currently, fair dealing is limited in Australia. Section 40 stipulates that 10% of the number of words in the work or adaptation applies to published literary work in electronic form (except a computer program or an electronic compilation, such as a database), a published dramatic work in electronic form or an adaptation.[326] These exemptions largely exclude a computer program. Hence, it could be argued that as computer technology becomes more sophisticated, the application of fair dealing-use may have to be reconsidered.

Moreover, in relation to the awarding of damages for an infringement, this was dealt with in the case of *Dallas Buyers Club*[327] where the court was

323 Ibid., sections 117 to 125.

324 *DLA Group Pty Limited v Western Australia* (Summons) [2023] ACopyT 1. https://www.copyrighttribunal.gov.au/decisions/judgments?sq_content_src=%2BdXJsPWh0dHBzJTNBJTJGJTJGd3d3Lmp1ZGdtZW50cy5mZWRjb3VydC5nb3YuYXUlMkZqdWRnbWVudHMlMkZKdWRnbWVudHMlMkZ0cmlidW5hbHMlMkZhY29weXQlMkYyMDIzJTJGMjAyM2Fjb3B5dDAwMDEmYWxsPTE%3D

325 There are specific laws for evidence that apply in civil and criminal matters, for example, *Evidence Act 1995*, Victoria.

326 Ibid., section 40.

327 *Dallas Buyers Club LLC v iiNet Limited* (No 5) [2015] FCA 1437. https://jade.io/article/421352

required to reconcile the operation section 115 of the Copyright Act 1968 that provides for damages. This pertained to the main issue of whether a party could re-litigate matters that had already been decided. The court stated it was an abuse of power.[328] The court noted that section 115(2), specifically provides for actions that deal with infringement, stating that

> subject to this Act, the relief that a court may grant in an action for an infringement of copyright includes an injunction (subject to such terms, if any, as the court thinks fit) and either damages or an account of profits.[329]

The court went on to say that a party had advanced this position:

> the Prospective Applicants contend that the infringer's conduct amounts to a distribution of DBC for which the infringer would ordinarily require a licence from the Prospective Applicants. By reason of the infringer's conduct in making DBC available online for others to download without a licence to do so, the Prospective Applicants have not received a licence fee and royalties which would have been payable had a licence been granted.[330]

The above indicates that the court will determine whether a licence exists, and the conduct of the party infringing the copyright. Third, the court is likely to ascertain whether a licence exists, and what, if any, fees or royalties apply when determining whether a level of relief should be sought under section 115. A year before Dallas, the court in *Tylor*[331] applied damages under section 115 of the *Copyright Act 1988* for an infringement of a copyright pertaining to photographs. As demonstrated above, in terms of both copyright and patent law, there is a need to understand not only the tests and steps handed down by the judiciary when interpreting and applying the legislation, but also that practitioners require a high level of skills and knowledge for statutory interpretation. This is because of the procedural nature of both legal frameworks. Finally, similar to the other states compared, Australia has a period of 70 years[332] for a copyright. However, a subtle difference is that if the work was made public, this period is reduced to 50[333] years.

328 Ibid., para 14.
329 Ibid., para 17.
330 Ibid., para 18.
331 *Tylor v Sevin* [2014] FCCA 445.
332 *Copyright Act 1968*, section 33.
333 Ibid.

5.3.2 European Union (EU)

Within and across the EU, there is some harmonisation of copyright law as it pertains to the implementation of the WIPO Copyright Treaty. In 2023, Paivi Hutukka undertook a comparison of the copyright laws of the EU, the US, and China.[334] This section will deal only with Directive 2009/29/EC, referring to this as 'the Directive'. Hutukka notes that the barriers to EU harmonisation of copyright law are predominantly driven by a 'low economic potential to exploit copyright involving literary and artistic works in trans-border transactions'.[335] However, Hutukka notes that this could be about to change due to the increasing 'economic interests involved in copyrighted works thanks to computer programs, databases and new communication technologies, copyright has gained economic prominence and, simultaneously, has become an increasingly important part of EU law'.[336] While outside the scope of this section, note that the EU in 2019 established Directive 2019/790/EC that amended Directive 2009/29/EC.[337] There are other EU laws pertaining to elements of copyright that will constitute part of further research.

On that basis, in recent times, the EU has reviewed copyright laws and made moves towards harmonisation. If and when achieved, it will bring this area of the law in line with the other areas of commercial law that have been harmonised by the EU. According to Hutukka, the overall

> architecture of copyright law in the EU[338] is thus a product of multinational efforts to unify the different copyright regimes of the EU Member States. Since no EU-wide unitary copyright exists, the same copyrighted work receives protection according to the different national laws of each EU Member State.[339]

While a level of harmonisation of copyright law has been achieved across the EU, there is still some way to go.

Against the backdrop of the above, Directive 2001/29/EC provides that at the

334 Paivi Hutukka. Copyright Law in the European Union, the United States and China. *IIC, 54* (2023), 1052. https://doi.org/10.1007/s40319-023-01357-0

335 Ibid., p. 1052.

336 Ibid.

337 Directive (EU) 2019/790 of the European Parliament and of the Council of 17 April 2019 on Copyright and Related Rights in the Digital Single Market and Amending Directives 96/9/EC and 2001/29/EC (Text with EEA relevance.) PE/51/2019/REV/1. *OJ L, 130,* (2019), 92–125.

338 Paivi Hutukka, Copyright Law in the European Union, the United States and China, *IIC, 54* (2023), 1052. https://doi.org/10.1007/s40319-023-01357-0, see also Directive 2001/29/EC of the European Parliament and of the Council of 22 May 2001 on the Harmonisation of Certain Aspects of Copyright and Related Rights in the Information Society. *OJ L, 167/10* (2002).

339 Ibid.

> Diplomatic Conference held under the auspices of the World Intellectual Property Organisation (WIPO) in December 1996 led to the adoption of two new Treaties, the 'WIPO Copyright Treaty' and the 'WIPO Performances and Phonograms Treaty', dealing respectively with the protection of authors and the protection of performers and phonogram producers. Those Treaties update the international protection for copyright and related rights significantly, not least with regard to the so-called 'digital agenda', and improve the means to fight piracy world-wide. The Community and a majority of Member States have already signed the Treaties and the process of making arrangements for the ratification of the Treaties by the Community and the Member States is under way. This Directive also serves to implement a number of the new international obligations.[340]

Specifically, in Preamble (19), the directive provides that:

> The moral rights of right holders should be exercised according to the legislation of the Member States and the provisions of the Berne Convention for the Protection of Literary and Artistic Works, of the WIPO Copyright Treaty and of the WIPO Performances and Phonograms Treaty. Such moral rights remain outside the scope of this Directive.[341]

Taking this approach, and while moral rights are outside the EU framework, they have generally been addressed at the member state level. While this section does not include a Member States laws, Slovenia[342] provides for moral rights. In Slovenia, there is no recognition of or reference to *original* works; there is only reference to works. However, under Directive 2001/29/EC, the works are reproductions of the original. The directive adopts the singular approach to separate the word 'original' from 'original works'[343] (which has had a complex history of harmonisation across the EU) as is the case in Australia. That is, the EU refers to 'original of works'[344] or 'copies'. Case C-479/04 concerns the interpretation and validity of Article 4(2) of Directive 2001/29/EC that pertains to the original or works.[345] Second, the court was also required to determine whether

340 Preamble (15), Directive 2001/29/EC of the European Parliament and of the Council of 22 May 2001 on the Harmonisation of Certain Aspects of Copyright and Related Rghts in the Information Society. *OJ L, 167/10* (2002).

341 Ibid., preamble (19).

342 Article 15 and Article 16, *Copyright and Related Rights Act* (Official Gazette of the Republic of Slovenia [*Uradni list RS*], No. 21/95 of 14 April 1995).

343 Eleonora Rosati, *Originality in EU Copyright: Full Harmonisation through Case Law*, Elga Publishing (2013), p. 27.

344 Preamble (28), Articles 2, 3, 4, Directive 2001/29/EC of the European Parliament and of the Council of 22 May 2001 on the Harmonisation of Certain Aspects of Copyright and Related Rights in the Information Society. *OJ L, 167/10* (2002).

345 Case C-479/04 (lASERDISKEN II). https://curia.europa.eu/juris/showPdf.jsf;jsessionid=E70F5259AE60F7EBA8350E9603150E27?text=&docid=63876&pageIndex=0&doclang=EN&mode=lst&dir=&occ=first&part=1&cid=14135968

> the national court asks whether Article 4(2) of Directive 2001/29 precludes national rules which provide that the distribution right in respect of the original or copies of a work is exhausted where the first sale or other transfer of ownership is made by the holder of that right or with his consent outside the Community.[346]

Notably, the court stated that:

> Article 4(1) of Directive 2001/29 enshrines the exclusive right for authors, in respect of the original of their works or of copies thereof, to authorise or prohibit any form of distribution to the public by sale or otherwise. Article 4(2) contains the rule pertaining to exhaustion of that right. According to that provision, the distribution right is not to be exhausted in respect of the original or copies of the work, except where the first sale or other transfer of ownership in the Community is made with his consent.[347]

Hence, Article 4 provides for an exclusive right. The right is relinquished upon the sale or transfer of the right through a licence, contract or other binding arrangement. The court responded to the second point above by stating that

> it follows that for the right in question to be exhausted, two conditions must be fulfilled: first, the original of a work or copies thereof must have been placed on the market by the rightholder or with his consent and, second, they must have been placed on the market in the Community.[348]

Moreover, Bently and others note that the *Software Directive*[349] Articles 1(3), 4(3), and 6 1(c) clearly refer to the original computer program, which can be protected by copyright law. This was reinforced in the 2009 case of *Infopaq*.[350] However, this case not set out a test for determining originality. This a[p] pears to be undertaken on a case-by-case basis. In *Infopaq*, the court looked at the extent to which a part was original, by considering the 'the five words which come before and after the search word are captured ("extract of 11

346 Ibid., para 17.
347 Ibid., paras 19, 20.
348 Ibid., para 21.
349 Lionel Bently, Brad Sherman, Dev Gangjee, *Intellectual Property Law*, Oxford University Press (2022), p. 105. Also see, Directive 2009/24/EC of the European Parliament and of the Council of 23 April 2009 on the Legal Protection of Computer Programs (Codified version) (Text with EEA relevance). *OJ L, 111* (2009), 16–22. https://eur-lex.europa.eu/legal-content/EN/ALL/?uri=CELEX%3A32009L0024
350 Case C-5/08, *Infopaq International A/S v Danske Dagblades Forening* [2009]. https://eur-lex.europa.eu/legal-content/EN/TXT/PDF/?uri=CELEX:62008CJ0005

words")'.[351] The court also pointed out that the 'reproduction of parts of the scanned printed articles since the extract of 11 words is stored and those 11 words are printed out on paper'.[352] More importantly, the court also considered the 'reproduction of parts of the scanned printed articles since the extract of 11 words is stored and those 11 words are printed out on paper?'.[353] Can they be protected? Most pertinent, the court ruled that words cannot be protected.[354] While there was a computer program was used for the collection and storage of the words, the court considered the words rather than the technology. Arguably, this is because the technology is the facilitator of the collection and storage of the words that were subject to the protection. Drawing a salutary conclusion, the court will look to what has been protected or otherwise. If a computer program is protected by copyright, then the court will consider the extent of the breach related to that computer program. Significantly, the court will exclude such technology if it is used to facilitate an activity that uses copyright material.

Furthermore, the court stated that in relation to the

> right of distribution, the WIPO Copyright Treaty fulfils its harmonisation objective in providing for the exclusive right of authors to authorise the making available to the public of the originals of their works and copies thereof through sale or other transfer of ownership.[355]

This specific reference to the WIPO Treaty is it has been incorporated into EU framework. The court ruled that Article 4(2) of Directive 2001/29 is to be interpreted as precluding national rules providing for the expiration of the distribution right in respect of the original or copies of a work placed on the market outside the European Community by the rightholder or with his consent. Therefore, this provision is to be applied to the internal market.

In addition to this, the application of fair dealing/use has been integrated into the EU legal framework or this directive, where the directive provides for a 'fair balance of rights and interests between the different categories of rightholders'.[356] This relates to the rights pertaining to the copyright holder. However, the fair dealing-use doctrine applied in Australia, US, India and UK is the reverse of the above, as it allows a limited use of a copyright by an individual or entity that is not the rightholder. Nonetheless, there is the right to

351 Ibid., para 20.
352 Ibid., para 24.
353 Ibid., para 26(8).
354 Ibid., paras 46–76.
355 Ibid., para 71.
356 Preamble (31), Articles 2, 3, 4, Directive 2001/29/EC of the European Parliament and of the Council of 22 May 2001 on the Harmonisation of Certain Aspects of Copyright and Related Rights in the Information Society. *OJ L, 167/10* (2002).

fair compensation,[357] which is equivalent to damages under the common law jurisdictions. While the directive does not provide for specific licences, it does however, allow for collective licences that have been delegated to Member States, and contractual licences for the administration of copyrights.[358] Under the civil law regime of the EU and the Member States, the copyright laws largely replicate the process, principles and concepts of the common law. This is because the EU has adopted the WIPO (international) copyright framework. Under the EU framework there is protection afforded to the same works of authorship, amongst others. Therefore, it is argued that amongst the concepts, principles and doctrines identified by copyright law, one of the most important starting points is that the work is original. In conclusion, copyright protection is given for a 70-year time period.

5.3.3 United Kingdom (UK)

Following BREXIT, the copyright law in the UK has largely stayed the same. However, it has not adopted the EU's 2019 copyright Directive 2019/790,[359] and no longer strictly follows the EU framework, even though many elements are similar.[360] Today, in regards to the EU copyright law, the UK is treated as a third country.[361] The UK will continue to be influenced by the EU courts' decisions regarding copyright law. However, one of the major changes post-BREXIT was that the UK no longer applies the 'Orphan Works Directive, which provided for the mutual recognition of orphaned works across Europe'.[362] Of further importance is that in 2021, the EU implemented the 'Marrakesh Treaty in its Directive for the benefit of persons who are blind, visually impaired, or otherwise print-disabled. The international Treaty entered into force in a national capacity on 1 January 2021'.[363]

Alison Harcourt notes that in its amendment, the 'UK removed the compensation mechanism. The Directive ensures that accessible format copies made by authorised entities in any Member State can be circulated and accessed by beneficiary persons and authorised entities throughout the Union'.[364] Now

357 Ibid., Article 5.

358 Ibid., Preamble (18), (30), (35).

359 Directive (EU) 2019/790 of the European Parliament and of the Council of 17 April 2019 on Copyright and Related Rights in the Digital Single Market and Amending Directives 96/9/EC and 2001/29/EC (Text with EEA relevance.) PE/51/2019/REV/1. *OJ L, 130* (17 May 2019), 92–125.

360 Alison Harcourt, Brexit and Copyright. In *Brexit and the Digital Single Market*. Oxford (2023). https://doi.org/10.1093/oso/9780192899378.003.0011

361 Ibid., p. 197.

362 Ibid., p. 206. See also: Directive 2012/28/EU of the European Parliament and of the Council of 25 October 2012 on Certain Permitted Uses of Orphan Works Text with EEA Relevance, *OJ L, 299* (2012), 5–12.

363 Ibid., p. 209.

364 Ibid.

in 2024, and with a change of government likely to take place, there may be further changes on the horizon. A new government may want to get closer to the EU or distance itself further, which could result in the copyright laws of the UK undergoing a further review and change.

Bently and others have written extensively on copyright law of the UK,[365] noting that, similar to the EU, Australia, and other jurisdictions compared, the copyright legal framework of the UK has been influenced and shaped by the international framework of the WIPO Copy Right Treaty, Berne Convention and TRIPS [Trade-Related Aspects of Intellectual Property Rights].[366] The principal legal instrument for copyright in Australia is the Copyright, Designs and Patents Act 1988 (CDPA),[367] in which section 1 stipulates that copyright applies to 'original literary, dramatic, musical or artistic works; sound recordings, films [or broadcasts], and the typographical arrangement of published editions'.[368] The CDPA varies from the EU and Australia law by conferring a 'design right in original designs'[369] and not the original of works or original works. Section 213 makes it clear that the 'design is not "original" if it is commonplace'.[370] In the case of *THJ*,[371] the court stated clearly that 'in order for copyright to subsist in an artistic work it must be "original" section 1(1)(a) of the 1988 Act'.[372] The test applied by the court was multilayered. The court made five points:

> First, the test is an objective one. Secondly, the test is not one of artistic merit: section 4(1)(a) of the 1988 Act expressly provides that graphic works qualify as artistic works 'irrespective of artistic quality', and nothing in the case law of the CJEU suggests otherwise. Thirdly, the burden of proof lies on the Claimants. Fourthly, particularly given that we are concerned with graphic works, a key item of evidence is the works themselves. Fifthly, as counsel for the Defendants rightly emphasised, the functionality of the Software is irrelevant to this question. The enquiry concerns the visual appearance of the R & P Charts. Given the informative purpose of the R & P Charts, the visual appearance is primarily a matter of the layout of the R & P Charts.[373]

365 Lionel Bently, Brad Sherman, Dev Gangjee, *Intellectual Property Law*, Oxford University Press (2022), p. 38.

366 Ibid., p. 46.

367 *Copyright, Designs and Patents Act 1988.* https://www.legislation.gov.uk/ukpga/1988/48/contents Note also the *Copyright and Related Rights Regulations 2003*, providing for licences amongst other matters.

368 Ibid., section 1.

369 Ibid., part 1.

370 Ibid.

371 *THJ Systems Limited v Sheridan Options*, [2023] EWCA Civ 1354.

372 Ibid., para 13.

373 Ibid., para 24.

By taking the objective approach, the court was not only referring to EU case law, but also interpreting the legislation which, arguably, was based on the purposive approach. The court applied the original test to the actual relevant provisions of the law, and then turned to the evidence provided by each party to determine the level of originality that was claimed. This will vary depending on the issue. For instance, the originality test for art will vary from that of an author's intellectual creation. Interestingly, this case did not apply a test for original design. Therefore, originality is a standard. On the other hand, section 213 goes further into detail in relation to the design right as it pertains to originality.

More importantly, a design right will not be granted for a method or principle of construction, features of shape or configuration of an article which enable the article to be

> connected to, or placed in, around or against, another article so that either article may perform its function, or are dependent upon the appearance of another article of which the article is intended by the designer to form an integral part, or surface decoration.[374]

However, and worth noting, a design is not original for the purposes of this Part if it is 'commonplace in a qualifying country in the design field in question at the time of its creation; and qualifying country has the meaning given in section 217(3)'.[375] Such a right exists where the

> design qualifies for design right protection by reference to the designer or the person by whom the designer was employed, or the person by whom and country in which articles made to the design were first marketed, or in accordance with any order.[376]

In order to maintain a consistent approach to the comparison of concepts and principles of the UK law, in this section, the overarching rights of copyright are examined. Arguably, it has two important components: the general rights afforded to the owner of the copyright, and the moral rights. Also of note, is the extension of the general rights to economic rights.[377]

On the other hand, the concept of fair dealing requires one not 'not infringe any copyright in the work provided that it is accompanied by a sufficient acknowledgement'.[378] Section 29 goes further than other laws compared in that it outlines what does not constitute fair dealing. For instance, it is not

374 *Copyright, Designs and Patents Act 1988*, section 213
375 Ibid.
376 Ibid., and note sections 218, 219, 220, 221.
377 *Copyright, Designs and Patents Act 1988*, Chapter 2.
378 Ibid., section 29.

fair dealing to convert a computer program expressed in a low-level language into a version expressed in a higher-level language.[379] The question is whether this applies to AI, algorithms and code that would be used by blockchain. This is because, as stated in Chapter 1, blockchain utilises code and algorithms to facilitate the development of smart contracts and token transactions.

Arguably, the concept of fair dealing needs to be tested by the judiciary to confirm its application. Moreover, section 30[380] allows an individual or entity to criticise a work by means of conceptual analysis; this is not considered an infringement of copyright. Thus, prima facie, is fair dealing in the UK a concept different from the notion of fair balance in the EU? However, as noted by Bently and others, these concepts are interlinked.[381] That said, in the case of *England*,[382] the court was required to respond to the notion of fair dealing. The court stated that it is

> impossible to lay down any hard-and-fast definition of what is fair dealing, for it is a matter of fact, degree and impression. However, by far the most important factor is whether the alleged fair dealing is in fact commercially competing with the proprietor's exploitation of the copyright work, a substitute for the probable purchase of authorised copies, and the like.[383]

Under UK law, the court further noted that the fair dealing defence will almost certainly fail. If it is not, and there is a 'moderate taking and there are no special adverse factors, the defence is likely to succeed, especially if the defendant's additional purpose is to right a wrong, to ventilate an honest grievance, to engage in political controversy, and so on. The second most important factor is whether the work has already been published or otherwise exposed to the public'.[384] Thus, arguably, the courts are going to apply the tests of breach of confidence, amount and importance, and the 'extent of permissible work to be taken'[385] (what was the percentage taken?).

Significant too, the ECJ [European Court of Justice] in Dirk[386] takes the rights-based, approach stating that to

379 Ibid., section 29(4) and (4A).
380 Ibid., sections 29, 30 and 32.
381 Lionel Bently, Brad Sherman, Dev Gangjee, *Intellectual Property Law*, Oxford University Press (2022), p. 246, footnote 24.
382 *England and Wales Cricket Board Limited (2) Sky UK Limited v Tixdaq* [2016] EWHC 575 (Ch).
383 Ibid, para 81.
384 Ibid.
385 Ibid., paras 84–85.
386 Case C-161/17 *Land Nordrhein-Westfalen v Dirk Renckhoff* [2018], para. 31. See also *The Copyright and Related Rights Regulations 2003*, which specify fair dealing.

> allow such a posting without the copyright holder being able to rely on the rights laid down in Article 3(1) of Directive 2001/29 would fail to have regard to the fair balance, referred to in recitals 3 and 31 of that directive, which must be maintained in the digital environment between, on one hand, the interest of the holders of copyright and related rights in the protection of their intellectual property, guaranteed by Article 17(2) of the Charter of Fundamental Rights of the European Union and, on the other hand, the protection of the interests and fundamental rights of users of protected subject matter, in particular their freedom of expression and information guaranteed by Article 11 of the Charter of Fundamental Rights, as well as the public interest.[387]

Therefore, the notable difference between the UK and the EU approach is that the EU takes a rights-based approach. Whereas, it can be argued that the UK takes a more interest-based approach. What I mean by 'interest' is the level of interest that the non-rightholder is using to use the original works.

In relation to the aforementioned rights[388] which are extended to the copyright holder and non-rightholder under a licence[389] or other agreement will be afforded the rights to use the copyright. Copyright licences can be issued according to section 116, and authorise the performance of any of the acts restricted by copyright. A

> licence or licensing schemes covering works of more than one author do not include licences or schemes covering only a single collective work or collective works of which the authors are the same, or works made by, or by employees of or commissioned by, a single individual, firm, company or group of companies.[390]

In the UK, a copyright 'expires at the end of the period of 70[391] years from the end of the calendar year in which the author dies, subject as follows'.[392] However, there is a 50-year copyright for

> sound recordings, films, broadcasts, and where the work is computer-generated the above provisions do not apply and copyright expires at the end of the period of 50 years from the end of the calendar year in which the work was made.[393]

387 Ibid., para 41.
388 *The Copyright and Related Rights Regulations 2003*. https://www.legislation.gov.uk/uksi/2003/2498/contents
389 *Copyright, Designs and Patents Act 1988*, section 16.
390 Ibid., section 116. (4).
391 Ibid., section 12.
392 Ibid., section 12.
393 Ibid., sections 12, 13A, 13B, 13C.

A unique but important feature of the UK laws is found in section 296ZD that provides a 'right/s and remedies in respect of devices and services designed to circumvent technological measures effective technological measures and/ or a computer program'.[394] This is a complex provision that requires careful consideration of the section as a whole and any specified exemptions or other obligations. Another significant right is the ability to register a design.[395] Also, in the case of *Original Beauty*[396] the court was required to deal with multiple issues such as infringement, damages, unregistered design, and original designs. At issue was the infringement of an unregistered design,[397] which was infringed upon, with the claimant being awarded financial damages. Under the legislation, damages can be awarded for breach of licence, or an unregistered of design amongst other provisions. Of further note, section 205N provides for remedies to be available where it has been determined that moral rights have been infringed upon. This brief outline has explained the important concepts and principles within the UK legal framework. To fully understand the copyright laws of the UK, the Act will need to be engaged with so as to reconcile the many elements that were not discussed above.

The ensuing challenge will be the evolution of technology related to artificial intelligence and cybersecurity, amongst other issues. In the *Eva*[398] case, the court made the point that a human creation can be protected.[399] Even though this was an EU case, the UK is likely to adopt the same approach. Nevertheless, Bently et al. state that a computer-generated work is entitled to copyright protection even where it has been generated by a computer in circumstances where there is no human author.[400] Bently et al. also state that products generated by a computer could be classified as works.[401] Problematic will be the assessment of a computer-generated work to determine the amount of human input. This will certain skills and will come out in the evidence provided by the parties. New judicial tests will need to be developed by the courts. That said, a possible starting point would be for the courts to consider: 1) where the program or code was developed, 2) the location the program or code was installed on the computer and by whom, 3) the owner of the computer on which the code or program was installed, 4) the purpose for which the code or program was installed, and 5) the elements or parts that constitute

394 Ibid., section 296ZD.
395 Ibid., section 224.
396 *Original Beauty Technology Company Limited & others v G4K Fashon Limited & others* [2021] EWHC 3439. https://www.bailii.org/ew/cases/EWHC/Ch/2021/3439.html
397 Ibid., para 2.
398 Case C – 145/10, *Eva-Maria Painer v Standard VerlagsGmbH.* https://eur-lex.europa.eu/legal-content/EN/TXT/PDF/?uri=CELEX:62010CJ0145
399 Ibid., para 150.
400 Lionel Bently, Brad Sherman, Dev Gangjee, *Intellectual Property Law,* Oxford University Press (2022), p. 127.
401 Ibid., p. 127.

the originality of the computer-generated work. There are likely to be additional factors that make up such a test. This is an area requiring vigilance as it is evolving rapidly and is far from settled. The next section looks at India.

5.3.4 India

Copyright law in India has followed the laws of other common law countries, particularly the UK.[402] The Copyright Act, 1957,[403] (CA) is the principal legislation that sets out the legal framework for copyright protection in India. Section 13 of the CA concerns original works pertaining to literary, dramatic, musical and artistic creations,[404] reaffirmed by the Delhi High Court in *Super Cassettes.*[405] Further, as part of registering a copyright under section 48,[406] the work must be original. That said, the application of 'original' will vary depending on the different creations seeking copyright, such as cinematographic and literary works.

The case of *Yash*,[407] highlighted that the word 'original' is missing in section 13(1)(b), yet the requirement stipulating originality or intellectual creation is found in sections 13(3)(a) and 2(b).[408] The court further pointed out that the 'scope of protection of a film is at par with other original works, the test laid down in *R.G. Anand v M/s Deluxe Films and Ors.* (1978) 4 SCC 118 would apply'.[409] The test applied in *Anand* is multilayered and looks to intention, impression, level of difference and dissimilarities, and has been applied to determine whether there has been an infringement of original works. In taking the wider view, 'author' is defined in section 2 of the CA to include a computer that 'generates literary, dramatic, musical or artistic work which is computer-generated, the person who causes the work to be created'.[410] The point is that the computer that has a programme installed can, over time, learn from itself today more than ever before, and can generate this work on its own.

Further to the above, a computer program is defined as a 'set of instructions expressed in words, codes, schemes or in any other form, including a machine-readable medium, capable of causing a computer to perform a particular task

402 Shyamkrishna Balganesh, David Nimmer, *Fair Use and Fair Dealing: Two Approaches to Limitations and Exceptions in Copyright Law.* In Harbir Singh, Padmanaghan Ananth, Emanuel Ezekiel (eds), *India as a Pioneer of Innovation,* Oxford Academic (2018), p. 124. https://doi.org/10.1093/oso/9780199476084.001.0001

403 *Copyright Act 1957.* https://copyright.gov.in/documents/copyrightrules1957.pdf

404 Ibid., section 13.

405 *Super Cassettes Indus. Ltd.* v *Chintamani Rao.*

406 Copyright Act, 1957, section 48.

407 *Yash Raj Films Pvt Ltd vs Sri Sai Ganesh Productions & Ors* on 8 July 2019. https://indiankanoon.org/doc/175297328/

408 Ibid., paras 13–14.

409 Ibid., para 15. *R.G Anand vs M/S. Delux Films & Ors* on 18 August 1978. https://indiankanoon.org/doc/1734007/

410 *Copyright Act 1957*, section 2.

or achieve a particular result'.[411] Given these definitions, in part, the Indian law is already accounting for code that relies on algorithms and is evident within a blockchain that could produce creative works. For instance, blockchain is being used to produce artistic works such as music.

Pertinent too, the general rights of the holder of copyright for original works are protected. Section 38B provides for the moral rights of a performer.[412] While not compared fully in this chapter, an interesting issue has emerged. This is because under the CA, a performer is defined by section 2 as an 'actor, singer, musician, dancer, acrobat, juggler, conjurer, snake charmer, a person delivering a lecture or any other person who makes a performance'.[413] Thus, it can be argued that a performer could be a robot or some other technological device or invention that can conduct these activities. For instance, there is technology that responds to humans' requests to answer a question, play music, or a song. Where the technology responds by singing a song on its own and not referring to the original song sung by an artist, it can be argued that the technology is performing. In the future, the law may need to be amended to account for this development. The court in *Amar*[414] argued that 'moral rights of the author are the soul of his works. The author has a right to preserve, protect and nurture his creations through his moral rights'.[415] The court also stated that moral right is a form of integrity.[416] More specifically, the court drew on the international law and stated that Article 6bis of the Berne Convention enjoins the members of the Berne Union to provide legal recognition for the moral rights of attribution and integrity in a work in which copyright exits.[417] Hence, the principle of integrity is an important part of the international framework in applying to moral rights. The moral rights protect the economic rights of individuals works, and are in the public interest and promote social attitude.[418] These developments while not new continue to be important to the application and practice of copyright law no matter the jurisdiction or nation-state.

Despite the related rights[419] afforded to the copyright holder, fair dealing has been preferred by India, similar to that of the UK. This is another example of how the Indian law continues to follow the UK legal framework. Noteworthy too is that scholars have described the Indian copyright law as 'consolidate(ing) various limitations and exceptions in one principal section of

411 Ibid.
412 *Copyright Act 1957*, section 38B.
413 Ibid., section 2.
414 *Amar Nath Sehgal vs Union of India (Uoi) And Anr.* on 21 February, 2005. https://indiankanoon.org/doc/1990275/
415 Ibid., para 24.
416 Ibid., para 25.
417 Ibid., para 27.
418 Ibid., para 41.
419 *Copyright Act 1957*, sections 56, 57, 58.

the statute, section 52. Dealing with actions that do not constitute copyright infringement, this section contains what are in essence two principal kinds of exceptions to infringement'.[420]

Shyamkrishna Balganesh and David Nimmer are of the view that the first exception involves what are true

> fair dealing provisions, which qualify their description of the activity that is exempted by the phrase 'fair dealing', thereby suggesting that the activity described is entitled to an exemption only when assessed to be a fair dealing under the law, not simply when found to have been undertaken as a factual matter.[421]

The authors go on to identify that the 'second kind' does just the opposite.

Centrally, these latter provisions describe an activity in some detail, and allow the exception to be invoked upon a mere showing that the 'factual elements identified in the provision (in its description of the activity) have been met'.[422] Strictly speaking, although these latter types of exceptions do not qualify as fair dealing, inasmuch as they are interspersed amongst the true fair dealing ones, the rules of construction and interpretation that courts apply to one generally carry over to the other as well. More specifically, and as noted by the authors, section 52 provides for 'certain acts not to be infringement of copyright, such as, a fair dealing with any work, not being a computer programme, for the purposes of – (i) private or personal use, including research'.[423]

The case of *Hubbard*[424] is another example of India drawing on judicial decisions of the UK to reconcile the application of copyright concepts and principles. This case involved an interpretation of section 6 of the UK Act from an interesting perspective. The Church of Scientology had commenced an action for copyright infringement (through its founder, L Ron Hubbard) against a former member who had published a book criticising the organisation. The plaintiff alleged that the defendant's book contained material that had been copied from the plaintiff's own books and writing. The defendant raised the defence of fair dealing, and succeeded. Writing for the Court of

420 Shyamkrishna Balganesh, David Nimmer, *Fair Use and Fair Dealing: Two Approaches to Limitations and Exceptions in Copyright Law.* In Harbir Singh, Padmanaghan Ananth, Emanuel Ezekiel (eds), *India as a Pioneer of Innovation,* Oxford Academic (2018), p. 124. https://doi.org/10.1093/oso/9780199476084.001.0001

421 Ibid.

422 Ibid. See also *Copyright Act 1957*, section 39: infringing performer's rights.

423 Ibid., section 52.

424 *Hubbard v Vosper*, [1972] 2 QB 84. https://uniset.ca/other/cs3/vosper.html. Shyamkrishna Balganesh, David Nimmer, *Fair Use and Fair Dealing: Two Approaches to Limitations and Exceptions in Copyright Law.* In Harbir Singh, Padmanaghan Ananth, Emanuel Ezekiel (eds.), *India as a Pioneer of Innovation,* Oxford Academic (2018), p. 124. https://doi.org/10.1093/oso/9780199476084.001.0001

Appeal, Lord Denning – a legendary law figure – took the opportunity to clarify the scope of the fair dealing defence and its meaning:

> It is impossible to define what is 'fair dealing'. It must be a question of degree. You must consider first the number and extent of the quotations and extracts. Are they altogether too many and too long to be fair? Then you must consider the use made of them. If they are used as a basis for comment, criticism or review, that may be fair dealing. If they are used to convey the same information as the author, for a rival purpose, that may be unfair. Next, you must consider the proportions. To take long extracts and attach short comments may be unfair. But, short extracts and long comments may be fair. Other considerations may come to mind also. But, after all is said and done, it must be a matter of impression. As with fair comment in the law of libel, so with fair dealing in the law of copyright. The tribunal of fact must decide. In the present case, there is material on which the tribunal of fact could determine this to be fair dealing.[425]

Hence, and as mentioned earlier in this chapter, jurisdictions are using different language to apply the fair dealing concept. Essentially, in India and the UK, Lord Denning defines fair dealing in terms of the number and extent of the quotations and extracts, their use and how they are conveyed, proportions (short or long), and their impression. However, and while this test was applied in 1957, it is arguable that it is nuanced and would change to suit the matter being decided. That is, this test might not be a one-size-fits-all test, because scenarios and copyright issues vary greatly.

Moreover, the Delhi High Court in *Super Cassettes*[426] case noted that the 'use of the copyright works by India TV is fair use, fair dealing and fair comment for the purpose of review and criticism and for reporting current events'.[427] Most noteworthy is that the term 'fair use' was recognised by the court. However, that is as far as the court went in using the term and applying it to the CA. What the court confirmed is that section 52 allows that

> the literary, dramatic, musical or artistic work may be reproduced without fear of infringement of copyright in such works, if such reproduction is a fair dealing of the copyright work in question, for the purpose of criticism or review whether of that work or any other work.[428]

The court went further, stating that:

425 Ibid.
426 Ibid., *Super Cassettes Indus. Ltd.* v *Chintamani Rao. https://indiankanoon.org/doc/576454/*
427 Ibid., para 17.
428 Ibid., para 27.

> firstly, it has to be 'fair dealing' of the work in question. This means that the dealing with the copyrighted work is not an unfair dealing. Only that part of the literary, dramatic, musical or artistic work may be utilized for the purpose of criticism or review, which is absolutely necessary, and no more. The purpose – ostensibly or obliquely, should not be to ride piggy back on the work of another. A person cannot, in the name of 'fair dealing', lift or copy literary, dramatic, musical or artistic work of another to such an extent that it ceases to be a 'fair dealing'.[429]

Arguably, by taking this position, the court was building on the 1957 UK case of *Hubbard*, and taking the purposive approach to the use of the copyright that is absolutely necessary, and no more. Civil remedies are available according to section 55 of the CA.[430] Simply put, the test here will be that the court will look to what was 'absolutely necessary' as part of utilising the copyright. Arguably, this will vary from case to case and be applied reasonably to suit the circumstances of the matter so as to protect the right of the copyright holder while balancing that protection with a fair use by the non-copyright holder.

When addressing these concepts and principles in copyright law they are by and large interconnected with other concepts and principles. For instance, the right of fair dealing is interconnected with infringing general rights of the copyright holder. Arguably copyright has evolved into a complex statutory right across all the jurisdictions compared.

Chapter VI of the CA provides for a number of different licences that enable the use of copyright. For India they have adopted the use of compulsory licences, withheld from public, unpublished works, and for the benefit of the blind.[431] Exclusive and non-exclusive licences are also available. Section 61 of the CA states that in 'every civil suit or other proceeding regarding infringement of copyright instituted by an exclusive licensee, the owner of the copyright shall be made a defendant'.[432] The case of *Super Cassettes*,[433] was heard on appeal from an

> order dated 20th October, 2003 passed by the Copyright Board at New Delhi in Case No. 10/2003. Appellant's main grievance is against the direction of the Copyright Board directing the Registrar of Copyrights to grant a compulsory license under section 31(1)(b), of the Copyrights Act, 1957.[434]

429 Ibid.
430 *Copyright Act 1957*, section 55.
431 *Copyright Act 1957*, sections 31, 31A, 31B. Note exclusive licences are defined in section 2.
432 Ibid., section 61.
433 *Super Cassette Industries Ltd. v Entertainment Network* (India) Ltd. on 30 June, 2004. https://indiankanoon.org/doc/1885590/
434 Ibid., para 1.

The court was required to reconcile the operation of section 31, and ruled that:

> the language of the section 31 (1)(b) question of compulsory license would arise only when the artistic work or music has been withheld from the public. In the instant case, admittedly licenses have already been granted to other broadcasters, who have substantial presence, in that event, whether the appellant can be compelled to grant compulsory license to others, would really be decided on the facts and circumstances of each case. When the licenses have already been granted to other broadcasters, who have substantial presence, then perhaps the application for grant of compulsory license will be treated differently, in a situation where the artistic work has been totally withheld from the public.[435]

The court was differentiating between an artistic and a compulsory broadcaster licence, and the rights that would be afforded on the issuing of the licence. Most notably, the court in relation to section 31, concluded that:

> legislature in its wisdom has used the expression 'may' in section 31. According to section 31 it is not imperative for the Board to grant license to each and every complainant. In our considered view the license can be granted or denied on valid grounds. Section 31 itself envisages that the decision to grant or refuse a license should be made after holding such inquiry as it may deem necessary. While granting compulsory licenses the Board must take into consideration whether the work has been totally withheld from public or licenses have been granted to other broadcasters and to what extent public interest is served. In the instant case licenses were granted to other broadcasting agencies. The Board ought to have taken into consideration this vital factor while arriving at a decision to grant compulsory license to the respondent.[436]

In deciding whether to grant a licence, the court directed the issuing authority that, in applying section 31, several factors were to be considered. First, it needs to consider the number of applicants and that a licence does not have to be granted to all entities when there is more than one in the application. Second, a compulsory licence can be denied or granted on valid grounds. Three, a compulsory licence should not be granted until after the fully inquiry has been concluded by the issuing authority. Fourth, the granting of a compulsory licence for broadcasting rights has to consider the public interest. This section has only touched the surface of the copyright law of India. Further research is needed to determine the extent and reach of the CA. Nonetheless,

435 Ibid., para 84.2.
436 Ibid., para 84.2.

the principles and concepts that India has adopted are consistent with those of the other common countries, with minor variations. It is these minor divergences that will need to be reconciled by the practitioner when representing a client, to ensure that any cross-border copyright issues are dealt with according to the local national legal regime. This will be further challenged as technology continues to develop. Finally, the major difference between India and the other jurisdictions compared is that the time period for a copyright has been shortened to 60 years.[437] This should not be an issue as a ten-year period is not a lot of time in the large scheme of things. However, practitioners need be aware of this difference. The next section examines the approach to copyright taken by the United States.

5.3.5 United States (US)

The US has developed a copyright framework similar to those of its other common law counterparts. It was not until 1989 that the US ratified the Berne Convention,[438] and the 1976 Copyright Act, the broad reach of US copyright law extends to form are '(1) original, (2) works of authorship, and (3) fixed in a tangible expression'.[439] Chapter 13 deals with original designs, whereby section1301 provides that a

> designer or other owner of an original design of a useful article which makes the article attractive or distinctive in appearance to the purchasing or using public may secure the protection provided by this chapter upon complying with and subject to this chapter.[440]

Notably, there are exemption for the department of defence, which arguably is a sensible addition to protect national security.

That said, in emphasising the concept of original, the laws define original as applying to the result of the 'designer's creative endeavour that provides a distinguishable variation over prior work pertaining to similar articles which is more than merely trivial and has not been copied from another source'.[441] Protection will not be afforded to a design where it is not original,[442] or otherwise referred to as having originality.[443] This is a common feature of copyright law all over the world.

437 *Copyright Act 1957*, sections 22, 23, 24,

438 Ibid., p. ix. Paivi Hutukka, *Copyright Law in the European Union, the United States and China*. IIC 54, 1044–1080 (2023). https://doi.org/10.1007/s40319-023-01357-0 Title 17 of the United States Code (2022), https://www.copyright.gov/title17/title17.pdf

439 Ibid., p. 1056.

440 Title 17 of the United States Code (2022), section 1301. https://www.copyright.gov/title17/title17.pdf

441 Ibid.

442 Ibid., section 1301.

443 Pamela Samuelson, The Originality Standard for Literary Works Under U.S. Copyright Law, *The American Journal of Comparative Law*, *14* (1994), 393.

Nevertheless, Pamela Samuelson referred to a very early US Supreme Court case law decision in *Feist Publications, Inc. v Rural Telephone Service Co.*,[444] where the court ruled that the white pages listings of a telephone directory did not exhibit sufficient creativity in selection, coordination, or arrangement of data to satisfy the originality standard of US copyright law.[445] Importantly, the above came much later following the 1936 case of Sheldon where the court clearly stated that like 'a patent, a copyrighted work must be not only original, but new'.[446] Thus, the test is whether the work is new or otherwise. It is a simple but important text.

Furthermore, and while the *Copy Right Act* does not include the concept of moral rights, generally, it has been viewed as important in the US as it is in the other states compared. While out of scope to compare state the laws of the US and the adoption of the concept, it is widely understood that across the US

> various federal and state laws arguably protect moral rights, in addition to explicit protection through an amendment to the *US Copyright Act* by the *Visual Artists Rights Act* of 1990. Some states, such as New York and California, also have moral rights protection for visual artists.[447]

For example, federally, the Latham Act and Visual Artists Act have adopted the concept.[448] By acceding to the Berne Convention, the US have embraced the concept of moral rights. Even though these laws do not concern computer technology specifically, the visual arts domain, together with other areas of works that are subject to copyright protection, are all being challenged and influenced by new technology that is enabling its development and availability to the broader community.

Karyn A Temple, makes the point that the *Copyright Act* grants authors six exclusive rights. For instance, section 106(2) gives the right to 'prepare and to authorize the preparation of derivative works based upon the copyrighted work'.[449] The Act defines a 'derivative work as one based upon one or more pre-existing works in which the original is "recast, transformed, or adapted"'.[450] Temple also states that an

444 Ibid., case 111 S.Ct. 1282 (1991).

445 Ibid., p. 394.

446 *Sheldon v Metro-Goldwyn Pictures Corporation*, 81 F.2d 49 (2d Cir. 1936), para 54. https://law.justia.com/cases/federal/appellate-courts/F2/81/49/1475281/

447 Karyn A. Temple, *Authors, Attribution, and Integrity: Examining Moral Rights in the United States, A Report of the Register of Copyright*, United States Copy Right Office. https://www.copyright.gov/policy/moralrights/full-report.pdf. Also see Moral Rights in US Copyright Law. https://www.copyrightlaws.com/moral-rights-in-u-s-copyright-law/

448 Ibid., pp. 4–5.

449 Ibid., p. 101, and Title 17 of the United States Code (2022), section 106. https://www.copyright.gov/title17/title17.pdf

450 Ibid.

> author (who is also an owner) can therefore enforce their integrity interests by bringing an infringement action under section 106(2) against a party making modifications to their work that results in the creation of an unauthorized derivative work.[451] Moreover, the unauthorized derivative work does not even have to be prejudicial to the author's honour or reputation to be infringing.[452]

In the case of *Andy*, the court reaffirmed that:

> The Copyright Act encourages creativity by granting to the author of an original work 'a bundle of exclusive rights'. In reconciling §106 and §107 that relates to fair use, the two are not mutually exclusive. But an overbroad concept of transformative use, one that includes any further purpose, or any different character, would narrow the copyright owner's exclusive right to create derivative works. To preserve that right, the degree of transformation required to make 'transformative' use of an original must go beyond that required to qualify as a derivative.[453]

What the court was considering was the inclusion of the 'actual use' and the 'transformative use'. Transformative use is another way of looking at the purpose of the use. Arguably, it is applying the purposive approach to determining the exclusive right. The court went further by pointing to other case law, noting thatcomputer programs are primarily functional, which makes it difficult to apply traditional copyright concepts in that technological world.[454] More specifically, the court will look at the use of the code and whether the 'purpose of the use was significantly different from that of the original; and, second, to the strength of other justifications for the use'.[455] The point is that this begins to direct the test of assessing code that is used in technology for copyright works. Again, it would be the purposive approach that is likely to prevail as the judiciary considers the purpose of the code and its use. Arguably, this is a growing area of the law and will require a level of vigilance as national judiciaries grapple with the application and use of code in copyright. While not fully settled, it is my view that the purposive approach to the use and application of the code and technology will continue to be the first test.

In reconciling the above, Temple further notes that a work that is prejudicial in this way, but that does not meet the 'derivative work standard of being recast, transformed, or adapted, will likely not be considered a "derivative

451 Ibid.
452 Ibid.
453 *Andy Warhol Foundation for Visual Arts, Inc. v Goldsmith*, 598 U.S. (2023). https://supreme.justia.com/cases/federal/us/598/21-869/
454 Ibid.
455 Ibid.

work" at all, and thus there will be no finding of infringement'.[456] In section 106A, the above is extended by providing specific right to attribution and integrity related to visual arts, so as to

> claim authorship of that work, and to prevent the use of his or her name as the author of any work of visual art which he or she did not create; and also prevent the use of his or her name as the author of the work of visual art in the event of a distortion, mutilation, or other modification of the work which would be prejudicial to his or her honour or reputation.[457]

The principle of integrity has been a test of high importance and is arguably commonly used across national copyright law to confirm the status of the works.

Notably also, the 'Sonny Bono Copyright Term Extension Act, Title I of Pub. L. No. 105-298, 112 Stat. 2827, extends the term of copyright protection for most works to life plus 70 years), 1998'.[458] However, this will differ in respect to specific copyright areas, such as the visual arts, that extends to the full life[459] of the person.

Another emerging concept that is consistently applied across the jurisdictions compared is 'fair use', otherwise referred to as 'fair dealing'. Section107 provides for the fair use of a copyrighted work, including:

> such use by reproduction in copies or phonorecords or by any other means specified by that section, for purposes such as criticism, comment, news reporting, teaching (including multiple copies for classroom use), scholarship, or research, is not an infringement of copyright. The factors to be considered include the purpose and character of the use, including whether such use is of a commercial nature or is for non-profit educational purposes; the nature of the copyrighted work; the amount and substantiality of the portion used in relation to the copy- righted work as a whole; and the effect of the use upon the potential market for or value of the copy-righted work. The fact that a work is unpublished shall not itself bar a finding of fair use if such finding is made upon consideration of all the above factors.[460]

While there are subtle and important differences between the interpretation of fair use and fair dealing among the states compared, they are very similar in

456 Title 17 of the United States Code (2022), section 106. https://www.copyright.gov/title17/title17.pdf
457 Ibid., section 106A,
458 Ibid., p. xi.
459 Ibid., section 106A d.
460 Ibid., section 107.

that they provide for some use of the copyright. Fair use can be traced back to more than a century in the US. In 1841, Justice Joseph Story, when required to 'consider the collected papers of President George Washington', began his remarks by commenting that the case presented

> one of those intricate and embarrassing questions, arising in the administration of civil justice, in which it is not, from the peculiar nature and character of the controversy, easy to arrive at any satisfactory conclusion, or to lay down any general principles applicable to all cases (*Folsom v Marsh* 1841: 44).

Acknowledging that 'the lines approach very near to each other, and, sometimes, become almost evanescent, or melt into each other' (1841: 44), he articulated what would later be codified as the 'doctrine of fair use'.[461] Therefore, the test is the level of use that is assessed to be fair.

On that basis, 'the new work merely supersedes the objects of the original creation or instead adds something new, with a further purpose or different character, altering the first with new expression, meaning, or message'.[462] The courts considers whether the new work is original, adds something new, has a further purpose than an existing work, and is different by altering the expression. Even though this test has not been specifically adopted by the other states, it has many similar characteristics. Significantly, the text links directly back to original works and hence this is the first step in assessing whether a copyright exists or otherwise. Second is the purposive approach that has been applied to look at what is the purpose of the copyright claim. Third is the alteration or added value to a work.

Section115 provides for a compulsory licence that allows the use of music and other digital activities, in addition to voluntary licences that are applied to contracts, along with blanket and digital licences.[463] The regime gives a high level of accountability, certainty and protection to the original copyright holder. Licence agreements are now commonplace for data and cybersecurity within the digital economy. They facilitate the specific governance and use of a copyright between parties that may provide some economic benefit.

Against the backdrop of the above,

> rights management information (RMI) is digital metadata attached to copyright works or appearing in connection with those works that

461 Shyamkrishna Balganesh, David Nimmer, *Fair Use and Fair Dealing: Two Approaches to Limitations and Exceptions in Copyright Law.* In Harbir Singh, Padmanaghan Ananth, Emanuel Ezekiel (eds), *India as a Pioneer of Innovation,* Oxford Academic (2018), p. 118. https://doi.org/10.1093/oso/9780199476084.001.0001

462 Ibid., p. 123.

463 Title 17 of the United States Code (2022), section 115. https://www.copyright.gov/title17/title17.pdf

> provides intellectual property information such as the title of the work, the author, the copyright owner, or the conditions for using the work. Rights management information is legal metadata related to the moral rights, patrimonial rights and licensing conditions of the work. Public international law defines RMI within the context of copyright and neighbouring rights.[464]

This is important because, as stated above, code and computer programs can support these works. Drawing on this connection, Cadavid notes that the *WIPO Copyright Treaty* defines RMI as: information which identifies the work, the author of the work, the owner of any right in the work, or information about the terms and conditions of use of the work, and any numbers or codes that represent such information, when any of these items of information is attached to a copy of a work or appears in connection with the communication of a work to the public.[465] Further, Cadavid emphasises that the *WIPO Performances and Phonograms Treaty* defines RMI as: information which identifies the performer, the performance of the performer, the producer of the phonogram, the phonogram, the owner of any right in the performance or phonogram, or information about the terms and conditions of use of the performance or phonogram, and any numbers or codes that represent such information, when any of these items of information is attached to a copy of a fixed performance or a phonogram or appears in connection with the communication or making available of a fixed performance or a phonogram to the public.[466]

Moreover, Cadavid makes the point that The *WIPO Beijing Treaty on Audiovisual Performances* defines RMI as:

> information which identifies the performer, the performance of the performer, or the owner of any right in the performance, or information about the terms and conditions of use of the performance, and any numbers or codes that represent such information, when any of these items of information is attached to a performance fixed in an audiovisual fixation.[467]

The definitions have a similar structure: '(i) they refer to metadata providing related intellectual property information; (ii) they include identifiers (numbers

464 Jhonny Cadavid, *The Origin and Purpose of Legal Protection for the Integrity of Copyright Metadata, IIC, 54*(2023), 1179–1185. https://doi.org/10.1007/s40319-023-01364-1

465 Ibid. World Intellectual Property, The Copyright Treaty. https://www.wipo.int/treaties/en/ip/wct/

466 Ibid. See also World Intellectual Property, *The Performances and Phonograms Treaty 1996.* https://www.wipo.int/treaties/en/ip/wppt/

467 Ibid. See also World Intellectual Property, *Beijing Treaty on Audiovisual Performances 2012.* https://www.wipo.int/treaties/en/ip/beijing/

or codes); and (iii) the scope of the definition is technologically neutral: it applies to both digital and traditional media'.[468] The importance of this recent observation by Cadavid is that it provides a comparative view of the international approaches. It confirms that the codes and data being used by technology relate to various areas of IP law, including copyright. However, the application under national legal regimes is an area requiring further research.

There a number of laws that pertain to damages for copyright breaches. Notably, the *Digital Theft Deterrence and Copyright Damages Improvement Act* of 1999 specifies the statutory damages for copyright infringement.[469] Furthermore, for a breach of licence, damages and injunctive relief can be sought through the courts under section 115. More generally, proceedings can also be implemented when there is a breach of the wider copyright protections afforded to a copyright holder.

5.3.6 China

China's copyright laws, while different from those of the other jurisdictions and somewhat complex, provide a similar outcome in terms of protecting 'economic rights'.[470] However, this section does not compare the concepts and principles that have been discussed earlier, such as originality, time period of a copyright and fair dealing. The history of copyright law in China can be traced to the 1985 *General Principles of the Civil Law of the PRC*, which laid down that natural and legal persons were entitled to own copyright.[471] In tracing the developments of copyright law in China, Paivi Hutukka stated that it is set up under a framework that has been dispersed amongst several pieces of legislation, including:

> the Copyright Law (1990, revised 2001, 2010, 2020); second, the Copyright Law Implementing Regulations (1991, revised 2002, 2011, 2013); and finally, the Provisions on Implementing International Copyright Treaties (1992).[472]

For more than two decades, there were considerable changes made to the laws of China, which resulted in the country adopting the wider international approach. More recently though, in 2021, China undertook to make further changes to the laws. Importantly, the first Article of the Copyright Law of the People's Republic of China outlines the purpose of the statutes, that it

468 Ibid.
469 Title 17 of the United States Code (2022), https://www.copyright.gov/title17/title17.pdf, p. xii.
470 Paivi Hutukka, Copyright Law in the European Union, the United States and China, *IIC*, *54* (2023), 1044–1080. https://doi.org/10.1007/s40319-023-01357-0
471 Ibid., p. 1061.
472 Ibid.

> is enacted ... for the purposes of protecting the copyright of authors in their literary, artistic and scientific works and the rights and interests related to copyright, of encouraging the creation and dissemination of works that would contribute to the construction of a socialist society that is spiritually and materially advanced, and of promoting the development and flourishing of socialist culture and sciences.[473]

This is an area of further research. Apart from the economic rights that copyright affords to the copyright holder, China has adopted a level of moral rights. Apart from adopting a similar approach to the common law countries in relation to works being original, where there is an article that has, for instance, 'published your article without permission or crediting you, someone has edited the photograph you took, or someone has made copies of your brochure and has been using it for their company'.[474] These are all examples of moral rights infringement, which means you were not properly identified, the work was published without your permission and the work was distorted in a way that might harm your reputation. Moral rights are personal and cannot be waived, licenced or transferred. In infringing your moral rights, e.g. if a competitor uses your product images to promote their own counterfeit products, confusion is created, possibly resulting in loss of reputation or business.[475] A key feature is Article 10 that provides for personality and property rights.[476] Article 12 protects original works. A notably difference in China is that a copyright protection is only 50 years according to Article 21.[477] While there are no specific titled licences provided for under the law, generally a licence has been provided for in the form of certain rights. Finally, and in this short overview, Article 347 provides for the damages where there have been specific breaches of copyright. Unlike the other jurisdictions compared, China restricts the level of any damages for injury to RMB 500,00.[478] A more comprehensive comparison of the laws is needed. This section has not recommended any reform for China or commented on their policy or legal approach. It has only provided a short overview and highlighted similarities and divergence amongst the jurisdictions compared of copyright law.

473 Ibid., *Copyright Law of the People's Republic of China* (as amended up to the Decision of 11 November 2020, of the Standing Committee of the National People's Congress on Amending the Copyright Law of the People's Republic of China (hereinafter *Copyright Law of the PRC* (2020)). Article 1 (2020).

474 European Commission. *Copyright Protection in China: A Guide for European SMEs*, 2012. https://intellectual-property-helpdesk.ec.europa.eu/system/files/2020-10/EN_Copyright_guide_Aug_2010.pdf

475 Ibid.

476 World Intellectual Property Organisation, *Copyright Law of the People's Republic of China 2010*, Article 10. https://www.wipo.int/wipolex/en/text/466268#:~:text=Any%20work%20of%20a%20foreigner,protected%20in%20accordance%20with%20this

477 Ibid., Article 21.

478 Ibid., Article 49.

5.4 Conclusion

5.4.1 Patents

Patent law is complex. While the legal frameworks are procedural, the judiciaries of the states compared have developed principles and concepts that are important to understand. However, the adoption and various applications of these principles and concepts vary. Hence, there is a lack of harmonisation in this area.

This chapter has confirmed that the PCT has all but been adopted in its entirety across the jurisdictions examined. It is the PCT that has provided a level of harmonisation across the world for the governance pf patent applications. More recently, the WIPO has developed rules that now guide and direct national laws on the development, implementation and application of patent law.

The chapter has confirmed and demonstrated the importance of the principles and concepts of prior art, novelty, invention, specification requirements, breach of confidence, enablement, written description, non-obvious, opposition and purposive approach. These principles and concepts will be specific to certain states, and are not be applicable in all jurisdictions. Therefore, it is argued that the most settled principle emerging from the respective patent laws is the 20-year timeframe for the protection of a patent. There are, however, some minor differences between the states.

Importantly, the adoption and application of these principles and concepts vary across the states compared. Therefore, a high level of vigilance is required, particularly in relation to the way(s) that the respective courts have applied them. Adding to this complexity, there is a need to understand the application of patent law to the technology of blockchain and activities involving tokens.

This chapter has demonstrated that there is an emerging area of patent applications related to blockchain technology and, to a lesser extent, tokens. The patent applications themselves have largely focused on the technological components that support blockchain. This new area of patent application is likely to grow. It could involve applications for tokens themselves, provided such applications can meet the threshold tests for enablement, invention, and specification, amongst others.

Arguably, the most important element of a sought patent is the application itself. Without meeting the required threshold tests, the application will not succeed. There must be an invention and it must be new. However, it would be problematic for a token itself to be patented. As mentioned in this chapter, an application had been submitted for an authentication token using a smart card.[479] However, in this application, it was not the token itself that would be patented, but rather the 'system for generating secure passwords for use by at

479 Google Patent, *Authentication Token*. https://patents.google.com/patent/US7865738B2/en

least one authentication server in authenticating a user of an authentication token and an authentication token interface device'.[480] Prima facie the application is for the device supporting the security of the authentication process of the user of the token.

5.4.2 Copyright

Copyright law is becoming increasingly important nowadays. At the international level, the many concepts and principles of originality, rights, and moral rights, amongst others, have been developed to provide a high level of harmonisation across the world. Yet, as is the case with a lot of commercial law, there is some way to go before full international harmonisation will be achieved.

The common and civil law has generally adopted the above concepts, and provide for various forms of licences. India's laws are very close to those of the UK. Australia's laws are also similar. The EU is far from harmonised, and continues to leave it to Member States to implement their laws. Although, and while this book does not compare the laws of individual Member States, there is some general harmonisation as the EU applies the international framework.

Additionally, all jurisdictions provide for licences whether they be compulsory, mandatory, voluntary or those going by some other name. They are used to guarantee a right to copyright protection. They are valuable in that they can be included in contractual arrangements between entities and individuals.

The copyright of data has become a real issue. Internationally, metadata in particular, that is being applied and used by code and other technology are beginning to be considered as eligible for copyright protection. However, this protection is limited to what has been produced by the technology, but does not apply to the technology itself. Technology protection would come under patent law. Furthermore, the principle of integrity has also emerged as one of the tests to determine what constitutes new works.

In the US, for example, the concept of transformative use has been identified and applied to the assessment of the purposive approach. Significantly too, is the adoption and application of fair dealing-use. This book demonstrates that it is largely a matter of semantics. Some jurisdictions use 'fair use', while others use 'fair dealing'. In the absence of any formal definition of the concept, and using India and the UK as examples, a test considers the extent of the quotations and extracts, their use and how they are conveyed, proportions (short or long), and their impression. It has also developed as a right complementing the other rights that are provided by the respective laws.

More specifically, copyright is arguably a form of statutory rights enabling the use of original works under certain conditions such as the holding of a licence. This attempts to ensure economic and social rights. It protects the

480 Ibid.

economic interests of the copyright holder who developed the original works. It is transnational and there is, arguably, a high level of harmonisation attached to both patent and copyright law.

Simply put, the test here will be that the court will consider what was 'absolutely necessary' as part of utilising the copyright. Arguably, this will vary from case to case and be applied reasonably to suit the circumstances of the matter to protect the right of the copyright holder, while balancing that protection with a fair use by the non-copyright holder.

These concepts and principles in copyright law are, by and large, interconnected with other concepts and principles. For instance, the right of fair dealing is interconnected with the general rights of the copyright holder. Arguably, copyright has evolved into a complex statutory right in all the jurisdictions compared.

Generally, the life of a copyright is either for 70 years or for the life of the person who has been afforded the right. There are, however, some minor variations, particularly China which grants only 50 years of copyright.

China's copyright laws apply different moral rights when dealing with infringements of copyright. They consider whether or not the creator of the work was properly identified, whether the work was published without the creator's permission, and whether the work was distorted in a way that might harm the creator's reputation. Moral rights are personal and cannot be waived, licenced or transferred. Article 12 protects original works. A notably difference in China's law is that copyright protection is afforded for only 50 years according to Article 21. While there are no specific licences provided for under the law, generally a licence has been provided for in the form of certain rights.

In conclusion, this chapter has demonstrated that technology that can perform an activity similar to a human. For example, in the case where a robot produces its own song but not referring to an original song that it is mimicking, it could be said that it is the technology that is performing. Thus, over time, technology could be afforded a level of copyright protection. However, more research is needed to confirm this position over the coming years. Put another way, a computer programme comprises a set of instructions expressed in words, codes, schemes or in any other form, including a machine-readable medium, capable of causing a computer to perform a particular task. As mentioned, India appears to be further advanced than the other states as its laws have defined such technology where it produces work. Arguably, the code that supports blockchain could fall within this definition.

6 International Arbitration

6.1 Introduction

International arbitration is a suitable option for resolving complex transnational commercial and investor–state disputes that involve tokens and the technology that supports and facilitates their transactions. As stated briefly in Chapter 1, arbitration can be used to resolve token[1] disputes, such as those that have been assigned to a contract or smart contract on blockchain. Chapter 1 drew on recent rules established in the UK to govern disputes over digital assets. More specifically, the 2023 *UK Dispute Resolution Rule* states that 'a digital asset includes a crypto asset, digital token, smart contract or other digital or coded representation of an asset or transaction; and a digital asset system means the digital environment or platform in which a digital asset exists'.[2] On the other hand, there is no clear international definition of a token. With the current regulatory frameworks not being clear, there are likely to be investor–state arbitration disputes involving tokens over the coming years.

Against the backdrop of the above, contracts [smart] and other forms of agreements can be used across the token economy, where a level of obligation arises and binds a party. In turn, tokens can form part of smart contracts[3] and cybersecurity agreements, data agreements, data storage agreements, service level agreements, and, to a lesser extent, intellectual property such as patents and copyright. For a long time, international arbitration has been a very effective legal mechanism for resolving commercial disputes within these areas of commercial law.

Tokens reside on distributed ledger technology (DLT) and, thus,

1 Sir Geoffrey Vos, Francis Bautista, *ADR in the Blockchain Ecosystem: A Primer* (2023). https://arbitrationblog.kluwerarbitration.com/2023/12/14/adr-in-the-blockchain-ecosystem-a-primer/

2 *Digital Dispute Resolution Rules.* https://27221500.fs1.hubspotusercontent-eu1.net/hubfs/27221500/UKJT%20work/Digital%20Dispute%20resolution%20rules.pdf

3 Ali Sunyaev, Niclas Kannengießer, Roman Beck, Horst Treiblmaier, Mary Lacity, Johann Kranz, Gilbert Fridgen André Luckow, Token Economy *Business Information Systems Engineering, 63* (4) (2021), 457–478. https://doi.org/10.1007/s12599-021-00684-1

DOI: 10.4324/9781003511687-6

> come in many forms and shapes and offer a huge number of different use cases. They can be generated at the protocol layer inherent to a specific ledger, in which case they are frequently labelled as 'coins', or they can reside on the application layer and are minted by smart contracts.[4]

As noted by Sunyaev et al:

> Smart contracts are programmed to process sensor readings so that when events happen to the physical asset, such as a physical movement, a change of ownership, a change of status, or a physical transformation – its digital counterpart is updated on the DLT application. The supply chain partners, if given permission rights, all store identical replications of a tamper-resistant record of events.[5]

It is not necessary for legal scholars and practitioners to understand the complexities of the technology and the functional requirements of smart contracts. However, it is argued that where there is a commercial dispute involving these new and emerging modern-day financial products, practitioners, and arbitral tribunals will be forced to have a basic level of knowledge of this technology. Moreover, the formal and functional arrangement of the DLT, 'offers a new approach based on asset tokenization, smart contracts for processing transactions pertaining to the asset, and a tamper-proof ledger shared by all authorised parties'.[6] Most noteworthy is how the smart contract(s) and DLT,[7] are often talked of in the same breath but are distinct technologies – albeit complementary and, in some instances, symbiotically linked. However, the advent of 'DLT has created a platform on which smart contracts can be hosted and executed. This has brought smart contract concepts into the mainstream'.[8] However, the full extent of the application and use of smart contracts today is not fully understood. This may not be known for some years and many commercial operations will view this information as commercial in confidence.

4 Ibid., p. 464. See also ISDA Linklaters, *Whitepaper, Smart Contracts and Distributed Ledger – A Legal Perspective* (2017), pp. 4–5. https://www.isda.org/a/6EKDE/smart-contracts-and-distributed-ledger-a-legal-perspective.pdf

Smart legal contracts and smart contract code are two separate domains; the reality is that there is a relationship between them. For a smart legal contract to be implemented, it will need to embed one or more pieces of code designed to execute certain tasks if pre-defined conditions are met – that is, pieces of smart contract code. Smart legal contracts, therefore, are functionally made up of pieces of smart contract code – but, crucially, under the umbrella of an overall relationship that creates legally enforceable rights.

5 Ibid., p. 466.

6 Ibid.

7 ISDA Linklaters, *Whitepaper, Smart Contracts and Distributed Ledger – A Legal Perspective* (2017), p. 8. https://www.isda.org/a/6EKDE/smart-contracts-and-distributed-ledger-a-legal-perspective.pdf

8 Ibid.

Thus, the ensuing question is: how far and to what extent do these functional arrangements automate the smart contract?

Notwithstanding the above, it has been identified that 'one of the most powerful inter-relationships between smart contracts and DLT is how 'computers that can automatically execute code'.[9] Functionally, it requires the 'contracting parties to program a computer to automatically execute a payment under a contract [i.e. a transaction using a token] upon satisfaction of pre-defined conditions, for pre-defined price'.[10] However, a problem arises when one party does not accept and use the other party's code but develops their own separate code. To deal with this issue, in part, the code itself can be housed on the DLT. In short, this establishes a single point of contact for the transaction and contractual arrangements that are binding on the parties. It has been argued that with this approach, the contract itself is self-enforcing,[11] and would not require a court or arbitral tribunal to enforce it. However, this may not address a dispute where the DLT has not be used. This is because 'smart contracts and DLT are distinct from each other, and come with their own respective challenges'.[12] This has been highlighted where the DLT is the issue of situs:

> Under various legal regimes, it is necessary to identify the location of an asset or contract to determine the applicable legal jurisdiction for various legal questions relating to it – for example, whether a property right has been created. In the case of dematerialised financial assets where ownership is recorded on a register, it is often the place where the register is held or where the registrar is situated that is deemed to be the situs of that financial asset. However, the distribution of the register across nodes in multiple jurisdictions raises a seemingly intractable problem – under current legal principles at least – as to where the situs should be.[13]

Viewed this way, the situs is where and how to evaluate the location of the property. The situs provides the basis for where something exists and can be located. In the context of this book, the situs is where the token, the parties, the smart contract, and the ensuing transactions are located. That is, they are on the blockchain. Another problem is that the

> DLT and smart contracts suffer from legal issues relating to situs. It is important to note, though, that this legal issue is one relating to DLT rather than smart contracts. To be sure, smart contracts raise their own legal issues (although the degree to which such issues arise depends on

9 Ibid.
10 Ibid.
11 Ibid.
12 Ibid.
13 Ibid.

> the conception of what a smart contract is), but they are distinct issues from those that arise for DLT.[14]

Arguably, the legal status of smart contracts and DLT, whether combined or on their own, remains unsettled. Generally, the smart contract will fall within the contract legal framework of the place where the contract itself has been prepared. However, it is argued that this has not been fully settled by many states, and further research is required. The drafting stage[15] of the contract itself is likely to become more complex. Smart contracts know no national borders. Under transnational contract law arrangements, emerging research has affirmed that these contracts can apply to the *Convention on the Sale of Goods (CISG) 1980.* Additionally, in 2021, the UK Law Commission released its report in relation to smart contracts,[16] noting that under the law of England and Wales, there are several requirements for the formation of a legally-binding contract. These are:

- agreement;
- consideration;
- certainty and completeness;
- intention to create legal relations; and
- formality requirements.[17]

This, it can be argued, means that under these arrangements a smart contract will follow the existing concepts and principles of contract law, whether in common or civil law jurisdictions. Yet, within national legal frameworks of contract law, a level of clarification remains required. What has not been fully determined, and while outside the scope of this chapter, is that encoded contracts are not fully settled at law.

Despite the above, there is also emerging evidence whereby, in certain circumstances, disputes may be resolved solely via the smart contract that has been developed on an Ethereum blockchain. To govern a dispute:

> both parties agree on a set of arbiters. Should a dispute arise, the preselected arbiters can vote, within a specified time period, either yes or no on whether a breach occurred. Should a minimum number of arbiters

14 Ibid.

15 Maren K. Woebbeking, The Impact of Smart Contracts on Traditional Concepts of Contract Law, *JIPITEC, 10* (2019), 112.

16 Law Commission, *Smart Legal Contracts Advice to Government* (2021). https://s3-eu-west-2.amazonaws.com/lawcom-prod-storage-11jsxou24uy7q/uploads/2021/11/Smart-legal-contracts-accessible.pdf. In Robert Walters. *Commercial and Arbitration Law of the Digital Economy: A Comparison of Asian, European and North American Jurisdictions,* Routledge (2024), pp. 82–86.

17 Ibid., p. 39.

> vote, and the majority of those who voted agree that a breach occurred, the smart contract can automatically enforce monetary penalties.[18]

Under these arrangements, the arbiters are included in the technology and base a decision on votes. In practice, which has not been fully applied and remains at the conceptual stage, 'when instantiated, the lawyers must provide parameters to populate the text template, a list of parties who can update the state of the action, and a list of independent arbiters who can adjudicate disputes'.[19] Furthermore, the other parties and 'arbiters in the case of a disagreement, vote to decide whether to update the action state'.[20] However, what is not clear is the number of arbiters to be pre-selected. How will they be selected? Will the traditional arbitrator selection process be applied? Based on the above, the study by Rahman, Liu, and Kagal did not confirm whether they were human arbiters or technology arbiters created by an algorithm. Currently, arbitrators are renumerated for their time when assessing a case and handing down a decision (arbitral award). Significantly, would a voting arrangement constitute a decision-award under the current legal framework? This chapter will confirm or otherwise refute this proposition. Another difficult question that arises from a voting system, and the possible number (odd or even) of arbiters required to vote, is: are they all remunerated for their time when reviewing the contract itself? If so, this could potentially increase the costs of arbitration. This is because, prior to casting a vote (i.e. make a determination of a contractual breach), the arbitrator would need to undertake a high level of research to understand the dispute. No doubt more research is required to fully understand whether this scenario could be extended beyond Ethereum-based blockchain to other blockchain models. The study by Rahman, Liu, and Kagal raises many more questions than it answers. The current arbitration framework, arguably, has been designed to be implemented by humans[21] and not for technology to be the arbitrator. Should the above be realised, another question arises: how does the arbiter deal with evidence? The next section discusses evidence captured by blockchain and potentially used in arbitral proceedings.

6.2 Evidence

Evidence captured and used via a blockchain has the potential to transform the collection and use of evidence presented in international arbitration. Importantly though, when evaluating evidence on blockchain that can be used

18 Ravi Rahman, Kevin Liu, and Lalana Kagal, *From Legal Agreements to Blockchain Smart Contracts* (2020), pp. 3–4. https://blockhack.osive.com/_downloads/d03a87ab494069c6ab2ac242ec7a429e/49.pdf

19 Ibid., p. 2.

20 Ibid. The study generated another 100 one-action, one-clause agreements with between 10 and 100 parties and arbitrators.

21 Robert Walters, *Commercial and Arbitration Law of the Digital Economy A Comparison of Asian, European and North American Jurisdictions*, Routledge (2024), Chapter 2.

by an arbitral tribunal, there are two distinct elements: 1) the evidence that blockchain technology acquires, and 2) the rules or law of evidence that is applied by the arbitral tribunal during an arbitral proceedings.

In regard to the first point above, a recent study undertaken by Alvarez, Vidal, and Vallespinos, noted that the value of blockchain evidence provides the following:

1. As proof of transactions carried out within the system. The existence of a transaction can be proved through a blockchain receipt, as it is tracked, validated, registered and time-stamped in the chain through a hash. If admissible, it would be a verified proof of the time, place and nature of the transaction.
2. As an authentication system for information produced outside the blockchain. Deploying information on the blockchain, which functions as a tamper-proof, timestamping database, has a huge impact on the pre-constitution of evidence. For instance, uploading a design [patent and copyright see Chapter 5] on a blockchain platform would be proof that it existed at a certain time, a piece of information that would be key for any judge deciding on its ownership. Yet blockchain could be the solution to a challenging problem: the uncertainty of the source, integrity and authenticity of digital data in relation to the original document. By comparing the hash of the original external document to the one deployed on a blockchain, an expert can determine whether they are exact copies.[22]

In adopting this approach, a more efficient means of validation would easily be accepted by any arbitration tribunal. Problematic, though, is the 'functioning and security of blockchain, and they are uncertain about how to present digital evidence'.[23] On this basis, three challenges have emerged. First is blockchain evidence. Second is the application and use of blockchain to submit evidence such as documents. Third is the rules of evidence across the common and civil law divide. On this third point, a significant issue is that the rules of evidence in common law jurisdictions of Australia, the US, and the UK require that evidence be relevant and reliable. Therefore, unless blockchain evidence conclusively comes within these rules, the tribunal is likely to be reluctant to rely on its use and admit the evidence. On the other hand, and as highlighted below, the general rules for evidence are left to the tribunal to determine, which can allow a level of flexibility for the use of both blockchain evidence and submission of evidence by blockchain. Therefore, the tribunal will need to look at the institutional rules and the use of electronic documents as one element of evidence.

22 Omar Puertas Álvarez, Oriol Valentí Vidal, Laura Díaz Vallespinós, Unlocking Blockchain Evidence in International Arbitration, *Spain Arbitration Review, Revista del Club Español del Arbitraje, Wolters Kluwer España*, 43 (2022), 19.

23 Ibid., p. 20.

The rules pertaining to evidence in arbitration have been settled for some time, although they may vary depending on whether the rules established by the International Arbitration Institute are being applied. For instance, Article 27 of the Chartered Institute of Arbitrators [institutional rules] provides that 'each party shall have the burden of proving the facts relied on to support its claim or defence'.[24] Therefore, the burden of proof is a form of standard of proof. Put another way, 'the standard of proof has been defined as a rule whose function is to indicate the party bearing the burden of proof'. Arguably, the burden and standard of proof is far from settled when it comes to blockchain-related evidence.

In other words, it depends on 'how much cogent or convincing the evidence must be to conclude that a fact actually happened'.[25] In referring to well-understood cases from the US and UK, Ezurmendia and Gonzalez note that the Supreme Court of the United States held that the living motive of a standard of proof is 'to instruct the fact-finder about the degree of confidence our society thinks he should have in the correctness of factual conclusions for a particular type of adjudication'.[26] The authors further state that in England and Wales, this has been conceptualised by Lord Hoffman in *Re B (Children) (Sexual Abuse)* as follows:

> If a legal rule requires a fact to be proved (a fact in issue), a judge or jury must decide whether or not it happened. There is no room for finding that it might have happened. The law operates a binary system in which the only values are 0 and 1. The fact either happened or did not. If the tribunal is left in doubt, the doubt is resolved by a rule that one party or the other carries the burden of proof. If the party who bears the burden of proof fails to discharge it, a value of 0 is returned and the fact is treated as not having happened.[27]

Viewed this way, and applying the approach under the UK and Australian legal systems, the burden or standard of proof is based on the balance of probabilities for civil matters and beyond a reasonable doubt for criminal matters. Importantly, these tests have varying thresholds. It is well understood that the balance of probabilities is a lower threshold. Moreover, Ezurmendia and Gonzalez believe that the

24 The Chartered Institute of Arbitrators, *Arbitration Rules 2015*, Article 27. Also see, Chartered Institute of Arbitrators, *Guidelines for Witness Conferencing in International Arbitration* (April 2019).

25 Jesus Ezurmendia, Maria Gonzalez, A Comparison Between the Standard of Proof Applicable in Arbitration and Formal Adjudication, *The International Journal of Evidence & Proof*, *25* (1) (2021), 5. http.s://doi.org/10.1177/1365712720943333

26 Ibid., *In Re Winship* 397 US 358, 370 (1970).

27 Ibid., quoting *Re B (children)* [2009] AC 11.

general rule, evidentiary law is not vastly considered in this regard, by either the legislation or the parties, given the fact that one of the main features of arbitration relies on its flexibility and the possibility to avoid over-strict rules of proceedings.[28]

By adopting this approach, 'arbitrators practising their functions usually decide on the main evidence and proof matters, such as exclusion and admissibility, without specific or clear rules'.[29] More specifically, the arbitrator must 'establish a procedure for the gathering of evidence'.[30] Generally, this will be done according to the institutional rules that have been agreed upon to be used by the parties. This is usually achieved through the arbitration agreement[31] where the arbitration institution is identified and, by automatic default, those institutional rules will be applied. Therefore, the broader question indirectly related to evidence is: Can the courts force or oblige the parties to arbitrate, according to the arbitration agreement? Moreover, where there is no arbitration agreement, can the parties be forced into arbitration by the courts? Further, it will need to be reconciled as to whether the binding arrangements within the arbitration agreement are evident or otherwise. In the case of *Jagdish*, it is stated clearly that '[T]he words used should disclose a determination and obligation to go to arbitration and not merely contemplate the possibility of going for arbitration'.[32] An arbitration agreement has to be in writing. This long-standing requirement was expressed by the court in case No 44, where 'the requirement that an arbitration agreement be in writing under article 7 (2)'.[33] A failure to provide an arbitration agreement that places binding obligations on the parties to arbitrate will pose many challenges, and the courts will need to make a determination and possibly force the parties to arbitration. In responding to the above questions of forced arbitration, Article 8 would need to be considered. For an arbitration agreement claim before the court, Article 8 refers the 'parties to arbitration unless it finds that the agreement is null and void, inoperative or incapable of being performed'.[34] Article 8(2) also pro-

28 Ibid., p. 7.
29 Ibid., p. 7.
30 Ibid., p. 7.
31 United Nations Commission on International Trade Law (UNCITRAL) Model Law on International Commercial Arbitration, Adopted by the United Nations Commission on International Trade Law on 21 June 1985, 2006 Amendments. https://uncitral.un.org/sites/uncitral.un.org/files/media-documents/uncitral/en/19-09955_e_ebook.pdf
32 *Jagdish Chander v Ramesh Chander & Ors*, Supreme Court, India, 26 April 2007, para 8. https://indiankanoon.org/doc/1913246/
33 CLOUT case No 44 [*William Company v Chu Kong Agency Co. Ltd. and Guangzhou Ocean Shipping Company*, High Court – Court of First Instance, Hong Kong, 17 February 1993], [1993] HKCFI 215. https://documents.un.org/doc/undoc/gen/v93/899/70/img/v9389970.pdf?token=qhbsjFMMTDfiH3QVcr&fe=true
34 United Nations Commission on International Trade Law (UNCITRAL) Model Law on International Commercial Arbitration, Adopted by the United Nations Commission on Inter-

vides that where an action referred to in paragraph (1) of this article has been brought, arbitral proceedings may nevertheless be commenced or continued, and an award may be made, while the issue is pending before the court. In order to determine whether the arbitration agreement falls within the test of being null and void, inoperative, or incapable of being performed, the courts will look to consent,[35] intention,[36] not a party to the arbitration agreement but later become party to the commercial arrangements.[37] On the third point 'the assignee of a claim is bound by the arbitration clause contained in the contract out of which the claim arose'.[38] Moreover, the court will need to determine whether the arbitration agreement continues to be in effect.[39] The court in case No 382 refused to send the parties to the COA to arbitration in London, based on the interpretation of Article 8 that, the existence of a dispute was required in order to refer the parties to arbitration and that a court was entitled to consider this prerequisite in applying Article 8.[40] Another example of arbitration being refused because the arbitration agreement was invalid[41] is the case of *Dell* where the court pointed out that Article 8(1) of the Model Law is almost identical to that of Article II(3) of the New York Convention. What is more, Article 16 of the Model Law expressly recognises the competence–competence principle, whereby the tribunal may rule on its own jurisdiction, including any objections with respect to the existence or validity of the arbitration agreement.[42]

Furthermore, national laws must be taken into consideration. While it is out of the scope of this book to address all the national laws compared herein,

national Trade Law on 21 June 1985, 2006 Amendments, Article 8. https://uncitral.un.org/sites/uncitral.un.org/files/media-documents/uncitral/en/19-09955_e_ebook.pdf

35 CLOUT case No 507 *Liberty Reinsurance Canada v QBE Insurance and Reinsurance (Europe) Ltd.* 20 September 2002, Published in English: [2002] Ontario Judgments No 3599. https://documents.un.org/doc/undoc/gen/v04/600/35/pdf/v0460035.pdf?token=5VyywdlPeHKh2nl8Fj&fe=true

36 *Mariana Maritime S.A. v Stella Jones Inc.*, Federal Court – Court of Appeal, Canada, 24 May 2002, [2002] FCA 215, para 20. https://www.canlii.org/en/ca/fca/doc/2002/2002fca215/2002fca215.htm

37 CLOUT case No 1046 [*PS Here, L.L.C. v Fortalis Anstalt*, Court of Appeal of Quebec, Canada, 19 March 2009]. https://documents.un.org/doc/undoc/gen/v11/811/89/pdf/v1181189.pdf?token=sonxJegZJ6kWLIW6MZ&fe=true

38 Ibid.

39 CLOUT case No 382 [*Methanex New Zealand Ltd. v Fontaine Navigation S.A., Tokyo Marine Co. Ltd., The Owners and all Others*, Federal Court – Trial Division, Canada, 9 January 1998], [1998] 2 FC 583. https://documents.un.org/doc/undoc/gen/v01/847/23/pdf/v0184723.pdf?token=55BYOtHyxjVeXXg7Rj&fe=true

40 Ibid.

41 *Dell Computer Corp. v Union des Consommateurs,* Supreme Court, Canada, 13 July 2007, [2007] SCC 34, [2007] 2 SCR 801, para 74. https://decisions.scc-csc.ca/scc-csc/scc-csc/en/item/2374/index.do

42 Ibid.

in the *UK Arbitration Act 1996*,[43] section 34 provides that 'the tribunal to decide all procedural and evidential matters, subject to the right of the parties to agree any matter'.[44] Section 23J of the *Australian International Arbitration Act 1974* allows the tribunal or a person specified in the order to inspect, photograph, observe, or conduct experiments on evidence that is in the possession of a party to the arbitral proceedings and that may be relevant to those proceedings (the relevant evidence). For experts, Article 26 of the UNCITRAL Model law[45] applies according to section 23J. Therefore, the national laws of the other states compared will need to be assessed to determine whether they depart from the UNCITRAL Model Law.

Notably, the arbitrator 'must deal with more abstract rules of evidence. Therefore, the arbitrator will have to apply rules for bearing the burden of proof, and, as a consequence, the rules of the standard, to determine whether the burden has been discharged'.[46] Ezurmendia and Gonzalez also argue that the

> arbitrator should apply the rules of burden and standard contained in the law, or to suggest that he/she should use, necessarily, rules equivalent to those that the civil court would use when hearing the case. Nonetheless, inside the adjudicative process, it seems to be unavoidable for epistemological reasons – as part of the decision-making process – that the adjudicator will assign a burden to one of the parties and apply a given standard, although he/she may not explicitly mention it.[47]

Subsequently, the 'arbitrator could not arrive at a rational conclusion regarding the veracity of the facts proposed by the parties, to subsequently apply the proper law to those facts'.[48] This is reaffirmed by Article 19 of the UNCITRAL Model Law[49] whereby the parties are free to agree on the procedure to be followed by the arbitral tribunal in conducting the proceedings. Second, according to Article 19(2), failing such agreement, the arbitral tribunal may, subject to the provisions of this law, conduct the arbitration in such manner as it

43 *United Kingdom Arbitration Act 1996*, section 34. https://www.legislation.gov.uk/ukpga/1996/23/section/34
44 Ibid.
45 United Nations Commission on International Trade Law (UNCITRAL) Model Law on International Commercial Arbitration, Adopted by the United Nations Commission on International Trade Law on 21 June 1985.
46 Jesus Ezurmendia, Maria Gonzalez. A Comparison between the Standard of Proof Applicable in Arbitration and Formal Adjudication. *The International Journal of Evidence & Proof*, *25* (1) (2021), 7. https://doi.org/10.1177/1365712720943333
47 Ibid.
48 Ibid.
49 United Nations Commission on International Trade Law (UNCITRAL) Model Law on International Commercial Arbitration, Adopted by the United Nations Commission on International Trade Law on 21 June 1985 2006 Amendments. https://uncitral.un.org/sites/uncitral.un.org/files/media-documents/uncitral/en/19-09955_e_ebook.pdf

considers appropriate. The power conferred upon the arbitral tribunal includes the power to determine the admissibility, relevance, materiality, and weight of any evidence.[50] This could be applied according to the institutional rules that have been agreed upon by the parties. Importantly, here the rules of admissibility and relevance are considered and will again be applied according to the institutional rules or national laws of evidence, according to what the tribunal chooses to apply.

In addition, Article 24 is important as it provides that

> subject to any contrary agreement by the parties, the arbitral tribunal shall decide whether to hold oral hearings for the presentation of evidence or for oral argument, or whether the proceedings shall be conducted on the basis of documents and other materials. However, unless the parties have agreed that no hearings shall be held, the arbitral tribunal shall hold such hearings at an appropriate stage of the proceedings, if so requested by a party.[51]

When a party requests a hearing, it is important that the arbitrator takes this request seriously. Most significantly, in case 659, the court determined that according to Article 24[52] it had to reconcile with the position taken by the tribunal. That is,

> during the arbitral proceedings, the claimant requested an oral hearing. The arbitrator, however, informed the parties that he would decide the case on the basis of documents only and set a time limit of three weeks for the respondent to reply to the request.[53] The Court held:
>
> the refusal of an oral hearing did not constitute a violation of the right to be heard. The principle of oral hearing did not apply in arbitral proceedings to the same extent as in court proceedings. Thus, in arbitral proceedings the right of the parties to be heard is respected if the parties have at least the possibility to file a statement of defence. The peculiar manner in which the right of defence is exercised (i.e. in an oral hearing instead of written submissions) cannot be unilaterally decided by a party (art. 24 (1).[54]

50 Ibid., Article 19.
51 Ibid., Article 24.
52 CLOUT case No 659 [Oberlandesgericht Naumburg, Germany, 10 Sch 08/01, 21 February 2002]. https://documents.un.org/doc/undoc/gen/v06/567/83/pdf/v0656783.pdf?token=SswzBUWdkyMHV63SOC&fe=true
53 Ibid.
54 Ibid.

In the case above, the court decided that a statement of defence was necessary for the party's evidence to be heard. Arguably, Article 19 provides that parties are free to agree on the procedure, the Canadian court[55] noted that a

> written instrument: an arbitration agreement shall be evidenced in writing; it is deemed to be evidenced in writing if it is contained in an exchange of communications which attest to its existence or in an exchange of proceedings in which its existence is alleged by one party and is not contested by the other party.[56]

Additionally, 'an arbitration agreement which provides for the arbitration to be dealt with on written submissions only (thus without cross-examination of witnesses) was held to be valid and not contrary to the law or public policy'.[57] Therefore, an arbitration agreement can restrict the use of evidence by the tribunal.

Importantly, Article 27 allows for court assistance in taking evidence. However, this can be viewed as being discretionary as it is not a mandatory obligation on the parties to produce documents or evidence. It is left to the tribunal to determine the admissibility, relevance, materiality, and weight of the evidence offered.[58] Article 28[59] states the arbitral tribunal shall decide the 'dispute in accordance with such rules of law as are chosen by the parties as applicable to the substance of the dispute'.[60] The tribunal has some flexibility to determine the conditions for the presentation of oral evidence. This includes evidence presented in person or via video camera. However, the rules specify that the individual presenting the evidence must be within the camera's picture frame. That is, they must be able to be viewed. Article 28 further allows the parties to choose the institutional and national laws that will be applied to the arbitral proceedings.

Expert witnesses[61] are important to arbitral proceedings. In my view, they will become increasingly more important for commercial disputes related to tokens, distributed ledgers and blockchain. In the case of blockchain technology, code, storage of data, token development, facilitation, use and valuations,

55 *Desputeaux v Éditions Chouette* (1987) Inc., Supreme Court, Canada, 21 March 2003, [2003] 1 S.C.R. 178, 2003 SCC 17, available on the Internet at http://canlii.ca/t/1g2jh.

56 Ibid.

57 Ibid. See also UNCITRAL Digest of Case Law on the Model Law on International Commercial Arbitration, 2012. https://uncitral.un.org/sites/uncitral.un.org/files/media-documents/uncitral/en/mal-digest-2012-e.pdf

58 United Nations Commission on International Trade Law (UNCITRAL) Model Law on International Commercial Arbitration, Adopted by the United Nations Commission on International Trade Law on 21 June 1985, 2006 Amendments, Article 24. https://uncitral.un.org/sites/uncitral.un.org/files/media-documents/uncitral/en/19-09955_e_ebook.pdf.

59 Ibid., Article 28.

60 Ibid., Article 28.

61 Ibid., Article 29.

smart contracts, and the technology to facilitate digital forms of finance, there will be a new category of expert witnesses that will be called upon to give evidence. If the token is used on blockchain via a smart contract that is also on blockchain, the ensuing challenge will be to determine whether the token is commodities-backed. Thus, care will need to be taken when draughting the arbitration agreement to ensure that all evidence to be adduced is available.

Doug Jones notes that there are 'three broad categories of expert evidence that can be identified: strictly technical expertise, legal expertise, and expertise on delay'.[62] Jones goes on to say that the importance of 'technical experts is that they assist when a dispute involves a specialist area of knowledge on which the tribunal may require assistance'.[63] Jones further points out that under

> international arbitration, the procedure for the taking of evidence is a combination of both common law and civil law traditions. Subject to any express agreement between the parties, experts can be appointed by a party or by the tribunal. The use of party-appointed experts is the norm in practice, despite the extensive involvement of counsel and arbitrators with civil law backgrounds.[64]

Simply put, there can be party experts or tribunal appointed experts;[65] however, it is important to look at the institutional rules as they may vary. Article 26 of the UNCITRAL Model Law[66] provides for the appointment of experts and, in the Singapore case of Luzon,[67] both parties agreed to the appointment of Mr Shorland as an expert technical assistant for the tribunal.[68] However, Luzon put forward that the appointment of the expert went beyond what was required. The court also stated that it would

> not permit it to mount what appeared to be a [back-door] appeal by attacking the manner in which the tribunal had made use of the expert when there was no evidence but only speculation that the expert had overstepped his bounds.[69]

62 Doug Jones AO, Methods for Presenting Expert Evidence, *Global Arbitration Review* (2021). https://globalarbitrationreview.com/guide/the-guide-evidence-in-international-arbitration/1st-edition/article/methods-presenting-expert-evidence

63 Ibid.

64 Ibid.

65 For example, International Bar Association, *Rules on the Taking of Evidence in International Arbitration* (IBA Rules of Evidence). https://www.ibanet.org/MediaHandler?id=def0807b-9fec-43ef-b624-f2cb2af7cf7b. See also, The Chartered Institute of Arbitrators, *Arbitration Rules 2015*, Article 29.

66 United Nations Commission on International Trade Law (UNCITRAL) Model Law on International Commercial Arbitration, Adopted by the United Nations Commission on International Trade Law on 21 June 1985.

67 *Luzon Hydro Corp. v Transfield Philippines Inc,* High Court, Singapore, 13 September 2004, [2004] SGHC 204. https://www.elitigation.sg/gdviewer/s/2004_SGHC_204

68 Ibid., para 20.

69 Ibid.

The point is that experts are fundamental to arbitration in providing specific evidence. They have a specific role and parties should not appeal the award based on the supposition that the expert did not operate within the agreed parameters of the appointment. Undoubtedly, this will apply to experts who will be called upon in commercial disputes to provide evidence for smart contracts, tokens, blockchain, and code, amongst others. Finally, and while not covered in this chapter, where there are multiple parties, contracts, and arbitration agreements, the consideration of evidence will need to be carefully thought through according to the relevant institutional rules and national laws, along with the arbitration agreement. It is inevitable that this will have to be dealt with where smart contracts and blockchain, including tokens, are involved.

6.3 Forced Arbitration

This section examines selected cases from the jurisdictions compared, in relation to either forcing parties to go to arbitration or allowing parties to opt out of arbitration, as a result of a dispute with the arbitration agreement. An arbitration agreement is of importance and is developed and agreed upon by the parties. An arbitration agreement can also be established in the digital economy, in pre-printed consumer contracts for financial services, insurance contracts, amongst others. They could be applied to tokens in the future in a standard consumer contract binding the party using the token. Thus, the question is: where there is a dispute, can the parties be forced to arbitration based on the arbitration agreement?

First, beginning with the case of *Dialogue*[70] in Australia, the court was required to decide on the respondents' interlocutory application seeking of a stay of the proceedings under section 7(2) of the International Arbitration Act 1974 (IAA) be dismissed. The case concerned Dialogue's access to the social media platforms, Instagram and Facebook. It highlighted the growing issues surrounding the use of modern-day technology and the intersection with data and, to a lesser extent, cybersecurity. Dialogue alleges that by restricting access to Instagram, the respondents breached various implied terms of Instagram, LLC's Terms of Use.[71] Section 7(2) of the IAA applies where:

(a) proceedings instituted by a party to an arbitration agreement to which this section applies against another party to the agreement are pending in a court; and
(b) the proceedings involve the determination of a matter that, in pursuance of the agreement, is capable of settlement by arbitration; on the

70 *Dialogue Consulting Pty Ltd v Instagram,* Inc [2020] FCA 1846. https://jade.io/article/780603
71 Ibid., para 2–3.

> application of a party to the agreement, the court shall, by order, upon such conditions (if any) as it thinks fit, stay the proceedings or so much of the proceedings as involves the determination of that matter, as the case may be, and refer the parties to arbitration in respect of that matter.[72]

Viewed this way, and in confirming whether an arbitration agreement existed and what the agreement provided, the court stated that:

> The respondents say that prima facie there is a valid arbitration agreement that covers the matters in dispute in the proceeding before me save for the competition claims, and therefore the matter should be referred to arbitration. They say that according to the competence-competence principle, it is for the arbitrator to resolve any questions of jurisdiction, including any challenge to the existence of the arbitration agreement, as well as any dispute as to the scope of the arbitration agreement.[73]

The court went further by clarifying the operation of section 7 IAA, whereby it is obliged to refer the parties to arbitration under section 7(2). The court referred to the plaintiff Dialogue, who

> opposes the application, principally denying the existence of any arbitration agreement. Further, *Dialogue* has brought a cross-application asserting that if there is an **arbitration agreement,** then it should be declared void or unenforceable as in essence involving an unfair contract term or on the basis of statutory unconscionability [emphasis added, Article 8 UNCITRAL Model Law]. If these arguments fail, Dialogue then says that there has been a waiver of the right to arbitrate, and it seeks to invoke s 7(5) of the IAA.[74]

It was confirmed by the court that an arbitration agreement was formed between Dialogue and Instagram LLC, such that section 7(2) applies, but subject to section 7(5). Moreover, the scope condition in section 7(2)(b) is satisfied.[75] On the application of Australian law, the court made the point that 'under Australian law, arbitration agreements in contracts formed on the internet are valid and enforceable. As I say, on the evidence, an arbitration agreement was under Australian law formed'.[76] In referring to the original Terms of Use as they appeared on Instagram's website,[77] the court stated that

72 Ibid., para. 7. *International Arbitration Act 1974*, section 7.
73 Ibid., para 8.
74 Ibid., para 9.
75 Ibid., para 14.
76 Ibid., para 214.
77 Ibid., para. 254.

17 'Basic Terms' were set out. For the present purposes, save for clauses 13 to 17 which provided:

- You must not interfere or disrupt the Service or servers or networks connected to the Service, including by transmitting any worms, viruses, spyware, malware or any other code of a destructive or disruptive nature. You may not inject content or code or otherwise alter or interfere with the way any Instagram page is rendered or displayed in a user's browser or device.
- You must comply with Instagram's Community Guidelines.
- You must not create accounts with the Service through unauthorised means, including but not limited to, by using an automated device, script, bot, spider, crawler or scraper.
- You must not attempt to restrict another user from using or enjoying the Service and you must not encourage or facilitate violations of these Terms of Use or any other Instagram terms.
- Violation of these Terms of Use may, in Instagram's sole discretion, result in termination of your Instagram account. You understand and agree that Instagram cannot and will not be responsible for the content posted on the Service and you use the Service at your own risk. If you violate the letter or spirit of these Terms of Use, or otherwise create risk or possible legal exposure for Instagram, we can stop providing all or part of the Service to you.[78]

More specifically, in relation to arbitration, the court in referring to the arbitration clause noted that:

> Except if you opt-out or for disputes relating to: (1) your or Instagram's intellectual property (such as trademarks, trade dress, domain names, trade secrets, copyrights and patents); (2) violations of the API Terms; or (3) violations of provisions 13 or 15 of the Basic Terms, above, you agree that all disputes between you and Instagram (whether or not such dispute involves a third party) with regard to your relationship with Instagram, including without limitation disputes related to these Terms of Use, your use of the Service, and/or rights of privacy and/or publicity, will be resolved by binding, individual arbitration under the American Arbitration Association's rules for arbitration of consumer-related disputes and you and Instagram hereby expressly waive trial by jury. As an alternative, you may bring your claim in your local 'small claims' court, if permitted by that small claims court's rules. You may bring claims only on your own behalf. Neither you nor Instagram will participate in a class action or class-wide arbitration for any claims covered by this agreement. You also agree not to participate in claims brought in a private attorney general or representative capacity, or consolidated claims involving

78 Ibid., para 259.

> another person's account, if Instagram is a party to the proceeding. This dispute resolution provision will be governed by the Federal Arbitration Act. In the event the American Arbitration Association is unwilling or unable to set a hearing date within one hundred and sixty (160) days of filing the case, then either Instagram or you can elect to have the arbitration administered instead by the Judicial Arbitration and Mediation Services. Judgment on the award rendered by the arbitrator may be entered in any court having competent jurisdiction. Any provision of applicable law notwithstanding, the arbitrator will not have authority to award damages, remedies or awards that conflict with these Terms of Use. You may opt out of this agreement to arbitrate. If you do so, neither you nor Instagram can require the other to participate in an arbitration proceeding. To opt out, you must notify Instagram in writing within 30 days of the date that you first became the subject to this arbitration provision. You must use this address to opt out.[79]

While the court ultimately dismissed Dialogue's application, in so doing it stated

> under Australian law, the respondents waived their rights to rely on the arbitration agreement, when referring to the waiver. That waiver leads to the conclusion that the arbitration agreement is inoperative or incapable of being performed under s 7(5), and the stay should be refused.[80]

This case is a good example of the enforceability or otherwise of internet contracts. These contracts now appear in various forms that include clickwrap, sign-in wrap, and browsewrap. These are new forms of contracts that, until recently, had not been considered by the courts. First, clickwrap agreements 'require a user to scroll through the terms of use and to affirmatively click a dialogue box labelled "I agree" or similar words of assent before the user is able to further use the site's services'.[81] On the other hand, 'sign-in wrap' is a term that has been coined by the US courts and requires an individual to click on a hyperlink to sign-in.[82] A browsewrap is different again and 'contains a notice that by accessing or using the services of the website, the user is agreeing to be bound by the site's terms of service. A site that presents a browsewrap does not have an 'I agree' button or its equivalent. A user is able to use the website's services without being required to take any affirmative action to indicate his or her knowledge of or agreement to Terms of Use. The notice states that use of the site, 'something that the user is already doing when the

79 Ibid., para 260.
80 Ibid., para, 599–602.
81 Ibid., para. 242.
82 Ibid., para 250.

notice is displayed, is a manifestation of assent'.[83] Thus, the question that arises is: are such contracts enforceable? Generally, the clickwrap and sign-in wrap agreements are enforceable, whereas browsewrap ones are not.

According to section 7 of the IAA, Australian courts have forced parties to seek arbitration. While the *Dialogue* case has no relevance to technology, it demonstrates that subcontracts have been established to engineer, procure, construct, and commission works for mining, rail, and port projects. Similar subcontracts can and do exist in the digital economy where, for instance, an entity contracts another entity to undertake work on their behalf such as maintenance and development of software (by a programmer) that supports code and blockchain. Thus, the following case may apply to force parties to arbitration if they established similar sub-contractual arrangements across the digital economy, where arbitration can be used to reconcile modified terms. Thus, in the 2016 case of *Samsung*[84] there was:

> an unincorporated joint venture of the defendant, Duro, and Forge Group Constructions Pty Ltd (Forge) entered into a contract (the Subcontract) with the plaintiff, Samsung. The Subcontract contains a dispute resolution clause, cl 42, which includes an arbitration agreement. Samsung terminated the Subcontract. Samsung and Duro entered into a new contract (the Interim Subcontract) by executing a Term Sheet. A term of the Term Sheet provides that the Interim Subcontract is on the same terms as the Subcontract as modified by the terms set out in the Term Sheet and its schedules for the performance of the works. The Term Sheet contains a governing law clause and a jurisdiction clause but no separate arbitration agreement.[85]

Essentially, the court had to determine whether the combined contractual arrangements in their totality retained the requirement to go to arbitration when a dispute arose. The other party, Duro, contended that the 'Subcontract has become inoperative within the meaning of s 7(5) of the Act (IAA)'.[86] The court did not accept the argument put forward by Duro since:

> the court has a discretion to either determine that question of inoperativeness or to grant a stay and permit that issue to be resolved by the arbitral tribunal and that a factor relevant to the exercise of that discretion is whether there has been or will be related proceedings addressing the arbitrability issue between the parties. If the arbitrability dispute has

83 Ibid., para 244.

84 *Samsung C&T Corporation v Duro Felguera Australia Pty Ltd* [2016] WASC 193. https://jade.io/article/482094

85 Ibid., para. 1.

86 Ibid., para 15.

> been addressed or resolved in other proceedings, the court will be anxious to do what it can to minimise the risk of inconsistent judgments and provide for orderly case management. Therefore, Duro says the tribunal decision is relevant to this discretionary factor.[87]

After further analysing the contractual arrangements between the parties and determining how or whether arbitration would be applicable, the court stated that:

> In this case the arbitration agreement in the Subcontract does not apply to the Duro Claims because they arise out of the Interim Subcontract. The arbitration agreement in the Subcontract survives the termination of the Subcontract but it does not apply to claims which arise out of the Interim Subcontract not the Subcontract. The Interim Subcontract does not render the arbitration agreement in the Subcontract inoperative so far as the Duro Claims are concerned. The question is whether there is an arbitration agreement in the Interim Subcontract which applies to the Duro Claims. In my opinion the question of whether the Term Sheet renders the arbitration agreement in the Subcontract inoperative so far as the Duro Claims are concerned does not arise in this proceeding. Accordingly, there is no risk of inconsistent findings in this proceeding and in the proceedings before the arbitral tribunal whether the arbitration agreement in the Subcontract covers the Duro Claims or is inoperative so far as those claims are concerned.[88]

In the above, the court applied section 7 of the IAA and Article 8 of the UNCITRAL Model Law.[89] In so doing, it was contended whether the court could determine that there was an agreement to arbitrate under the Interim Subcontract. The court ruled a stay of proceedings and referred the matter to arbitration based on the fact that the 'Interim Subcontract includes an arbitration agreement in the terms of cl 42 of the Subcontract'.[90] Moreover:

87 Ibid., also para 16.
88 Ibid., paras 17–18.
89 United Nations Commission on International Trade Law, Model Law on International Commercial Arbitration 2006, Article 8. Arbitration agreement and substantive claim before court. (1) A court before which an action is brought in a matter which is the subject of an arbitration agreement shall, if a party so requests not later than when submitting his first statement on the substance of the dispute, refer the parties to arbitration unless it finds that the agreement is null and void, inoperative, or incapable of being performed. (2) Where an action referred to in paragraph (1) of this article has been brought, arbitral proceedings may nevertheless be commenced or continued, and an award may be made, while the issue is pending before the court.
90 Ibid., paras 75–76.

> the parties have agreed by the Interim Subcontract, incorporating an arbitration agreement in the terms of cl 42 of the Subcontract, that the Duro Claims are to be determined by arbitration. In substance the matter in controversy in this proceeding is whether the Duro Claims are within the jurisdiction of the arbitral tribunal to which disputes under the arbitration agreement are to be referred. The answer is that they are. This proceeding involves the determination of a matter that, in pursuance of the arbitration agreement in the Interim Subcontract, is capable of settlement by arbitration. Section 7(2) of the Act requires that the court stay the proceeding and refer the parties to arbitration in respect of that matter.[91]

Essentially, the cases above demonstrate how different subsections of section 7 of the Australian IAA are applied by Australian courts when determining whether or not to send parties to arbitration. In the case of Samsung, it can be argued that in applying section 7 of the IAA, the judiciary had the option to either force parties to arbitrate or dismiss the matter.

6.4 Partiality

Further to the above, privacy has increasingly become a complex issue to resolve, as has the concept of partiality. In the USA, in the recent case of *Cristo*,[92] when presenting the background of the case, the court noted that on 6 November 2017, the plaintiff, proceeding *pro se*, filed a First Amended Complaint (FAC) alleging grievances stemming from the Schwab defendants' submission of the plaintiff's financial records to the Internal Revenue Service without his knowledge or consent.[93] It was alleged that there had been a number of violations against the *Right to Privacy Act*.[94]

It also drew upon earlier cases in relation to the partiality of the arbitrator. Nonetheless, the Federal Arbitration Act (FAA) is codified in 9 U.S.C section 1–16,[95] which protects the integrity of many arbitration agreements by deeming them valid, irrevocable, and enforceable. That is, according to §3 and §4, the FAA provides for the stay of proceedings and, where there is a failure to arbitrate under the arbitration agreement, the court can compel the parties to arbitrate. As a result of this law, courts do not have the authority to set aside arbitration awards if the arbitration agreement is valid. Nevertheless, on 11

91 Ibid.

92 *Cristo v Charles Schwab Corp.*, No 17-cv-1843-GPC-MDD, 2021 WL 2633624, at *3 (S.D. Cal. 25 June 2021). 2021 WL 2633624.

93 Ibid., paras 1–3.

94 Ibid., 12 USC section 3403,3404(c), 3405(2),3410, 3412(b), violations of section 1519, 827, 1001, 1341.

95 Arbitration, 1947, https://www.govinfo.gov/content/pkg/USCODE-2019-title9/html/USCODE-2019-title9.htm

April 2018, the court granted the defendants' motion to compel arbitration and stayed the case. The order directed the parties to submit a joint status report within five days of the arbitrator's decision. Because no joint status report was ever filed, on 21 August 2019, the court directed the parties to file a status report on the arbitration proceedings. Both parties' status reports indicated that arbitration had not yet commenced; therefore, on 12 September 2019, the court directed the plaintiff to initiate arbitration within 30 days. On 17 September 2019, the plaintiff informed the court that he had filed an arbitration claim under protest.[96]

Importantly, a long-held tradition is that the arbitration agreement be valid and contain the necessary elements for an arbitration to be undertaken. Also, arbitration has often been considered to be a better choice for businesses because of its requirement that an arbitrator be impartial. In this case, the court referred to *re Sussex*, the Ninth Circuit, which granted the extraordinary relief of a writ of mandamus when the district court clearly erred in granting a motion to disqualify the arbitrator during a pending arbitration for obvious partiality.[97] The district court held that the disqualification of the arbitrator was warranted because the arbitration was in its early stages, the consolidated arbitrations involved 385 plaintiffs, and the court surmised that at the end of the arbitration, the moving party would likely prevail on a motion to vacate the arbitration award based on 'evident partiality', a basis for vacating an arbitration award under the FAA.[98] The court further explained that the undisclosed business ventures of the arbitrator would create a reasonable impression of bias sufficient to meet the FAA standard and if the award were vacated, the parties would have to repeat the arbitration process, which would result in a waste of time and resources.[99] Further, the court noted that:

> Under the Federal Arbitration Act, any time within one year after the award is made any party to the arbitration may apply to the court so specified for an order confirming the award U.S.C. § 9. At that time 'the court must grant such an order unless the award is vacated, modified, or corrected'. The court may vacate an arbitration award, upon the application of any party to the arbitration, 1) where the award was procured by corruption, fraud, or undue means; 2) where there was evident partiality or corruption in the arbitrators, or either of them; 3) where the arbitrators were guilty of misconduct in refusing to postpone the hearing, upon sufficient cause shown, or in refusing to hear evidence

96 *Cristo v Charles Schwab Corp.*, No 17-cv-1843-GPC-MDD, 2021 WL 2633624, at *3 (S.D. Cal. 25 June 2021). 2021 WL 2633624, paras 1–3. Also see https://www.govinfo.gov/content/pkg/USCOURTS-casd-3_17-cv-01843/pdf/USCOURTS-casd-3_17-cv-01843-6.pdf
97 Ibid.
98 Ibid.
99 Ibid.

> pertinent and material to the controversy; or of any other misbehavior by which the rights of any party have been prejudiced; or 4) where the arbitrators exceeded their powers, or so imperfectly executed them that a mutual, final, and definite award upon the subject matter submitted was not made.[100]

However, the Ninth Circuit rejected the district court's ruling as it was clearly

> erroneous on a showing of 'evident partiality' because the district court predicted that an arbitration award would likely be vacated due to 'evident partiality' but Ninth Circuit law requires evidence of a direct financial connection between a party and the arbitrator or a concrete possibility of such connections.[101]

The court went further to explain that a number of allegations pertaining to partiality had been made. It explained that the:

> Plaintiff alleges four instances of evident partiality to support his motion to vacate the arbitration award under 9 U.S.C. § 10(a)(2). First, he argues that 1) in 2019, FINRA 'staff' treated Plaintiff more harshly than Defendants due to deficiencies in their respective pleadings, 2) on November 19, 2020, FINRA 'staff' showed favoritism towards Defendants by informing them that Plaintiff had filed a separate federal court lawsuit attempting to enjoin the pending arbitration, 3) FINRA's procedure in appointing the original panel, its failure to respond to his objection to each of the arbitrators proposed by FINRA because they cannot rule on constitutional issues and the panel's selection solely from Defendants' ranking list show evident partiality in favor of Defendants, and 4) the arbitrators' failure, at the time he filed his statement of claim, to determine eligibility of Plaintiff's claims under FINRA Rule 12206(a) and instead improperly ruling on it two years later based on a different rule, Rule 12206(c), demonstrates evident partiality. To demonstrate an arbitrator's evident partiality, the Plaintiff must provide specific facts indicating actual bias toward or against a party or show that [the arbitrator] failed to disclose to the parties information that creates '[a] reasonable impression of bias. A plaintiff must show that the arbitration award resulted from the arbitrators' bias. The appearance of impropriety, standing alone, is insufficient' to establish evident partiality in actual bias cases. A party alleging evident partiality [in actual bias cases] must establish specific facts which indicate improper motives. Even repeated rulings against one party to the arbitration will not establish bias absent some

100 Ibid.
101 Ibid.

> evidence of improper motivation. The fact that an arbitrator consistently relied on evidence and reached conclusions favourable to one party, is not enough establish evident partiality.[102]

Accordingly, the court ruled that the plaintiff provided no basis for vacating the award under §10(a)(2). The court further ruled that the award was to stand as it could not be vacated under the FAA. Thus, for partiality to be accepted by the court, there is a rigorous threshold test where a party must demonstrate clearly that an improper motive needs to be established throughout the proceeding and within the arbitration award. It also requires that a level of bias be established. These two tests are highly complex, and partiality is hard to prove based on an arbitration award and the conduct of an arbitrator throughout a proceeding. Nonetheless, when applied, this two-stage test could prove particularly important under certain circumstances.

In the case of *Lamps*,[103] the court was required to confirm or otherwise whether it could compel arbitration. The notable difference was that this case was in relation to class-wide arbitration. Similar to the above case, the court was required to examine U.S.C. §9 of the F*ederal Arbitration Act*, in relation to enforcing an arbitration according to the terms of the agreement. Thus, the court was required to confirm or otherwise the status of the FAA in providing for class-wide arbitration. The court referred to the earlier cases of Stolt-Nielsen and Corp[104], where it had been ruled that a court does not have to compel parties to arbitration in relation to a class-wide action when the agreement is silent on the availability of arbitration itself, and this type of arbitration fundamentally changes the nature of traditional individualised arbitration. Further, under the FAA, a party may not be compelled to class-wide arbitration unless there is a contractual basis to do so. The court noted that the FAA requires courts to enforce arbitration agreements according to their terms. However, at issue in this case was the interaction between a state contract principle for addressing ambiguity and a rule that arbitration is a matter of consent, not coercion under the FAA.[105] In response to this point, the court held that arbitration is strictly a matter of consent, which is a principle that underpins all arbitrations. The court also emphasised that consent is essential under the FAA because arbitrators wield no more than the authority they have been given.[106] On the question of ambiguity in the contract, the court noted that:

102 Ibid., p. 21.

103 *Lamps Plus, Inc. v Varela,* 139 S. Ct. 1407, 1415 (2019). https://casetext.com/case/lamps-plus-inc-v-varela-1

104 Ibid. *Stolt-Nielsen v AnimalFeeds Int. Corp.,* 559 U.S. 662, 130 S.Ct. 1758, 176 L.Ed.2d 605 (2010) and Epic Systems Corp. v Lewis, 584 U.S. https://casetext.com/case/lamps-plus-inc-v-varela-1

105 Ibid., paras 1415–1416.

106 Ibid.

> Neither silence nor ambiguity provides a sufficient basis for concluding that parties to an arbitration agreement agreed to undermine the central benefits of arbitration itself. The Ninth Circuit reached a contrary conclusion based on California's rules that ambiguity in a contract should be construed against the drafter, a doctrine known as contra proferentem. The rule applies only as a last resort when the meaning of a provision remains after exhausting the ordinary methods of interpretation.[107]

The court also stated that:

> Unlike contract rules that help to interpret the meaning of a term, and thereby uncover the intent of the parties, contra proferentem is by definition triggered only after a court determines that is cannot discern the intent of the parties. When a contract is ambiguous, contra proferentem provides a default rule based on public policy considerations, it can scarcely be said to be designed to ascertain the meanings attached by the parties.[108]

However, the court also made the point that class arbitration, to the extent that it is manufactured by state law rather than consent, is inconsistent with the FAA.[109] That is, the court reaffirmed earlier precedents that they may not rely on state contract principles to reshape traditional individualised arbitration by mandating class-wide arbitration procedures without the parties' consent.[110] If courts have determined otherwise and allowed for such, this is not consistent with the FAA. Importantly, the application of the principle of equal treatment cannot pre-empt general rules that target arbitration either by name or by more subtle methods, such as by interfering with the fundamental attributes of arbitration. The court further stated:

> The general applicability of the rule did not save it from pre-emption under the FAA with respect to arbitration agreements, because it had the consequences of allowing any party to a consumer arbitration agreement to demand class proceedings, without the parties' consent.[111]

The point is that:

> [The American Congress] enacted the Federal Arbitration Act (FAA) in 1925 to enable merchants of roughly equal bargaining power to enter into binding agreements to arbitrate commercial disputes.[112]

107 Ibid., para 1417.
108 Ibid.
109 Ibid., 1418.
110 Ibid., 1418.
111 Ibid.
112 Ibid., 1420.

Viewed this way, and similar to the other jurisdictions compared, the FAA has been established as a cornerstone of the law of arbitration for governing commercial disputes in the US. Moreover, in further unpacking the provisions within the FAA, the court noted that:

> Section 4 of the FAA permits a district court to compel the parties to arbitrate their claim and § 16(b)(2) explains that an appeal may not be taken from an interlocutory order directing arbitration to proceed under section 4 of this title. Thus, the District Court order compelling arbitration was interlocutory and generally unappealable.[113]

Nonetheless, the court ruled that it would 'disregard the actual contract the parties signed. And to dismiss the neutral and commonplace default rule that would construc that contract against the drafting party. No matter what either requires, the majority will prohibit class arbitration'.[114] On that basis, the court dismissed the process for class-wide arbitration. The takeaway from this case is that careful drafting of the arbitration agreement needs to take place to ensure it is clear about the type of arbitration that can be allowed.

Notwithstanding the above, in the case of *Nori Holding*[115] the court was required to, as part of an

> ... application for a final anti-suit injunction to restrain the pursuit of court proceedings in Russia and Cyprus which are alleged to be brought in breach of an arbitration clause. It raises some interesting questions including: (1) how the court should proceed when an application for similar relief can be made to arbitrators; (2) whether such an injunction can or should be granted to restrain proceedings brought in accordance with the insolvency law of a foreign state to set aside transactions at an undervalue; and (3) whether the decision of the CJEU in *West Tankers Inc v Allianz SpA* (Case C-185/07) [2009] AC 1138 that a court in one European member state cannot grant an injunction to restrain proceedings brought in breach of an arbitration clause in another member state remains good law.[116]

The facts of this case were:

> The first and second claimants (Nori and Centimila) are companies incorporated in Cyprus. They are wholly-owned subsidiaries of O1 Group Limited, an investment holding company also incorporated in Cyprus,

113 Ibid., 1425.

114 Ibid., 1435. Note that state courts in California have based on the same that an arbitration agreement did not authorise class arbitration – *Nelsen v Legacy Partners Residential Inc.*, 207 Cal. App. 4th 1115, 1129–1131, 144 Cal. Rptr. 3d 198, 210–211.

115 *Nori Holding Limited, Centimila Services Limited, Coniston Management Limited, Public Stock Company* EWHC 1343 (Comm). https://www.bailii.org/ew/cases/EWHC/Comm/2018/1343.html

116 Ibid., para. 1.

> which owns and manages assets, including in real estate and finance. The ultimate beneficial owner of the group is Boris Mints. I refer to O1GL and the companies controlled by it as the O1 Group. The third claimant is a BVI-incorporated company, which has a minority shareholding in O1 Properties Limited. O1 Properties is a company incorporated in Cyprus which owns valuable real estate in Moscow. Its majority shareholders are entities within the O1 Group. Lira LLC, Leblanc Investments LLC and Semela LLC, companies incorporated in Russia, are or were at various times companies in the O1 Group. O1 Group Finance LLC is a company incorporated in Russia which raises money on the bond markets for companies within the O1 Group. According to the claimants it is not, despite its name, a company within the O1 Group but 'a special-purpose orphan vehicle which attracts financing in Russia through the issue of bonds traded on the Moscow Exchange'. The defendant ('the Bank') is a licensed bank incorporated and existing under the laws of the Russian Federation. I was told that Mr Mints was formerly one of its largest shareholders and its Executive Director. His precise role does not matter for present purposes.[117]

In relation to the arbitration, the court noted that:

> The Pledge Agreements were governed by the law of Cyprus. Each contained an arbitration clause, clause 19, which provided for arbitration in London under the rules of the LCIA in the event of any dispute or disagreement arising under, or in connection with, this Agreement, such dispute or disagreement shall be resolved by binding arbitration held in London under the rules of the London Court of International Arbitration (which rules are deemed to be incorporated herein; hereinafter – the 'Rules'), save that no requirements of the Rules as to the nationality of arbitrators shall apply, with 3 (three) arbitrators appointed in accordance with the Rules (where each of the Pledgee and the Pledgor shall appoint one arbitrator; the two arbitrators so elected shall appoint the chairman). The London Court of International Arbitration shall be the appointing authority. The working language of the proceedings shall be English. The Parties' addresses for service of process shall be the addresses specified in this Agreement.[118]

A total of ten arbitrations were noted by the court, which determined whether the termination of arbitration agreements could be established. The court stated:

117 Ibid., paras 1–6.
118 Ibid., para 9.

> On 2 January 2018 Nori and Centimila commenced eight arbitrations against the Bank by filing a Request for Arbitration with the LCIA. Two other arbitrations were commenced by Coniston on 14 February 2018. Accordingly, there are now ten arbitrations between the parties, one under each of the Pledge Agreements and the Pledge Termination Agreements. The same tribunal, finally constituted on 25 April 2018, has been appointed in each arbitration. The arbitrations have been or will be consolidated. In the arbitrations the claimants seek declarations that each of the Termination Agreements is valid and that each of the Pledge Agreements has been validly terminated. They seek also an anti-suit injunction such as is sought in the present application before me. By its response, the Bank has indicated that it intends to advance a defence and possible counterclaim based on its contention that the August transactions were fraudulent and that the Termination Agreements are void or should be set aside. However, this is without prejudice to its position that (1) the arbitrations were improperly commenced because the claimants ought to have filed a separate Request for Arbitration for each arbitration, and (2) the tribunal lacks jurisdiction.[119]

In relation to the legal framework, the court noted that:

> The legal framework within which this application has to be determined is well established. Where court proceedings are brought (otherwise than in the courts of an EU or Lugano Convention state) in breach of an agreement to arbitrate, the court will generally grant an anti-suit injunction to prevent any further breach unless there are strong reasons not to do so. The court's power to grant such an injunction is derived from section 37 of the Senior Courts Act. It does not depend on whether an arbitration has been or is about to be commenced. When such an injunction is sought, it is for the court to determine whether there is a binding arbitration agreement and whether the pursuit of the foreign proceedings constitutes a breach of the agreement. Moreover, an arbitration agreement is distinct from the contract of which it forms part and will be binding notwithstanding the invalidity of the main contract unless the ground for invalidating the main contract applies equally to the arbitration agreement according to section 7 of the Arbitration Act 1996.[120] [emphasis added]

Essentially, section 7 of the *UK Arbitration Act* provides that

> unless otherwise agreed by the parties, an arbitration agreement which forms or was intended to form part of another agreement (whether or

119 Ibid., paras 23–24.
120 Ibid., para 28.

> not in writing) shall not be regarded as invalid, non-existent or ineffective because that other agreement is invalid, or did not come into existence or has become ineffective, and it shall for that purpose be treated as a distinct agreement.[121]

It applies the concept of separability, whereby an arbitration agreement forms part of another agreement. On that basis, the court ruled that there can be no injunction to restrain the further pursuit of the bank's proceedings in Cyprus. However, as noted by the court,

> the proceedings against the claimants in Cyprus will continue. It may be that the Cyprus court itself will stay the proceedings against the claimants pursuant to Article II (3) of the New York Convention, but that will be a decision for that court to make. Or it may be that in due course the arbitrators will issue an order restraining the further pursuit of the Cypriot proceedings against the claimants. If so, an award will be entitled to recognition and enforcement under the New York Convention even in EU member states.[122]

The ability to restrain an arbitration must be weighed against the provisions of the *Arbitration Act*. While section 7 does not specifically provide for the court to restrain an arbitration, it allows for the court to determine whether an arbitration agreement is part of any other agreement.

In the more recent *Payward*[123] case, the UK court was required to determine the enforcement of an arbitral award in accordance with sections 101 and 103 of the *UK Arbitration Act 1996*. The court stated:

> This judgment concerns the Claimants' claim, by an arbitration claim form issued on 23 October 2022, for the enforcement of an arbitration award in the same manner as a judgment or order of the Court to the same effect. The award in question is the Final Award dated 18 October 2022 ('the Final Award') in an arbitration under the Judicial Arbitration and Mediation Services ('JAMS') Rules, Case No. 5100000163. The seat of the arbitration was San Francisco, California. The claim is brought pursuant to s. 101 of the Arbitration Act 1996.[124]

121 *Arbitration Act 1996*, United Kingdom, section 7. https://www.legislation.gov.uk/ukpga/1996/23/section/7

122 *Nori Holding Limited, Centimila Services Limited, Coniston Management Limited, Public Stock Company* EWHC 1343 (Comm), paras 99–100. https://www.bailii.org/ew/cases/EWHC/Comm/2018/1343.html

123 *Payward, Inc. (2) Payward Ventures, Inc. (3) Payward Limited v Maxim Chechetkin* [2023] EWHC 1780 (Comm). https://3vb.com/wp-content/uploads/2023/07/CL-2023-000029-Payward-v-Chechetkin-final-Judgment39.pdf

124 Ibid., para. 1.

However, the defendant, Chechetkin, put forward that the Final Award should not be enforced according to

> s. 103 of the Arbitration Act 1996, which relies on: i) Recognition or enforcement may be refused if it would be contrary to public policy: s. 103(3), and ii) Recognition or enforcement may be refused if the award deals with matters beyond the scope of the submission to arbitration: s. 103(2)(d).[125]

This case is of significant importance to the current-day developments in arbitration relating to digital payments and crypto assets that use blockchain in the digital economy. By way of background, Payward was/is the operator of the Kraken global digital online crypto-asset exchange.[126] The arbitration transcended the US and UK borders. Payward is a Delaware corporation with an address in San Francisco. Second, Payward Ventures is also a Delaware corporation and has the same address in San Francisco. Third, Payward Ltd is a company incorporated in England. Finally, 'Chechetkin is a British citizen resident in England'.[127] The complex corporate structure of many of these FinTech industries that transcend national borders is nothing new. However, they have been used with effect. Without delving into the background in relation to this matter, and turning directly to the contractual arrangements and the ensuing requirement to proceed to arbitration, the court noted that contractual clause 23 provided the following:

> 23. **Applicable Law; Arbitration**
>
> PLEASE READ THE FOLLOWING PARAGRAPH CAREFULLY BECAUSE IT REQUIRES YOU TO ARBITRATE DISPUTES WITH US AND IT LIMITS THE MANNER IN WHICH YOU CAN SEEK RELIEF.
>
> You and Payward agree to arbitrate any dispute arising from these Terms or your use of the Services, except for disputes in which either party seeks equitable and other relief for the alleged unlawful use of copyrights, trademarks, trade names, logos, trade secrets or patents. ARBITRATION PREVENTS YOU FROM SUING IN COURT OR FROM HAVING A JURY TRIAL ... You and Payward further agree ... (b) that any arbitration will occur in San Francisco, California; (c) that arbitration will be conducted confidentially by a single arbitrator in accordance with the rules of JAMS; and (d) that the state or federal

125 Ibid., para 2.

126 Ibid., para 3.

127 Ibid., paras 4–6. He qualified as a lawyer in Russia and has an LLM from the Connecticut School of Law in the US. He has worked as a lawyer for a number of international organisations but has never qualified as a lawyer in England or in the USA.

> courts in San Francisco, California have exclusive jurisdiction over any appeals of an arbitration award and over any suit between the parties not subject to arbitration ... Any dispute between the parties will be governed by these Terms and the laws of the State of California and applicable United State law, without giving effect to any conflict of laws principles that may provide for the application of the law of another jurisdiction.[128]

Given the above, the arbitration was conducted in the US under the rules of JAMS, whereby, Rule 1 provides that parties are deemed to have made the JAMS Rules a part of their arbitration agreement whenever they have provided for arbitration by JAMS. Rule 4 provides as follows:

> **Rule 4. Conflict with Law**
> If any of these Rules, or modification of these Rules agreed to by the Parties, is determined to be in conflict with a provision of applicable law, the provision of law will govern over the Rule in conflict, and no other Rule will be affected.[129]

Nonetheless, at issue was 'Chechetkin lost £608,534'.[130] The transaction undertaken by

> Chechetkin and the Payward group concerns deposits that Mr Chechetkin made between 15 March 2020 and 6 June 2020, totalling £613,000. These deposits were made by payments from his UK bank account to the UK bank account of Payward Ltd. I have received no evidence regarding any previous deposits, but I assume (a) that there will have been such deposits and (b) that they, too, will have been paid from his UK bank account to the UK bank account of Payward Ltd.[131]

On that basis, Chechetkin argued that Payward Ltd was in breach of ss 19, 22, 23, and 26 of the *Financial Services and Markets Act 2000.*

128 Ibid., para 18.
129 Ibid., paras 19–20. The court also relied upon JAMS Consumer Arbitration Minimum Standards. These apply: '... where a company systematically places an arbitration clause in its agreements with individual consumers and there is minimal, if any, negotiation between the parties as to the procedures or other terms of the arbitration clause. A consumer is defined as an individual who seeks or acquires any goods or services, primarily for personal family or household purposes, including the credit transactions associated with such purchases, or personal banking transactions'. Rule 3 of the JAMS Consumer Arbitration Minimum Standards provides as follows: 3. Remedies that would otherwise be available to the consumer under applicable federal, state, or local laws must remain available under the arbitration clause, unless the consumer retains the right to pursue the unavailable remedies in court.
130 Ibid., para 30.
131 Ibid., para 26.

During the arbitration, the arbitrators were replaced, and, ultimately, 'Chechetkin challenged the arbitration agreement, the applicability of the JAMS Rules and the applicability of the laws of California (or other US law)'.[132] Therefore,

> on 8 July 2022 and later on 12 July 2022, the arbitrator issued Prehearing Order No. 2. According to the JAMS rules. On 29 July 2022, the arbitrator issued a Partial Final Award, again flowing from the hearing on 8 July 2022 dealing with the same matters as Prehearing Order No. 2.[133]

The Partial Award stated that the 'Respondent's challenges to arbitrability and jurisdiction are denied. Payward's Motion to Confirm Arbitration and Jurisdiction is granted. Pursuant to JAMS Rule 11, the resolution of this issue by the Arbitrator is final'.[134]

On the point of enforcement and its consideration by the arbitrator, the court noted that:

> the arbitrator considered the enforceability of cl. 23 essentially by considering whether its terms had been brought sufficiently to Mr Chechetkin's attention, whether they were sufficiently comprehensible and whether he had indicated his acceptance. No points along these lines were developed before me. If they had been, my views on them would have been similar to the arbitrator's. Also, regarding the significance of the Financial Services and Markets Act 2000, and of English law more generally, they were given no consideration in her decision. My impression is that, having decided that cl. 23 was incorporated into the contract, and having had regard to the express choice of law that this provision contains, she had no further interest in any issue as to applicable law, or as to whether the enforceability of cl. 23 could be attacked on any other basis (as Mr Chechetkin sought to contend).[135]

In addition to the above, the court pointed out that

> Chechetkin relied primarily on the second limb of s. 103(3), on the basis that enforcement would be contrary to public policy. In this regard, he relies on the Consumer Rights Act 2015 and on the Financial Services and Markets Act 2000.

It also highlighted how

132 Ibid., para 51.
133 Ibid., para 57–58.
134 Ibid., para 58.
135 Ibid., para 59(ii).

> the Final Award was in respect of a matter that was not capable of settlement by arbitration (cf. the first line of s. 103(3)) and/or that the Final Award dealt with a difference beyond the scope of the submission to arbitration (cf. s. 103(2)(d)).[136]

In relying on the above, the court made a notable point in relation to cross-border arbitrations: that knowledge of both the US and UK is needed. It stated:

> A US arbitrator with no experience of English law, let alone the English regulation of financial services and marketing, is not obviously the ideal tribunal for this kind of claim. Where the arbitral institution makes it a priority to 'save time and money', and prioritises 'efficiency, speed and results', the arbitrator may well wish to favour the short and simple route over one that would require the investigation of foreign laws, and that this factor was heavily in play.[137]

Finally, in relying on the public policy elements of UK law, the court ruled that because there were no new fresh circumstances,

> enforcement of the Final Award would be contrary to UK public policy, within the meaning of s. 103(3) of the Arbitration Act 1996. This means that recognition and enforcement 'may be refused', in the words of that provision, and the arbitration claim fails.[138]

This case highlights a number of important matters that may arise in the future regarding the digital economy, arbitration, crypto assets, and cross-border law. Beginning in reverse, a significant matter emerged where the court made the point that arbitrators more or less need to have knowledge of the laws of more than one jurisdiction. Today, in the digital economy, they need to be cross-border experts to enable them to understand the laws of other jurisdictions. In some cases, this may require knowledge of multiple jurisdictions' laws at the same time. Second, the regulation of crypto assets is a new area of the law that has not been fully addressed. Third, crypto-asset transactions will come under not only banking and financial regulation, but may also be under consumer law depending on the contract. Fourth, and while this matter concerns a commercial transaction, it could result in investor–state arbitration had Chechetkin been an entity investing in Payward under the US regulation-legal framework. Much is to be learnt from this case. It will require arbitrators, legal counsel, and scholars to be vigilant as the judiciary increasingly is required to decide on the enforcement of arbitral awards that involve cryptocurrency, digital payments, tokens and other transactions within the digital economy.

136 Ibid., paras 67–68.
137 Ibid., para 95.
138 Ibid., paras 166–169.

6.5 Conclusion

Undoubtedly, international commercial arbitration will be an effective mechanism for the resolution of disputes that arise from tokens, smart contracts, and agreements that support digital finance. These include, but are not limited to, data agreements, cybersecurity agreements, licencing agreements, software agreements, joint ventures, data storage facility agreements, and service level agreements. This is because blockchain technology could be used to develop and govern these contracts and agreements. International arbitration institutions have emerged as important entities[139] that now offer specialist arbitration options.

Against the backdrop of the above, it has been argued that tokens reside on distributed ledgers in and on blockchain. Thus, they come in many forms and offer a huge number of different use cases. Additionally, they can be generated at the protocol layer inherent to a specific ledger, in which case they are frequently labelled as 'coins', or they can reside on the application layer and are minted by smart contracts. It is these contracts that will be one element of the evidentiary process in a dispute.

This chapter has confirmed that tokens and smart contracts that are supported by blockchain technology will be subject to the rules and evidence for arbitration. It has also confirmed that the rules of evidence are indirectly associated with an arbitration agreement, which could be rendered invalid on a number of grounds. On the other hand, it has been demonstrated that under certain circumstances, the courts can force the parties to arbitration in light of the arbitration agreement.

Problematic to the above, when related to the rules of evidence, is how the functioning and security of blockchain, and the uncertainty of digital evidence. This is far from being settled. As highlighted above, and more challenging, are the three difficulties that have arisen from blockchain technology. They are associated with 1) the blockchain evidence itself, 2) the use and application of blockchain to submit evidence, and 3) the rules of evidence across the common and civil law divide.

To address the third difficulty, the rules of evidence in the common law jurisdictions of Australia, the US, and the UK require that evidence be relevant and reliable. Therefore, unless blockchain evidence conclusively falls within these rules, the tribunal could be reluctant to rely on its use and admit the evidence submitted via blockchain. However, when the international arbitral rules of the UNCITRAL Model Law are applied, the general rules for evidence are left to the tribunal to determine.

Essentially, it is well understood that the rules of evidence in arbitration are all but settled. Although the rules of evidence may vary depending on

139 World Intellectual Property Organisation Arbitration and Mediation Centre. https://www.wipo.int/amc/en/center/specific-sectors/ict/fintech/

the rules of the International Arbitration Institute being applied, they may be specified by the arbitration agreement. Therefore, the burden of proof is a form of standard of proof. Hence, both parties are equally required to prove their respective positions. More specifically, the arbitrator must 'establish a procedure for the gathering of evidence'.

An arbitration agreement has to be in writing. A failure to provide an arbitration agreement that imposes binding obligations on the parties to arbitrate will pose many challenges, and the courts will need to make a determination and possibly force the parties to arbitration. In order to determine whether the arbitration agreement passes the test of being null and void, inoperative, or incapable of being performed, the courts will look to consent and intention, rather than whether a party to the arbitration agreement later they become party to the commercial arrangements.

Additionally, an arbitration agreement that provides for the arbitration to be dealt with on written submissions only (thus without cross-examination of witnesses) would be valid. The tribunal has some flexibility to determine the conditions for the presentation of oral evidence, such as in person or via video camera.

Significant too is the use of expert witnesses. This will, in my view, be crucial to arbitration that involves tokens, blockchain, and smart contracts. In the case of blockchain technology, code, storage of data, token development, facilitation, use and valuations, smart contracts, and the technology to facilitate digital forms of finance, there is a new category of expert witnesses that will be called upon to give evidence. Where the token is used on blockchain via a smart contract, the ensuing challenge will be whether the token is or will be commodities-backed. Thus, care needs to be taken when drafting the arbitration agreement to ensure that all evidence to be adduced is available.

To conclude, the arbitration agreement is of importance and is developed and agreed upon by the parties. It can be used to address some of the evidentiary difficulties. Moreover, the new and emerging landscape of tokens and the technology that supports their use will pose more questions than have been resolved in this chapter. It is a fascinating new addition to the arbitration world. However, it will require arbitrators, legal counsel, and scholars to be vigilant as technology evolves to support and facilitate transactions involving tokens, cryptocurrency, digital payments and other digital assets in the digital economy.

7 Conclusion

7.1 Introduction

One of the most pressing challenges facing the world is the evolution of digital finance. The benefits and challenges are far from being fully understood. A central position taken throughout this book is that tokens and the tokenisation of the economy are inextricably linked to smart contracts and, in turn, to blockchain technology and distributed ledgers.

It was explained that tokens can be grouped under four categories: fungible token – a token that is capable of mutual substitution among individual units; non-fungible token – a token that is not capable of mutual substitution among individual units; security token – a token with specific characteristics that meet the definition of a financial instrument or other investment instrument under applicable legislation in the relevant jurisdiction; or utility token.

What is remarkable is that most tokens generally fall into the NFT and FT categories. Arguably, and as demonstrated in Chapter 1, these categories represent the many emerging sectorial tokens that have emerged or are being developed to provide a commercial application for both goods and services, performing a functional transaction and having a certain value.

Most notably, tokens co-exist with existing commercial instruments and are directly or indirectly connected with smart contracts. Smart contracts are supported by blockchain technology and are used to govern the legal relationship between parties for the development and use of tokens. This means that tokens can have *any level* of content and therefore are not subject to the constraints of a limited number of instruments, as is the case in commercial law. Tokens are not subject to the typical limits of the literality principle, either. Through smart contracts, it is possible to include a complex suite of shareholder agreements, for instance.

Commercially, the application of smart contracts is increasing and is being applied to many areas of the legal profession. Smart contracts can be established via blockchain technology. The benefit of using smart contracts is multilayered. They will, in addition to token agreements, ensure a high level of governance of tokens. In addition to the four categories of tokens mentioned above, there are

DOI: 10.4324/9781003511687-7

subcategories of tokens such as security tokens, infrastructure tokens, energy tokens, real estate tokens, agriculture tokens, and fan tokens, amongst others.

Nonetheless, digital finance, which operates in the banking and finance sectors today, has been developing in different forms for a number of decades. For more than a century, there have been different forms of digital finance, seen in the development of both transaction modes and investment products. Finance and the money derived from these products has been, and continues to be one, of the most profound innovations in modern history. The transformation that will take place of the coming decade if the token economy is fully accepted by governments will be enormous. It will change the way financial transactions are facilitated making them more efficient and effective, and possibly in rela time without any delays. However, this will all be predicated on how government choose to regulate these activities.

Centrally, digital finance has been referred to as FinTech. In Chapter 1, it was described as constituting: 'i) credit, deposits, and capital-raising services; ii) payments, clearing and settlement services, including digital currencies; iii) investment management services; and iv) insurance'. In reaffirming these developments, FinTech, digital finance, and tokens (crypto assets, stablecoins, amongst others) as a collective have evolved over the past century.

Theoretically, the term 'tokenomics' is used to describe different aspects of a blockchain project such as: 1) the number of tokens issued and the way they are issued (vesting schedule, airdrops, etc.), 2) the economics of a consensus algorithm, largely referred to as crypto-economics, and 3) the general structure of the system: game-theoretic and economic incentives. More specifically, the concept of tokenomics is arguably a form of tokenisation. Arguably, the term 'tokenisation' is applied to those sectors in the economy that have been tokenised.

Today, there are tokens used across the economy at a functional and in different forms. Also, the tokenisation of all areas of the trading and investment economy is far from being fully realised. However, if fully realised, which is more likely than not, it will have significant implications worldwide. It will all but see the decline and elimination of cash from the economy.

Tokenomics considers blockchain tokens as a tool to exchange value within the blockchain. As highlighted in Chapter 1, the process of tokenisation encapsulates digital or real-world assets and assigns them a digital representation (token) that can be traded on the blockchain. More specifically, this process allows any kind of value to be managed and exchanged as a digital asset, and highlights the ability to shift from economics to tokenomics, where tokenomics represents the switch from economics, in which stakeholders react to changes, to token economics, where they adjust to the tokens.

Chapter 1 took the reader to the early beginnings of societal philosophy. The philosophies of Hobbes, Austin, Locke, Bentham, Weber, and others can be considered to reconcile the impacts and challenges that will likely evolve from tokenising the economy. Of note is that, in terms of social theory and law, society will be transformed significantly in many areas as a result of tokens and the digital finance economy.

The transformation of society, brought about by the transition from the use of clay, paper, and metal-based tokens (amongst many others) to modern-day technology that uses tokens, is remarkable. The formal and functional differences are that the earlier tokens were tangible, physically held, and used for transactions between humans. In the modern period, the token is not as tangible because it is developed and used within and by technology (e.g. a computer-Iphone which is the tangible item). An individual does not physically hold the modern-day token; it is computer-generated.

This means that it will require nation-states and supranational polity of the EU to establish laws. This is far from settled, and it is argued that Singapore and the US are leading the way, as indicated by the comparisons made in this book. It has not accounted for other nation-states that are also working on developing a legal framework for this new area of finance.

On the other hand, the laws can be informed by the above and other well-established philosophers. Most importantly, it will be to ensure that any rules set maintain the rule of law, which is based on a set of principles and values applicable to each of the sovereigns. Doing so will ensure that the legal framework is coherent and not a highly fragmented regime.

Another, more important point is that technology is supporting the growth of the digital finance sector. The layperson who does not have a technology background finds these products difficult to understand, as is the case with lawyers, practitioners, scholars, students, governments, and regulators. They require new skills being developed. Notably, blockchain is underpinned by AI technology, code, and algorithms that are changing the landscape of digital finance significantly. The real challenge is for non-technology-savvy people to understand the operation and application of this technology. Knowledge of the function of a distributed ledger will be paramount.

The stark reality is that for machine learning alone, expert systems that rely on pre-determined norms encoded in a program, leverage extensive sample data to extract relevant algorithms. For this to occur, the data is inputted by a human into a computer program that is also encoded by a human. The data then interacts with the program, algorithms, and codes to learn. Over time, as this learning expands, similar to the human brain, the ML becomes more intelligent.

A further formal and functional arrangement is the learning algorithms that produce other algorithms, enabling computers to self-generate programs. This is achieved by a program capable of identifying repeated patterns in the data. As a result, the computer can perform human functions.

Put another way, technology-enabled devices can now perform some functions that are or were being performed by a human. It is this technology that is rapidly transforming the modern world of finance and presenting significant challenges. It is also problematic for the law when determining the extent of the changes driven by technology. The legal frameworks to facilitate and enable the commercialisation of these products are largely in place, such as corporate law and intellectual property law, to protect the invention or copyright. Nonetheless, these developments are a function.

An emerging negative aspect of this technology is the potential for bias and the infringement of individual rights, segregating certain ethnic and religious groups in society. This could in and of itself be used to restrict, block, or exclude certain groups and classes of people from participating in digital finance activities and the use of tokens. This problem, in addition to the challenges and risks to the broader economy, cannot be underestimated. That is, cybersecurity has developed into its own economic activity.

Arguably, it has emerged as a major economic, social, and national security risk. More than ever, the financial sector is now under threat every day from cybersecurity breaches that are exposing the functions of economies, personal wealth, and transactions, along with the functions of government departments.

Pertinent too, cybersecurity is a major threat to blockchain technology that will be used to facilitate the development and use of tokens and digital finance. In responding to cybersecurity intrusions globally, the ethical and legal challenges differ significantly from one jurisdiction to another, and present daily challenges that make it difficult for these jurisdictions to respond effectively. It is of the utmost importance that any framework developed for the use and application of tokens and other digital financial products provides a high level of consent and trust in the public and private sectors. In part, this is already evident, given the number of products on the market that are accessible via a mobile phone.

The accentuating challenges that will emerge from cybersecurity is cybercrime. That is, although cybercrimes are categorised as criminal law, increasingly, they are being called upon to protect economic activity. Cybersecurity is a major economic activity. Today, it requires extensive investment by governments and entities to protect commercial activities. This area will be further challenged under a tokenised economy, as every transaction will be undertaken online. Even the security of a blockchain and other distributed ledgers might not be able to deter any state and non-state actors determined to breach the protective barriers.

It is well understood that cybercrime comes in many forms, some examples of which are identity fraud, data theft, ransomware attacks, copyright infringement, and phishing campaigns. Organisations consider the loss of personally identifiable information of customers or employees as one of the most dangerous outcomes of cyberattacks. The loss of sensitive information can have serious repercussions for companies, such as a damaged reputation and loss of revenue.

Hence, more research is needed. There needs to be greater coordination at the international level. The world is possibly heading down the road of another commercial sector being highly fragmented, not only legally but also, operationally. On a positive note, there is international law that can assist in this area. However, more collaboration is needed to strengthen the international legal regimes.

Centrally, this legal research posed the following questions: 1) What is the current status of the national and international regulatory framework pertaining to digital finance, specifically tokens? 2) What are the gaps in the current law? and 3) How effective can international arbitration be in resolving commercial disputes within the digital economy?

In response to the above, it is argued that, to begin with, digital technologies that are being used in the digital finance domain are revolutionising the world. However, in terms of law, these technologies are challenging governments, regulators, nation-states, and the broader community. The law is slowly catching up, but more work is needed as a matter of urgency.

This book has compared the laws of banking and finance, confirming that the law(s) pertaining to tokens [crypto assets and stablecoins] are evolving rapidly. Most noteworthy is that under the regulatory frameworks of the banking and finance sectors, it could be argued that the large banks as we know them at present might no longer exist in the new world of digital assets. Problematic for regulators and governments will be their having to balance the innovation in this new area of the economy while ensuring that there is an adequate level of protection and controls in place to ensure trade and investment continue with a high level of certainty. Additionally, the book has confirmed that currently, most jurisdictions have well-established national laws for these sectors. Notably though, the exceptions are Australia and the US. Challenging too is that the laws are very quickly diverging from each other, and while there appears to be a consensus that this digital financial activity will be authorised through a licence or some other mechanism, it has been defined very differently.

It has been argued that, as the first step, the definition(s) provided by the US 2022 *Executive Order* are the most specific, direct, and coherent. Collectively, blockchain, cryptocurrencies, digital assets, and stablecoins are all defined separately, but upon analysis, they have blockchain in common and constitute a digital asset. Other economies should adopt this definition. Arguably, the definition(s) provided by the US 2022 Executive Order collectively define blockchain, cryptocurrencies, digital assets, and stablecoins separately and constitute a digital asset. There is a general theme emerging of licencing as the preferred regulatory model. It is argued that the Swiss model has gone further, requiring a level of licencing and regulating the DLT as a trading facility. It is the trading facility that enables the facilitation of token transactions. On the other hand, Liechtenstein is the first state to establish token-specific laws. More and urgent work is needed to understand how these laws operate in practice.

Furthermore, this book has made the case for greater collaboration internationally and regionally through the many extant organisations and institutions. For instance, it was argued that ASEAN, APEC, and the Commonwealth Secretariat could be very important to the development of the law. Additionally, the African Union should be consulted along with BIS, IMF, World Bank, UNCITRAL, and UNIDROIT. The importance of implementing this proposal cannot be underestimated. This is an area urgently needing attention at the regional and international levels to ensure there is a high level of certainty, and to counter any developments by regional blocs that could assume a level of control that would not benefit the current economic certainty the world enjoys. What I am advocating is that, whatever framework is adopted, there should be a high level of international and regional agreement no matter who is first to develop their national laws. This is not a geopolitical matter; it is intended to protect investors and merchants. By providing a high level of certainty, this helps to ensure that the global economy remains as stable as possible.

Another pressing and complex issue that is not often examined is the area of taxation law. The imposition of tax in a token-driven economy will be problematic, to begin with. There is little to no work being undertaken to reconcile the issues of taxation as it relates to tokens. At this early stage, tokens are considered a form of property in the economies that are working on this issue. On the other side, there are a number of challenges that lie ahead. A further problematic area is the general taxing of products and services within the digital economy. More specifically, this applies to: 1) double taxation of digital suppliers; 2) revenue recognition arising from the need to monetise value; 3) tax impact of legal structures; 4) monetisation strategies used by digital business models; and 5) the double revenue threshold mechanism. Fundamentally, addressing the above has to be a priority where entities are establishing offices throughout the countries examined. In other words, a FinTech company with its central office in Sydney, Australia, and with satellite offices in Singapore and India, will be subject to different national tax laws.

In a similar way to the above, insurance law is also being challenged with regard to blockchain technology. Arguably, the insurance sector has been one of the rapid adopters of smart contracts. It is challenging the existing and longstanding contractual doctrines such as 'good faith', which is well entrenched in both statutory and case law. To understand this point alone, the concrete nature of smart contracts can eliminate the subjective *good faith* or *reasonableness* that is often contained in traditional contracts. That is, in common law countries, this will be difficult to reconcile, and the judiciary may need to address it at some point. A possible resolution could be that, when establishing a smart contract, the concept of 'good faith' must be encoded. However, to date, this has not been successfully accomplished. A further accentuating problem will be the total application of smart contracts to tokens and digital finance. This issue will be challenged by the law in cases where the code was installed to facilitate these activities. Contractual clauses will be crucial to minimising confusion.

A further development concerns the intellectual property rights for tokens and the technology that supports their use. This book has demonstrated that both patent and copyright law will be important components of the overall legal landscape. WIPO will be crucial in the development and response to token disputes. WIPO provides guidance and rules on the resolution of disputes through arbitration. It is an international organisation that is responsible for all intellectual property law. The international laws for patents and copyright are well settled. They provide a framework that has been generally adopted by the economies compared throughout this book. It has been demonstrated that the principles and concepts of prior art, novelty, invention, specification requirements, breach of confidence, enablement, written description, non-obvious, opposition and purposive approach are important to patent applications. These have all but been fully adopted by national laws.

Most significant is that the patent and copyright laws have a high level of harmonisation. This is on the backdrop that across the EU, generally, the Member States have responsibility for the administration of patent and copyright law. Of note is that patent applications, to date, have focused on elements of the technology that supports blockchain, and not the overall blockchain itself. On the other hand, for tokens to be afforded a patent, they must be an invention. This could be a step too far. Authentication systems could well be used to allow the use and transaction of tokens to be afforded patents.

Copyright law is becoming increasingly important nowadays and is another area of law that will need to evolve as the digital economy expands. At the international level, many concepts and principles of originality, rights, moral rights, and licencing, among others, have been developed to provide a high level of harmonisation across the world. The common and civil laws have, generally, considered these concepts for various types of licences. India's laws are very close to those of the UK. Australia's laws are also similar. However, the EU laws are far from harmonised, and it is left to Member States to implement their own laws in this regard.

In the future, a difficulty may arise in cases where technology can perform an activity similar to a human, such as a robot producing its own song without referring to an original song that it is mimicking. This scenario begs the question: can the robot be afforded a copyright? Additionally, there are numerous and very different computer applications, and in some cases, the national laws do not provide a definition of a computer programme. A computer programme is a set of instructions expressed in words, codes, schemes, or in any other form, including a machine-readable medium, capable of causing a computer to perform a particular task. Demonstrably, India appears to be more advanced than other states whereby, the laws have defined a computer programme where it produces work. Arguably, the code that supports blockchain could fall within this definition.

Arguably, as digital finance expands and the token economy is realised, commercial disputes will ensue. This book has demonstrated how arbitration will be important in resolving these disputes. Arbitration has evolved into a well-recognised and effective mechanism for resolving commercial disputes. The rules of evidence in arbitration will be challenged by this new economic activity.

Importantly, tokens and smart contracts that are supported by blockchain technology will be subject to the rules of evidence in arbitration. Simply put, the rules of evidence are indirectly associated with an arbitration agreement and could be rendered invalid on a number of grounds.

The multiple factors that need to be considered include the rules of evidence in relation to the functioning and security of blockchain when the blockchain is providing digital evidence. This is far from being settled. Therefore, the formal and functional arrangement pertaining to blockchain can be summarised as blockchain evidence itself, the application and use of blockchain to submit evidence, and the application of the rules of evidence to both the common and civil law. These areas have not been fully addressed and require further research. A possible way to address part or all of the evidentiary issues is through an arbitration agreement. The application of international arbitration rules [the UNCITRAL Model Law] and institutional rules may overcome this difficulty as the Tribunal has the discretion to determine the rules of evidence. However, the rules of evidence may differ for different arbitration institutions.

Finally, it has been argued that one of the most important challenges that need to be addressed by the legal profession is that the judiciary needs to understand the operation of the technology that facilitates crypto exchanges and transactions. Today, the legal profession will need to be more multidisciplinary. It will, arguably, require new skills and capacities to be developed within the legal profession. This book has demonstrated that the judiciary will be required to address issues such as transactions undertaken by mistake, transactions where crypto assets [tokens] have been stolen, and whether the current national laws address digital payments, along with the obligations of software developers whose software is used to facilitate these transactions, among other technology-enabled commercial activities. In the current cybersecurity environment, the aforementioned issues are likely to be heightened even further. While there is a need for ongoing research as emerging cases become more complex, this book has established the groundwork for further research and, more importantly, has identified a number of legal gaps and dilemmas that currently exist in various legislatures. Can they be resolved? In short, yes. However, it requires the international community to collaborate in order to ensure that the law is consistent and coherent, so as to give investors and traders a high level of certainty as they make the transition to a fully functional digital finance [token] economy.

Index

Kolibri 360 GmbH
Ferdinand-Jühlke-Straße 7
99095 Erfurt, Deutschland
produktsicherheit@kolibri360.de